ASK
THE
CHILDREN

ASK
THE
CHILDREN

▼ What
America's
Children
Really Think
About
Working
Parents

ELLEN GALINSKY

WILLIAM MORROW AND COMPANY, INC. NEW YORK

Library of Congress Cataloging-in-Publication Data

Galinsky, Ellen.
   Ask the children : what America's children really think about working parents / Ellen
Galinsky.
     p. cm.
   Includes bibliographical references and index.
   ISBN 0-688-14752-6
   1. Children of working parents—United States—Attitudes.   2. Working mothers—
United States.   3. Dual-career families—United States.   4. Work and family—United
States.   5. Parent and child—United States.   I. Title.
HQ777.6.G35   1999
306.89—dc21   99–34354
                 CIP

Printed in the United States of America

First Edition

1 2 3 4 5 6 7 8 9 10

FIGURE DESIGN BY JANIN/CLIFF DESIGN, INC.

BOOK DESIGN BY OKSANA KUSHNIR

www.williammorrow.com

For my mother, Leora Osgood May, who is a treasure and an inspiration, and for her mother, my admirable grandmother, Bessie Osgood. Both have shown me how the past can inform the present and the future.

For my daughter, Lara Galinsky, and my son, Philip Galinsky, who show me every day how the future can inform and strengthen the present. Lara set the standard for this book by conducting the first and the very insightful interviews of children. Philip worked side by side with me, making me laugh and reminding me of what's important, as he finished his dissertation and I finished this book.

And for Norman Galinsky, my husband of 34 years, for his nurturing support, practical help, and deep and abiding goodness. He shows me how to draw from the past, prepare for the future, but be in the present.

ACKNOWLEDGMENTS

This book would not have been possible without the help of many talented and dedicated individuals. My deepest thanks go to them:

Terry Bond for his skill as a researcher, his creative approach to the conceptual model, his precision in thinking about the study design, his patience with my never ending questions, his work on the data analyses, his joy in the discovery process, and his wise counsel every step of the way. There is no one more wonderful to work with than Terry.

Judy David for the strength and wisdom she brings to understanding parenthood—what it's really like and what we need. Judy's insights in interviewing parents and children and in synthesizing the findings from these interviews have added joy and depth to this book.

Carter McJunkin for the 3 years he has worked on this book, as he puts it, "from beginning to end." Carter began as a college intern helping me frame the one-on-one interviews and then traveled around the country with me conducting interviews. After he graduated from college, he returned to manage the book's completion. His contributions to every page are immense.

Kimberley Poppe, Nicole Young, and Stephanie Aubrey—each in a unique way—have contributed to the "poetry" of this project as they conducted insightful interviews and organized findings from the one-on-one interviews and from the open-ended questions in the children's survey.

Toni Sciarra for being the kind of editor authors dream of having. Day in, day out, Toni has offered her profound knowledge to every facet of the book, illuminating all she touches. My daughter says the highest praise a child can give a parent is "being there for me." Toni has been "there for me" beyond measure.

To the staff at the Families and Work Institute, who deeply and respectfully supported me over the years as I followed my passion in writing this book, working harder and longer to make my venture possible. Special thanks to Lois Backon, who has brought a commitment to excellence and creativity to the enormous contribution she has made to this book; Nina Sazer O'Donnell, whose inventive and sound thinking add to my work in incalculable ways; to Donna McPherson, for her invaluable wisdom; to Jim Levine, who brought his considerable talent to bear in assisting me—from conceptualizing the study to presenting the results; to Arlene Johnson, for sharing her in-depth understanding of work and family life; to Nik Elevitch, for his creative design help; to Barbara Norcia and Diane Kirschner, for helping to manage the practical realities of a project as all-consuming as this one; to Robin Hardman, for helping with the media; and to Wanda Moore, for her insights about parenthood.

To Dana Friedman, the cofounder—and for many years copresident—of the Families and Work Institute, for the deep reservoir of knowledge she has about work and family life and the humor and many profound insights she has shared with me as I worked on the book.

To the talented and creative people at William Morrow: Michael Murphy, Lisa Queen, Marly Rusoff, Sharyn Rosenblum, Michele Corallo, Katharine Cluverius, and the rest of the Morrow team who worked on this book.

To the funders who made this book possible: Betty Bardige, Luba Lynch, and Victoria Frelow of the A. L. Mailman Family Foundation; Donna Klein of the Marriott Corporation; and Michele Peterson of Merck & Co., Inc. And to Milton Little and Marilyn Resnick of the AT&T Foundation, for supporting a meeting of researchers on the impact of parental employment on children; to Michael Levine of the Carnegie Corporation of New York, for supporting a review of the literature on this subject; to June Zeitlin of the Ford Foundation, for supporting the dissemination of our work; and to Margaret Mahoney of MEM associates for being a mentor in so many ways.

To the following scholars who met at the Families and Work Institute in September 1994 to share findings from their research as a prelude to our study: Ann Crouter, Pennsylvania State University; Judy David, parent educator and consultant; Carollee Howes, University of California at Los Angeles; Diane Hughes, New York University; Susan Kontos, Purdue University; Shelly MacDermid, Purdue University; Toby Parcel, Ohio State University; Chaya Piotrkowski, Fordham University; Judy Smith, Teachers College, Columbia University; Marybeth Shinn, New York University; and Marlene Zepeda, California State University.

To Allison Sidle Fulgini and Michelle Poris, for working with me in reviewing the literature about the impact of parental employment on children. And to Mary Ann Clawson of Wesleyan University, for supervising my daughter's independent study project in interviewing children for this book.

To all of the individuals who helped to arrange the one-on-one interviews—especially Mary Greene, whose overall assistance was especially invaluable; Dana Friedman, Nina Sazer O'Donnell, Claudia Hedensköj, Donna Klein, Steve Huston, Denise Feldman, Britt McJunkin, Gerry Nottingham, Jennifer Perry, Michele Peterson, Anita Pretlow, Bea Romer, Monica Harris, Jennifer Swanberg, Sally Vogler, Barbara O'Brien, and Cass Casillas. To Lois Backon, Buffy Wallace, Judy McJunkin, Lara Galinsky, Connie Nestor, Younghee, Stacy Kim, Simone Durandisse, and Andrea Camp for helping me arrange the photography. And to David Gottlieb for his help with scanning photographs.

To Dana Markow, Alan Steinberg, and Elizabeth Cooner of Louis Harris and Associates, for their thoughtful and thorough assistance in developing the surveys and administering them.

To Rosalind Barnett of Brandeis University; Urie Bronfenbrenner of Cornell University; Faye Crosby of Smith College; Peter Fraenkel of the Ackerman Institute; Wendy Goldberg and Rachelle Strauss of the University of California at Irvine; Rhona Rapoport, who with her late husband, Robert Rapoport, was instrumental in establishing this field, now a consultant to the Ford Foundation; Rena Repetti of the University of California at Los Angeles; and Marybeth Shinn of New York University for advising on the content of the parent and children surveys.

To the thoughtful and creative people who helped me find the right word to replace *balancing*: especially my college roommate and close friend, Karen Diamond; Nancy Dunbar; Mark Morris of Ted Bates; Paul Saffo of the Institute For The Future; Bill Ryan of Lamont-Doherty Earth Observatory of Columbia University; Janet Chan of *Parenting Magazine*; Dory Devlin of the Newark *Star-Ledger*; Julia Lawlor of *The New York Times*; Phil Mirvis of the London School of Economics; Edwin Nichols of Nichols and Associates, Inc.; and Keith Devlin of Saint Mary's College of California.

To the many people who transcribed the one-on-one interviews: Barbara Schaefer, Norm Conley, Troy O'Dend'hal, Melanie Nanez, Patricia Chang, Rafael Arias, David Shulman, Anita Chikkatur, Yvon Beaubrun, Emma Jacobson-Sive, and Julie Tutor.

To Cynthia Cliff and her colleagues at Janin/Cliff Design for their very creative design for presenting data in the figures.

To Andy Boose, my lawyer, for his wise assistance with legal issues.

To Camille McDuffie and Lynn Goldberg of Goldberg McDuffie Communications, Inc., for their outstanding help in developing and implementing a communications strategy for the book.

To Ginger Barber, my exceptional agent, who has supported me enormously since the day we met 25 years ago, when she said, "You have many books in you."

In memory of Nancy and Walter Sawyer. I wrote this book on your desk.

And finally to my family. In addition to Mother, Norman, Philip, and Lara, I would like to thank my sister, Sally Ruth May; my niece, Sasha Rau; and my children's "second" mother, Simone Durandisse, for all of their help.

C O N T E N T S

Why Ask the Children, and Why Now?

Researching and writing *Ask the Children* has been a journey that has lasted well over 15 years, but one that has its origins 15 years ago. It has been a journey of traveling through what seemed like a dense thicket, trying to make sense of the complex lives we lead, then of soaring with new insights and new understandings. Most of all, it has been a pioneering journey. I feel deeply privileged to have been among the first to have covered this territory.

Why has a book that asks the children how they see their working parents never been written? Why has a comprehensive and in-depth study that pursues this question never been conducted? Because we have been afraid to ask, afraid to know.

Whenever I mention that I am working on a book about how kids see their working parents, the response is electric. People are fascinated. Parents want to know what I have found, but inevitably they are nervous, too. Sometimes they say, "You should talk to my children. I wonder what they would say." Or they say, "I wonder what *other* people's children would say. I'm not sure that I'm ready to hear what mine have to say!"

Having spent many years exploring the worlds of work and family life, I feel the time is right to know. The answers of children are illuminating, not frightening. They help us see that our assumptions about children's ideas are often at odds with reality. Ultimately, this information will help us be better parents—and better employees, too. In fact, adding children's voices to our national conversation about work and family life will change the way we think about work and family life forever.

OUT WITH THE OLD DEBATES

In looking at the views of parents and of children, I often feel as if they are both looking through the same picture window but seeing an entirely different landscape. As I have examined these landscapes, I've discovered that many of the debates we've been having about work and family miss the mark. For example, we have been locked in a long-standing debate about whether mothers' working is "good or bad" for children. Numerous studies have found that having a working mother doesn't harm children, yet the debate rages. In our Ask the Children study of a representative group of more than 1,000 children in the third through the twelfth grades, having a working mother *is never once predictive* of how children assess their mothers' parenting skills on a series of twelve items that are strongly linked to children's healthy development, school readiness, and school success. Other characteristics of their mothers' *and their fathers'* lives are very important in predicting how children assess their parents' parenting skills, but whether their mother works is not one of them.

If the findings in this book are simply read and reported as another study that weighs in on whether mothers should or shouldn't work, that would be a terrible misreading, a black-and-white rendering of a full-color portrait. This study, like many others, shows that the impact of parental employment on children *depends* on a number of factors, including whether the parent is doing what he or she thinks is right. The point of *Ask the Children* is to look at *why* parental guilt is so deeply embedded in us, when the research indicates that it needn't be and to use the insights from our study to move beyond the current debate and to develop new ways to think about and "live" work and family that are more successful than many of our current attempts to "balance" the two.

I believe that the reason we have been stuck in the "should she/shouldn't she work?" debate is that there is a problem, but we have put the wrong label on that problem. The problem isn't *that* mothers (and fathers) work: It is *how* we work.

For example, we asked the children in this study, "If you were granted *one* wish to change the way that your mother's/your father's work affects your life, what would that wish be?" We also asked a representative group of more than 600 parents to guess what their child's response would be. Taken together, 56 percent of parents assume that their children would wish for more time together and less time at work.

But *time* is not on the top of children's lists. The largest proportion of children (23 percent) say that they want their mothers and their fathers to make more money. I suspect that money is seen as a stress-reducer, given children's other answers. Why? Because if we put together the number of children who wish that their parents would be less stressed or less tired by work, 34 percent make this wish for their mothers and 27.5 percent make this wish for their fathers. Perhaps children think that their parents would be less burned out if they made more money. In contrast, only 10 percent of children wish that their mothers would spend more time with them and 15.5 percent say the same thing about their fathers. (Interestingly, only 1 percent of parents guess that their children would want them to be less stressed and 1 percent guess that their children would want them to be less tired.)

Perhaps surprisingly, children with employed mothers and those with mothers at home do not differ on whether they feel they have too little time with their mothers. Again, why is this the case? Because simply asking children whether they want more time with their parents leaves out the issue of what they do when they are together. An at-home mother is not automatically an attentive mother, nor is an employed mother necessarily inattentive.

As another example, take the "quality time/quantity time" debate. We find that it is older children—more than younger children—who are yearning for more time, and they are yearning for more time with their fathers. Clearly fathers, as well as mothers, are very much needed by children.

The quantity of time does matter, but so does the content of the time. A very special contribution of the Ask the Children study is that I have been able to identify those aspects of togetherness that affect children's development in positive or negative ways. One of those factors is focus: our ability to really focus on our child when we are together. In contrast to the idyllic (and often exhausting) notion of "quality time," focusing on our child can involve grappling with tough situations as well as having fun together doing any number of everyday activities.

A NEW LANGUAGE FOR THE LIVES WE LEAD

It has also become increasingly clear to me that the language we have been using to describe everyday realities of employed parents and their children is out of sync with what really matters. We need new nondichotomous, non-either/or terms to replace the quality/quantity time conundrum. I suggest we use *focused time* and *hang-around time*.

We also need to replace the notion of "balancing" work and family life. Balancing implies an either/or situation—a scale on which if one side is up, the other is down. It is thus a win/lose seesaw. Yet the research conducted for this book reveals that if work life is "up" or family life is "up," the other side is very likely to be up as well. This is not a zero-sum game in which giving to one side takes away from the other.

I suggest the phrase *navigating work and family life*. I make this suggestion on the basis of developing and testing a theory of how work affects how we parent. There is a flow between work and home, a dynamic interrelationship in which positive—or negative—aspects of one area can spill over, enhancing or impairing the other. In later chapters, we look at how work affects our moods and energy levels in parenting, and how these, in turn, affect our interactions with our children and our children's development—including whether or not our children have behavior problems. We also show how our parenting experiences spill back into work, affecting our job performance.

WHAT WORKS AND WHAT DOESN'T?

I have identified several key aspects of work and of family life that can help us be the kind of parents and employees we want to be. These include the support of others, autonomy, and effective alignment of home and work demands with our priorities. Understanding how these and other factors affect us can help us steer a steadier course.

I also propose numerous other practical suggestions for navigating work and family life successfully, drawn from one-on-one in-depth interviews with close to 175 parents and children in fifteen states around the country, our findings from the Ask the Children surveys, and my own experiences from working from this field for more than two decades.

PLAYING DETECTIVE, "MOOD CLUES," AND OTHER SURPRISES

The findings from this study hold many surprises. We found that children learn more about the world of work from their mothers than from their fathers. We found that many children don't think we like our work as much as we really do. That's probably because many of us have said to our kids, "I have to go to work." Or "I wish I didn't have to leave." We seem to talk *around* children rather than *with* them about our jobs.

As a result, many children play detective to figure out what is going on in our jobs that upsets or elates us. They study our moods at the end of the workday. For example, listen to several children:

> *You can tell [whether your parent is in a bad mood] because you get a short and simple answer.*

> *If they had a bad day, they won't talk. Or they will just go off by themselves . . . I guess to try to think about their day rather than blowing up.*

> *When they are in a good mood, they ask [me] a million questions.*

One child even calls her parents at work to get a reading on how they are feeling so she can determine whether she should clean up the house before they come home! Other children look for "mood clues" in the way that their parents open the door and walk into the house, and they adjust their behavior accordingly. One child says:

> *If they have had a bad day, I just leave them alone. I just give them time to cool down.*

Another adds:

> *When [my mother] is really angry, we stay away. I don't want to get my head bitten off. So I just back down. Sit down. Go out of the room.*

Of course, children would try to read our moods whether we were at home all day with them or at work. The point is that our reluctance to talk to our children about our work has meant that children are getting haphazard rather than *intentional* information about our lives at work. This study finds that such information frames how children feel about their place in the world of work in the future.

In fact, when we ask the children, we find that they want us to like our work, but not more than we love them. As one said:

> *I think that something that goes on with kids is: "Wouldn't you rather be with me than do this other thing?" I want my mother to* like *her job, but not more than she* loves *me.*

The same goes for fathers, too.

Children have many wise things to say to us. In fact, the last question of our survey asks children, "What would you like to tell the working parents of America?" In Chapter 11, I share ten essential messages from them, messages that are funny and poignant, heartfelt and direct, and very powerful. Listen to one child:

> *If you are trying as a parent, if you are leading by example, if you are following what you preach, then your kids will turn out pretty good.*

Why and How This Study Was Conducted

Ask the Children has its genesis in a study that I and other colleagues at Bank Street College conducted more than a decade ago, during the early days of our attempts to understand work and family life. Until that time, there had been studies of work and studies of family life, but few attempts to understand how these two domains fit together. At the time, we* didn't even know what aspects of life on and off the job to assess in our quantitative questionnaires. Of course, we reviewed the research literature, but we also felt that we had to listen. In our first study—at Merck & Co.—we interviewed employees and the top management of the company before developing questionnaires. In our second study of three small companies in New Jersey and New York, we expanded our reach and interviewed employees, their husbands, wives, or partners and—importantly—their children. We called it the Family Study.[1]

One of the findings of the Family Study has intrigued me ever since: Parents and children often see the same issues quite differently. For example, we asked the 100 or so children ages 6 through 18 whom we interviewed what could be done to improve their family lives. We also

*You will notice that throughout the book, I use "we" whenever my research involved the assistance of others.

asked the parents to guess what their children would say. Most guessed that their children would say "more time together as a family."

Some of the children did comment that having more time together would be "nice." They then talked about what they might do if they had more time together—not going on expensive outings, as parents might assume, but doing very mundane things together like walking around the block on a nice summer evening. But what would really help, many of the children said, would be for their parents to come home less "wired." "Wired?" we asked. "Yes," children answered, and proceeded to tell us exactly what was going on in their parents' workplace that caused their parents to be stressed:

> *My mother's boss is asking her to do things that a person at her level shouldn't have to do.*

> *Someone just got hired in my father's work group who is a jerk, and my father is supposed to train him. How can my father possibly train someone who is so stupid?*

We wondered whether parents talked about their work in front of their children. Some parents said that they did: "When I've had a bad day, I talk about it." In fact, parents mentioned talking more about the bad days than the good days. Other parents, however, said they never talked about work. As one parent put it, "I take off my work hat and put on my parenting hat." However, many of their children knew what was going on at work, too—they knew about difficult bosses, conflict with coworkers, impossible deadlines, and frantic schedules. How had the children whose parents said they never talked about work obtained such accurate information? Did they listen at the top of the stairs or through the radiators when their parents talked at night? Did they eavesdrop when one of their parents had a telephone conversation with a friend? However they found out, they seemed to know.

What's more, children had techniques for handling the situation when one of their parents came home from "one of those days." They could tell by the way the doorknob was turned, by the footsteps into the house, by the way that their parents put their "stuff" down. One girl said:

> *If it has been one of those days, I jump into the bathtub right away. I am too old for my parents to walk in on me. I can stay in the bathtub as long as I want . . . even until my skin gets all wrinkled. I turn the water on loud and it drowns out their nasty voices.*

And a boy said:

> *If it has been one of those days, I pick a fight right away. I know that there will be a fight eventually so you might as well get it over with as soon as possible.*

Since the time of the Family Study, there have been studies indicating that the conditions of parents' jobs can affect children, but very few attempts to explore how children view their working parents.[2] Although I knew that such a study must be done, I felt that there were a number of steps that must be taken to do it right.

The first step was to convene a group of some of the most respected researchers on work, family, and children. With funding from the AT&T Foundation, this group met at the Families and Work Institute in September 1994. The participants at the September meeting were asked to address the question of how their own research would inform a study of how children see their working parents.

With funding from the Carnegie Corporation of New York, staff at the Families and Work Institute—Allison Sidle Fuligni, Michelle Poris, and I—conducted a literature review on how parental employment affects children. This literature review, which was conducted between 1994 and 1995, served a dual purpose: informing this book as well as providing background information for a policy statement on working and children being prepared by the American Academy of Pediatrics.

Since this project is a pioneering one, I wondered, however, whether the research to date had captured the real issues on children's minds. From my own interviews conducted for the Family Study, I felt there was a gap between how children think and what researchers have studied. Since I wanted to start this project without any preconceptions that might limit my thinking. I felt that a perceptive and articulate young person might be the best source of this kind of insight. I turned to one of the most perceptive, articulate people I know—my daughter, Lara Galinsky, who was 21 years old at the time and a senior at Wesleyan University. I asked her to talk free-form with a diverse group of children of differing ages and backgrounds to see what they thought the important issues were, to probe for the points of pain and the points of joy. In the fall of 1995, Lara went to housing projects, public and private schools, and playgrounds. In all, she interviewed twenty children in depth. Not surprisingly, she found that the literature had not touched some of the issues that are central to children, including whether parents are "there for their children," children's guilt, and children's feelings about the busyness of their parents.

The next step was to interview parents and children from the same families to ascertain whether we had captured the right issues, to determine to what extent children and parents converge or differ in their perceptions, and to frame the survey questionnaires. We wrote and rewrote the questions for the one-on-one interviews throughout 1996 and in the beginning of 1997 and set out to "ask the children" and their parents about work and family life.

In the spring of 1997, the coauthor of my book *The Preschool Years*, the educator Judy David, and I conducted focus groups in the Washington, D.C., metropolitan area. Judy continued to interview there and in California. With the help of research assistants, interviews with a nonrandom sample of parents in fifteen states and the District of Columbia were conducted, including 78 parents and 93 children—171 individuals from 69 families.

The next step was to use what we had learned thus far to develop questionnaires for surveys of nationally representative groups of children and of parents. In the one-on-one interviews, we had heard certain themes again and again. Over and over, we heard that parents felt good about themselves as workers and as parents when they could focus on what they wanted to focus on and when they had support for doing so. On the negative side was the piling up, the often steep escalation of demands at work and at home. These four constructs—focus, autonomy, support, and demands—became the basis for building a model for understanding parents' stress and satisfaction that I would use in the questionnaires.

Parents wondered what children were going to remember from this period in their lives. Sometimes parents asked this question from the haze of guilt:

What are my children going to blame me for later?

Sometimes it was curiosity:

I often think about the memories that stick and they certainly aren't the moments my parents might have anticipated. Like I remember driving in the car to a family vacation, not the vacation itself. That makes me wonder what my children are taking away from the present time.

So we asked the children. Children did remember the moments when their parents were truly focused on them. A 10-year-old said, "Right before we go to bed, Mom usually tells us these stories about a cow, a pig, and a chicken." Every night, this girl or one of her sisters made up a sentence and then her mother wove a story from this starting point. It was a tradition in their family. So, I learned, focus is important to children as well.

We also asked the parents about their best and worst memories of their own working parents. One woman recalled coming home from school, eager to tell her father what had happened to her that day. He was a musician and was practicing at home at the end of her school day. He never looked up; he pretended she wasn't present. She said:

> *I now have a great relationship with my father and have forgiven him, but I will never forget the pain of being invisible. I wouldn't have minded it if he had just looked up and said, "I'm busy— I'll talk to you later." But to be invisible!*

The one-on-one interviews reinforced the model I was developing. I found that some of the same constructs—such as focus—that were central to parents' satisfaction at home and at work were possible predictors of how children view their parents and how they assess their parents' parenting skills.

I also used the one-on-one interviews with children and parents to determine the comparisons I wanted to make between children's and parents' perceptions of the same issues based on the surveys. I selected the following issues amid many others: Is time at home seen as calm or rushed? Do parents seem like the same or different people when they are at work? Do parents tell children much about work? Do parents like their work? Are they more likely to share the good things or the bad things that happen? How well are parents managing their work and family responsibilities?

As one might imagine, we began with enough questions for questionnaires that would take well over an hour to complete. But, in this era of telemarketing and school pressure, it is impossible to have questionnaires that long. We were restricted to questionnaires that lasted approximately 25 minutes. The work on constructing the questionnaires began in fall 1997. A group of renowned work and family experts reviewed the final questionnaires.

With funding from the publisher William Morrow, Merck & Co., the Marriott Corporation, and the A. L. Mailman Foundation, the questionnaires were then administered. Parent interviews were conducted on the phone by Louis Harris and Associates with a nationally representative sample of 605 employed parents with children 18 years old or younger in June 1998. A nationally representative sample of 1,023 children in the third through the twelfth grades were given a self-administered questionnaire during their English classes in April–May 1998.[3]

So what did we learn? This book tells the story.

Reframing the Debate About Working and Children

hy have we never asked children how they feel about working parents? Yes, they tell us, of course, from time to time, whether we want to hear from them or not. But why is it that whenever I mention that we are studying children's views of their employed parents, parents inevitably respond, "I wonder what my children would say?" They wonder because they have never asked.

Why has a book like this one never been written, a comprehensive study like the one I have conducted never been done? After all, increasingly dual-earner families have become the norm. In all this time, have we not wanted to know what our children think?

The parents who first wonder what their children would say just as inevitably stop short and add, "I don't know if I want to know." "I would feel too guilty." "My child might say awful things about me." And for many mothers: "My child might tell me to stop working—to stay home."

Yet there is curiosity: "Don't tell me about what my own children say, but do tell me about what other people's children think."

Although many of us probably have not asked our own children, we are ready to listen. Over the years that I have worked on issues of work and family life, I have seen an evolution in our interest in understanding social change. At different times, there is a "societal readiness" to take on certain issues. I believe that we are ready to listen because it is finally the right time. More important, we are ready to listen because we really do need to know.

Recently, the Families and Work Institute cohosted a meeting of business leaders at which a neuroscientist presented an overview of what we know about the brain development of young children. He showed slides revealing that the brain of the child is wired by experience, both positive and negative. There were several other presentations, and then a strong discussion among the business leaders present. As the meeting was wrapping up, the moderator asked the audience, "What should the business community do in response to this information about the brain development of young children?" The room stilled; the heated discussion of moments before seemed frozen in time. Finally, Faith Wohl, president of the Child Care Action Campaign, broke the silence. "For the twenty years that I worked for a corporation," she began, "whenever the topic turned to the business community's responsibility for young children, we would say, 'That's the government's role.' Then I went to work for the federal government, and there we would say, 'It's the business community's role.' This subject is a hot potato, passed from unwilling player to unwilling player. And it is because we are still ambivalent about whether or not mothers should work."

Yet our feelings about whether or not mothers should work have changed over the past 30 years. They have changed because of what I think of as a national conversation about mothers' and fathers' roles in work and family life. Including children and their views of their working parents is the logical next step in this conversation.

Why do I call it a conversation? Essentially because the debate about the changing roles of women and men has taken place publicly. A controversial or tragic occurrence—a school shooting, a study, a book, a television show, a custody case, a trial—will arise that captures the public's attention because it presents a topic about which we are unsure or strongly divided. This topic will be widely discussed—at gatherings at work, around our kitchen tables, at parties with our friends and neighbors. One can almost chart the course of evolving public opinion by looking at these incidents.

Importantly, the conversation thus far has hinged on an either/or premise. I've found, however, that bringing *both* children and parents into the picture moves us beyond a black-and-white view.

THE ONGOING DEBATE ABOUT CHILDREN
AND PARENTAL EMPLOYMENT

▼ **Is having a working mother good or bad for children?** The debate in the 1960s centered on the question, Is having a working mother good or bad for children? It was first fueled by studies of children in orphanages showing that children separated from their mothers for long periods and raised in environmentally depressed conditions failed to thrive, even though they received adequate physical care.[1] Some social scientists and experts drew the conclusion that therefore mothers' working was bad for children. This opinion was countered by a number of researchers who said that the prolonged separation from mothers of children in an orphanage and the daily separations involved in child care could not be compared; therefore the jury was out on working mothers.

Between the 1960s and the late 1980s, a number of reviews of the research showed that there was little reason to be concerned about older children whose mothers worked. Although the public didn't necessarily agree, the public debate then shifted to infants. In 1988—perhaps not so coincidentally the very first year that a majority of mothers of infants were in the work force—Jay Belsky of Pennsylvania State University reported that a few studies indicated that infants whose mothers worked more than 20 hours a week in their child's first year of life were less likely to become securely attached to their mothers.[2] Since insecure attachments have been shown to lead to developmental problems in older children, and since some studies indicated that children with early experiences in child care are more aggressive, a public alarm was sounded.

Researchers immediately lined up on both sides of this issue on talk shows, and articles were published pro and con. Ultimately, the National Academy of Sciences convened a meeting bringing together what was informally called "the warring parties in the debate." This meeting led to a longitudinal study in the 1990s of approximately 1,300 children from ten communities by ten teams of researchers funded by the National Institute of Child Health and Human Development (NICHD).

▼ **Can mothers who work have just as good relationships with their children as mothers at home?**[3] How do working parents feel about this issue? In our Ask the Children study, we asked a representative group of employed parents how strongly they agreed or disagreed with the following statement: "A mother who works outside the home can have just as good a relationship with her children as a mother who does not work." Overall, 76 percent of employed parents agree somewhat or strongly with this statement. One would expect employed parents to endorse their own life-style, but it is noteworthy that one in four parents disagrees.

Who are these parents who disagree? Fathers are much more likely to disagree (30 percent) than mothers (18 percent). However, there are no differences between fathers and mothers in dual-earner couples on this issue, whereas—as one might expect—there are large differences between fathers with employed wives and those with wives at home.

Among all family types, employed mothers who are single parents are the most likely to agree that mothers who work can have just as good relationships with their children as mothers who are at home. In fact, 90 percent agree with this statement. Thus, mothers who have little or no choice about working are the most adamant in their belief that mothers' working doesn't harm the mother-child relationship.

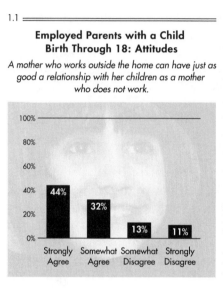

1.1

**Employed Parents with a Child
Birth Through 18: Attitudes**

A mother who works outside the home can have just as good a relationship with her children as a mother who does not work.

Over time, there has been a steady increase in the number of people who feel that employed mothers can have just as good a relationship with their children as at-home mothers. I attribute this largely to the gradual social and cultural change as women have moved into the work force in larger and larger numbers and as families have become more dependent on their income. Twenty years ago, the same question was included in the 1977 Quality of Employment Survey conducted for the Department of Labor. Among all employees—whether or not they were parents—the number climbed from 58 percent who agreed in 1977 to 67 percent in 1997, according to the Families and Work Institute's 1997 National Study of the Changing Workforce conducted by researchers Terry Bond and Jennifer Swanberg and me.[4]

In fact, one working mother we interviewed for the Ask the Children study said:

> I've seen growth in [my daughter] and I think a lot of that has to do with my own growth, and I think a lot of my own growth has to do with the fact that I had that extension of my life in the world of working. I may have had other interests and done other things had I not worked and been a stay-at-home mom, but I think I gained more and was able to give more to her as a result of having that amount of independence in my own life.

Is this mother speaking from experience or is this wishful thinking? The research shows that parents are speaking from experience. The most definitive study on the subject, conducted by the NICHD research team, found that mothers' working and a child's being in child care in themselves do not affect the bond between the mother and the child. It is very simple. Infants are more likely to be securely attached to their mothers when their mothers are *warm and responsive*. And mothers can be warm and responsive whether they are employed or not. A parent we interviewed put it well:

> I think you can be just as good a parent working or staying at home. It depends on where the parent is coming from and what their skills are.

The NICHD study did find cases in which mothers' working had a negative impact on the mother-child bond. This was more likely to occur when mothers were less warm and responsive *and* when the children experienced one or more of the following conditions: poor-quality child care, more than minimal amounts of time in child care, or more frequent changes in the child care arrangement.[5]

These nuances have been largely lost in the public debate, however, dismissed by the people who want to see maternal employment as an either/or proposition: A working mother is *either* bad *or* good for children. They are also dismissed by the people who see this finding as an indictment of mothers who stay at home: If working doesn't harm children, then what's the justification for staying at home? Mothers at home will say that they *know* that their being at home has been good for their children. And typically they are right! Typically, so are the mothers who say that their working has been good for their children. Because it is not an either/or proposition. It depends on the people and the circumstances of their lives. And what's right for one person may not be right for another.

So although the debate to this point has assumed an either/or stance, the research indicates that "it depends"—on the quality of parenting the child receives at home and on the child's experiences in child care.

▼ | **Is it better if men earn money and women care for the home and children?** Breadwinning is another highly charged issue in the debate about parents' roles. So we asked parents to respond to the statement "It is much better for everyone involved if the man earns the money and the woman takes care of the home and the children." Fifty-one percent of employed parents somewhat or strongly agree.

Again, employed fathers are more likely to support this statement than employed mothers. The difference, however, is not between fathers and mothers in dual-earner families. It is fathers with wives at home who feel most strongly about this statement.

One might ask, Why is there such strong support for the traditional family when fewer and fewer families are living that way? Among married fathers in the labor force, the proportion with employed wives has climbed from 49 percent in 1977 to 67 percent by 1997.[6] Arlene Skolnick, a family sociologist at the University of California at Berkeley, argues that in any period of social transformation such as the one we are in at the advent of the twenty-first century, people look at the recent past with nostalgia. They grasp at old images before developing new ways of handling reality.[7]

I believe that the views of employed parents are more complicated than those who would interpret this finding as a call for mothers to leave the work force and return home realize. Why? Because my study also finds that more than seven in ten employed mothers and fathers agree that it would be OK for the woman to be the economic provider and the man to be the nurturer. Most employed parents are not simply endorsing the traditional family;

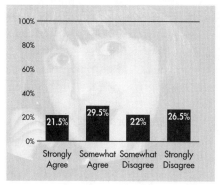

1.2

Employed Parents with a Child Birth Through 18: Attitudes

It is much better for everyone involved if the man earns the money and the woman takes care of the home and children.

- Strongly Agree: 21.5%
- Somewhat Agree: 29.5%
- Somewhat Disagree: 22%
- Strongly Disagree: 26.5%

Not all figures here and throughout the book add up to 100 percent, due to rounding.

rather, they seem to be yearning for a less stressful life. It certainly seems as if *both* mothers and fathers would like someone at home who cares for them and the children.

▼ **Is it right or wrong for a mother to work if she needs the money?** Economics is the backdrop for the latest discussions about whether it is right or wrong for a mother to work. This public conversation intensified with the presidential campaign in 1991 and the push to "end welfare as we know it." Welfare recipients were often portrayed in the media as only too happy to live off the work of others. This largely distorted depiction stuck and affected public opinion.

Since welfare reform passed, has this debate been resolved? At first glance it appears so. Virtually all employed parents (97 percent) somewhat or strongly agree that "it is okay for mothers to work if they really do need the money." But a closer look reveals that there is still ambivalence, particularly among fathers, who are less likely than mothers to believe that mothers should work—even if they need money: 67 percent of fathers strongly agree compared with 81 percent of mothers.[8]

In our one-on-one interviews, a mother described how it feels to be the brunt of these blaming attitudes:

> *So many women have to work just to even eat, but a lot of people look at them and think "You know you should stay home; you're not being the kind of parent you should be" or "Why are you having children?"*

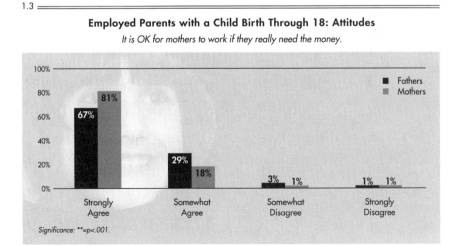

1.3

Employed Parents with a Child Birth Through 18: Attitudes

It is OK for mothers to work if they really need the money.

- Fathers
- Mothers

	Strongly Agree	Somewhat Agree	Somewhat Disagree	Strongly Disagree
Fathers	67%	29%	3%	1%
Mothers	81%	18%	1%	1%

Significance: **=p<.001.

This mother argues that mothers "don't need any more guilt than they already feel":

Life is hard enough when you work [and have] children that you don't need anything but SUPPORT.

Study after study confirms parents' views that maternal employment can be, in fact, good for low-income children. There are many well-documented risks for the children who grow up poor compared with those who don't. In the early childhood years, the risks are delayed development and behavior problems. In the school-age years, the risks are inferior school performance, behavior problems, grade failure, and learning and attention problems. In the teen years, they include dropping out of school, antisocial behavior or juvenile delinquency, teen pregnancy, and drug and alcohol use.[9]

The quality of child care becomes even more important for children in low-income families. The NICHD study has found that such children in poor-quality child care suffer what one of the researchers, Deborah Phillips of the National Academy of Sciences Board on Children and Families, calls a "double whammy." Thus, although we can say that it is typically good for poor children to have employed parents who can raise the family's standard of living, we must also say that "it depends" to some extent on other factors, including the quality of child care these children receive.

▼ **Is it right or wrong for mothers to work when they don't need the money?** Given the either/or framework in which most of our national conversations take place, it is not surprising that there is more disapproval of mothers who work when they don't need the money than of those who truly need the income. This conversation has, at times, become very polarized, as it did in 1997, after the publication of a book called *The Time Bind*. The author, Arlie Hochschild, argued that some women are turning to work as a refuge from the hassles of home and hearth.[10] Since she had conducted research at a corporation where the employees are well paid, this book unleashed strong opinions on all sides. During the call-in radio shows that I did at the time, I heard repeatedly from callers who could accept women's working if it was necessary to put food on the table and a roof over the family's heads. But many of these callers said, "Forget it," if a mother could afford to stay home. And particularly "forget it" if a mother actually liked her work. There was almost a puritanical tone to some callers' comments: For mothers, work should be a duty, certainly not enjoyable.

Likewise, in 1997, the so-called nanny trial of Louise Woodward for the death of the 9-month-old infant in her care suddenly turned on the mother, Deborah Eappen. This woman, an ophthalmologist married to another physician, worked 3 days a week and went home regularly to have lunch with her baby. Nevertheless, she was criticized so sharply for working that she finally asked when the climate had changed such that she had become the villain rather than the victim of a crime. In fact, the *New York Times* stated at the time, "Working mothers, not a nanny, often seem on trial."[11]

Through the 20 years that I have been following this debate, the media have regularly profiled highly paid mothers who quit their jobs. The latest of these mothers is Brenda Barnes, who left PepsiCo and a very high salary to be at home with her children—though she hinted at the time that she might look for a job that would be more accommodating.[12] Moreover, I have even seen the media report a trend that women are returning home when no such trend has actually occurred. Such are the public's strong feelings about women who can afford to be at home and yet work.

How do employed parents feel about mothers who work but could afford to stay home? Our study reveals some ambivalence on this question. Overall, 47.5 percent agree that mothers who really don't need to earn money shouldn't work compared to fully 97 percent who agreed that "it is okay for mothers to work if they really need the money."

Not unexpectedly, fathers with nonemployed wives endorse their own life-style by being more likely to agree (60 percent) than fathers with employed wives (48 percent) that mothers who don't need the money shouldn't work.[13]

Many of the mothers we interviewed described this as a no-win situation. Working mothers are chastised for *leaving* the home, and stay-at-home moms are chastised for *being* at home! One mother described this dilemma:

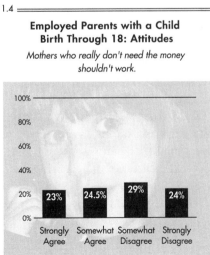

1.4

Employed Parents with a Child Birth Through 18: Attitudes

Mothers who really don't need the money shouldn't work.

Strongly Agree	Somewhat Agree	Somewhat Disagree	Strongly Disagree
23%	24.5%	29%	24%

> *I think it's easy to see that neither life-style is respected as it should be: That if you stay home you can't have value as a person, and that if you work you can't be a good parent.*
>
> *I think that both are valuable and that both are difficult and neither one of those are going to go away. Women are always going to work either because they choose to or because they have to, and women will always stay home because they can.*

My forays into talk radio over the past few months have confirmed this mother's point of view. While many social commentators continue to push the either/or debate, they are beginning to seem out of touch with the American people, who are moving to a more holistic outlook. Our experiences are reshaping the debate. Many mothers move in and out of the work force so that sometimes they are employed and sometimes they are at home. Furthermore, almost everyone has an employed mother somewhere in his or her family. Thus, the hard lines between the two camps are softening. The time has come to move the debate past the "One is good, therefore, the other is bad" mentality. As this mother says, both need to be valued. Because after all, there are wonderful and terrible mothers who work and wonderful and terrible mothers who stay at home.

What does the research say? After several decades of studies in which the children of employed mothers have been compared with the children of mothers not working outside the home, the conclusion reached is that maternal employment in and of itself has very little impact on children. As a 1999 study following children from infancy through their twelfth year found: "Early maternal employment status and the timing and continuity of early maternal employment were not consistently related to children's development."[14] There are, simply, no clear-cut results. The effect on children of being separated from their mothers on a daily basis *depends* (there's that word again) on many other factors, such as the income that the mother's job brings into the family, the mother's and father's attitudes toward her working, the stresses and satisfactions that parents bring home from their work, and the quality of the child care the children receive.[15]

▼ **Are mothers putting their material needs and their desire for success ahead of their children's well-being?** When federal child care legislation was introduced in 1998, I reviewed numerous articles for and against the enactment of such legislation. It was not uncommon to find writers opposing child care legislation with the argument that today's parents (more often, mothers) are selfish, putting their material desires and their strivings for success ahead of their obligation to care for their children.

Our study shows that a majority of employed parents disagree. However, sizable proportions (42 percent) of employed parents feel that employed mothers care more about being successful at work than meeting the needs of their children.[16]

▼ **Are fathers putting their material needs and their desire for success ahead of their children's well-being?** Since the debate has tended to center on mothers, it is perhaps surprising that employed parents are more likely to see *fathers*—not mothers—as putting their desires for success ahead of their concerns for their children. Overall, 62 percent of employed parents feel this way, with no difference between mothers and fathers in holding this opinion.[17]

Our one-on-one interviews with parents reflected both agreement and disagreement with the idea that men put their desires for suc-

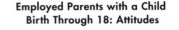

1.5

Employed Parents with a Child Birth Through 18: Attitudes

Many working **mothers** seem to care more about being successful at work than meeting the needs of their children.

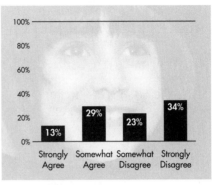

1.6

Employed Parents with a Child Birth Through 18: Attitudes

Many working **fathers** seem to care more about being successful at work than meeting the needs of their children.

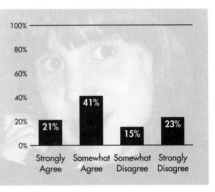

cess ahead of their children. Most men we talked to worked longer hours than their wives. Some women attributed a father's propensity toward having his own pursuits as a gender difference:

> *I think it may be a male thing, and that's a terrible stereotype, but [my husband] has a greater sense of entitlement and making sure his needs are being met first. He's aware that I think he's got a little bit too much entitlement so there's at least the open*

communication. And he's even declared jokingly that "this is the year of me," meaning himself. And so I appreciate that he's seeing the humor in it.

A father speaks of some of his male coworkers:

I know guys that are married and have kids and they love to travel and my theory is that it's their way to get away from all the action, so to speak. They look for trips.

On the other hand, many men we met had made conscious efforts to put family before work. One father says:

My choice was to be leaning toward my family as opposed to leaning toward a career. Because I think I could put a lot more effort into my career and do a lot better than I'm probably going to do, be a lot further along than I am today. So I think I have the capability but I don't have the drive or energy because I funnel that into the family.

Others tried to narrow the gender gap by turning down travel opportunities:

It's not fair; my wife works, and she has a business to run and the more I'm [not home] at night, [the more] it makes it difficult for her because she does a lot of her work at night. So if I'm not here at night it gets kind of crazy. Plus the kids miss me.

Although clearly there are selfish parents—I imagine we all could name some—the research paints a picture of a somewhat different reality of what author Betty Holcomb describes as the media's tendency to stigmatize ambition, particularly among working mothers. In the Families and Work Institute's 1997 National Study of the Changing Workforce, we found that despite the rapid influx of mothers into the work force over the past 20 years, household income for employed families with children had not changed during that period. Expressed in 1997 dollars, household income was about $57,500 for workers with children in 1977 *and* in 1997.[18] (This average masks the fact that the rich have become richer, the poor have become poorer, and the middle has stayed more or less the same.) Although there was a slight increase in family income in 1998, most parents are not running to get ahead:

Essentially, they are running to stay in place, to preserve their standard of living.

In addition, our 1997 National Study of the Changing Workforce found that children appear to be receiving somewhat *more* attention from their employed parents today than was the case 20 years ago (see Chapter 3 for a fuller discussion). On the basis of mothers' and fathers' reports of how much time they spend with their children, we found that the time mothers spend has remained constant, while fathers' time has increased. Since families also have fewer children, this means that children see their parents slightly more.[19] The National Study of the Changing Workforce didn't assess what is happening in the time that parents and children are together—for example, whether it is rushed or calm or whether parents are doing several other tasks while they are with their children. In terms of these two findings, parents in general do not appear to be putting their material needs blatantly ahead of their children, though, of course, there are always exceptions.

▼ **Is it right or wrong for the mother to be the primary bread-winner and the father to care for the children?** There have been a number of movies about "Mr. Mom." There have also been magazine articles and books about fathers who are primary care givers in two-parent families. However, such men remain relatively few in number.

Our National Study of the Changing Workforce reveals, however, that increasing numbers of men are raising children alone. Among single parents, 27 percent are now men.[20] Thus, much of the national conversation about fathers as primary nurturers has been triggered by bitter wrangling in cases in which fathers fight for custody.

There is the case of Jennifer Ireland, a student at the University of Michigan in 1994, who lost custody of 3-year-old Maranda in a lower court simply because she placed her in a child care center while she attended classes. Although the Michigan Court of Appeals reversed this decision in 1995, stating that the use of child care is not a sufficient basis for removing a child from her mother's custody, this case generated a great deal of media coverage because it included the twin taboos of an unmarried mother and a mother's choosing nonfamily care for her child.[21]

Another potential taboo for mothers: working long hours. Should such a mother be granted custody rather than a father who has been more of a stay-at-home or very involved dad? These issues have had their day in actual courts as well as in the court of public opinion. There was Sharon Prost in 1994, a counsel to Senator Orrin Hatch of Utah, who lost primary custody to her husband. In the newspaper reports, she was described as taking a work-related phone call during her child's birthday party. Marcia Clark, the Los Angeles County prosecutor, was arguing the O. J. Simpson case while fighting to keep custody of her children, in jeopardy because of her 16-hour workdays during the trial. In 1998 in Miami, another lawyer, Alice Hector, lost primary custody of her children to her husband, who had for the past two years assumed their care and who also volunteered in their school. There was testimony that she once took a law book to a school performance. Since virtually all employed parents have, at one time or another, paid attention to work rather than to their children, assertions like this can send shivers of fear through most employed mothers (and fathers).

Still another issue about which we are divided: mothers earning more than fathers. According to the 1997 National Study of the Changing Workforce, 24 percent of employed mothers in dual-earner households earn more than their husbands.[22] Still, we haven't resolved how we feel about this issue. Alice Hector, the Miami lawyer, was reportedly very upset that her former husband didn't do more to bring in money.

And finally, we haven't fully sanctioned the idea of fathers gaining custody. Although more dads are winning custody fights, many fathers argue that they have an uphill battle. Writing in the *New York Times* about Alice Hector and her former husband, Robert Young, Melody Petersen says, "Whatever the final outcome of this case, it is a cautionary tale for mothers—and fathers—who try to balance parenthood with professional ambition."[23]

What does the research say about fathers' involvement with children? As James A. Levine and Todd Pittinsky state in *Working Fathers*, until recently, "most eyes [of researchers] were focused on working mothers."[24] They report on studies showing that father involvement is positive for children's development. For example, children whose fathers were more involved when they were infants score better on tests assessing their mental and motor development[25] and manage stress better in the school-age years.[26] Children whose fathers are more involved in the preschool and school-age years demonstrate a greater ability to take initiative.[27] Father involvement also seems to reduce the risk of drug use, juvenile delinquency, and teen pregnancy.[28] As with mothers, the point is not simply to have fathers involved. Children fare better when their fathers are warm and responsive in their involvement.[29]

What about children whose fathers take the primary responsibility for child care? Kyle Pruett of Yale University followed such families

over a number of years. He found
that it isn't that children lose a
mother to gain a father, but rather
that they reap the benefits of having *both* parents involved.[30]

Where do employed parents
stand? Our study shows that
almost three quarters of parents
agree that "children do just as well
if the mother has primary responsibility for earning the money and
the father has primary responsibility for caring for the children."

Taking on the role of a nurturer
is more acceptable today as men
are becoming aware of the satisfy-
ing nature of that role and its importance to children's development.
One stay-at-home dad explains:

1.7

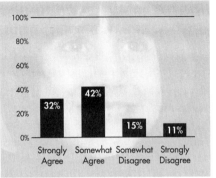

**Employed Parents with a Child
Birth Through 18: Attitudes**

*Children do just as well if the mother has primary
responsibility for earning the money and the father has
primary responsibility for caring for the children.*

- Strongly Agree: 32%
- Somewhat Agree: 42%
- Somewhat Disagree: 15%
- Strongly Disagree: 11%

> *In the back of your mind you
> think about the macho man who is supposed to be the bread-
> winner, but your children still love you and respect you as you
> are, even [though you're not] actually fulfilling the role as the
> breadwinner.*

▼ **Is child care good or bad for children?** Woven through the
decades of debate about work and family life has been the subject of child care. A number of "cautionary tales" have riveted
public attention. There was the McMartin sexual abuse case in child
care in California in the 1980s. There was Jessica McClure, the toddler
who fell into an uncovered well at the home of her unlicensed child
care provider in Texas in 1987. While the country cheered as Jessica was
rescued, parents asked themselves, "Weren't those special circumstances?" Or they noted, "I would be more careful about the child care
I choose."

Then in the early 1990s, Diane Sawyer showed that parents might
not know what really goes on behind the closed doors of child care centers once they say good-bye in the morning. In a special feature on *Prime
Time Live*, she followed well-meaning, diligent parents through their
search for child care. Then, through the use of hidden cameras, she

played back for these parents and the public what was happening to their children: babies left, unchanged and hungry, in cribs all day; toddlers being slapped for crying. It was unthinkable. "Could this possibly happen to my child?"

It became clear that the answer might be yes. Three community-based studies were released—in 1988, in 1994, and again in 1995—indicating that the quality of child care was mediocre at best, and that between 12 and 21 percent of children are in child care arrangements that could be considered potentially harmful to their safety and development.[31] The findings instantly became headline news. One of the studies was conducted by the Families and Work Institute, and its results were featured above the centerfold on the front page of some of the nation's leading newspapers, fueling the debate Is it bad or good for a mother with young children to work and to use child care?

What does the research show? Again, the answer is not the black-and-white finding so desired by the commentators who want a point/counterpoint argument. Essentially, studies, including the one conducted by NICHD, show that parents are first and foremost in children's lives and have the greatest impact on how they develop. Yet, they also show that the quality of child care does matter: Good child care can add value to parental care giving and bad child care can diminish the best of parenting.[32] In other words, once again, "it depends."

MOVING BEYOND THE EITHER/OR DEBATE

As you can see, our national debate about working and children has been conducted as if the answer is either yes or no, as if one path is inherently good and the other bad. But more than four decades of research has shown that reality is not so simple. Outcomes for children "depend" primarily on what parents do with their children when they are together and secondarily on what happens to the children when they are away from their parents.

Until now, the language that we have used to describe work and family life similarly has been either/or language. Implicit in this way of speaking is the notion that work and family are "separate, non-overlapping worlds."[33] In 1997, Rosalind Barnett of Brandeis University wrote that we have to move beyond the notion of separate spheres toward understanding that work and family are inextricably interconnected, and that, in fact, multiple roles can energize rather than deplete us.[34]

There is also an either/or notion of balancing work and family, which has been endlessly promulgated in books and other media. Balancing connotes a set of scales. If one side is up, the other side is down. The goal, as working parents typically see it, is to keep both sides even or equal. Although the notion of balance is correct in considering both work and family on the same continuum, the connections are more dynamic than balance implies. Both sides can be up and both sides can be down. What works for one person doesn't work for another.

Finally, there is the concept of quality time versus quantity time. This concept implies that *either* the amount of time *or* the quality of time is more important. Yet, as you will see, this study of parents and children makes it very evident that one can't separate the amount of time from what happens during that time.

When we ask the children, not only are we able to see what we do in a new way, we also reframe the debate. In the chapters that follow, I will suggest a new language to describe today's realities and new ways of handling them. Asking the children is clearly the next step in what has been an ongoing national conversation. From my many discussions with parents across the country, I believe that we are ready to listen to children and in so doing to embrace a more accurate and more empowering view.[35]

How Children See Their Parents' Parenting Skills

Being a parent is unlike any of life's other experiences. As one mother puts it:

> *With everything else I do, I know that if I do A, it will almost certainly lead to B. But as a parent, I don't really know what the results of my actions will be. If I do A, will it lead to C or D or X?*

Another parent said:

> *You get such conflicting advice. From one person I hear that if I pick up the baby when she cries, I will spoil her. From another person I hear that if I don't pick up the baby when she cries, I won't give her a sense of basic trust that the world is a good place, that her parents will respond to her needs and that her parents are reliable. Who is right?*

Yes, being a parent is different from any other endeavor we undertake and there are no surefire, absolute answers. As I discussed in the previous chapter, the debate about working and parenting has swung from extreme to extreme: It's bad for children if their mothers work—it's good for children if their mothers work. So when we examine how children view their parents, one of our goals is to assess whether having an employed mother or a mother at home makes a difference in how children feel about their mothers and fathers. In other words, do families really have to choose work *or* family?

There is a growing body of research that has examined the connections between what parents do and how children turn out. At the Families and Work Institute, we have reviewed this research, including studies on the brain development of children, to determine what parents can do to promote their children's healthy development, school readiness, and school success. Our interviews with parents and children provided an additional opportunity to probe the question, What makes a good parent? From these, I postulated eight critical parenting skills and then looked at how children from third through twelfth grades assess their parents on each of these skills.

EIGHT IMPORTANT PARENTING SKILLS

1. Making the child feel important and loved

One of the most important parenting skills is making one's children feel important and loved. This is certainly common wisdom—parents know this, and it is confirmed by decades of scientific research. Children who receive warm and loving care are more likely to feel safe and secure with the adults who take care of them. In research parlance, these children are *securely attached.* Such children can rebound from stress more easily when they are older, are more curious, get along better with other children, and perform better in school than are children who are less securely attached. Conversely, children who receive erratic care are more likely to become dependent and anxious later in life.[1] As the well-known developmental psychologist of Cornell University Urie Bronfenbrenner has often said, in order to thrive, every child needs someone who is crazy about him or her.

2. Responding to the child's cues and clues

Children become securely attached when parents and other care givers try to read their cues and clues and respond to them, starting at the beginning of life. Infants begin to trust that when they smile, someone will smile back; that when they are upset, someone will comfort them;

that when they are hungry, someone will feed them. This trust becomes the basis of feelings of security.

It is very important to note that the child is not a passive recipient of how he or she is treated but an important actor. Development involves the parent *and* the child and how they interact. Both are givers, both are takers, though of course the parent as the adult takes the lead. This dynamic interplay is at the heart of the concept of responsiveness.

There are biological processes that underlie this psychological concept, that both nature and nurture, which are inextricably entwined, shape development and perhaps even influence survival. In studies of mother rats and their babies, Myron Hofer of Columbia University College of Physicians and Surgeons has shown that the nature and timing of the contact between mother and infant actually regulate the infant's biological systems. Particularly important is the mother's responsiveness to the infant's rhythms and behavioral signals. In experiments in which the mother rat and her newborn are separated 2 weeks after birth, biochemical changes in the infant can be observed within 24 hours, including changes in the level of growth hormones, heart rate, blood pressure, sucking, and responsiveness to stimulation. Hofer has found that infant rats who are permanently separated from their mothers are more likely to be vulnerable to stress as they grow up. Because of the powerful influences of normal interactions between care giver and child on newborns' biological systems and developing brain, Hofer has termed them "hidden regulators."[2]

The importance of the give and take between the young child and the care giver can be dramatically demonstrated in videos when one camera is on the child and one camera is on the adult, but the interactions between them are viewed on a split screen where the faces of both can be seen. These interactions can also be graphed, moment by moment, as they have been in studies by Ed Tronick and T. Berry Brazelton at Harvard University. The child will do something, and the adult will respond, typically imitating the child, for example, repeating the noise the child has made. This give and take will begin to crescendo, until the child appears to have had enough stimulation and turns away, only to turn back, beginning the cycle again. In experiments in which the care giver (mother or father) is told to "freeze," to stop responding, the child will typically look startled, do everything to reengage the parent, then become red-faced, flail, and cry.

According to Daniel Siegel of UCLA, these patterns of communication can have direct effects on the child's development.[3] Other corroborating research by Megan Gunnar at the University of Minnesota shows that by the end of the first year, children who have received consistent, warm, and responsive care produce less of the stress hormone cortisol than those who have not, and that when they do become upset, they can "turn off" their stress reaction more quickly. This suggests that well-nurtured children are better equipped to respond to life's challenges.[4]

These studies do not imply that the daily separations between employed parents and their children or the periodic bad mood and lack of responsiveness of a parent will irreparably harm a child or that it's all over when the child becomes a preschooler. That is simply not so. It is the persistent extremes that *can* cause harm. These studies are described to make visible how important the normal give and take between the parent and child is. I know that after being steeped in this research, I now see the normal interactions between a parent and child, such as the game of peekaboo, in an entirely different way.

Responsiveness encompasses being emotionally as well as intellectually responsive. It includes comforting a child who is upset, whether that child is a toddler who falls and is hurt or a teenager who thinks he or she has been spurned by a friend (being emotionally responsive). It also includes caring about the child's learning, whether by bringing home a book about fire engines for the preschooler who is excited by them or listening to the teenager's paper on El Niño (being intellectually responsive). If we as adults think back to the moments in which we really learned something, we will undoubtedly realize that they occurred during a moment of give and take with another person.

Studies have found that there are certain techniques that parents use that affect children's intellectual development, which, in turn, can affect how well the children do in school:

▼ Talk to children in a way that engages them in the conversation. Talking includes listening as much as it does speaking.

▼ Ask children to discuss what has happened to them during the day. Specific questions work better than general ones (rather than "What did you do in school today?" ask, "What book are you reading and what do you think of it?").

▼ Read to children regularly and interactively "in a manner that actively involves the child through responses to parent questions about pictures and story figures."[5] Pose challenging questions when you are reading: "How do you feel? How does the person in the story feel? What would you do if you were in her situation?"[6]

▼ Help children learn to think about sequencing: "What do you think will happen next?"

▼ Encourage children to use their imaginations, to be creative.

▼ Ask children questions that encourage them to think beyond the here and now: "What do you think will happen when we get to Grandmother's house?"[7]

▼ Make reading and writing materials available.[8]

▼ Limit television watching, be selective in what children watch, and discuss programs with them.[9]

Douglas R. Powell of Purdue University warns that although parents can do a great deal to strengthen children's learning, they are certainly not entirely responsible for either children's successes or failures. Other people in children's lives, including teachers, make a difference, and the child plays a part as well.[10]

3. Accepting the child for who he or she is, but expecting success

As most parents note, some differences in each of their children seem inborn and are apparent very early on. Children do have different temperaments: One child is shy and slow to warm up, and another child is outgoing; some children are easygoing, and others are more intense and less adaptable to daily routines.[11]

Children's ideas about themselves—including their self-esteem—reflect to an important degree their parents' attitude toward them. The parenting expert Penelope Leach uses the concept of a mirror suggesting that children initially come to see themselves as parents see them.[12] Thus, parents and families play an important role in shaping children's self-concepts, which of course are also affected by the child's friends and community. Specific praise works better than general praise (rather than "You are the most wonderful person in the world," you can say, "The story you wrote has a lot of suspense in it").

Studies have found that children develop more positively when parents have realistic views of who their children are and accept them;[13] for example, when parents with a musical child don't keep saying, overtly or more subtly, that they wish their child were less artistic and more of a jock. On the other hand, parents who are unaware of their children's interests and abilities are more likely to create situations in which the children are bored or pushed beyond their abilities.[14]

Another factor that emerges from the parenting literature is the importance of expecting one's child to succeed, to be competent, to do well.[15] When we expect our children to succeed, we are also more likely to create a home environment that promotes children's competence.[16]

4. Promoting strong values

A study conducted by Public Agenda reveals that most people do not think that children are being raised with good values. When asked to use any word to describe "kids these days," more than two thirds of the adults—some of whom had little contact with children; some of whom had a great deal of contact, as parents or teachers—used derogatory descriptions like "rude, irresponsible, and wild." Although people tend to feel good about their own children, they are not necessarily positive about "other people's children." But they are very concerned about imbuing all children with strong morals and values.[17]

Families help shape children's values.[18] Parents communicate values not only by talking about values but by living them as well. Although parents are first and foremost in their children's lives, the influence of the children's group of friends can undermine or reinforce the values that parents are trying to teach. Studies of teenagers have found that their friends' lack of support for academic achievement can erode what parents are trying to accomplish.[19] So parents need to be mindful about what their children's friends are promoting as well as what they themselves are teaching.

5. Using constructive discipline

Discipline is one of the most difficult tasks we have as parents. It makes us feel good about ourselves to comfort a distressed child or to acknowledge a child's accomplishment, but it doesn't feel as wonderful to tell a child, "Stop," "You can't," "I won't let you." Even though we know that children feel safer when there are limits on their behavior, we may feel like "bad cops" when we discipline. Yet studies reveal that the ways we set limits influence whether or not children listen to us at the time as well as how they turn out later.[20]

A number of different approaches to setting limits can work, as long as they aim to teach children to internalize the limits rather than to humiliate, hurt, or demean them. Children seem to thrive when discipline is firm but caring. You can:

▼ focus the child's attention on what will happen next: "It will be time to leave in a few minutes."[21]

▼ be selective about when you say no, so children learn to recognize the important "nos."

▼ use neutral or positive language, and try to accompany "no" with a "yes" that directs the child's behavior: "Throw the ball outside, not inside."[22]

▼ give the reason for a rule: "It is not safe for you to go there."

▼ provide consequences for misbehavior that at best are connected to the child's action, such as repairing something he breaks or cleaning up something he spills. It can be very helpful to specify consequences in advance so children know what to expect.

▼ follow through on the consequences you have set.

▼ give limited tasks: "Pick up your clothes from the floor" (not "Clean your room").

▼ acknowledge children's feelings, but set limits: "I know you're angry, but you cannot hit your sister."

▼ help children see how their actions affect others: "Your brother is upset because of how you talked to him."[23]

▼ acknowledge positive behavior: "You did a good job with your homework."

▼ teach problem-solving skills to toddlers and older children: "What ideas do you have for solving that problem? How would each of those ideas work?"[24]

Conversely, studies show that parents who explode, who demean their children, and who are harsh and hurtful may have children who toe the line in the short term, but they tend to rebel and be less cooperative in the long run.[25]

6. Providing routines and rituals

As parents, we always wonder which experiences are going to have a lasting impression on our children. So we asked the children in our one-on-one interviews what they thought they would remember most from their childhoods. If our interviews with children are any indication of the future, children mentioned family rituals as being especially memorable in a positive way. Children talked about the made-up bedtime stories such as an ongoing story about a cow, a pig, and a chicken that went on night after night. Children talked about a family tradition of speaking silly languages such as double talk or pig Latin. Children talked about taking a walk every evening with a parent, or always singing "Michael, Row Your Boat Ashore" in the car. Likewise, studies have found that routine and tradition are important components in children's school readiness and school success.[26,27] As

Daniel Siegel has demonstrated in his book, *The Developing Mind*, *repeated* patterns of predictable, collaborative communication can have a positive effect on the child's social, emotional, and cognitive development.[28]

Routines make life predictable and understandable. Children (and adults too) manage more difficult transitions if they have rituals to get through them. For example, children who have a set way of going to bed each night are more likely to comply than children for whom bedtime is never the same from one night to the next. Children can also leave their parents more easily if they have ritualistic ways of saying good-bye.

Traditions are treasured rituals that we carry from childhood into adulthood. The way that birthdays or holidays are always celebrated, the songs that are always sung, the favorite family stories or jokes tend to stay with us throughout our lives.

7. Being involved in the child's education

Studies have found that when parents are more involved in their children's education, children's achievement is higher. Being involved means participating in the child's school or child care.[29] It also means encouraging at-home learning activities.[30] These activities include talking with the child about what happens in school, monitoring the child's performance, helping with homework, and reading with the child. In line with the importance of being intellectually responsive, parental involvement does not mean pouring information into the child, but engaging in a give-and-take discussion in which the child contributes, thinks, imagines, and problem solves. This concept can be illustrated by the story of a father of a first- and a second-grader:

> *I used to think that it was important for me to read two books aloud to my children every night, like it or not. I have since learned that this is not the point of reading aloud. Even if we only get to page one, but have a wonderful conversation, I have found out that that's what's important. Like I ask the children to pick out certain things in the pictures, or ask them "What if . . ." or "How would you feel?"*

8. Being there for the child

When my daughter, Lara, interviewed children as a prelude to the surveys we conducted for *Ask the Children*, she found that children judge their parents on whether or not they are "there for me." Although the definition of "being there for me" shifts as the child grows, becoming less and less limited to the parent and child's being physically together, we heard repeatedly from parents and children about two crucial issues: It is important to both parents and children that parents be present at the important events in the child's life and that parents be there for the child when the child is sick. When parents tell you about their failings or regrets, often these center on missing an event or leaving a sick child:

> It was the night of a school play and I got caught in a horrific traffic jam in the tunnel leaving the city. I was stuck. Trapped. There was nothing I could do about it. I felt so helpless. I walked into the school auditorium just as the audience was applauding at the end of the play. I don't think I will ever forget my daughter saying to me, "I kept looking for you in the audience and you weren't there."
>
> MOTHER OF A 12-YEAR-OLD DAUGHTER

> If I have any regrets it is how we handled my daughter's sicknesses. She has asthma so she has been sick often. Her father [they are now separated] and I would always end up fighting about who missed work. No matter what I was doing, it was never as important as what he was doing. I hated fighting in front of her. I certainly didn't want her to feel that she was less important than our work. But I also hated it that he would never stay with her. Now that she is about to leave for college, I wish I could roll back the clock and handle her sicknesses differently.
>
> MOTHER OF A 17-YEAR-OLD DAUGHTER

A WORD ABOUT ASKING THE CHILDREN

Before we explore how children view their parents' parenting skills, I want to talk about the issue of asking children for their views. Most people will see this study as providing enlightening information that can "keep the communication channels open" on a national, not simply on a family, level. This is especially necessary in the wake of school shootings where we wonder, Do parents know what is really going on with their children? But I can also imagine that some people might see this as abdicating our parental power to the children, as one more sign of permissive parenthood, in which parents can't make decisions, so they turn to their children.

Thus, it is very important to me to delineate the context in which I think we should ask the children. We are the adults, the parents, the authority figures, the disciplinarians. When we ask the children, we do so in that capacity. We are encouraging children to share how they feel about our working—as part of being a "responsive parent." But we are still the parents. The information we receive from children helps *us* make better decisions as parents—it doesn't at all imply that we are abdicating our responsibility for parenting to children.

HOW DO CHILDREN SEE THEIR PARENTS' PARENTING SKILLS?

Why we asked children to "grade" their parents

I have learned repeatedly from my own research and the research of others that people tend to say that they are "very satisfied" with whatever aspect of their lives you ask them about. For this study I searched for ways of assessing how people feel other than asking about satisfaction. Since parents and children are very familiar with the concept of grades, I felt that this construct would provide as accurate an assessment of how employed parents are doing—from both children's and parents' vantage points—as any other survey question I might ask.

I want to make the point very strongly that asking children to "grade" parents is simply a *research technique* to get more accurate answers. I am in no way suggesting that your children or mine "grade" us. This would be inappropriate. But it wouldn't be inappropriate for families to have discussions about these parenting skills. Nor would it be inappropriate for you to grade yourself. So before you look at the grades that a representative group of children give their parents on each parenting skill, you might want to ask yourself some questions:

▼ What grade do I think my child(ren) would give me? Why?
▼ What grade would I give myself? Why?
▼ Is there a discrepancy between the grade I think my child(ren) would give me and the grade I would give myself? Why?

▼ **Who is included in this study?** The research questions for parents were asked of a nationally representative group of employed parents with children birth through 18 years old. In our analyses, we include mothers, fathers, stepmothers, stepfathers, and guardians who live with the child at least half-time.

The research questions for children were asked of a nationally representative group of children in the third through the twelfth grades. They lived in two-earner families, single-parent employed families, unemployed parent families, and traditional families.

In our analyses, we define *mother* as either the biological mother or the stepmother (whom the child sees as filling the mother role) who lives with the child most of the time. We define *father* in the same way: the biological father or stepfather (whom the child sees as filling the father role) who lives with the child most of the time. In a few instances, children provide information about someone other than a parent or stepparent whom they view as filling the role of mother or father. Often these are relatives such as grandmothers or grandfathers, and they are included in our analyses.

Because there are many children who do not live with their father or with the person whom they consider their father figure (23 percent of the children in this study), we focus in every instance first on fathers who live with the children—resident fathers. So when we report a grade for fathers, it includes *only* resident fathers. Then we conduct additional analyses comparing children's views of resident fathers and nonresident fathers. There are far fewer children who do not live with their mother or the person who fills the role of mother for them (3.5 percent of the children). This group is too small to make reasonable comparisons and thus they are excluded from these analyses.

For most of the analyses conducted for the remainder of the book, we examine how children feel about their *employed* and *resident* mothers and fathers. But in determining how children assess their parents' parenting skills, we also include children's views of their parents who are not employed, either because they chose to stay at home and care for their children or because they were out of work when we surveyed their children. For each question, we look at differences in the grades given by children according to their gender, family type, family economics, and so forth.[31] We report only differences that are statistically significant.[32]

Later we will compare the grades children give their parents with those that parents give themselves. We'll also explore how the work and family lives of parents and children are linked to how well parents manage their work and family responsibilities. At this point, however, let's begin by asking the children.

Making the child feel important and loved

In order to assess the extent to which their parents are warm and caring, we asked children to grade both their mothers and fathers on "making me feel important and loved."

Most children give their mothers high marks on making them feel cared about, with 72 percent giving their mothers an A and only 12.5 percent give their mothers a C or lower. Children give their mothers higher grades when:

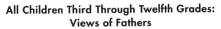

All Children Third Through Twelfth Grades: Views of Mothers

*What grade would you give your **mother** on... Making me feel important and loved?*

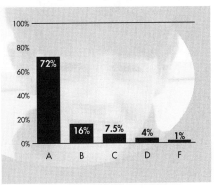

▼ the children are younger: 81 percent of children in the third through the sixth grades give their mothers an A compared with 64 percent of children in the seventh through the twelfth grades.

▼ they believe that their family is economically healthy (their family has no problem buying the things they need and they can also buy special things) compared with those who see their families as struggling (their family has a hard time buying the things they need or their family has just enough money for the things they need).

Because the debate about working and parenting has at times assumed that children fare differently in families in which the mother is employed compared to those in which the mother stays at home, we looked for a difference in the ways employed and nonemployed mothers are viewed by their children. There is none. Neither is there a difference in the grades given by children whose mothers work part-time and those who work full-time.

Children grade fathers lower than they do mothers on making them feel important and loved: 65.5 percent give their fathers an

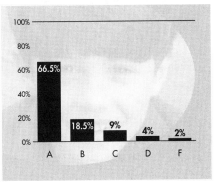

All Children Third Through Twelfth Grades: Views of Fathers

*What grade would you give your **father** on... Making me feel important and loved?*

A compared with 72 percent for their mothers, and 15 percent give their fathers a C or lower compared with 12.5 percent for mothers.

Although conflict and tension between teenagers and their parents can be standard fare, it is very striking that only 57 percent of children in the seventh through twelfth grades give their fathers an A compared with 80 percent of children in the third through the sixth grades. Children also give their fathers higher grades when:

▼ they see their families as economically healthy.
▼ their fathers are employed; in fact, only 37 percent of children give their nonemployed fathers an A.

We also conducted analyses comparing children's views of their resident and nonresident fathers. Not surprisingly, children give their nonresident fathers poorer marks—29 percent give them a C or lower compared with 15 percent for resident fathers.

Responding to the child's cues and clues

We used four questions to assess how children grade their parents on being responsive to their cues and clues. To examine parents' emotional responsiveness to their children, we asked about "being someone I can go to when I am upset," "spending time talking with me," and "knowing what is really going on in my life." To assess how intellectually responsive parents are, we asked about "encouraging me to want to learn and to enjoy learning." (Because we were quite limited in the length of the questionnaire we could administer to children in the third through sixth grades, some of these questions were asked only of children in the seventh through twelfth grades.)

▼ **Being someone the child can go to if upset** Mothers get lower marks on this parenting attribute than they do on making their children feel important and loved. Just over half of the children (57 percent) give their mothers an A, whereas one in four (25 percent) give their mothers a C or below.

Again, we find no differences in grading of employed mothers versus at-home mothers. Children give their mothers higher grades when:

▼ the children are younger.
▼ they see their families as economically healthy.

There is a significant difference in the number of children who give their mothers an A for being someone they can go to when they are upset (57 percent) and the number who give their fathers an A (48 percent). Just under one third of children (32 percent) give their fathers a C or lower. Children give their fathers higher grades when:

▼ the children are younger.
▼ they see their families as economically healthy.
▼ their fathers live in their households.

In our one-on-one interviews with children across the country, we heard how important it is to be able to go to a parent if they are upset. One 10-year-old boy says:

> It's better to talk with your parents than baby-sitters because you automatically feel more comfortable talking with them because they're part of your family.

2.3 ═══════════════════════

All Children Third Through Twelfth Grades: Views of Mothers

*What grade would you give your **mother** on... Being someone I can go to when I am upset?*

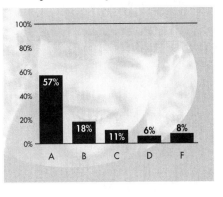

2.4 ═══════════════════════

All Children Third Through Twelfth Grades: Views of Fathers

*What grade would you give your **father** on... Being someone I can go to when I am upset?*

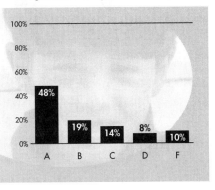

A 9-year-old girl knows that her parents want to help:

> When I'm upset they talk to me. They want to know why I'm upset. Which is comforting because I can't talk to myself. They help me deal with problems.

▼ **Spending time talking with their child** Forty-eight percent of children give their mothers an A for "spending time talking with me" and 21 percent give them a C or lower. Children give their mothers higher marks when:

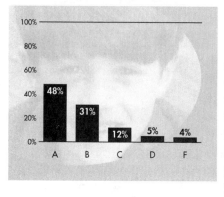

2.5

**All Children Third Through Twelfth Grades:
Views of Mothers**

*What grade would you give your **mother** on...
Spending time talking with me?*

- ▼ they are girls.
- ▼ they are younger.
- ▼ their fathers work full-time (versus part-time).
- ▼ they see their families as economically healthy.

Perhaps surprisingly, there is no significant difference in the grades children give to their mothers and their fathers on their "spending time talking with me." As we have found before, older children give lower grades to their fathers (33 percent give a C or lower) than younger ones (20 percent give a C or lower). The economic health of the family does not make a difference, but where the father lives does. Forty percent of children with nonresident fathers give them a C or lower compared with 28 percent of children with resident fathers.

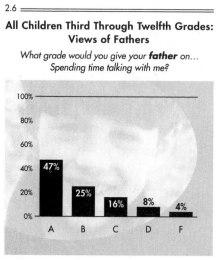

2.6

**All Children Third Through Twelfth Grades:
Views of Fathers**

*What grade would you give your **father** on...
Spending time talking with me?*

According to the children we interviewed in person, talking to their parents was seen as "the glue" that binds the parent and the child together. Conversations can occur in all sorts of places, as this 9-year-old girl notes:

> *In the car on the way there and in the car on the way back, and at home when we're sitting in front of the fire we talk about me, what's been going on at school and if there're any problems.*

One teenage girl (17 years old) initially resisted the idea that talking was important, but she has now changed her mind:

I heard that so many times—[talking is important]. I was like, "It's not it, that's not it." But it IS. It's talking, you know, communication. Telling your mother about your day; your mother telling you [about her day]. That's what we do.

▼ | **Knowing what is really going on in the child's life** 2.7

This question was asked only of children in the seventh through twelfth grades. Of all the skills graded by the older children, this was one of the lowest rated skills, with just more than one third of the older children (35 percent) giving their mothers an A. Comparable numbers (34 percent) give their mothers a C or lower.

Children who see their families as less economically healthy give their mothers lower grades (40 percent give a C or lower) than children in families in which money does not seem to be a problem (29 percent give a C or lower).

Fathers and mothers are graded similarly by their children when it comes to knowing what is really going on in their children's lives. These are disturbing findings given the concern raised by recent school shootings. Children give fathers higher grades when:

▼ they are boys.
▼ they believe their families are economically healthy.
▼ their fathers live in their household—57 percent of nonresident fathers receive a C or lower compared with 39 percent of resident fathers.

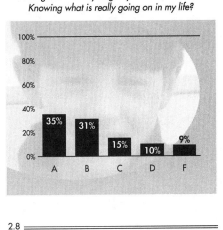

All Children Seventh Through Twelfth Grades: Views of Mothers

*What grade would you give your **mother** on ... Knowing what is really going on in my life?*

2.8

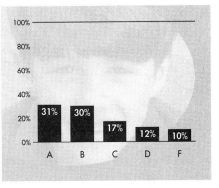

All Children Seventh Through Twelfth Grades: Views of Fathers

*What grade would you give your **father** on... Knowing what is really going on in my life?*

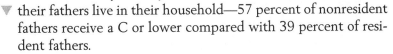

These low grades given to fathers and mothers alike by teenagers make me wonder whether teenagers' sense of distance from parents is part of the normal culture of growing up in the United States, or whether there could be greater closeness. As I will discuss later, children across the board in this study seem to yearn for closer relationships with their fathers. These findings are unexpected, since much of the debate about children and parental employment has centered on women.

2.9 ═══════════════════════════

All Children Seventh Through Twelfth Grades: Views of Mothers

*What grade would you give your **mother** on...*
Encouraging me to want to learn and to enjoy learning?

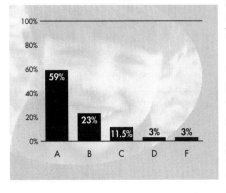

any demographic factors. It is also interesting that male and female chil-

2.10 ═══════════════════════════

All Children Seventh Through Twelfth Grades: Views of Fathers

*What grade would you give your **father** on...*
Encouraging me to want to learn and to enjoy learning?

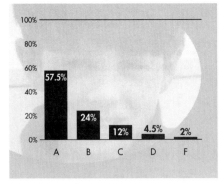

▼ **Encouraging the child in learning** This question also was asked only of children in the seventh through twelfth grades. Both mothers and fathers are seen fairly positively in terms of being intellectually responsive.

Almost three in five of the older children (59 percent) give their mothers an A in "encouraging me to want to learn and to enjoy learning," while 17.5 percent of children give their mothers a C or lower. Breaking with the pattern we have seen thus far, the grades children give their mothers do not differ by dren do not differ on their assessment of their mothers. Although there is concern about teenage girls' being turned off to learning,[33] perhaps this process is triggered more by children's friends than by their parents.

Fathers are graded comparably, with 57.5 percent of children giving their fathers an A whereas 18.5 percent give them a C or lower. Only two demographic factors make a difference in how children grade their fathers. Children give their fathers higher grades when:

▼ their fathers work full-time.

▼ their fathers live in their households.

A number of the children we talked with reported how their interest in learning had been enhanced by active parental involvement.

Accepting the child for who he or she is, but expecting success

Children of all ages were asked to grade their parents on "appreciating me for who I am." Mothers are given high marks for their acceptance and appreciation of their child, with 72 percent receiving an A. Children give their mothers better grades when:

▼ the children are younger.
▼ their mothers are married as opposed to being single parents.
▼ they see their families as doing well economically.

2.11

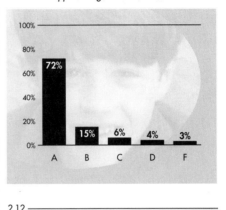

All Children Third Through Twelfth Grades: Views of Mothers

*What grade would you give your **mother** on... Appreciating me for who I am?*

2.12

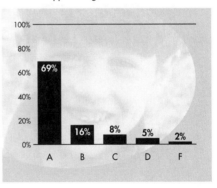

All Children Third Through Twelfth Grades: Views of Fathers

*What grade would you give your **father** on... Appreciating me for who I am?*

Notably, there is no difference between the marks given to mothers who are employed and those who are not.

There is also no significant difference in how children grade their mothers and fathers for appreciating them for who they are: 69 percent of children give their fathers an A, and 15 percent give their fathers a C or lower. But there is a steep drop in ratings given by older children compared with those given by younger children: 83.5 percent of younger children give fathers an A compared with 58 percent of older children—a finding that is consistent with the parent/child struggles of adolescence. Children also give their fathers better grades when they live with them.

2.13 ═══════════════════════════

All Children Seventh Through Twelfth Grades: Views of Mothers

*What grade would you give your **mother** on... Raising me with good values?*

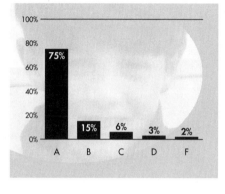

2.14 ═══════════════════════════

All Children Seventh Through Twelfth Grades: Views of Fathers

*What grade would you give your **father** on... Raising me with good values?*

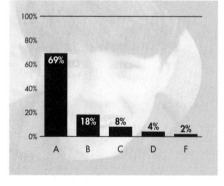

Promoting strong values

Children in the seventh through twelfth grades were asked to judge their mothers and fathers on "raising me with good values." Given the fact that older children consistently tend to give their parents lower marks, it is impressive that 75 percent of these older children give their mothers an A on this aspect of parenting. The only predictor of transmitting good values is family economics. Among children whose families are more marginal economically, 67 percent give their mothers an A compared with 80 percent of children with no perceived economic problems.

There is no statistical difference in the way that children judge their fathers and their mothers in terms of transmitting good values. Children give their fathers higher grades when:

▼ they see their families as economically healthy.
▼ they live in the household with their fathers.
▼ they are Latino or white (versus African American).

These findings show that there is obviously a dissonance between the public views and children's views about values. Whereas the public believes that children are being brought up with a "values deficit" and that parents are to blame,[34] only 11 to 14 percent of children give their parents bad marks on this score.

It is, of course, impossible to know whether the public is misguided or whether children have little perspective on the only reality they know, but my guess is that there is some truth in both views. I feel that the public focuses on the few children who have severe and very devastating problems, but overlooks the many, many children who have good values, who are committed, and who live right. At a 1999 town meeting run by the nonprofit organization Do Something designed to provide a forum for national leaders to hear from students, one child accused the media of portraying young people as monsters. With a passion that brought the group to cheers and applause, she said, "We are people, just like you. We are just younger people."

Likewise in our one-on-one interviews, we heard from many children about the positive values passed on by their parents:

She made me wise. You know, I'll watch these [other] children make the mistakes that I will never make because she taught me so well.

DAUGHTER OF A SINGLE MOTHER, 16 YEARS OLD

When I have lots of money and I'm an architect, I'm going to give some money to the homeless.

I want to be rich, but I wouldn't want to live in a really big fancy house. I would give my money to homeless people, donations and stuff like that. My mom always says, "If we win the lottery, I'm going to open up a house, a shelter for homeless people."

SISTERS, 9 AND 13 YEARS OLD

My mother is hard working. I ain't going to be lazy working. She tries to get that out of me 'cause I am lazy now, but I'm going to try to be better at that, work harder at that. You know she tries to perfect herself. She's persistent. You know that's a good quality.

11-YEAR-OLD BOY

Using constructive discipline

Of all of the parenting skills we included in this study, the lowest rating by children is given to their mother for "controlling her temper when I do something that makes her angry." Granted this is only one aspect of using constructive discipline, but I chose it because parents who lose control are likely to use other less effective disciplinary techniques. Overall, only 28 percent of children give their mothers an A and 41 percent give their mothers a C or lower. Surprisingly, there is no difference between younger and older children on the issue of temper control. Children in single-parent-mother families give their mothers lower marks (49 percent give their mothers a C or lower) than children in two-parent homes (38 percent give their mothers a C or lower). That finding is not surprising. Having others at home to turn to when our children inevitably upset us can help us recover. It also means that disciplinary duties may be shared, so that one parent does not always have to be the "bad cop." Children in families who are having a harder time economically give their mothers lower grades than children in families in which affording what they need is not a problem—a trend that we have seen throughout.

There is no statistical difference in the way that children grade their mothers and their fathers on controlling their tempers. Once again, family economics makes a difference: In economically marginal families 50.5 percent of the fathers are given a C or lower compared with 35 percent of fathers in families in which money is not seen as a problem.

We found throughout the course of our interviews that children are very sensitive to the moods of their parents. As kids tell it, their parents' ability to control their tempers depends on what kind of day they had at work:

2.15 ═══════════════════════════════

All Children Third Through Twelfth Grades:
Views of Mothers

*What grade would you give your **mother** on...*
Controlling her temper when I do something
that makes her angry?

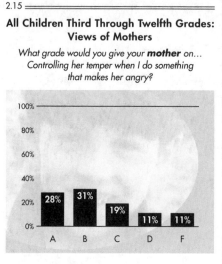

2.16 ═══════════════════════════════

All Children Third Through Twelfth Grades:
Views of Fathers

*What grade would you give your **father** on...*
Controlling his temper when I do something
that makes him angry?

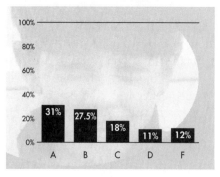

If my brother and I are fighting or if I don't do something the minute she tells me, she yells at me. It's usually because she's had a bad day at work. Because some days she doesn't care and sometimes she does. She'll say, "I've had a really bad day. Just leave me alone."

13-YEAR-OLD GIRL

My mom, when she has a bad day at work, she starts yelling at us. I say it's not all right. I understand you had a bad day at work, but it's not fair to take it out on us.

14-YEAR-OLD BOY

I get worried if she starts yelling too much. My brother was calling his friend and she was really getting mad. She said, "That's it; it's too late to call; you're grounded for the week." If she had had a good day it would have been, "It's a little too late to call, could you please get off the phone?"

12-YEAR-OLD GIRL

Later in the book I will explore how work affects parents' moods. For now, suffice it to say that all of us as parents could stand to improve how we control our tempers when we get angry.

Providing routines and rituals
I asked children in the seventh through the twelfth grades to assess their parents on "establishing family routines and traditions with me." Whereas just more than one third of the children (38 percent) give their mothers an A, another third (33 percent) give their mothers a C or lower. There are no demographic differences between children who give their mothers higher and lower grades.

Fathers and mothers are graded comparably on this skill. Only one demographic factor makes a difference: Among fathers, nonresident fathers are given lower grades (55 percent receive a C or lower) than resident fathers (33.5 receive a C or lower).

2.17

All Children Seventh Through Twelfth Grades: Views of Mothers

*What grade would you give your **mother** on... Establishing family routines and traditions with me?*

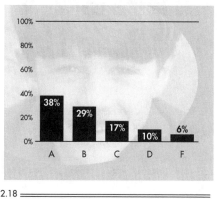

2.18

All Children Seventh Through Twelfth Grades: Views of Fathers

*What grade would you give your **father** on... Establishing family routines and traditions with me?*

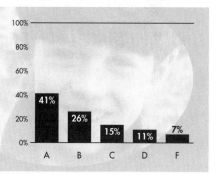

Children speak fondly of the traditions that develop in their families. An older boy who has already left for his first year of college remembers family meals:

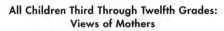

2.19

All Children Third Through Twelfth Grades: Views of Mothers

*What grade would you give your **mother** on... Being involved with what is happening to me at school?*

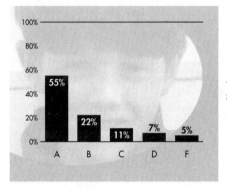

2.20

All Children Third Through Twelfth Grades: Views of Fathers

*What grade would you give your **father** on... Being involved with what is happening to me at school?*

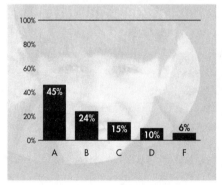

I really do miss having that dinner. . . . I always have this picture of having chicken—because that's what we had every night—and us sitting down and having dinner.

A 17-year-old girl talks about spontaneous family activities:

We just kind of talk and have a little family moment, and we just do really silly stuff, like when we were in the car we'd start singing harmony or something. It's like the Brady Bunch or something, and I can't believe—I don't think the other families do that.

I suspect that when parents hear the voices of children saying how important family traditions and rituals are, we will all work harder to establish them. After all, if one in three children gives his or her mother and father a C or lower, this is a skill that could stand improvement.

Being involved in the child's education

Although 55 percent of children overall give their mothers an A for "being involved with what is happening to me at school" they give their mothers higher grades when:

▼ the children are younger.
▼ they see their families as economically healthy.

Fathers are graded lower than mothers on being involved in their child's education (45 percent are given an A compared with 55 percent for mothers). As we have been finding, children give their fathers higher marks when:

▼ the children are younger.
▼ their fathers live in their households.

Parents can make a significant difference in the course and quality of their children's schooling. One 10-year-old boy who was having a problem at school describes how his parents took matters into their hands—for which he was thankful:

> *I introduced them to my library teacher, who I don't like, who I don't feel is doing the best job she can do. And my mom sort of agreed with me and [so] she talked to her and stuff.*

An 18-year-old boy told us about how his parents ensured he got the most out of his education:

> *They were extremely involved because they had such a stake in it. My dad would go to the PTA meetings. They have always wanted to get involved, always making sure that I was getting everything out of the school that I could. I'm extremely glad now because I think it did a lot to shape me.*

Being there for the child

The two questions we asked to assess the extent to which parents are "there" for their children do not cover the range of ways children know that their parents are, in fact, there for them but simply look at two examples that are important to both parents and children: "Being there for me when I am sick" and "Being able to attend important events in my life."

2.21 ═══════════════════════════

All Children Third Through Twelfth Grades:
Views of Mothers

*What grade would you give your **mother** on...*
Being there for me when I am sick?

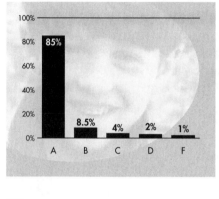

2.22 ═══════════════════════════

All Children Third Through Twelfth Grades:
Views of Fathers

*What grade would you give your **father** on...*
Being there for me when I am sick?

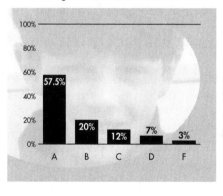

▼ **Being there for the child when the child is sick** Of all of the parenting skills we investigated, children give their mothers the highest marks for feeling that they can count on them if they are sick: 85 percent receive an A. In addition, younger children and children who see their families as more economically healthy give their mothers higher grades.

Fathers are less likely than mothers to receive high grades when it comes to being there for their sick children. Only 57.5 receive an A—27.5 percentage points lower than mothers in receiving an A. In keeping with previous findings, younger children, children whose families are more economically healthy, and children who live with their fathers give their fathers higher marks.

Attending to a sick child can be difficult for many working parents. One 12-year-old girl gratefully explains how her parents arrange their schedules to ensure that they are "there for her":

> *Like my mom would stay with me in the morning and then goes to work in the afternoon, and my dad comes and stays with me in the afternoon while my mom is at work. [Together], they take the day off but still go to work.*

▼ **Being able to attend important events in the child's life** Fewer mothers are given an A for being able to attend the important events in the child's life (69 percent) than for being there when the child is sick (85 percent). Children give their mothers better grades when:

▼ the children are younger.
▼ they live in two-parent households.
▼ they see their families as economically healthy.

The lowest scores for mothers are given in families in which the father is not employed (44 percent receive an A) compared with families in which the father is employed (74 percent receive an A)—a 30 percentile point differential. Perhaps these mothers have to work especially hard to bring in needed income, precluding their attendance at important events in their child's life.

Fewer fathers receive an A than mothers when it comes to being able to attend the important events in the child's life (60 percent for fathers compared with 69 percent for mothers). Children give their fathers better marks when:

▼ the children are younger.
▼ they see their families as economically healthy.
▼ their fathers are employed (versus nonemployed).
▼ their fathers live at home with them.

Children take the special events in their lives seriously and consider the attendance of their parents at those events to be quite important. What matters more, however, is that parents care: that they are making an effort, even if they can't come. An 18-year-old girl explains:

They're usually always there; they usually make time. They'll tell the boss, "I really have to do this. This is really important to me." Sometimes if it's not that important they'll

2.23 ═══════════════════════════

All Children Third Through Twelfth Grades: Views of Mothers

*What grade would you give your **mother** on... Being able to attend important events in my life?*

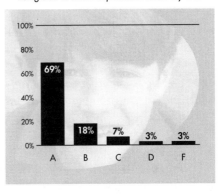

2.24 ═══════════════════════════

All Children Third Through Twelfth Grades: Views of Fathers

*What grade would you give your **father** on... Being able to attend important events in my life?*

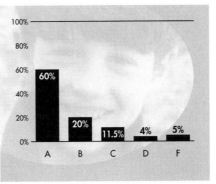

say, "I'm not going to come this time but next time I will because this is not as important as graduation."

As I have said, "being there" means availability, both physical and emotional. Particularly among older children, emotional availability is key. Children told us again and again how important it is for their parents to be there for them:

If I am in a bad situation, I think that they need to be there to help me out. 'Cause I do not think that I am old enough to get out of these situations. Maybe when I am in a bad mood, or broke up with a girlfriend they need to be there for me. Comfort me and hug me. Yeah, yeah, they're there. They find time out of their busy schedule to help.

16-YEAR-OLD BOY

My mother listens to me. I can tell her anything, I think that's "there for you." It's not just physical—physically being there, you know, it's not just picking me up every afternoon at 3:30; it's talking to me about what happened at school on the way home and it's laughing with each other. And I think that's being there for someone, emotionally there for someone, not just physically.

16-YEAR-OLD GIRL

I'll be at work and one of the workers—I didn't think he was doing as much work as he could've been doing. And I come home and she'll be like, "How was your day at work?" And I don't want to say anything, and she'll still try to talk to me anyway even though I'm in [a bad] mood. I realize, I have a really good mother. She tries to help me [even] when I don't feel like it.

17-YEAR-OLD GIRL

WHICH PARENTING SKILLS ARE GRADED
HIGHEST AND LOWEST?

To synthesize children's evaluations of their mothers, we compare the assessments for children in the seventh through the twelfth grades, since those children were asked all of the questions.

Mothers are given the highest grades for being there when the child is sick and for raising their children with good values. They receive the lowest grades for controlling their tempers when their children make them angry and for knowing what is really going on in their children's lives. It is also noteworthy that less than half of mothers are given an A by their teenagers on being involved in the children's education, in being someone whom their children can turn to if they are upset, in spending time talking with their children, in establishing family routines and traditions, in knowing what's going on in their children's lives, and in controlling their tempers.

We also compared the grades given to fathers by their older children. Note that in this analysis, we only include the fathers who live with their child most of the time—so that it will be comparable to the analysis of mothers, all of whom are resident mothers. However, if the ratings for nonresident fathers were included in this table, the scores, as we've seen repeatedly, would be quite a bit lower.

Children in the seventh through the twelfth grades judge their fathers less favorably than their mothers in some important respects—such as making their child feel important and loved and being someone whom the child can go to if upset. Fathers are not seen as very emotionally available to their children—with only 43 percent of children giving their fathers an A on spending time talking with them, 38 percent for being someone whom they can go to if they are upset, and 31 percent for knowing what is really going on in their children's lives.

WHICH CHILDREN ARE MOST LIKELY TO GIVE THEIR
PARENTS THE HIGHEST—OR LOWEST—MARKS?

In later chapters, I will explore those aspects of parents' lives on and off the job that make it more likely that children will give their parents high marks for their parenting skills and for managing their work and family responsibilities. Here, however, we'll look at key demographic differences.

2.25

All Children Seventh Through Twelfth Grades: Views on Mothers

What grade would you give your MOTHER on . . .

	A	B	C	D	F
Being there for me when I am sick?	81%	11%	5%	2%	1%
Raising me with good values?	75	15	6	3	2
Making me feel important and loved?	64	20	10	5	1
Being able to attend important events in my life?	64	20	10	3	3.5
Appreciating me for who I am?	64	18	8	6	5
Encouraging me to want to learn and to enjoy learning?	59	23	11.5	3	3
Being involved with what is happening to me at school?	46	25	14	10	6
Being someone I can go to when I am upset?	46	22	14	8	9
Spending time talking with me?	43	33	14	6	4
Establishing family routines and traditions with me?	38	29	17	10	6
Knowing what is really going on in my life?	35	31	15	10	9
Controlling her temper when I do something that makes her angry?	29	27.5	20.5	12	11

2.26

All Children Seventh Through Twelfth Grades: Views on Fathers

What grade would you give your FATHER on . . .

	A	B	C	D	F
Raising me with good values?	69%	18%	8%	4%	2%
Appreciating me for who I am?	58	21	11	8	2
Encouraging me to want to learn and to enjoy learning?	57.5	24	12	4	2
Making me feel important and loved?	57	22	13	6	2
Being able to attend important events in my life?	55	22	13	5	5.5
Being there for me when I am sick?	51.5	20	16	8	4
Spending time talking with me?	43	24	19	10	4
Establishing family routines and traditions with me?	41	26	15	11	7
Being involved with what is happening to me at school?	38	24	19	12	7
Being someone I can go to when I am upset?	38	22	15	12	13
Controlling his temper when I do something that makes him angry?	31	27	20	10	12
Knowing what is really going on in my life?	31	30	17	12.5	10

The age of the child makes a difference

In the questions asked of children of all ages (third through twelfth grades) in this study, the only parenting skill to which age does not make a difference is in the way children view their mothers' and fathers' ability to control their tempers when something that their children do makes them angry. Interestingly, this is among the very lowest rated skills of all we looked at. In other parenting skills, younger children consistently rate their parents more favorably than older ones.

Is this age difference inevitable? The lower scores given by older children are certainly related to the fact that teenagers are separating from their parents and may not want to turn to them. As they differentiate themselves, children often need to see their parents as less perfect, as more fallible. Yet although there is a normal developmental push toward separating, parents can and do find new ways to connect. Our interviews with teenagers reveal that they certainly do want their parents to hang in there so that they can go to them when they need to. When there is open communication between parents and their teenagers, these older children do respect their parents:

> Sometimes [my mother and I] will talk forever and ever, you know for a real long time, and another day, it's kind of quiet. Sometimes, I have bad days for no reason, and I'll think—a lot of people think—that when you are a teenager, you kind of want to be on your own, so I figure that maybe that's it, maybe it is the teenager thing. I'm starting to realize that I want to do stuff on my own. And I don't want to depend on her all the time, but she's so supportive.
>
> I am proud of the fact that she deals with me even though I try to push her away. She's still there. Like if we get into a bad argument, she'll still try to talk to me until it really gets handled.
>
> 16-YEAR-OLD GIRL WITH SINGLE PARENT

Family economics matters

In analysis after analysis, the children's perception of their families' economic health is strongly linked to how they rate their parents' parenting skills. The only times when the families' economic health does not make a difference are in parents' encouragement of their children's love for learning, in parents' establishment of family routines and traditions, and in fathers' involvement in what is happening to their children in school. Obviously, children may not have an accurate sense of the family's actual household income. As a woman with two teenagers says, "We were very poor when I was growing up, but I never knew it." For those children who *believe* that their family is less healthy economically, however, there are repercussions.

This is an interesting finding in light of the fact that the public opinion research reveals that the problems of children are seen as primarily moral in nature and that parents are considered responsible. They don't see family economics as making much difference in how parents parent.[35] Yet several decades of research show that parents in families who are struggling to survive economically are less able to focus on their children and less able to be warm and responsive.[36] Studies also show that many (but not all) otherwise healthy children born into poverty do less well as they grow older and that these changes are "related to adverse living conditions, not inherent factors and traits within [the] child."[37] Other studies have found that children's friends and the communities they live in also have an important impact on their development.[38]

Although families' push to improve their material well-being may be depicted as selfish and greedy in the public discourse, our analyses show that families who do not have to worry about putting bread on the table may have more to give to their children emotionally. They also may be able to raise their children in more positive, cohesive communities.

Maternal employment is *not* linked to children's assessments of their parents

In *not a single analysis* is the mother's employment status related to the way a child sees his or her mother or father. Neither is her working part-time or full-time. This is clearly one of our most important findings.

This finding may surprise many people: How can children whose mothers are at home caring for them full-time fail to see them as more supportive? After all, they are devoting themselves to their children. In my view, this would be exactly the wrong way to interpret these findings because it slips back into the either/or paradigm. A mother who is employed can be there for her child or not, just as mothers who are not employed can be. It is who the mother is as a person and the relationship she establishes with her child that are the important factors. Rather than search for the *one* way that is best, we should support mothers in having real choices of being employed or staying at home. Studies have found again and again that when mothers are doing what they think is right for themselves and their families, their children are more likely to prosper.

On the other hand, children of nonemployed fathers give these fathers lower grades when it comes to making their children feel important and loved and to participating in important events in the children's lives. Fathers who work part-time are less likely to be seen as encouraging their children's learning. Other studies offer several plausible explanations for these findings. Perhaps fathers who work less than full-time or who are unemployed are feeling financial and role strain, which could affect how they interact with their children. A 1988 study found that fathers experiencing job loss were more likely to be inconsistent and arbitrary, and that tendency increased the prospects of children's having behavior problems and thus could also affect how children grade their fathers.[39]

Expectations may also make a difference.[40] Because many children and families expect fathers to play an economic provider role, family relations can become strained when they don't.[41] Clearly, our society has moved to give mothers more latitude in their roles as nurturer *and* economic provider, but not fathers. To me, this is a disturbing finding.

A 9-year-old girl describes how her father's underemployment affects him, providing insight into why children may be giving lower grades to fathers who are unemployed or who work part-time. Her father is a musician who, after losing a job in music several years ago, has had to support the family by doing manual labor. Sometimes he can find work for 40 hours a week; sometimes he can't.

> *He has been getting 20 hours a week instead of 40, which has been really hurting his paycheck. When he doesn't get his full paycheck, it makes him feel bad. It makes him feel like he's not doing enough for the family.*
>
> *A lot of time, especially in December, he feels like he's not doing enough for the family and he's not going to get through Christmas very well. And last year, around Christmas, he got really, really sick and so did Mom and it was just kind of a lousy Christmas for us all. And right now [it's Christmastime again], he's got strep throat . . . so he'll take a few days off so he can get rest and I'll help him with Christmas.*

When the father is consumed with worry, so is his daughter:

> *It doesn't make me feel very good to see him worried about that. I told him last year, I said, "Dad, I don't care if there is nothing under the tree. All I care about is that we are all together on Christmas Day."*

Living in single-parent homes and having nonresident fathers affect children's feelings

In all but one of the results, both sons and daughters see their fathers less positively, sometimes dramatically so, when they don't live with them. Since this family form affects 23 percent of the children in our study—and considerably more throughout the life cycle of children in this country—it is a cautionary finding for parents today.

Our one-on-one interviews with children echoed this finding. For example, a 17-year-old girl told us about her nonresident father:

> *I get very angry at him. There's some things that I think he should do but he doesn't. My school is really family oriented; we have Mother-Daughter this, Father-Daughter that. I would invite him and he'd be like, "No, I don't want to go," and it's like, well, I mean, I think we should. It's like, we don't have quality time really, cause I mean we don't spend time together like that.*

Gender differences for the children of employed resident parents

There is only one difference between boys and girls in the grading of their parents—boys are more likely than girls to give their fathers higher marks in "knowing what is going on in my life."

Since a few studies have found that boys with employed mothers fare less well than girls, I decided to take a closer look, comparing the responses of boys and girls with *employed* resident mothers and fathers. I did find a few differences. Girls are more likely than boys to give their mothers higher marks for "making me feel important and loved," for "spending time talking with me," and for "knowing what is really going on in my life." Boys are more likely than girls to give their fathers higher marks for "knowing what is really going on in my life." Although these are not dramatic findings, they indicate that some mothers who are employed may favor their daughters over their sons.

DOES MATERNAL EMPLOYMENT AFFECT THE BONDS BETWEEN MOTHER AND CHILD?

As we've discussed, this study finds that the way children judge their parents is *not* linked to whether their mother is at home or employed. However, one could argue that what parents and children *say* about their relationships is not as accurate as *direct observations* of parents and children together or as research assessments of children's development. Thus a comparison of these studies and our findings is in order.

Many observational studies have focused on mother-child attachment.[42] Does this mean that father-child attachments are unimportant? I certainly don't think so, but the research in this field has been guided by an assumption of the overriding salience of the bond between mother and child; thus that is the topic studies have investigated.

In studies of children's overall development, infants with secure attachments to their mothers are found to be better able to solve problems, to explore, and to be independent in the toddler years. In the preschool years, securely attached children tend to be more constructively involved at school, to play better with other children, and to be cooperative with adults. In the school-age years, these children are more likely to form friendships and are judged by their teachers to be more engaged in group activities, more confident in approaching new experiences, and more flexible in managing their behavior.[43]

Researchers have worried that employed mothers who are away from their infants on a regular basis might be less tuned in to their children's cues and clues and thus might respond less warmly and sensitively to them. Babies might therefore doubt the availability of their mothers, and that doubt might interfere with attachment.[44] In the late 1980s and early 1990s, a few studies fueled this concern, finding that infants who spent long hours in child care in their first year of life were more likely to be insecurely attached to their mothers.[45] In contrast, other studies came to the opposite conclusion: that infants who spend time in child care are no more likely to be insecurely attached to their mothers than infants who are with their mothers full-time.[46]

To address these conflicting results and the public debate they aroused, in the early 1990s, the federal government funded a longitudinal study of the impact of maternal employment and infant care on children through the National Institute of Child Health and Human Development (NICHD). Called the NICHD Study of Early Child Care, it consists of ten research teams who study the experiences of children and families in ten sites around the country at specific intervals from the time the children are born until they are 7 years old.

The researchers also examined a number of other questions that have been debated over the past decade. One question that had been raised was whether the child's temperament made a difference in attachment. Perhaps mothers might find it more difficult to bond with children who have more difficult temperaments (who are fussy, cry a lot, are harder to soothe), but it turned out that this is not the case. Mothers can be equally warm and responsive with babies who are easygoing and with those who are more difficult to soothe.

The main question of the NICHD study is: Does child care affect the attachment relationship? The answer is no. As the authors state: "Even in extensive, early, unstable or poor-quality child care, the likelihood of infants' insecure attachments to mother did not increase, nor did stable or high-quality care increase the likelihood of developing a secure attachment to mother."[47] In other words, the relationship between mother and child is affected primarily by that relationship, not by the other experiences the child has.

Further statistical tests yielded what the researchers call "small, but consistent effects."

▼ When the relationship with the mother is lacking, that is, when it is less warm, sensitive, and responsive, child care does make a difference. If the mother is less sensitive and responsive *and* the child care provider is less sensitive and responsive, children are at *dual risk*. These children have the highest rates of insecure attachments.

▼ Children whose mothers are less warm and responsive are more likely to develop a secure relationship with their mothers when they spend more time with them. The researchers speculate that this may be a *dosage effect*—children with less involved mothers may need more time with them to develop a secure and trusting relationship.

▼ Children in low-quality child care are more affected by their mothers' behavior than are children in higher-quality child care. When children don't form secure attachments to their nonparental care givers, the relationship with their mothers becomes more salient.

These analyses provide evidence that "high-quality child care served a compensatory function for children whose maternal care was lacking."[48]

In further analyses, conducted when the children were between 2 and 3 years old, the researchers looked at whether the family has less of an impact on children who spend long hours (which they defined as 30 hours or more a week) in child care. They conclude that overall "the influence of the family is not reduced (or changed) by full time non-parental care."[49] The conditions of family life found to be most important for children's positive intellectual and social development are higher family income, less maternal depression, less authoritarian child rearing, and greater maternal warmth and sensitivity.

This study also found that mothers' attitudes make a difference. When mothers are doing what they think is the right thing to do—whether it is staying at home with their children or working—their children are more likely to flourish:

> . . . children in full-time *nonparental care* were more socially competent and had fewer behavior problems if their mother believed that maternal employment was beneficial for children and . . . children in full-time *maternal care* were more socially competent and had fewer behavior problems if their mothers believed that maternal employment was not beneficial for children.[50]

Do the daily absences of employed mothers affect the attachment between the mother and child? Although the overall answer is no, as you can see from the studies just described, child development is complex and there aren't simple either/or results. An interplay of several factors makes a difference:

▼ The income that working brings to the family, which for many families means the difference between living in better neighborhoods and having more resources to provide for their families.
▼ The mother's warmth, sensitivity, and responsiveness to her children (which, as I will argue later, can be affected by her job).
▼ The child care provider's warmth, sensitivity, and responsiveness.
▼ The mother's attitude about working—whether she believes she is doing the right thing either by working or by being at home.

DOES MATERNAL EMPLOYMENT AFFECT CHILDREN'S SOCIAL AND EMOTIONAL DEVELOPMENT?[51]

Children's development does not stop in the early childhood years. Overall, studies have either found no impact or a positive impact of maternal employment on older children's emotional and social development.[52]

In terms of self-esteem, one study found higher ratings for the 10-to-12-year-old children of single employed mothers than in a comparable group of children of nonemployed mothers.[53] Another study of similarly aged children in two-parent families found no differences in self-esteem between children of employed and children of nonemployed mothers.[54]

Studies consistently find that families with employed mothers encourage their children to be more independent than families with nonemployed mothers.[55] One study found that young children with employed mothers are more self-sufficient, whereas children of nonemployed mothers solicit more help from adults.[56] Older children of employed mothers reported a greater emphasis on independence in their homes than children of at-home mothers.[57]

Researchers also have investigated whether maternal employment has an impact on how children interact with other children. One study of children attending group child care programs found that preschoolers with employed mothers are more oriented toward other children than those with nonemployed mothers.[58] As children age, maternal employment appears to become a less important influence on children's relationships with their friends: It has been found that adolescents' social competence does not differ for children whose mothers are employed and those whose mothers are not.[59]

Other researchers have found that preschool boys with employed mothers are more defiant than boys with nonemployed mothers. However, among low-income children of both genders, children of employed mothers have been found to be less defiant than the children of nonemployed mothers. A study of behavior problems in adolescent children found no difference between children with employed and those with nonemployed mothers.[60]

Thus, whether or not a mother works does not tell us very much about how her children develop socially and emotionally. Rather, a number of other factors come into play:

▼ Mothers' satisfaction with the way they are living—working or staying at home—is one such factor.[61]

▼ The quality of child care is a factor. Although some studies have found that children who have employed mothers and/or who have nonparental child care are more aggressive, other studies have found that children's aggression is also affected by the way discipline is handled in the child care setting.[62]

▼ Parents' aspirations for the children matter. For example, when mothers have higher educational aspirations for their children, their children are more competent socially.[63]

DOES THE IMPACT OF MATERNAL EMPLOYMENT AFFECT CHILDREN'S INTELLECTUAL AND LANGUAGE DEVELOPMENT?

Few if any differences in children's intellectual ability or achievement are related to maternal employment. Studies of infants of employed and nonemployed mothers have not found any differences in intellectual or physical development.[64] A large study found that toddlers' language development isn't affected by maternal employment.[65] Studies with moderately sized samples of school-age children found that children of employed mothers have higher math and reading achievement levels than children of nonemployed mothers.[66] Studies of adolescents found that the children of employed and nonemployed mothers had comparable scores on tests of their intellectual functioning,[67] but the adolescents of employed mothers had higher creativity scores.[68]

Thus, when one compares the children of employed versus nonemployed mothers, most of the differences between the two groups wash out. As we have noted before, other factors have an impact:

▼ Children's home environment obviously has an effect on their intellectual development. When parents are more involved in their children's education,[69] and when mothers are satisfied with how they are living—whether working or being at home[70]—children's intellectual development is better.

▼ The amount of television viewing has also been linked to children's school achievement.[71]

▼ The quality of the child care and school setting makes a difference, particularly in homes where mothers are less sensitive and responsive.[72]

▼ Maternal employment has the most positive effect on children's development when children are from low-income families and when they receive warm and responsive care at home and in their child care arrangements.[73]

THE BOTTOM LINE

These findings from other research on children's development support our own findings on how children grade their parents: Whether or not a mother is employed has very little to do with how her children grade her. For the most part, fathers' work is not linked to the way children see their fathers, with the occasional exception of fathers who are not employed or who work less than full-time. In other words, this is not an issue of work *or* family.

Although our findings are new, those from observational research are fairly well known. Yet, despite this strong evidence that working per se does not affect children, the either/or debate about whether or not a mother should work has persisted. Why? Are there vested interests in society that want to keep mothers at home? Is it mothers' own guilt that clouds their personal and public thinking? Or is something going on that we feel but haven't identified? Why does our concern continue despite all of the books, articles, and studies we read that proclaim that working is okay for children, that tell us not to feel guilty?

In the next chapter, we begin to find out why.

Is It Quality Time or Quantity Time?

espite all they hear and read proclaiming that working is okay or even good for children, if parents feel there is a problem about work and family life, they define the solution as *simply* having more time with their child.

We asked parents in our Ask the Children survey, "If *you* were granted one wish to change the way that your work affects your child's life, what would that wish be?" The largest proportion of parents—22 percent—wished to "have more time with their child." An additional 16 percent wished to "work less time."

We also asked parents another open-ended question: "If *your child* were granted one wish to change the way that your work affects his/her life, what would that wish be?" The largest proportion of parents—21 percent—thought their child would want "more time with me." An additional 19 percent thought their child would want them to work less time, and 16 percent thought their children would want them "not to have to go to work." Taken together, 56 percent of parents mentioned time.

In this chapter, we explore the issue of time. Why does the debate about quality time versus quantity time persist? Does the amount of time that children say that they have with their parents affect how they feel about their parents' parenting? Do other aspects of time matter, such as the kinds of activities parents and children do together and whether children's time with parents is rushed or calm? What does the research say about the impact of time together on children's development? Is this another either/or debate—quality time *or* quantity time—as many have portrayed it? And finally and very importantly, do children and parents feel the same way about having time together?

WHY WON'T THE DEBATE ABOUT QUALITY TIME VERSUS QUANTITY TIME GO AWAY?

This debate reminds me of a punching bag that is slugged, even beaten down, but rebounds right back up. For four decades, this debate has had real staying power. Clearly it strikes a resonant cord.

In the 1960s, researchers looked at children in orphanages who failed to thrive and extrapolated this result to children who experienced daily separations from their employed mothers. Others countered that it is not the *quantity* of time that matters, but what happens in that time— the *quality* of time—that is important. And besides, they noted, the prolonged separations children experience from parents in orphanages are not the same as daily separations. The embers of this debate were fanned into flame again in the 1980s when findings from a few studies found that infants whose mothers were away from them for more than 20 hours a week were at risk for being insecurely attached.

Many parents don't seem to like the notion of quality time. In our one-on-one interviews, some described it as a rationalization for parents to spend less time with their children. A cellular phone advertisement that ran in the late 1990s became a symbol—in fact, a lightning rod— for the issue of quality versus quantity time. In this ad, a child approaches her mother just before the mother is to leave for work. She and her siblings want to go to the beach. When the mother refuses, the child asks when she can be a "client." The mother pauses—then tells her children that they have 3 minutes to get ready to go the beach. The last shot shows the mother sitting on the beach making a conference call on her cellular phone while her children play nearby in the sand.

A mother of a 9-week-old child, who has just returned to work from maternity leave, comments:

> *I would say that in general this generation of children may be getting signals that my generation didn't get—that they come in second. It is in this ad about this woman on the phone and the kid wants to go to the beach [and says to her mother,] "When am I going to be a client?" [The mother] gives such a mixed message. Instead of saying, "You're right. We are going to the beach," it's "We are going to the beach and I'm doing my conference call while you play around. And I'll [at least] make sure that you don't cut your foot on shells."*

It is clear to many parents that one shouldn't make a distinction between the amount of time one spends with his or her children and what happens in that time. Both the quality and quantity of the time that parents and child share are important. Yet, when asked about their *one* wish to change the way their work affects their child, parents emphasize the *quantity* of time per se: They wish for "more time." What is going on?

WHAT IS GOING ON ABOUT TIME IN TODAY'S FAMILIES?

▼ **How much time are employed parents spending with their children?** To answer the question of time employed parents spend, let's compare two studies that were conducted 20 years apart: the Families and Work Institute's 1997 National Study of the Changing Workforce and the U.S. Department of Labor's 1977 Quality of Employment Survey (QES).[1]

My colleagues Terry Bond and Jennifer Swanberg and I find—no surprise—that in dual-earner families[2] with children under 18, mothers spend more time doing things and caring for children than fathers on workdays (3.2 hours for mothers versus 2.3 hours for fathers). We also find—again no surprise—that mothers today spend more time than fathers with their children on days off work (8.3 hours for mothers versus 6.4 hours for fathers).

But we find—to the surprise of many—that the gap between mothers and fathers in dual-earner families has narrowed considerably in the past 20 years. Although the amount of time that mothers spend with their children on workdays has not changed in a statistically significant way, fathers have increased the amount of time they spend with children by a half hour.

The 1997 National Study of the Changing Workforce also found that over the past 20 years fathers have increased the time they spend with their children by slightly more than 1 hour on nonwork days, whereas mothers' time has again remained the same.

When the Families and Work Institute released these findings in 1998, the media and public reactions were swift and strong. A few women wrote prominent editorials skeptical of the veracity of the findings, stating, for example, in *The New York Times* that "super dads need a reality check,"[3] whereas many men, like Matt Lauer, host of the *Today* show, gave the findings a high five sign. At last, good news for dads, he said to me.

The public reaction echoes the private fault line between men and women on the subject of time with children. Women ask, "Is he really caring for the children or is he just 'Dad, the helper,' 'Dad, the baby-sitter?' " "Why does he always wait until I ask him to be with the kids?" "Why doesn't he know what they like to eat for lunch and who their friends are?" Men ask, "Why does she always criticize what I do? When I try to do more, all I get are complaints, complaints, complaints." Or, "I am doing more, but nobody seems to notice."

Are men exaggerating? Are they really spending more time with their children? The 1997 National Study of the Changing Workforce didn't ask parents to keep time diaries, but it did have a reality check, as *The New York Times* called it: We asked fathers and mothers how much time their *partners* spent with the children. Although of course our findings are estimates, we found—again a surprise to many—that mothers' estimates of their husbands parallel the amount of time fathers report spending with their children. So fathers do not seem to be exaggerating—at least according to wives.

Furthermore, because employed mothers have managed to keep constant the amount of time they spend with their children, because fathers have increased their time, and because families have fewer children today than they did 20 years ago, it appears that employed parents indeed are spending somewhat more time with their children than they were two decades ago.

Where do parents get more time? Certainly not from their workdays. For employed fathers with children under 18, the 40-hour workweek is a myth. On average, including paid and unpaid time and including part-time and full-time work, fathers work 50.9 hours per week and mothers work 41.4 hours. By our calculations, fathers' total work time has increased by 3.1 hours per week in the past 20 years, and mothers' time has increased by 5.2 hours.[4]

There has also been an increase in the amount of time that parents spend on their jobs while at home. Almost one in three parents spends time on a weekly basis doing work at home that is directly related to his or her job. The proportion of parents who take work home from the job once a week or more has increased 10 percent since 1977, while the proportion who never take work home from the job has decreased by 16 percent.

So if parents are spending more time at work and fathers are spending more time with their children, where has this increased time come from? Employed parents know the answer to that question. They are spending less time on themselves:

> *I haven't set aside time for myself all these years. That's one thing I really need to start working on, just for my own sanity.*

On average, fathers in dual-earner families report they have 1.2 hours for themselves on workdays. Mothers have about 18 minutes less—0.9 hour per workday. This figure has decreased quite significantly over the past 20 years. On average, fathers in dual-earner families in 1997 had 54 fewer minutes for themselves on workdays than fathers did in 1977, while mothers have 42 fewer minutes for themselves on workdays today than mothers did in 1977.[5]

Even on days off work, fathers' time for themselves has also decreased—from 5.1 hours to 3.3 hours, a change of 1.8 hours over the past 20 years. Mothers' time for themselves on days off work has also decreased from 3.3 hours to 2.5 hours, a change of 0.8 hour.[6] So while both parents are sacrificing "time for themselves" to spend more time with their children, fathers have done so more than mothers (who, granted, were spending more time with their children to begin with).

WHAT DID WE FIND ABOUT TIME, EMPLOYED PARENTS, AND CHILDREN?

▼ | How much time are employed parents spending with individual children? In the Ask the Children study,[7] we looked at how much time employed parents spend with just one of their children, randomly selected. Overall, employed mothers report spending about an hour more with their child than employed fathers on workdays (3.8 hours for mothers compared with 2.7 hours for fathers). On

3.1

Employed Parents: Hours Spent with Their Child on Workdays

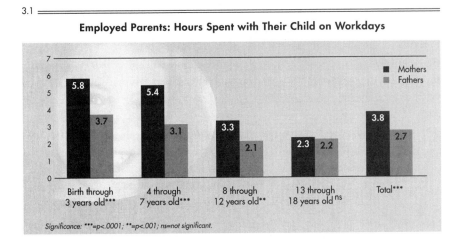

Significance: ***=p<.0001; **=p<.001; ns=not significant.

nonworkdays, mothers also report spending about an hour more with their child than employed fathers: 7.7 hours for mothers and 6.6 hours for fathers.[8]

When we look at the amount of time parents spend with children of different ages, there are shifts over time. Mothers spend more time with younger children than fathers do. By the teenage years, the amount of time that both parents spend declines—mothers' time more sharply than fathers'—to the point where there are no statistical differences in the amount of time mothers and fathers spend.

The same pattern applies to nonworkdays: Mothers reduce the amount of time they spend considerably as children age, dropping from

3.2

Employed Parents: Hours Spent with Their Child on Nonworkdays

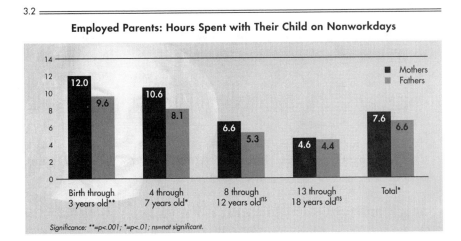

Significance: **=p<.001; *=p<.01; ns=not significant.

12 hours a day with a very young child to 4.6 hours with a teenager. Again, the difference in the amount of time mothers and fathers spend narrows and then disappears as the child grows up.[9] It is not simply that parents with an older child don't pay attention to that child; rather, children of these ages can be quite busy, doing their own thing. A mother with a teenage daughter says:

> *I would like to be with my teenage daughter more, but she is so involved with schoolwork, activities, and her friends. Inevitably I will hang around the house weekend after weekend, and the one day that I make plans, she will come up to me and say, "Let's do something together today."*

Since a few studies have found differences between how boys and girls are affected by their mothers' and fathers' work, I wondered whether there are gender differences here. I found that mothers spend more time with their daughters on workdays: 42.5 percent of mothers report spending 4.5 hours or more with their daughters on workdays compared with 24 percent who spend this much time with their sons. These differences occur during the teenage years, not when children are very young. In contrast, there is no difference in the amount of time mothers report spending with their daughters and their sons on non-workdays. Moreover, there are no differences in the amount of time that fathers report spending with their sons and their daughters of all ages on workdays and nonworkdays.

How much time do children say they spend with their mothers and fathers?

Now we turn full circle and look at children's estimates of the time they spend with their parents. Children in the third through twelfth grades were asked about how much time they spend with each of their parents—just the two of them or with other people—on a typical workday and on a typical nonworkday.[10]

▼ | **Time spent with employed parents on workdays** The majority of children report spending considerable time with their mothers on workdays, although the amount of time fluctuates, depending on the age of the child. Twenty-nine percent of younger children (8 through 12 years old) say they spend 2 hours or less compared with 35 percent of older children (13 through 18 years old). At the other end of the spectrum, 47 percent of younger children and 35 per-

3.3

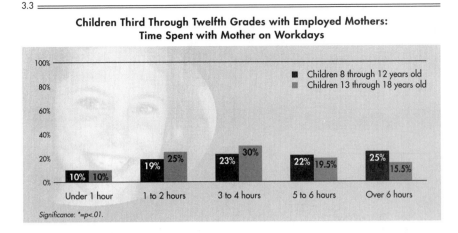

**Children Third Through Twelfth Grades with Employed Mothers:
Time Spent with Mother on Workdays**

■ Children 8 through 12 years old
■ Children 13 through 18 years old

	Under 1 hour	1 to 2 hours	3 to 4 hours	5 to 6 hours	Over 6 hours
Children 8–12	10%	19%	23%	22%	25%
Children 13–18	10%	25%	30%	19.5%	15.5%

*Significance: *=p<.01.*

cent of older children spend 5 hours or more with their mothers on workdays.

There is no difference in the amount of time that sons and daughters report spending with their mothers on workdays (although recall that mothers report spending more time with their teenage daughters than their teenage sons). It is not clear to me why there is a discrepancy between children's and parents' viewpoints, though children have less reason to overestimate than parents.

Children spend less time with their fathers than their mothers on workdays. Overall, 44 percent of children ages 8 through 18 years old report spending 2 hours or less with their fathers on workdays while 27 percent spend 5 hours or more. Interestingly, there is no significant difference in the amount of time younger and older children report spending with their fathers. Neither are there differences between boys and girls.

▼ **Time spent with parents on nonworkdays** An impressive 68.5 percent of both younger and older children say that they spend 5 hours or more with their mothers on nonworkdays. Although mothers do not report spending any more time with their daughters on nonworkdays than with their sons, children do report differences—girls say they spend more time with their mothers on nonworkdays than boys do. Here again, the discrepancy is hard to figure out.

Although children spend less time with their fathers than their mothers on nonworkdays, the amount of time they report spending with their

3.4

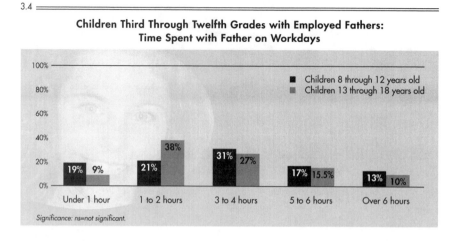

Children Third Through Twelfth Grades with Employed Fathers:
Time Spent with Father on Workdays

■ Children 8 through 12 years old
■ Children 13 through 18 years old

	Under 1 hour	1 to 2 hours	3 to 4 hours	5 to 6 hours	Over 6 hours
8–12	19%	21%	31%	17%	13%
13–18	9%	38%	27%	15.5%	10%

Significance: ns=not significant.

fathers is still high: 66 percent of children—boys and girls alike—say that they spend 5 hours or more with their fathers on nonworkdays.

Do parents and children feel they have enough time together?

▼ **Enough time—according to parents** It is one thing to know the *amount* of time that parents and children report spending together, but it is another to know the *psychological meaning* of that time. Do parents feel they have enough time with their child? Do children concur? I especially wondered about fathers. Since fathers spend less time with their children—both by their own and by their children's estimates—are they more likely than mothers to want more time?

Overall, 50 percent of parents with children, birth through 18 years old, say that they have too little time with their child; however, beneath this overall figure *fathers*— much more so than mothers— seem to be yearning to be with their child: 56 percent of fathers versus 44 percent of mothers feel deprived of time with their child!

3.5

Employed Parents with a Child
Birth Through 18:
Enough Time with Their Child

■ Mothers
■ Fathers

	Too little time	Just enough time	Too much time
Mothers	44%	52%	4%
Fathers	56%	42%	2%

*Significance: *=p<.01.*

Because fathers work longer hours, they have less time for their lives off the job. One father of a 9-year-old boy reflects on the fleeting nature of time:

> *Time is something, once it's gone, it's gone forever. So, you can look back and think, "Well, gee, I wish I would have spent more time with my kids when they were younger, I wish I would've spent more time with them when they were in high school," whatever. But once time is gone, that's it.*

Mothers and fathers with a son or a daughter are equally likely to feel that they have too little time with this child. Moreover, parents of children of different ages—from infants to teenagers—are also equally likely to feel they have too little time.

Enough time—according to children The majority of children 8 through 18 years old feel that they have enough time with their employed mothers and fathers: 67 percent say that they have enough time with their mothers and 60 percent say they have enough time with their fathers. Paralleling the overall difference in the amount of time fathers and mothers spend with their children, children are more likely to feel that they have too little time with their *fathers* than with their mothers.

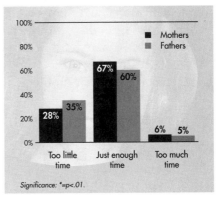

3.6

Children Third Through Twelfth Grades with Employed Parents: Enough Time with Mothers and Fathers

Significance: *=p<.01.

In our one-on-one interviews, a number of children talked about wanting more time with their fathers. One 12-year-old girl whose father takes frequent business trips says:

> *I miss him. He's gone for short times. He calls from where he is. I'd rather have him at home during that time, but I know he has to do it because it's part of his job.*

We heard a similar story from another girl whose father often works hard, including on weekends:

> *I can't spend much time with him because he's working. Sometimes I go with him to work on the weekends. But I just wish that he wouldn't work so much.*

Moreover, as has been the pattern thus far, children are far, far more likely to feel that they spend too little time with nonresident fathers (67 percent) than with resident fathers (35 percent).

These findings illustrate why it is so important to ask the children rather than to rely on our own assumptions. The issue of time with children has typically been framed in the public debate as mothers' issue. But when we ask the children, we see that fathers need to be front and center in this discussion as well.

▼ **Enough time—comparing children's views of employed and nonemployed mothers** All of the analyses in this chapter focus on employed mothers, but we also asked the question about having enough time with parents of children who have nonemployed mothers. Children with employed mothers are no more likely to feel they have too little time with their mothers than children with nonemployed mothers. Stated differently, children with mothers at home and children with mothers who work are equally likely to feel they have enough time with their mother.

▼ **Enough time—comparing children and mothers** What is also striking—and I must say unanticipated—is the discrepancy between the views of children and those of their mothers on whether they have enough time together. Almost half of mothers (49 percent) with a child 13 through 18 years old feel that they have too little time with their child, whereas less than one third of children (30 percent) this age concur. The results comparing mothers and younger children do not reach statistical significance but follow the same pattern. Perhaps mothers of teenagers anticipate the soon-to-occur loss of everyday contact with their child as the child grows up, goes to college, moves out. So they often long for more time, whereas children may be more eager (though ambivalently so) to separate from their mothers.

▼ **Enough time—comparing children and fathers** Teenagers are more likely than their younger counterparts to want more time with their fathers. Thirty-nine percent of children 13 through 18 years old feel they have too little time with their fathers compared with 29 percent of children 8 through 12 years old. On the other hand, children do not feel as strongly about this issue as fathers. For example, almost two thirds of fathers (64 percent) with a child 13 through 18 years old feel that they have too little time with this child, but only 39 percent of children this age feel the same way about time with their fathers.

3.7

Employed Mothers and Children with Employed Mothers: Enough Time Together		
	Children 8 through 12 years old	Children 13 through 18 years old
Too little time		
Mother	31%	49%
Child	24.5	30
Just enough time		
Mother	68%	50%
Child	69	65
Too much time		
Mother	1.5%	1%
Child	6.5	5
Significance:	ns = not significant;	*** = p < .0001.

3.8

Employed Fathers and Children with Employed Fathers: Enough Time Together		
	Children 8 through 12 years old	Children 13 through 18 years old
Too little time		
Father	64%	64%
Child	29	39
Just enough time		
Father	35%	34%
Child	65	56
Too much time		
Father	1%	2%
Child	5.5	5
Significance:	*** = p < .0001;	** = p < .001.

Unexpected findings about employed parents and time

In sum, while 53 percent of employed parents with a child 8 through 18 feel they have too little time with their child, only 31 percent of children with employed parents feel the same way.

Typically, when issues of employed parents and time are discussed, the focus is on comparing children with employed versus nonemployed mothers. When we "ask the children," however, we find that there is no statistically significant difference between these two groups of children in feeling that they have too little time with their mothers.

Second, the public discussion has been more concerned with mothers than with fathers. When we turn to children, we find that children 8 through 18 years old are more likely to feel that they have too little time with their employed *fathers* than with their employed mothers. We also find that fathers—more so than mothers—feel they have too little time with their child.

Third, the public discussion about employed parents and time has centered on younger children, but we find that older children are more likely than younger children to feel that they have too little time with their fathers. Asking the children helps us see that the hidden story about working parents and time is about fathers and teenagers.

DOES THE AMOUNT OF TIME THAT CHILDREN SAY THEY SPEND WITH THEIR PARENTS AFFECT THEIR VIEW OF THEIR PARENTS?

If children are more likely than their parents to think they spend "just enough" time together, should parents stop worrying about the amount of time they spend with their children? Flipping this question around: Do children who spend more time with their parents give their parents higher marks on their parenting skills?

We also asked children to assess their parents on three other outcomes: (1) how successful their parents are at managing work and family life, (2) whether parents put their families before their jobs, or (3) whether parents put their jobs before their families.

Overall, more than two thirds of children feel their mothers and fathers are very successful at managing work and family life.

3.9

Children Third Through Twelfth Grades with Employed Parents: Views of Parents' Success in Managing Work and Family Life

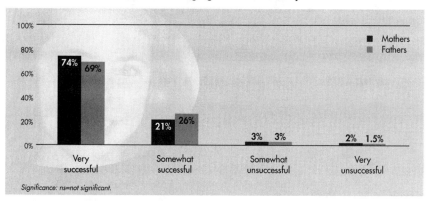

Significance: ns=not significant.

A 16-year-old girl summarizes this finding when she says:

I don't want [my mother] to change much. She's done a wonderful job.

Children do see their mothers making the decision to put family first more often than their fathers—though the vast majority of children are positive about both parents putting family first.

Next we looked at the reverse question: How often do children feel their mothers and their fathers put work first? Again parents get high

3.10

Children Third Through Twelfth Grades with Employed Parents: Views of Parents' Putting Family Before Job

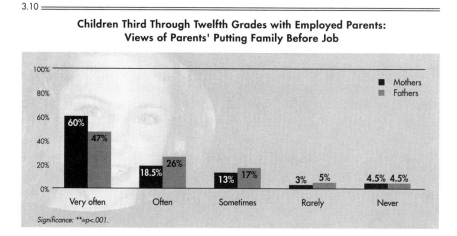

Significance: **=p<.001.

ratings. More than three in four children feel that their mothers and fathers rarely or never put their jobs before their families, but in cases in which work does come ahead of family, fathers do this more frequently than mothers. When this happens, an 11-year-old reveals that it can hurt.

Sometimes, it's like the job is more important than the child.

3.11

Children Third Through Twelfth Grades with Employed Parents: Views of Parents' Putting Job Before Family

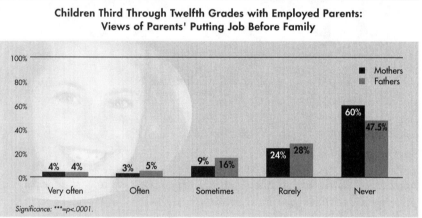

Significance: ***=p<.0001.

▼ **Does the quantity of time matter?** Again and again—in fact, *in all but one* of the analyses conducted to address this issue—we found that the quantity of time with mothers and fathers does matter a great deal. Children who spend more time with their mothers and fathers on workdays and nonworkdays grade their parents higher, feel their parents are more successful at managing work and family responsibilities, and see their parents as putting their families first.

For the most part, these statistics are quite striking. For example, far more children who spend 6 hours a day with their mothers on workdays give their mothers an A for making them feel important and loved (83 percent) than those who spend less than 1 hour with their mothers on workdays (62 percent). The same pattern holds for raising the child with good values: Ninety percent of those who spend 6 hours a day with their mothers on workdays give them an A compared with 55 percent of children who spend less than 1 hour with their mothers on workdays. Likewise with fathers: Eighty-four percent of children give their fathers an A for "appreciating me for who I am" when they spend more than 6 hours on workdays compared with 63 percent who spend less than 1 hour with their fathers on workdays.

So the *amount* or the *quantity* of time that children say they spend with their parents clearly makes a difference in how we parent. But what are the implications of this finding for the "quality versus quantity time" debate?

WHAT ACTIVITIES DO PARENTS AND CHILDREN DO TOGETHER?

One way of moving beyond simply cataloging the number of hours children and parents spend together is to look at what parents and children do while they are together. We investigated this by asking about a series of activities parents and children commonly do with each other: eating a meal together, playing a game or sport or exercising together (for those parents with a child over 5) doing homework with their children, and watching TV together. This list is certainly not inclusive of all important activities, nor do the questions we ask get at the nature of the interaction between children and their parents. A meal could be a time of warm conversation or a time of throwing insults across the table; working with a parent on homework could be a time of excitement and learning or a time of pitched battle; a child and parent could watch television discussing what they see or they could sit, side by side, like automatons, and the program they watch could be informative or violent and scary.

Employed mothers and employed fathers who live with a child at least half the time were asked how often during a typical week they engaged in each of these activities with their child. Children were asked how often they engaged in the activities "with at least one of their parents."[11] As you read about what we found, you might enjoy thinking about how you would answer each question and then compare your answer with that of typical parents in the United States today.

> **Eating a meal together—according to parents** The younger the child, the more likely parents are to report that they eat a meal with that child. For example, 78 percent of parents with a child

age 4 through 7 years report that they eat a meal with this child every day, whereas just less than half (49 percent) of parents report that they eat with their 13- through 18-year-old child every day. In fact, about a third of parents with a child 13 through 18 years old report eating with their child four times a week or less. Although fathers are more likely to eat with their sons than with their daughters for children 8 through 12 years old, mothers are equally likely to eat with children of both genders from birth through age 18 years.

3.12

During a typical week, how often do you eat a meal with your child?	Birth through 3 years old	4 through 7 years old	8 through 12 years old	13 through 18 years old	Total
Never	0%	2%	1%	1%	1%
One or two times a week	6	2	6	8	6
Three or four times a week	7	6	9	23.5	13
Five or six times a week	14	12	16	18	15.5
Every day	73	78	68.5	49	65

Employed Parents: Eating a Meal with Their Child

Significance: *** = p <.0001.

Many parents consider dinner to be a special ritual time for the family to bond and take measures to ensure that it is uninterrupted. One mother of two teenagers says:

We never have the television on during dinner, we try not to take phone calls, and we really try to be available.

A divorced mother with a 10-year-old son explains:

Family dinner hour is so important. I can remember that when we were married we would eat a lot as a family in front of a TV and it so limited our conversation and that sharing hour. Now I really make it a point for us to sit down and just say, "No, I'm sorry, we're not watching The Simpsons *and we're going to take these 30 minutes." Once you put your foot down and say this sharing time is important then it's okay.*

How would you answer this question? Do you eat with your child more or less often than the typical parent with a child your child's age?

▼ **Eating a meal together—according to children** Younger children also report that they eat a meal with at least one of their parents more frequently than older children do. Whereas 58 percent of children 8 through 12 years old eat a meal with a parent every day, only 34 percent of children 13 through 18 years old do. There is no difference between boys and girls in how often they say they eat a meal with their parents.

▼ **Eating a meal together—comparing parents and children** Because the children in our survey were asked about activities with "at least one of their parents," this parent might or might not be employed. In order to make precise comparisons between what parents and children say, we look at (1) children and parents in families with two employed parents and (2) children and parents in families with a single employed parent. (Note that these numbers differ from those of *all* children, reported above.)

3.13 ══

Parents and Children in Dual-Earner Families: Eating a Meal Together

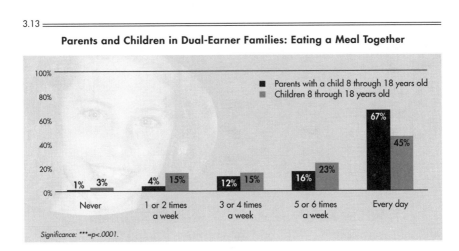

Significance: ***=p<.0001.

We found a very substantial discrepancy in dual-earner families between parents' and children's views of how often they eat together: 67 percent of parents say they eat with their child every day, compared with only 45 percent of children! Although we are not assessing children and parents from the same families, both are representative samples of the U.S. population. If we were assessing children and parents from the same families, the disparity might be smaller, but the magnitude of difference I find here is simply too great for it to disappear.

Since children are reporting about "at least one of their parents," one would expect the frequency of eating together to be higher for children than for parents. For example, if a child ate with only his mother and not his father every day, the child would say he ate with a parent every day. On the other hand, if a mother ate with a child every day, but the father did not, the combined parents' rating would be lower than the child's rating. But that is not at all the case here. Parents are far more likely to report that they eat frequently with their child than children of the same age are to report that they eat frequently with a parent.

Who is exaggerating? I can't say definitively—but there is more reason for parents to be susceptible to *social desirability* (a research term meaning that the individual wants to say what is socially correct to an interviewer) than for children.

3.14

Parents and Children in Employed Single-Parent Families: Eating a Meal Together

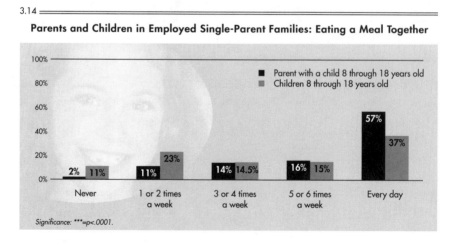

Significance: ***=p<.0001.

The same level of discrepancy is apparent in comparing employed single parents and children in employed-single-parent families. Slightly more than one third (34 percent) of the children say they never or rarely eat a meal with their parents compared with 13 percent of parents.

▼ **Playing, exercising together—according to parents** Not surprisingly, far fewer parents report that they "play a game, sport, or exercise" with their child regularly than they report eating a meal together. For example, 49 percent of parents with a child 13 through 18 years old say they eat with their child every day compared with 9 percent of parents who say they play or exercise with their child every day. Even among parents with children from birth through 3 years of age, 87 percent report eating with their child between five and seven times a week and 72 percent report playing with their child that often. The younger the child, however, the more likely the parent is to say that they play or exercise together.

Fathers are more likely to report playing or exercising with their sons from birth through 8 years old than with their daughters. Mothers are more likely to play or exercise with their daughters than their sons during the teenage years but not during other periods.

How would you answer this question? How do you compare to the typical parent?

3.15

During a typical week, how often do you play a game or a sport or exercise with your child?	Birth through 3 years old	4 through 7 years old	8 through 12 years old	13 through 18 years old	Total
Employed Parents: Playing, Exercising Together					
Never	0%	2%	3%	24.5%	9.5%
One or two times a week	8	14	35	40	27
Three or four times a week	19.5	25	34	21	25
Five or six times a week	7	13	11	5	8.5
Every day	65	46	17	9	30

Significance: *** = p < .0001.

▼ | **Playing, exercising together—according to children** According-
ing to children, the younger the child, the more likely he or
she is to play a game, sport, or exercise with his or her parents. However, only 3 percent of older children and 9 percent of
younger children say that they play or exercise with their parent
every day.

▼ | **Playing, exercising together—comparing parents and children**
As happened with the issue of shared meals, there are large differences in dual-earner families between parents' and children's perceptions of how often they play a game, sport, or exercise
together. For example, more than four times more children (31 percent) than parents (7 percent) say they never play or exercise
together. It is possible that children and parents might interpret this
question differently, but clearly not to the extent of the discrepancies
reflected here.

3.16

Parents and Children in Dual-Earner Families: Playing, Exercising Together

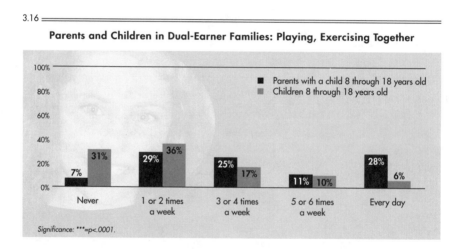

Significance: ***=p<.0001.

The contrast between parents and children in employed-single-
parent families is similarly phenomenal: More than three times more
children (47 percent) than parents (14.5 percent) say that they never
play or exercise together. In fact, just over three fourths of children in
these families say they rarely (once or twice a week) or never play or
exercise with their parent!

I find these discrepancies astounding. Do parents and children have
such different views of togetherness? I hope that these findings pro-

3.17

Parents and Children in Employed Single-Parent Families: Playing, Exercising Together

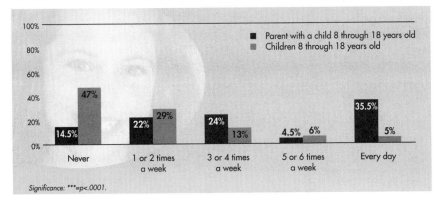

Legend:
- Parent with a child 8 through 18 years old
- Children 8 through 18 years old

	Never	1 or 2 times a week	3 or 4 times a week	5 or 6 times a week	Every day
Parent	14.5%	22%	24%	4.5%	35.5%
Children	47%	29%	13%	6%	5%

Significance: ***=p<.0001.

voke family discussions. So, practicing what I preach, I asked my now 25-year-old daughter to comment on them. She said:

> *Everything in this country is about parenting. Parents have to feel good about what they do. We live in a blame culture. If something goes wrong, people always look for someone to blame, so parents want to avoid being blamed. They want to feel good about what they are doing, so they probably exaggerate—probably unconsciously—how often they do things with their kids.*

What do you think?

▼ **Doing homework together—according to parents** Parents who had a child 5 years old or older were asked how many times a week they do homework with their child. One in four parents with a child 5 through 7 years of age never or rarely (defined as one to two times a week) does homework with his or her child.

As children get older, their parents are even less likely to help with homework—two in three parents with a child ages 13 through 18 never or rarely get involved. Overall, it is mothers more than fathers who help their children with homework. These differences between mothers and fathers are most pronounced with children 8 through 12 years old.

How often do you help your school-age child with homework?

3.18

During a typical week, how often do you do homework with your child?	5 through 7 years old	8 through 12 years old	13 through 18 years old	Total
Never	11%	7%	36%	21.5%
One or two times a week	13.5	23.5	31	25
Three or four times a week	18	28	16	20.5
Five or six times a week	23	10	5	10
Every day	35	31	13	23

Employed Parents: Doing Homework with Their Child

Significance: ***=p <.0001.

▼ | **Doing homework together—according to children** Older children echo parents' responses, reporting that their parents are less involved in doing homework with them than younger children report. In fact, three times as many older children (68 percent) as younger children (22 percent) say that their parents never do homework with them.

Since educators strongly promote parental involvement in children's education (though this goes beyond doing homework with children), I was interested to learn whether children whose parents are more involved in helping them with homework receive better or worse grades in school, as reported by children. We found no relationship. There could be any number of reasons why this is true. What do you think?

Doing homework with one's parents can be a pain, according to children:

My mom likes to check my homework, but I really don't like her to, because then we spend the whole night going over it and copying it over about a million times.

But it can also be satisfying:

> *It's sort of special if I let [my mom] check my homework. She likes to do it.*

▼ | **Doing homework together—comparing parents and children**
Parents and children in dual-earner families have quite different views of how often they do homework together. These differences are simply too large to have happened by chance: More than twice as many children (46 percent) as parents (18 percent) say that they never do homework together.

3.19 ═══

Parents and Children in Dual-Earner Families: Doing Homework Together

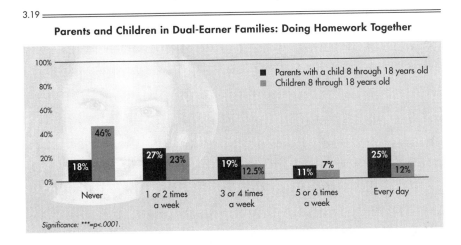

Significance: ***=p<.0001.

3.20 ═══

Parents and Children in Employed Single-Parent Families: Doing Homework Together

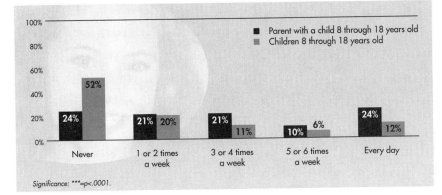

Significance: ***=p<.0001.

This two-to-one discrepancy also holds in single-parent homes, in which 24 percent of parents say they never do homework with their child compared with 52 percent of children who make the same claim.

▼ **Watching television together—according to single parents** Although a study from the University of Michigan indicates that television viewing among children declined between 1981 and 1997, nevertheless we found that parents watch television with their children more often than they help with homework or play or exercise with them.[12] For example, four times fewer parents never watch television (8 percent) with their 13- through 18-year-olds than never do homework with their child (36 percent). There is no difference between mothers and fathers in how frequently they watch television with their child.

How would you answer the question of how often you watch TV with your child? How does this compare with how often you help your child with his or her homework?

3.21

During a typical week, how often do you watch TV with your child?	Birth through 3 years old	4 through 7 years old	8 through 12 years old	13 through 18 years old	Total
Never	5%	2%	4%	8%	5%
One or two times a week	23	16	24	31	24
Three or four times a week	19	21	18	26	22
Five or six times a week	7	11	12	10	10
Every day	47	50	42	24	38

Employed Parents: Watching Television with Their Child

Significance: *** = p <.0001.

▼ **Watching television together—according to children** Among older children 13 through 18 years old, almost three quarters (74 percent) report watching television with their parent three times a week or more. More than one in four (27 percent) watch television with their parent daily. Among children 8 through 12, the figures are higher: Of these, 79.5 percent watch television with their parent three times a week or more and 45.5 percent do so daily. There is no difference between boys and girls in how often they say they watch television with a parent.

▼ | **Watching television together—comparing parents and children**
It is fascinating that there are no statistically significant differences in how frequently parents and children say they watch television together. Finding congruence here makes the discrepancies between parents and children in how often they say they are involved in other activities all the more intriguing. Obviously, parents and children can see eye to eye, but often they don't. This finding lends more credence to my hunch that parents are answering questions about the other activities in a "socially desirable way." When it comes to television, however, there is social pressure against "sitting in front of the boob tube" for too long, so here we probably answer more realistically or even underestimate the time we spend.

In later chapters, as we continue to explore other findings, we will see many instances in which parents and children have a very different take on reality, shaded by their own strong feelings about the subject. I saw similar disparities in the one-on-one interviews. When asked about what she did when her mother came home from work tired, a young girl said she put a pillow under her mother's head, covered her with a blanket, and tiptoed around so her mother could rest. When I asked the mother about how her child responded when she came home from work tired, this mother said her daughter was loud, was noisy, and never let her rest. Or when asked about how they spend evenings together, a father told of long walks with his son as dusk was falling, whereas his son described the father as locked in front of the computer, never looking up. The experience of both the parent and the child is real, but the prominence of the experience and the perceived frequency with which these experiences occur are clearly filtered by our feelings. I think we, as parents, want to believe that we are more often involved in certain activities with our children than we really are.

When I have shared the finding that parents and children differ in how often they say they do activities together—except watching television—both children and their parents have been astonished. Why? I think that we don't know how different our views of reality are because we so seldom talk about these issues. That, of course, is the purpose of this book.

DOES THE FREQUENCY OF ENGAGING IN ACTIVITIES WITH PARENTS AFFECT HOW CHILDREN FEEL ABOUT THEIR PARENTS?

We find that children who eat a meal more frequently with one of their parents:[13]

▼ feel that their mothers and fathers are more successful at managing their work and family responsibilities.

▼ are more likely to feel that their mothers and fathers put their family before their job and are less likely to feel that their fathers put their jobs before their families.

▼ give their mothers and fathers higher grades for making them feel important and loved, for being someone they can go to if they are upset, for spending time talking with them, for knowing what is really going on in their lives, for encouraging them to want to learn and to enjoy learning, for appreciating them for who they are, for raising them with good values (fathers only), for controlling their tempers, for establishing family routines and traditions, for being involved with what is happening to their children, for being there for their children when they are sick, and for being able to attend the important events in their children's lives.

The same patterns hold for *all* of the other activities we looked at. There is a very large number of significant findings that indicate that *the sheer regularity of parent-child interaction* in activities is linked to the way the child feels about his or her mother and father. This hearkens back to the importance of routines and rituals, discussed in Chapter 2. Although this study didn't tap what really happens when parents and children do activities together, we find that the parents who are involved in doing things with their children have children who feel more positive about them. Clearly, we cannot with certainty separate the chicken from the egg in these analyses: Do parents who get more involved in activities already have better relationships with their children, or does becoming more involved lead to better relationships? However, it is important to know that doing things with our children goes hand in hand with their feeling more positive about us.

HOW RUSHED IS THE TIME THAT PARENTS AND CHILDREN SPEND TOGETHER?

Many observers of family life worry about the fast pace of today's world. In one of her weekly columns for the *Wall Street Journal* in 1998, the staff writer Sue Shellenbarger describes focus groups of teenagers that she conducted in Lincoln, Nebraska, as revealing a pressure-cooker life for both teenagers and parents:

> "We don't have enough time to do all the things we need to succeed," says one. Another feels "bogged down with this ridiculous amount of obligation." . . . Many teenagers are mounting a juggling act that rivals anything their parents might conduct.[14]

I investigated this issue of rushing as another aspect of the tenor of the time parents and children spend together. We asked how employed parents and children with employed parents feel about their time together: Has their time in the past 3 months been very rushed, somewhat rushed, somewhat calm, or very calm? How would you answer this question?

▼ | **Rushed time—according to parents** Although only 4 percent of parents with children 18 years old and under feel that their time with their child is "very rushed," fully one third (33 percent) feel their time with their child is either "somewhat rushed" or "very rushed." There are no differences for parents with older or younger children.

3.22				
Employed Parents: Rushed Time with Their Child				
During the past three months, would you say that your time with your child has been typically	Birth through 3 years old	4 through 7 years old	8 through 12 years old	13 through 18 years old	Total
Very rushed	3%	2%	7%	3%	4%
Somewhat rushed	22	27	31	33	29
Somewhat calm	50	37	45	42	43.5
Very calm	24	34	17	22	24

Significance: ns = not significant.

Many parents told us stories about the pressure their hurried daily routine puts on their children. The mother of a 13-year-old girl and a 9-year-old boy says:

> I'm sure they feel it. They respond sometimes by demanding more, wanting me to spend more time with them. They feel the tension. They come home and everything is in chaos. It's not the time when we can sit down and talk and hear about what happened at school or there's no time to go and get the perfect pencil they need for the next day. Everybody's trying to get a little time to do what we need to do and we can't always do it.

There never seems to be enough time after work for some families. A mother of a 9-year-old girl explains:

> The evenings feel way too short. It seems like we have no evenings at all. We're always rushing into the next day. We're rushing into bed so that we can get ready for the next day, so we can get home and get ready for the next.

▼ **Rushed time with mothers—according to children** More than two in five (44.5 percent) children feel that their time with their mother is rushed. Given the pressures of the junior high/high school years, it is no wonder that children ages 13 through 18 are more likely to feel rushed than children ages 8 through 12.

Children told stories about rushing through the day as well. Some mentioned mornings as particularly hectic times for their families.

> She's rushing and telling me to rush. So I sort of try to rush but I can't really because it's early in the morning and I can't rush. And my backpack weighs a ton, so if she walks me to school, it's like running down the street. I'm like "wait up" because I can't run in the morning. Afternoons maybe I can run, but not in the morning.
>
> 12-YEAR-OLD GIRL

> I would say that it is rushed. You always have something to do. Somewhere to go. Somebody to talk to. Somebody is on the phone. The times you really have to spend together are Sundays; Sundays we all go to church together. So those are good days. We are not as rushed. In the mornings we are rushed.
>
> 18-YEAR-OLD GIRL

▼ **Rushed time with father—according to children** Since mothers take more responsibility for the care of children, I would have expected children to feel the brunt of rushing more with their mothers than with their fathers. But I was wrong. Children are equally likely to feel rushed with their fathers as with their mothers. Thirty-seven percent of children—younger and older alike—feel their time with their father is rushed.

▼ **Rushed time together—comparing parents and children** Whereas parents and children disagree quite strongly about whether they have enough time together, children and their mothers agree on the extent to which their time together is rushed.

3.23 ══

Employed Mothers and Children with Employed Mothers: Rushed Time Together

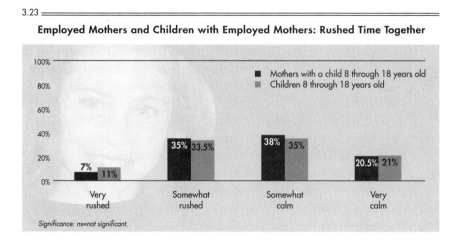

- ■ Mothers with a child 8 through 18 years old
- ■ Children 8 through 18 years old

	Very rushed	Somewhat rushed	Somewhat calm	Very calm
Mothers	7%	35%	38%	20.5%
Children	11%	33.5%	35%	21%

Significance: ns=not significant.

Similarly, there is no significant difference in how rushed children 8 through 18 years old and fathers with a child of the same age feel.

DOES FEELING THAT TIME WITH THEIR MOTHERS IS RUSHED AFFECT HOW CHILDREN JUDGE THEM AS PARENTS?

Of the analyses we conducted to address the question of children's judgments of mothers in relation to feeling rushed when they are together, *most are significant*. Specifically, children are more likely to see their mother positively if their time with her is calmer. For example:

3.24

Employed Fathers and Children with Employed Fathers: Rushed Time Together

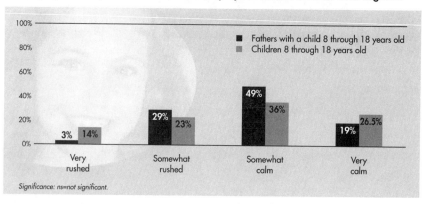

Significance: ns=not significant.

▼ Of children 8 through 18 years of age who rate their time with their mothers as "very calm," 85 percent feel that their mothers are "very successful" in managing their work and family responsibilities compared with 56.5 percent who rate their time with their mothers as "very rushed."

▼ Among those who feel that their time with their mothers is very calm, 71 percent feel their mothers "very often" put their families before their jobs, compared with 58 percent who rate their time with their mothers as very rushed.

▼ Among those who see their time with their mothers as very calm, 86 percent give their mothers an A for "making me feel important and loved" compared with 63 percent who rate their time with their mothers as very rushed.

The only findings that did not reach significance are the grades given to mothers for establishing family routines and traditions, encouraging their children to want to learn and to enjoy learning, and raising their children with good values.

DOES FEELING THAT TIME WITH THEIR FATHERS IS RUSHED AFFECT HOW CHILDREN JUDGE THEM?

Every analysis we conducted revealed a significant link between rushed time and how children perceive their fathers, indicating that children are highly sensitive to the pace of time with their fathers. For example, 80 percent of children who feel their time with their fathers is very calm give their fathers an A for "appreciating me for who I am" compared with 50.5 percent who rate their time with their fathers as very rushed. Even more telling are the grades given to fathers for "being someone I can go to when I am upset." Sixty-four percent who rate their time with their fathers as very calm give their fathers an A compared with 36 percent of those who see their time with their fathers as very rushed.

"Focus" Is Key

In one-on-one interviews, we asked parents to describe moments when they felt particularly successful at home. Over and over, we heard the word *focus*. The mother of a 12-year-old says:

> "It's the time you spend with your children [when] you are really focused on them that's good; it is a focused time, not a distracted time.

The mother of an 8-year-old and a 2-year-old says:

> "I feel good when I can focus on my kids and I can feel like I am in the present tense and not always kind of figuring out the next step.

A father says:

> When I focus, I pay attention to what my children are doing and I can feel the connection between us.

On hearing the word *focus* again and again, from parent after parent, I began to listen to how and when we use this word in everyday conversation. I call it the *focus test*—it is almost as if a buzzer goes off now whenever I hear the word. A friend is diagnosed with an illness but responds, "The benefit is now that I can *focus* on what is most important." Another friend is distressed by a family problem but finds that *focusing* on her children helps her begin to heal. Another friend says that one of the reasons that exercise helps him feel better is that exercise commands your complete *focus*—you don't feel distracted from within or bombarded from without. People reserve the word *focus* for what matters. When people focus, they seem to feel energized.

I talked with Daniel Siegel of the University of California at Los Angeles, a child and adolescent psychiatrist who specializes in the neurobiology of the developing mind, about what I was hearing. He said that there is a reason why parents are using the word *focus*. They are talking about an important biological reaction:

> When parents and children align their focus on each other, there is a neurobiological process involving the sympathetic branch of the autonomic nervous systems that is activated. This process, which mediates a sense of well-being, joy and elation, is at the heart of emotional attunement when one person feels "felt" and understood by the other person. This form of contingent communication is at the heart of developing secure attachments. It begins in infancy and continues throughout the life span.[15]

To focus is to calm down as well as to feel energized. Try my focus test: Listen to how often this word is used when there is really something important at stake.

▼ **Focus—according to parents** The vast majority of parents with children from birth through 18 years of age report that it is either very easy (62 percent) or somewhat easy (31 percent) to focus on their child when they are together. Only 7 percent of parents find it difficult to focus on their child. Mothers find it easier than fathers to focus on a child 8 through 18 years of age, although mothers and fathers find it equally easy to focus on their daughters and their sons.

When my daughter interviewed children for this book, she concluded that children ultimately judge their parents on whether they are "there for me." Our study makes it clear that among other things "being there" means "focusing." A number of the parents we interviewed concurred and described the effort they put into focusing on their children—especially after a tough day at work. A single mother of an 8-year-old boy says:

> *You have to be there for your kids, you have to be there mentally. Don't think just because you work and you give them what they need . . . that that's it. It doesn't stop there.*

A mother of a 16-year-old girl tells us:

> *It's more being attuned to a person's needs, physical and emotional. So when she wants to talk, even though I am tired and I don't feel like talking, I force myself. Actually I shouldn't say force, but I say, "Okay, let's talk."*

Another woman describes the similarity to marriage:

You have to decide to pay attention [to your spouse], even when you are tired and don't want to. Being willing to focus shows that you care.

▼ **Focus—according to children** Children were asked how easy or difficult it is for their parents to focus on them. The vast majority of children in the seventh through twelfth grades—boys and girls alike—report that it is either very easy or somewhat easy for both their mothers and their fathers to "really focus" on them when they are together. Nevertheless, children do report differences between mothers and fathers: 62 percent say that mothers find it "very easy" and 52 percent say that fathers find it very easy to focus on them when they are together.

Children are very attuned to the extent to which their parents are focused on them:

They're really involved in what they're saying to me. They're not just saying normal things like "uh huh . . . uh hmmm." They seem to be very intent on what I'm saying, they're not just looking away.

10-YEAR-OLD BOY

As you will see in Chapter 7, some children even have "tests" of whether their parent is focusing on them. For example, a 13-year-old boy throws nonsense statements—"a goldfish on the grass"—into the middle of a sentence to check out whether his parents are really listening to him.

When we compared children's and parents' views of the ease or difficulty of focusing, we found no differences.

DOES THE EASE WITH WHICH PARENTS FOCUS ON THEIR CHILDREN AFFECT HOW CHILDREN FEEL ABOUT THEM?

Every analysis we conducted revealed a significant association between children's assessment of their parents' ease in focusing on them and how children judge their parents. When children feel that their mothers and fathers can focus on them, they are much more likely to feel that their parents manage their work and family responsibilities more successfully and put their families before their work, and they give their parents much higher marks for all of the parenting skills we examined. Although very few children believe that their parents have trouble paying attention to them, those who do see their mothers and their fathers in an extremely negative light.

SO, IS IT QUANTITY TIME OR QUALITY TIME?

When we ask the children, we find that the *amount* of time they report spending with their mothers and their fathers certainly does affect how they see their parents. But so do the content and quality of time: the activities they engage in with their parents, whether or not the time they have together is frenetic or calm, and whether they believe that their parents are really focusing on them when they are together. So whereas the national discussion on work and parenting has polarized the issue of time into quality versus quantity, our data indicate that *both* quality *and* quantity matter. An either/or debate simply doesn't make sense.

As the parent of 13-year-old twins puts it:

> *Downtime is important. Car time is important because you're just stuck in the car. If there is something on their minds, they can talk about it. Or going to bed time. It is interesting to me that my 13-year-old kids still have to be tucked in. Why is that? It is not like every night we talk, but once in a while if something is bothering one of them, we talk.*
>
> *There is a balance between quantity and quality. The quantity of time isn't enough. It is very hard to create quality without quantity. Particularly as they get older, they have to be able to unwind and relax into being with you.*

The words we're using to describe time within the family are wrong. To change the debate, we need new words. Since *focus* is the word that parents use to describe the *quality* of time they treasure most, I suggest we use it. And since parents and children highly value the *quantity* of time they spend being together, whether sharing a meal or just being around each other in a nonrushed way, we need a phrase for that, too. Children need *focused times and hang-around times*.

WHAT CHILDREN WISH THEY COULD CHANGE ABOUT THEIR PARENTS' WORK AND FAMILY LIVES

Recall that we asked parents, "If your child were granted one wish to change the way that your work affects his/her life, what would that wish be?" Parents guess that their children will wish for "more time with me" (21 percent); that "I work less time" (19 percent); and that "I wouldn't have to work" (16 percent). All told, a total of 56 percent of parents assume children would wish for more time with them. Furthermore, 14 percent wish that "I would earn more money." Only 1 percent, respectively, think their children would wish that they would be less stressed by work or less tired by work when they are together.

So we asked the children the same question: "If you were granted one wish to change the way that your mother's/your father's work affects your life, what would that wish be?" I was fascinated to find that, in contrast to parents, children do not put time at the top of their list.

First, children say that they wish their mothers would make more money (23 percent). Is that because children are overly materialistic? It is clear that families are under increasing financial pressure and that the definition of what it means to live a good life today costs more and more, according to Juliet Schor of Harvard University.[16] Children may be the youngest to fall prey to the lure of consumer culture, or they may hear their parents worry out loud about money. We can't fully know,

3.25

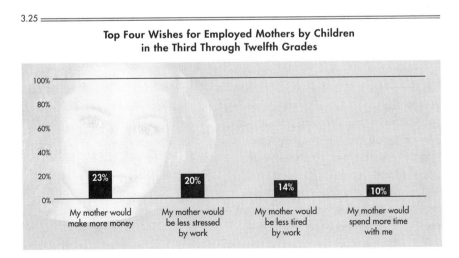

Top Four Wishes for Employed Mothers by Children
in the Third Through Twelfth Grades

3.26

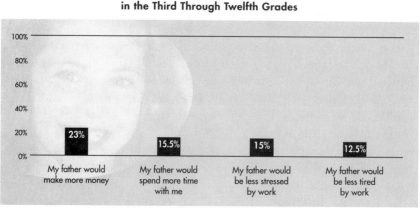

Top Four Wishes for Employed Fathers by Children in the Third Through Twelfth Grades

My father would make more money	23%
My father would spend more time with me	15.5%
My father would be less stressed by work	15%
My father would be less tired by work	12.5%

but I suspect that children may hear their mothers wish for money to reduce the pressure and stress they feel. That would make sense, given children's other answers: that their mother would be less stressed by work (20 percent) and would be less tired by work (14 percent). Putting those two answers together, 34 percent of children wish that their mothers would be less stressed and tired. Only 10 percent say that they wish mothers would spend more time with them.

When asked about their wish for their fathers, children's most frequent answer is the same: making more money (23 percent). As we have seen previously, many children yearn for more time with their fathers, and that answer is second (15.5 percent), and being less stressed by work (15 percent) and being less tired by work (12.5 percent) are third and fourth. Taken together, 27.5 percent of the children wish that their fathers would be less stressed and less tired.

When we ask the children, we see that the time parents spend with children does not occur in a vacuum. It is clearly affected by work. Again, there is a big disparity between what parents think their children think and what children actually think. Rather than simply wanting to have more time together, children want their mothers and fathers to be less stressed by work and less tired by work, and perhaps they think that more money would alleviate those problems.

I wonder whether parents say that their children would wish for more time because parents are projecting their own desires on to their children. And perhaps having too little time has become the major explanation for all that's wrong with life today. But rather than addressing life in its complexity, we simplify it into an either/or debate about time.

It is fascinating that parents almost *never* guess that their children would want them to be less tired and stressed. This mother, however, joins the 2 percent in the survey who do guess what many children want:

> *If you are stressed by work, the amount of time that you spend with your children might be exactly the same, but you are not really available when you are at home.*

This mother knows there is something about work that can affect parents—and thereby children—at home. Identifying that "something" is my goal in the next chapter.

There Is Something About Work

hen I first began conducting research on work and family life, I thought that once there were studies that elucidated how children are affected by the fact that their mothers work, the debate would change: that I would no longer be asked the same question, year after year: "Are children harmed when their mothers work?"

Twenty years has passed. During that time, studies have built a stronger and stronger knowledge base: The fact that a mother works tells us very little about how her child turns out. But the question doesn't change. I still get calls from the media asking this question. I am asked it at speeches I give. Even my dentist, while I am rendered speechless by dental apparatus in my mouth, asks.

Kathleen Gerson of New York University says it well in a paper she presented to a Radcliffe Public Policy Institute in November 1997:

> When the public debate turns to children's well-being, the focus inevitably turns to the reputed harmful effects of employed mothers. Yet after decades of research on this subject, what is most striking about the cumulative findings is the lack of evidence that employed mothers have any harmful effects at all. What is striking is how much trouble people have gone through

to try to show that women's employment harms children and
how very little they have been able to demonstrate.[1]

So my question has changed. Now I ask myself: Why do we hold on
to this idea of harm?

Clearly, there are many reasons. First, we tend to hold parents responsible for *all* the problems children face. That certainly was the finding of
a series of focus groups conducted for the Ad Council. They were interested in how the public responds to children's issues. When the plight
of children—the number of children born in poverty, the number of
children born prematurely, the number of children harmed by guns, and
so on—was described in focus groups across the country the reaction of
the participants in focus groups was unequivocal. First, there was shock,
then disbelief, and then the groups turned on the parents of the children
in trouble: "Those children wouldn't have problems if it weren't for
their parents . . . their terrible parents." The language used against the
parents was harsh, even demonizing. In fact, when the focus group leaders played back some of the accusations levied at parents, the group
members were often shocked at the venom in their words.[2]

When fingers are pointed at parents for causing children's problems,
working mothers are often singled out. Recently, I served as a commen-
tator for a political debate among gubernatorial candidates. One of the
candidates proclaimed that *all* the problems children today face would
simply disappear if their mothers accepted the responsibility they had
incurred by choosing to have children and stayed at home with them.
When I participated as an adviser to a new study of working parents, children, and child care, I heard a colleague from the U.S. Department of
Education talk about the distress among teachers over a perceived decline
in children's performance in school—a decline teachers attributed *primarily* to working parents (read working mothers). Interestingly—perhaps ironically—these two critics were working mothers themselves!

Another reason we hold on to the notion of harm resides within us.
One of my friends, the director of a private school, calls it the "saber-
tooth tiger" response: "I believe that parents are programmed to protect
their children against danger, against the saber-tooth tigers of the
world." According to his analogy, born out of years of working with parents as an educator, the suggestion that our working might harm children can be so threatening to our role as protectors that we don't really
want to examine it. In today's vernacular, "We don't want to go there."

The extent to which protective feelings are rooted in our biological
nature is open to question, but I am nonetheless struck by how often

animal images occur when parents talk about the pull they feel to be with their children and how separations can elicit feelings of danger. In my book *The Six Stages of Parenthood*, I quote the mother of a 6-week-old child as saying that her desire to be with her child is so strong that everything else is an "annoyance, an interruption." What she would really like to do is to "get into a little burrow with this baby." And when she is separated from her child for a while, she says, "My image of myself is of an elephant mother charging through the jungle because she hears her babies squeal."[3]

Our own studies have increasingly pointed to an answer to my question. There is a problem, but the problem is not the fact that mothers—and fathers—work. The problem is that jobs themselves can be stressful or satisfying. Jobs can drain us or energize us. Jobs can overwhelm us or support us. The problem is not *that* we work; it is *how* we work.

ARE EMPLOYED MOTHERS MORE STRESSED THAN MOTHERS AT HOME?

What does the research on work and family life say about *how* we work? The earliest research on the impact of jobs on parents focused on mothers, not fathers, and had a simpler paradigm; it investigated what is labeled *role occupancy*. The question asked was, Do women who have more roles (wife, mother, worker) fare better or worse than women who have fewer roles (wife, mother)? Underlying some of these studies is the theory of *role stress* or *role strain*: Having more roles has the potential to make us feel overloaded.

Contrary to role strain/role stress theory, however, many of these studies tend to find that employed mothers have better physical health and mental health than at-home mothers. Such findings led to another theory: *role expansion*. According to this theory, having multiple roles is more likely to ensure our well-being because they provide separate sources for feeling good about ourselves and for receiving support. Problems at home can have less of an impact on us if things are going well at work, and vice versa.[4]

On the other hand, studies, including our own national study of the changing workforce, have found that employed women with children have higher levels of stress or role strain than employed women without children. So which role hypothesis is correct? In a very real sense, both hypotheses are true. Employed mothers are typically healthy, mentally and physically, but they are also stressed.

Our one-on-one interviews with mothers and fathers make it clear that staying at home doesn't remove stress; it simply exchanges one set of stresses for another, which can affect different individuals in different ways. In a speech she gave at the Association for Work/Life Professionals conference in February 1997, Carol Madole describes her decision to leave a corporate job to stay at home to care for her young son and daughter. She made this decision after moving out of a city to a more rural community and facing the logistical difficulties of finding child care and of commuting into the city for her job:

> To say the least, I was overwhelmed by the complexity of our logistical arrangements [caused by the move].
>
> So after a lot of discussion about finances, working, working part-time, not working, day care, no day care, etc., my husband and I decided I should stay at home.
>
> I was going to be the cohesive unit, the glue that would make all of these changes possible and even positive.
>
> For me, the season to change my life had arrived.
>
> But honestly, I was ready to pack it in—I was stressed and I was resentful.
>
> 1) I had enough of getting up at 5:30 in the morning to get myself and everyone else ready;
> 2) I had enough of picking up tired, grumpy kids at night and serving bowls of cereal for dinner;
> 3) I had enough of grocery shopping at 10 at night just to have something to prepare for lunch the next day;
> 4) I had enough of the corporate pressures and worrying about work when I was home;
> 5) I had enough of the "beat the clock" schedule; I had enough of the juggling act.
>
> I wanted a real, stay-at-home Mom experience. I wanted to give my kids all of the benefits of my being at home more often and being more involved in their lives.
>
> And so the dreams and fantasies began. In my imagination, there was no end to how wonderful our lives would become:
>
> 1) No more temper tantrums (on my part as well as the kids');
> 2) No more rushed mornings and missed trains;

3) *No more homework at 8:00 at night with tears and frustration;*
4) *No more fights with my husband over who stays home with a sick kid.*

I even went so far as to imagine:

1) *Greeting my son at the end of the day with a smile and a plate of home-baked cookies;*
2) *Total peace and tranquility daily;*
3) *Preparing a home-cooked dinner for my family every night;*
4) *Being awake enough and relaxed enough to have a conversation with my husband when he comes home at the end of the day;*
5) *In short, I thought our life would be like a Norman Rockwell painting: the family sitting around the fire laughing and playing games.*

And so, the more I thought about not working, the more I was convinced that THIS was the answer to all of our problems; THIS was the key to sanity!!

I thought that life would be easy simply *because the work portion of my work/life struggle was being eliminated.*

Not only did I NOT eliminate the stress in my life, I merely traded one source of stress for another.

Anyone who thinks that being home almost all day with a demanding and irrepressible five-year-old is NOT stressful is wrong.

I learned very quickly I was not going to be sitting around eating bonbons all day and getting my nails done.

Here's my reality, the flip side to my fantasy:

1) *I am a chauffeur, a maid, a waitress, a cook, a social director, a therapist, and a baby-sitter;*
2) *I deal with all of the workmen and contractors and take full responsibility for every aspect of our house;*
3) *I wait around all day for deliveries that don't come;*
4) *I am on a first-name basis with the garbage man, the mailman, and the UPS man and actually look forward to their visits;*
5) *I put over 200 miles a week on the car without really going anywhere;*

6) *I do at least eight loads of laundry a week and clean the kitchen at least five times a day;*

7) *I still scream and yell and get frustrated easily;*

8) *I still serve cereal for dinner (because I don't like to cook and not working hasn't changed that);*

9) *I am still exhausted at the end of the day when my husband comes home and needs me for support;*

10) *My kids still don't want to get ready in the morning or go to bed at night (because kids are kids and they're going to do their own thing whether I work or not);*

11) *We still have temper tantrums and we still do homework too late at night;*

12) *And worse yet, my family doesn't fully understand what my day is like and why I may not have gotten to do a particular errand. Because after all, to quote my 6½-year-old, "What did you do today? You don't even work anymore."*

At times I feel misunderstood and not quite sure what my role is.

I have eliminated my work at the office, a move which I always ASSUMED would give me the balance I was looking for. I was sure that my stresses were the result of the traditional work/life balancing act.

But what I have found is that I have simply substituted my work outside the home with more work at home.

And to make matters worse, I don't have working, corporate stresses, and the frenetic pace of life to blame for whatever is not perfect in my life.

So what have I gained?

▼ *Good, bad, or indifferent, I am with my kids much more. I am there to get them off to school each morning, to arrange play dates, to shuttle them to their various activities, and to be the shoulder they cry on at the end of the day when things did not go their way.*

▼ *And because I am home, their friends come to our house a lot, and this allows me to know their friends and to be more connected and involved in their lives.*

▼ *I see my husband more focused on his career. No longer is he torn between our work/life responsibilities; no longer does he feel guilty watching me handle both sides of the equation.*

▼ *I am learning to be a more relaxed, patient parent. Parenting is more difficult than I had imagined, and because I thought that it would magically be easier when I didn't work anymore, I have had to rethink my whole approach toward parenting.*

▼ *BUT MOST OF ALL, I see my kids thriving and doing beautifully in their new schools and new environments, and this is extremely gratifying.*

There is no established formula; what works for one person may provide stress for another.

But at this point in my life, taking this time has been right for me and for my family. Overall, it has been an invaluable and rewarding experience.

And besides, had I never taken this time, I'd still be rushing to the train living with the fantasy that life could be great if only . . . [5]

As the reflections of Carol Madole reveal: It is not *that* we work, it is *how* we work and how we manage family life that make a difference. And the "we" includes fathers as well as mothers.

A NEW MODEL FOR MAKING SENSE OF WORK AND FAMILY LIFE

When I first began to conduct research on work and family life in the early 1980s, researchers—including me—tended to look at the influences of these spheres in unidirectional ways: How does work affect family? How does family affect work? Since that time, each study that the Families and Work Institute has conducted has brought us closer to a model for understanding how work and home life fit together. In addition, excellent research by many others has illuminated our knowledge.

The study conducted for *Ask the Children* gave me an opportunity to create and test a new framework for making sense of the complicated, confusing lives we all live. That's why I spent so many years in framing this project and why I turned to the best minds in the field—conducting a literature review, bringing in experts. That's why I put everything we "knew" aside and went to fifteen states to talk with parents and children. In those interviews, I felt as if we tucked our years of research into a packet, sealed it, and filed it away. We listened as if we had never before heard a parent or a child talk, with no preset agenda, no hypotheses to prove. We listened as if we had landed in a foreign land, trying to decipher the ways that people in this land see the world, speak, and behave.

Out of this welter of information, I have developed a model for understanding work and family—a model that I hope is both illuminating and practical.

A WORK-FAMILY MODEL, BEGINNING WITH WORK

Over the next chapters, we'll examine the components of this model for employed parents with a child from birth through 18 years old, first looking at work, then at family life, then at the spillover from work to family, and vice versa, and finally at how all of this affects our success as parents and our children's development.[6] Throughout we'll test this model to determine how well it fits our empirical data.[7]

Job demands

The first component of this model is *job demands*. When I think of job demands, I think of a recent meeting of an ongoing council of work-life business leaders in which I participate. The topic on the agenda was overwork. Normally, the tone of these meetings is very professional (we have met together for 16 years on the subject of work life). But this topic engendered an extremely personal response. Member after member described feeling overwhelmed by work. All are hard workers; all enjoy the challenges of work. But there are clearly problems with the way many of us work today. It is the relentless volley of work, the seemingly never-ending requirements and responsibilities, the fact that there is no safe haven from work, that are very difficult. Email, voice mail, cell phones, and portable computers all have eroded the boundaries between work time and nonwork time. They foster expectations of an instant response, of 24-hour-a-day availability. Work continues to pile on so that even if we took a break, we would return to mountains of "things to do"; a perfect description of excessive job demands.

Job demands represent the requirements of our jobs. I use the word *demands* because our work often feels this way—our jobs make demands on our time and energy. Obviously, some of these demands are imposed on us and others are self-imposed. Some job demands are *objective*—such as the number of hours we are required to work—and some are *subjective*, such as how pressured our jobs make us feel.

Objective job demands

Researchers have found each of these conditions of jobs linked to employees' well-being.[8]

JOB DEMANDS
Number of jobs
Number of hours worked per week
Number of days worked per week
Work location
Work schedule
Overnight travel
Taking work home
Job pressure

▼ **Number of jobs** In the study conducted for *Ask the Children*, we found that 84 percent of employed parents with children 18 and younger have one job, and 16 percent have two or more jobs. Although one might imagine that fathers are more likely to hold more jobs than mothers, this is not the case. Fathers and mothers are equally likely to work more than one job.

▼ **Number of hours worked per week** As I noted in Chapter 3, fathers' total work time has increased by 3.1 hours per week in the past 20 years, while mothers' time has increased by 5.2 hours.[9] Today, only 12 percent of employed parents work fewer than 35 hours and almost half (48 percent) work more than 40 hours a week.

As expected, there are substantial differences between mothers and fathers in how much time they work. Whereas almost one in four mothers (23.5 percent) works what is typically considered part-time, fewer than 35 hours a week, only 2 percent of fathers do. At the other end of the spectrum, almost three times as many fathers (30 percent) as mothers (11 percent) work more than 50 hours per week.[10]

4.1

Employed Parents with a Child Birth Through 18: All Paid and Unpaid Hours Worked Each Week			
	Fathers	Mothers	Total
Less than 35 hours	2%	23.5%	12%
35–40 hours	36.5	43	40
41–50 hours	32	22	27
More than 50 hours	30	11	21

Significance: *** = p <.0001.

▼ | **Number of days worked per week** There are large differences between mothers and fathers in terms of the number of days they work. Three times more mothers (16 percent) than fathers (5 percent) work fewer than five days per week. However, as with work hours, it is clear that most employed parents are working a great deal of time. In fact, one in five mothers (21 percent) and almost two in five fathers (38 percent) work 6 to 7 days a week.

▼ | **Work location** Seventy-nine percent of parents work from a location other than their home, whereas 7 percent work regularly at home and 14 percent sometimes work at home and sometimes at another location. Employed parents with more years of education and higher household income are likely to work either at home or at home and at another location, indicating that more advantaged parents have greater flexibility in where they work.

▼ | **Work schedule** Sixty-nine percent of parents—mothers and fathers alike—work a regular daytime schedule, whereas almost one in three (31 percent) works a nondaytime schedule, including a regular evening schedule, a regular night shift, a rotating shift, a split shift, or a flexible schedule. As expected, mothers and fathers in households with higher income levels are more likely to work regular daytime schedules. At the other end of the continuum, 45.5 percent of employed parents with annual household income at or below $25,000 work nondaytime schedules.

▼ | **Overnight travel** Three in four employed parents report that they have not spent any nights away from home because of their work in the past 3 months. On the other hand, 15 percent have spent between 1 and 9 nights away from home and 8.5 percent have spent 10 nights or more away. Fathers are more likely to travel and be away from home than mothers: Thirteen percent of fathers spent 10 or more nights away from home because of their work in the past 3 months compared with 4 percent of mothers.

▼ | **Taking work home** Employed parents were asked, "On a typical workday, how much time do you do any work at home before you leave for work or after you return home?" Although more than two in five (43 percent) parents report doing "no" work, almost one in three (32 percent) spends more than an hour at home doing work around the edges of the workday.

Employed Parents with a Child Birth Through 18: Amount of Time Working at Home on Workdays	
None	43%
0–1 hour	25
More than 1 hour–3 hours	21
More than 3 hours	11

Although there is no difference between mothers and fathers in how much work they do at home on workdays, there is a difference for non-workdays: On nonworkdays 38.5 percent of fathers and 28.5 percent of mothers spend more than an hour working.

Subjective job demands: job pressure

As I've noted, job demands also have a powerful psychological component. This construct has been well defined and quantified in the seminal research of Robert Karasek of the University of Massachusetts at Lowell. He and his colleagues use a measure of job pressure—a measure that I also use in this study—that includes such items as "My job requires that I work very fast" and "I never seem to have enough time to get everything done on my job."

Karasek and his colleagues found that feeling pressured by our jobs (job demands), having little say about how to do our jobs (little job autonomy), and not feeling challenged by our jobs (little job challenge/few learning opportunities) all work together. Their research overturns the "role strain" paradigm that assumes that the greater the number of roles a person holds, the more likely he or she is to experience role strain. Now, role strain is reconceptualized as job strain and is seen as resulting from the actual conditions of our jobs: specifically, heavy job pressure with little decision-making authority or control and little job challenge.

Karasek and his colleagues found that men who reported that their jobs were very pressured and that they had little decision-making authority—little power to fix what wasn't going well—were much more likely to have cardiovascular problems 6 years later.[11] They also found that men who worked in hectic jobs with little influence over their work pace and few opportunities to learn new things were at much higher risk for heart attacks than men without these job conditions. Other studies have also found high strain jobs (high demands and little control) are associated with poorer health as well as sleep problems, depression, psychosomatic symptoms, even mortality.[12]

Debra Lerner at the Health Institute, New England Medical Center, and her colleagues have identified four types of jobs:

1. High strain = high in demands and low in control
2. Low strain = low in demands and high in control
3. Active = high in demands and high in control
4. Passive = low in demands and low in control

Intuitively, it is clear that having a demanding job in and of itself is not necessarily stressful, nor is it bad for one's health. We all know people who thrive on pressure, who live long and productive lives amid very hectic and demanding circumstances. Similarly, Lerner and her colleagues found that employees with jobs that are low-strain (low in demands and high in control) or active (high in demands and high in control) are the healthiest—physically, socially, and emotionally. The group with passive jobs fall in the middle and the group with high-strain jobs have the poorest health.[13]

In the Ask the Children study, employed parents—both mothers and fathers—have quite demanding jobs. Sixty-five percent either somewhat or strongly agree with the statement "My job requires that I work very fast" and 61 percent somewhat or strongly agree that "I never seem to have enough time to get everything done on my job."[14]

4.3 Employed Parents with a Child Birth Through 18: Job Pressure				
	Strongly agree	Somewhat agree	Somewhat disagree	Strongly disagree
My job requires that I work very fast.	34%	31%	22.5%	12.5%
I never seem to have enough time to get everything done.	30	31	20	19

There has been a striking increase in job pressure over the past 20 years. Comparing our 1997 National Study of the Changing Workforce with the Department of Labor's 1977 Quality of Employment Survey, Jennifer Swanberg and I found a 10 percentage point increase among parents with children under 18 in response to the item "My job requires that I work very fast," and a 21 percentage point increase in response to the item "I never seem to have enough time to get everything done."[15] These findings confirm what many employed parents have been saying: "I am now doing the job that two people used to do"; "I feel like I'm on a treadmill every day, running in place because I don't feel that I am accomplishing that much"; "I am drowning in work." Given their links to poor health, escalating job demands are worrisome.

▼ **Putting the pressures together** In our 1997 National Study of the Changing Workforce, Terry Bond, Jennifer Swanberg, and I found that employed parents whose jobs were more demanding—both objectively and subjectively—were much more likely to feel burned out by their jobs, to be in worse moods at home, and to have less energy for their families.[16]

Focus

There is little if any research on the importance of *focus*, the second component of this model. Yet we heard about it again and again in our interviews with parents. In response to the question "When do you feel most and least successful at work?" a mother of two said:

> At the end of the day, if I'm feeling great, I've been able to focus on the work I needed to do. And if I'm feeling shot, the phone rang every time I turned to my work, or someone came into my office, or some crisis interrupted me.

A father of three who worked in a youth agency described when he felt least successful:

> If you're working on your computer and you get interrupted, you are most likely to forget certain things. And when you go back to your work, it's upsetting because you made mistakes and missed things. You get frustrated at yourself for allowing yourself to get distracted.

Parents' comments reminded me of a study that Lotte Bailyn from Massachusetts Institute of Technology and her colleagues conducted at Xerox. The purpose of this project was to experiment with changes at the workplace that could improve both productivity and family life. Bailyn and her team shadowed employees, seeing how they spent their time and looking at the implicit assumptions that lay beneath their actions. They unearthed a number of assumptions:

▼ We should operate as if we are in perpetual crisis mode.
▼ If there is a problem, we throw more time at it.
▼ Time—at least at work—is an infinite resource.
▼ The hero at work is the individual who slaves long hours and solves the crisis at the very last minute.

Sound familiar? At one site, the employees were always interrupting each other's work. They were thus barraged, working in fits and starts throughout the day. They felt as if they could only do their "real" work around the edges of the day—early in the morning and late in the evening.

Among other experimental changes, employees at this Xerox site decided to set aside a certain period of each day when no interruptions were permitted. In other words, they created a period of *focused time*. It is a seemingly simple solution to a sense of fragmentation. But not so simple, it turned out: The idea engendered resistance because many people thought "it couldn't work with my job." Nonetheless, they tried it at this Xerox site, along with several other experiments in increased flexibility. The result: This team made its production deadline on schedule—for the first time in years. In addition, employees felt that their home lives had improved in the bargain.[17]

I was a member of this Ford Foundation–funded research project, doing research at another site. The wisdom of having "uninterrupted time" at work made sense to me at the time, but it made even more sense several years later as I was conducting interviews for this book. I found that parents feel most successful at work and at home when they can *focus* on what they consider important and have *support*

> FOCUS
>
> Difficulty in focusing on work
> Multitasking
> Interruptions

for doing so. The interlocking construct of *focus, autonomy,* and *support* became an important component of my model for understanding how work and home life fit together and how these aspects of our jobs impact us and the way we parent.

I define focus as encompassing three components: the difficulty of focusing on work, work on too many tasks at the same time, and interruptions that make it difficult to get one's work done.

▼ | **Difficulty in focusing on work** We asked parents, "Please tell me, during a typical week, how often is it very difficult to focus on the work that you have to do? Would you say very often, often, sometimes, rarely, or never?" The majority of parents do not report that it is difficult to focus on their work. In fact, only 19 percent say that they experience difficulty either very often or often. If one adds the parents who say, "sometimes," to this total, the percentage rises to 47.5. On the other hand, 53 percent say that they rarely or ever experience this difficulty.

▼ | **Too much multitasking** The fact that within the last few years a new term—*multitasking*—has entered the popular lexicon should tell us something about the work climate today. With downsizing and labor shortages fewer people are available to do the same amount of work, and with the demands of a 24-hour economy, increasingly jobs call on employees to keep several balls in the air at the same time. One mother who manages many international clients describes her work:

> *All of the subsidiaries throughout the world with whom I work—and there are many—communicate primarily by email. When they send an email, they expect my response immediately, which is fair, and they assume that their problem is the most important problem of anyone, that they are the most important of my clients; and that's correct. But I've got maybe a hundred people all needing me at once, and that is pressure!*

We asked parents to tell us how often during a typical workweek they "work on too many tasks at the same time." Since people differ on the number of tasks they can comfortably juggle, we wanted to gauge when multitasking moves beyond parents' comfort level—when they feel they are working on *too many* tasks at the same time. It is striking that 55.5 percent of employed parents experience this situation "often" or "very often."

Mothers experience this situation more often than fathers: 64 percent of mothers and 47 percent of fathers reported that they work on too many tasks often or very often during a typical week. This is a thought-provoking finding. Is it that mothers' and fathers' jobs are different? Or since parenting today also often calls for multitasking, perhaps mothers are more attuned to it than fathers? Or perhaps mothers try to cram more into their time at work. We certainly heard from a

number of employed mothers that they used the time at work differently after the birth of a child. Minutes at work were then seen as minutes away from one's child. Chatting can be seen as a luxury. A number
of the mothers we interviewed talked about trying to squeeze as much
productivity as possible into the time they have at work so that they can
leave on time or so that they can have a "reasonable to-do list" when
they arrive at work the next day.[18]

▼ | **Interruptions** Two in five employed parents (41 percent) report
  | that they are interrupted very often or often during the work-
  | day, making it difficult for them to get their work done. Con-
versely, 31 percent say that they are rarely or never interrupted. Fathers
and mothers are equally likely to experience interruptions.[19]

Job quality

Although job autonomy or job
control has a strong effect on us at
work and at home, we feel it is
one component of a larger construct: the third component of
this model, which I call *job quality*. On the basis of the findings of

JOB QUALITY
Job autonomy
Learning opportunities
Job challenge
Meaningful work

our own and others' research, we define job quality as consisting of
three components: doing work that gives us autonomy and gives us a
say about how to do our jobs, doing work that is challenging and gives
us an opportunity to learn, and doing work that we see as meaningful.

▼ | **Job autonomy** Research by Robert Karasek, Debra Lerner, and
  | others has found that when we have very pressured jobs in com-
  | bination with little control or decision-making authority, we are
at greater risk for health problems. As this research has become more
widely known, there has been a parallel change in business thinking
whereby employees are given more authority. This business strategy,
however, results less from a commitment to improve the health of
employees (thus saving on health care costs) and more from a desire to
increase productivity in a high-stakes economy. Taking root in the
1980s, total quality management (TQM) has among its goals the notion
of replacing command/control hierarchical decision making. Employees
at every level of the organization are seen as possessing the expertise to
help solve business problems. No longer are managers, sitting in remote
offices, deemed the repository of all knowledge and wisdom. The

employees who manufacture the products or who provide the services are recognized as having the capacity to come up with potentially better ideas to improve productivity because they are closer to the nuts and bolts of production or sales processes. Likewise, the emphasis on teams in business today depends on infusing decision-making authority into the ranks of employees. Even the concept of business leadership has evolved so that leadership is no longer seen as simply the province of "the leader," but a quality within us all.

To measure job autonomy, we asked parents whether they somewhat agree, strongly agree, somewhat disagree, or strongly disagree with the following statements related to job autonomy:

▼ "I have the freedom to decide what I do on my job."
▼ "I have a lot of say about what happens on my job."

Since these items were also included in the 1977 Quality of Employment Survey and in the Families and Work Institute's 1997 National Study of the Changing Workforce, we were able to make useful 20-year comparisons between work as it used to be and work as it is today. Given the business emphasis on increasing employees' decision-making authority, it is not surprising to find that employed parents today have more job autonomy than they did two decades ago. The proportion who feel they have freedom to decide what they do on their jobs has increased by 16 percentage points and the proportion who feel that they have a say about what happens on the job has increased by 10.5 percentage points.[20]

Almost three quarters of parents with children 18 and younger somewhat or strongly agree that they have freedom to decide what to do on their jobs (74 percent) and a lot of say about what happens on their jobs (73 percent). Although this is a sizable and impressive proportion, still one in four employed parents has little decision-making latitude. Although one might expect men to have more authority to make decisions than women, there are no differences in their responses to these two items.[21]

A construction manager who has children of his own understands the importance of job autonomy in his work and in his employees':

> You never make anybody happy when you have some manager saying go do something this exact way. The staff have to own the work that they're doing. The managers that help me get this work done also have to own [their work]. I have to know what they're doing but I don't have to own it.

One mother who is a benefits executive talks about her ability to "own" her own work:

> *I had to get stuff done for this closing and I had two weeks to do it, and I just said to my secretary, "Absolutely no conference calls, and no meetings, except on this project." And I had people calling me with "Well, you know, this just came up, and we really need to do it." And I had some people telling me, "Well, we have to do it tomorrow, because I'm going on vacation next week." I just said, "I'm sorry. I can't."*

Another mother finds that conflicting interests sometimes make it difficult to maintain this kind of control:

> *Working smarter is ignoring things that don't need to get done. Taking control of your life. Doing what the priorities are. But the fact is, what we think are priorities, what the client thinks are priorities, and what in fact are priorities, are all different things, so it's very hard.*

When this father of two encounters barriers to his job autonomy, he finds a way to make up for it outside work by being a soccer referee:

> *The way I cope is I go out on the soccer field. The soccer referee is in total control of the game. When he blows the whistle and when he makes a ruling it's final, right? Nobody gets to debate about it and that's the way I keep my sanity. Because otherwise everybody else is influencing everything that goes on around me and a lot of times it's negative.*

▼ **Learning opportunities and job challenge** In order to assess learning opportunities, we asked parents to respond to the following:

▼ "I am satisfied with the opportunities that I have at work to learn new skills that could help me get a better job or find another equally good job if this one doesn't work out."

And to assess job challenge, parents were asked to respond to two more statements:

▼ "My job requires that I keep learning new things."
▼ "My job requires that I be creative."

About four in five employed parents somewhat or strongly agree that they are satisfied with the opportunities they have at work to learn new skills (79 percent), that their jobs require that they keep learning new things (85 percent), and that their jobs require that they be creative (79 percent). Although these numbers are high, it is important to note that only 49 to 59 percent of parents strongly agree with each of these statements. Parents who have managerial or professional occupations and higher household incomes have more challenging jobs than their counterparts.

A mother of three who is a nurse describes how important tackling challenging cases in the emergency room is to her:

> *The docs in the group laugh at me because when we get a bad GI bleed, I'm just like "Let me go help." And they're like "Ruth, you are sick." I'm like "No, man, I love this. I love taking care of this stuff. I love being able to do this, and I love seeing that what I did and how I handled it made a difference, and whether maybe it affected whether that person lived or died." It's not a God complex. It's just that I really love it. I love the challenge. I absolutely love it.*

We find that over the past 20 years there has been an increase in the number of parents who report that their jobs are challenging. There has been a 7 percentage point increase in the number of parents who feel that their jobs require that they keep learning new things and a 14 percentage point increase in the number who feel that their jobs require that they be creative.[22]

▼ **Meaningful work** The vast majority of employed parents— mothers and fathers alike—agree somewhat or agree strongly that the work they do is meaningful to them (89 percent), although those in managerial and professional occupations and those with higher household income find more meaning in their jobs. As with other aspects of job quality, there has been a 6 percentage point increase over the past 20 years in the number of parents who feel that their work is meaningful.[23]

Parents who feel their work is meaningful tend to enjoy that work. A mother of two who works for an employment agency says:

We place these ads in the paper and it's almost like a gamble. You place them, you look for them in the Times *on Sunday: "Oh my god!" Monday, you get [to the office]. 400 calls, "Wow!" I feel successful and so does everybody there, you know? You're doing a great job and then people refer you to other people because you're so good.*

A mother of a 5-year-old son works knowing the good that it accomplishes:

Enjoying what I'm doing and feeling like it has some purpose and it's not just a job to make money. I'm doing cancer research so it feels like there's a purpose to it. It benefits somebody other than my wallet.

Support at work

In the 1980s, in our first study of work and family life at Merck, we asked an open-ended question in a census of workers: "If you could make one change in the workplace that would improve your family life while maintaining or improving your productivity, what would it be?" We used this question because we weren't really sure which aspects of life on the job mattered most. We got the answer in no uncertain terms. Employee after employee wrote about his or her boss.[24]

SUPPORT AT WORK
Supervisor support
Coworker support
Culture support

On the basis of this insight gained almost two decades ago, we have elaborated our notion of *support at work:* the fourth component of this model. I define support at work as consisting of three parts: the relationship with one's supervisor, the relationship with one's coworkers, and the supportiveness of the workplace culture.

▼ **Supervisor support** At the time we conducted the study at Merck, there was research on supervisor support. However, virtually all of those studies focused on what we call *task support:* support from one's supervisor for doing job tasks well.

Yet Merck employees wrote about the need for another type of support: work-family support. They felt their bosses didn't "get it that family life had changed." They wrote about how awful they felt when they had to call in sick in order to get time off to be with a sick child. They wrote about telling their boss that they were leaving work to attend a meeting when, in fact, they were going to see their child in a school play or a sports competition. They wrote about bosses who squirmed when the employee brought up a family or personal issue.

So we asked employed parents whether they strongly or somewhat agree or disagree with the following statements:

▼ "My supervisor is understanding when I talk about personal or family issues that affect my work."

▼ "I feel comfortable bringing up personal or family issues with my supervisor."

▼ "My supervisor really cares about the effect that work demands have on my personal and family life."

We found that employees with supportive supervisors fared better. They experienced less conflict in managing their work and family responsibilities and felt less stressed. Benefits also accrued to the company. The employees with more supportive supervisors were more likely to say that they would recommend their company to a friend, were more loyal to the company, and were more satisfied with their jobs.[25]

Employed parents who have management support feel lucky. Their descriptions of the trust and support they enjoy can sound almost corny, but they are deeply felt:

> The whole management team—I just can't say enough about how wonderful and supportive they are. There were a couple of crises that happened before I had even gotten there, but I've heard about how everyone just pulled together. They're just so supportive. I'm just amazed because I've never run into it before—where the support from management is actually there.
>
> MOTHER OF TWO GIRLS, 8 AND 12 YEARS OLD

> [My bosses and I] have a lot of respect for each other. They know my work caliber. They know I don't just say, "Oh, I want to take the day off," and go. They know if I tell them I have to leave that they don't ever need to ask me what I have to leave for. They never say, "What's wrong? What do you need? Are you sure you have to?" They don't ever question me. They say, "Take care of [your child]." And I go. I like that, because they know I'm going to be there for them. If I need to stay late and help with things, I do. But if I need to leave and come home, I do.
>
> MOTHER OF THREE TEENAGERS

As we continued to conduct research on this issue, my colleagues Terry Bond and Dana Friedman and I began to wonder whether it took a special kind of skill to support employees with personal or family issues. In other words, are supervisors who are supportive about family or personal issues different from the supervisors who manage work tasks well? Essentially, we found that competencies in these two domains go hand in hand. In other words, a good boss is a good boss is a good boss.[26]

In addition, we found that it is possible to train supervisors to become more supportive of employees. In 1990, supervisors at Johnson & Johnson received work-family management training and efforts were undertaken to make the workplace culture more family-friendly. An evaluation of this initiative that we conducted in 1992 indicated that employees viewed their supervisors as significantly more supportive 2 years after the management training.[27]

It's tempting to wonder, Are women supervisors more supportive than men? Are younger supervisors more supportive than older ones? Does the mix of genders (who supervises whom) matter? Our 1992 National Study of the Changing Workforce revealed—to our surprise—that the age and the gender of the supervisor did not matter. What did matter was whether the supervisor had an employed spouse and/or child care responsibilities. At first we were taken aback because we had heard critics say that being a parent (read mother) at the workplace is a handicap in managing workers. Then this finding began to make sense. After all, when one has a husband or wife who works or when one has children, it is easier to empathize with the work-family needs of others. And isn't that the essence of a good boss—someone who can look at the world from "both sides," who can take the needs of the company and the needs of employees into account when making decisions?[28]

A manager who has children of his own illustrates this understanding:

> I have four or five people that report to me and I'm pretty flexible with them, I think because I have kids and I understand how kids are. So I know when Tommy, who works for me and has a rug rat, and he's got a call from school, and he says, "My son threw up on the bus. I gotta go home." I mean you know, it's like, "Yeah, go, it's no problem."

We also found that indicators of productivity are strongly linked to having a supportive workplace environment (which includes having a supportive supervisor). A supportive work environment increases employed parents' satisfaction with their jobs, their loyalty, their commitment to going that extra mile for their employers, and their desire to remain with their organizations. Furthermore, we found that employees with support at work are less burned out by their jobs and less likely to experience what we call "job-to-home spillover"—being in a bad mood at work or having insufficient time and energy for themselves, their family members, or their friends because of their jobs.

Although supportive workplaces offer some protection against the effects of a demanding and hectic job, we found that not even the most supportive workplace can eliminate this problem entirely. As other studies have shown, different features of the workplace—including job demands and support—join forces to affect us in positive and negative ways.[29] That's why the work-family model developed for this book includes four important elements: job demands, focus, job quality, and support.

In the Ask the Children study, the majority of employed parents (79 percent) have a supervisor to whom they report. Of these, most rate their supervisors as supportive in terms of work-life issues. In fact, 85.5 percent either somewhat or strongly agree that their supervisors are understanding when they talk about the personal or family issues that affect their work, 69 percent feel comfortable bringing up personal or family issues, and 75 percent feel that their supervisors really care about the effect that work demands have on their personal and family life.

Given how much complaining I hear about supervisors, I should be surprised by these findings, but I'm not: They don't differ from results of other studies we've conducted over the years. I have concluded that most people have good supervisors, but those who don't are loud and vociferous about it. Furthermore, I have learned that a difficult supervisor has radiating power: Those around a difficult supervisor thank their lucky stars they don't work for that person. They feel, "There, but for the grace of God, go I."

4.4

Employed Parents with a Child Birth Through 18: Supervisor Support

	Strongly agree	Somewhat agree	Somewhat disagree	Strongly disagree
My supervisor is understanding when I talk about personal or family issues that affect my work.	53%	32.5%	7.5%	7%
I feel comfortable bringing up personal or family issues with my supervisor.	37	32	15	16
My supervisor really cares about the effect that work demands have on my personal and family life.	39	36	12	13

Fathers are less convinced than mothers that their supervisors really care about the effects of work demands on home life: Only 29 percent of employed fathers strongly agree when asked to respond to "My supervisor really cares about the effect that work demands have on my personal and family life" compared with 50 percent of employed mothers. Otherwise, there are no differences between fathers and mothers.

Over the past 5 years, employed parents' ratings of the work-life support provided by their supervisor has increased. This is a very short period in which to see any evidence of change, but, in fact, it has occurred. Although most of these shifts are small in magnitude, there is a sizable increase (10 percentage points) in the number of parents who feel comfortable in raising family or personal issues with their supervisors.[30]

▼ | **Coworker support** In the 1992 National Study of the Changing Workforce, we found that employees who have better relationships with their coworkers feel less burned out by their jobs, are more loyal to their employers, are more willing to work hard to help their companies succeed, are more satisfied with their jobs, and are more committed to doing their own jobs well.[31] One mother of a teenage daughter explains what a supportive working environment means to her:

> I feel satisfied when the values that I care about—trust, respect—are a part of the fabric of the institution and where the human resources are valued over the image of the organization or the bottom line. I believe that if you create an environment in which people feel trusted, feel valued, feel respected, then people are willing to go the extra mile to get the job done.

Working parents describe coworkers in such a supportive environment as a "safety net" for maintaining work and family life. Here is the father of two teenage children:

> I would say, "Hey, my son's got a ball game at so and so; my daughter's got something going on here at so and so time, so I'm going to be about two hours late. I'll stay late for you the next day." Generally, we guys were all about the same age, had kids the same age. Most guys were kind of flexible and we would work that out. That was a luxury too. They kind of allowed us that flexibility as long as we got our hours in.

In the Ask the Children study, we asked parents to evaluate these statements:

▼ "I feel I am really a part of the group of people I work with."
▼ "I look forward to being with the people I work with each day."

Most employed parents report that they have positive coworker relationships: A total of 88.5 percent somewhat or strongly agree that they feel a part of the group of people they work with and 89 percent look forward to being with their coworkers each day.

4.5

Employed Parents with a Child Birth Through 18: Coworker Support

	Strongly agree	Somewhat agree	Somewhat disagree	Strongly disagree
I feel I am really a part of the group of people I work with.	59.5%	29%	7%	5%
I look forward to being with the people I work with each day.	44	45	8	3

▼ | **Culture support: understanding "they"** When we were asked to assess the impact of Johnson & Johnson's Balancing Work and Family Program, a comprehensive effort to address employees' work-life needs, we conducted employee and manager focus groups and individual interviews in order to frame the study. We kept hearing a similar story: "My boss would let me wait with my child for the school bus even if it is late," "My boss would let me stay at home with a sick child," "My boss would let me check on my grandmother during lunch"— "but *they* won't let my boss do it."

Who is this "they"? we asked. "They," we were told, is the boss's boss, or the boss's boss's boss. After probing, it became clear that "they" is the company's work-life culture: the agreed-upon atmosphere of the company that "smiles" or "frowns" on how the boss acts.

Over the years, my colleague Dana Friedman and I also found that whenever we went into a company to study work-life issues, people would say, "Oh, you should talk with so and so." The "so and so" was usually someone who reflected the company's stance toward personal or family concerns. At one organization, this person was a woman who took a phone call related to work en route to her cesarean section. At another, it was a woman who showed up at work when her children were sick. At still another, it was a man who took a last-minute trip to Japan just after his wife had had twins. Sometimes, this person was a woman or a man who took time off to be with a child, who interrupted a business meeting to take a phone call from a child, who refused a business trip that necessitated a Saturday night stay-over, or who fought hard to get the company to be more family-friendly *and* was well respected and productive at work. These people reflected the work-family culture.

We used this kind of information in framing our measure of what we call *culture support*. We used the words of employees in creating our research items. For example, "If you have a problem managing your work and family responsibilities, the attitude is 'You made your bed, now lie in it!' " And again and again, we found that when employees feel that their organization supports what *USA Today* once described as having a job and having a life, they fare better. At Johnson & Johnson, for example, we found that employees who feel that the company culture is supportive of their family and personal needs are less stressed, feel more successful in balancing work and family life, are more loyal to the company, are more likely to recommend J&J as a place to work, and are more satisfied with their jobs.[32]

In this study, we asked employed parents whether they agreed or disagreed with two statements about the culture where they work:

▼ "There is an unwritten rule at my place of employment that you can't take care of family needs on company time."

▼ "At my place of employment, employees who put their family or personal needs ahead of their jobs are not looked on favorably."

4.6

Employed Parents with a Child Birth Through 18: Culture Support				
	Strongly agree	Somewhat agree	Somewhat disagree	Strongly disagree
There is an unwritten rule at my place of employment that you can't take care of family needs on company time.	12%	18%	26.5%	43%
At my place of employment, employees who put their family or personal needs ahead of their jobs are not looked on favorably.	18	23.5	23	35

Overall, 30 percent of employed fathers and mothers somewhat or strongly agree that it is not acceptable at their organizations to take care of family needs on company time, and 41.5 percent agree that employees who put their family or personal needs ahead of their jobs are not looked upon favorably.

So, although most supervisors are seen as supportive, "they"—the company culture—is seen as less so. And this assessment by parents has not changed in the past 5 years.[33]

HOW DO JOB DEMANDS, FOCUS, JOB QUALITY, AND SUPPORT AT WORK AFFECT OUR FEELINGS ABOUT WORK? TESTING THE WORK-FAMILY MODEL

I began this chapter by saying that we have been unable to move beyond the "should mothers work or not" debate, because we sense that there is a problem. My contention is that the problem is not simply the fact that mothers and fathers work: It is *how* we work. I use the work-family model to test this idea and to assess how these four features of work are linked to our stress, frustration, and success at work. First, let's look at stress.

Stress at work

We asked employed mothers and fathers with a child birth through 18, "In a typical workweek, how much stress do you experience in your job—a large amount, a moderate amount, very little, or none at all?" Almost one in four parents reports that he or she experiences a large amount of stress on the job, and another 45 percent experience a moderate amount. Only 31 percent of parents report that they have very little or no stress at all.

As we explore these findings later, consider your own life. Which of these aspects of your

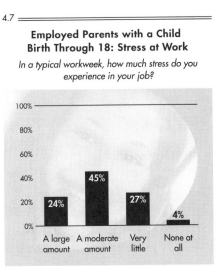

4.7

Employed Parents with a Child Birth Through 18: Stress at Work

In a typical workweek, how much stress do you experience in your job?

A large amount 24%
A moderate amount 45%
Very little 27%
None at all 4%

job or your workplace environment is linked to the amount of stress you feel? Is it the hours you work or the way your boss treats you? Is it constant interruptions?

▼ **Job demands and stress at work** Employees who work fewer hours, who work fewer days per week, who travel less frequently, who do less work at home before or after their workdays, and who experience less job pressure typically experience less stress at work. Some of these numbers are very dramatic:

▼ Only 15 percent of employed parents who work fewer than 35 hours a week report a large amount of stress at work compared with 36.5 percent of parents who work more than 50 hours a week.

▼ Only 12 percent of parents who strongly disagree that their job requires that they work very fast experience a large amount of stress at work compared with 40 percent of parents who strongly agree with this statement.

▼ Only 11.5 percent of parents who strongly disagree that they never have enough time to get everything done in their jobs experience a large amount of stress at work compared with 42 percent of parents who strongly agree with this statement.

▼ **Focus and stress at work** There are very strong connections between being able to focus on work (having little difficulty in focusing on work, not having too many tasks to do, and having infrequent interruptions) and feeling less stressed at work:

▼ Only 16 percent of parents who rarely experience interruptions feel a large amount of stress compared with 41 percent who are interrupted very often.

▼ **Job quality and stress at work** Employed parents who feel that they have a say about how to do their jobs and who feel that their work is meaningful experience less stress at work.

▼ **Support at work and stress** When parents have more supportive supervisors, better relationships with coworkers, and a supportive work-life culture, they are less likely to feel stressed at work. Again, many of the statistics are quite striking:

▼ Only 21 percent of parents who strongly agree that their supervisor is understanding when they talk about personal or family issues that affect their work report a large amount of stress compared with 54.5 percent of parents who strongly disagree with this statement.

▼ Only 21 percent of parents who strongly agree that they look forward to being with the people they work with each day experience a large amount of stress compared with 62.5 percent who strongly disagree with this statement.

▼ Only 19 percent of parents who strongly disagree that at their workplace employees who put their family or personal needs ahead of their jobs are not looked upon favorably report that they experience a large amount of stress compared with 37 percent who strongly agree with this statement.

The diagram on page 126 summarizes these findings, with those that are statistically significant in italics. How did your own assessment compare with that of our representative group of employed mothers and fathers?

Frustration at work

Because we heard from parents in our one-on-one interviews that they were feeling frustration at work, we asked parents with a child birth through 18 about these feelings in our survey: "In a typical workweek, how much frustration do you experience in your job—a large amount, a moderate amount, very little, or none at all?"

Fewer parents experience frustration in their jobs than experience stress: 11 percent report a large amount of frustration compared with 24 percent who report a large amount of stress. Similarly, 45 percent report very little or no frustration compared with 31 percent who experience very little or no stress.

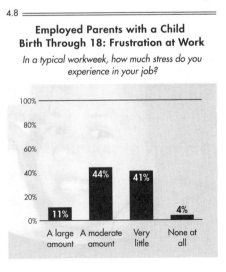

4.8

Employed Parents with a Child Birth Through 18: Frustration at Work

In a typical workweek, how much stress do you experience in your job?

	A large amount	A moderate amount	Very little	None at all
	11%	44%	41%	4%

PREDICTING STRESS AT WORK

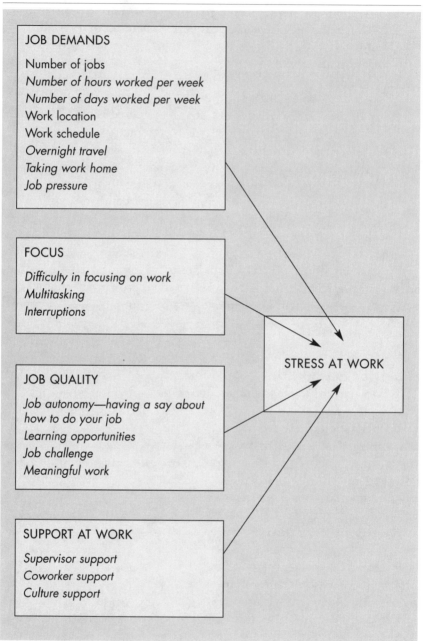

▼ **Job demands and frustration** There are some differences between factors associated with frustration and those associated with stress at work. For example, the number of hours worked, the number of days worked, and taking work home are no longer significant, but the work schedule is. Parents who work daytime shifts, who travel less often, and who feel that their job is less pressured experience less frustration at work.

▼ **Focus and frustration** When parents can really focus on their work, they are much less likely to feel frustration. Our interviews with parents strongly support this contention as well.

▼ **Job quality and frustration** Employed parents who have more decision-making authority or autonomy on the job feel less frustrated. So do employed parents who find meaning in their work and are satisfied with their opportunities to learn new skills that keep them employable.

▼ **Support at work and frustration** Experiencing less frustration is linked to having a supportive supervisor, good coworker relationships, and a culture that doesn't jeopardize employees for putting personal or family needs ahead of their jobs. For example:

▼ Of employed parents who strongly agree that they feel comfortable bringing up personal or family issues with their supervisor, 55 percent experience little or no frustration on the job compared with 29 percent who strongly disagree.

▼ Likewise, 54 percent who strongly agree that their supervisor really cares about the effect of work demands on their personal or family life report little or no frustration compared with 23 percent who strongly disagree.

Feeling successful at work

About one in three parents with a child birth through 18—mothers and fathers—feels successful very often. At the other end of the continuum, 23 percent feel successful sometimes or rarely. Although one might assume that employees with more education or with more money might feel successful more often than employees with less education or with lower income, that is not the case. There are no differences among these groups.

4.9

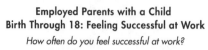

**Employed Parents with a Child
Birth Through 18: Feeling Successful at Work**

How often do you feel successful at work?

Very often   Often   Sometimes   Rarely   Never

▼ **Job demands and feeling successful** Having a demanding job is linked to feeling stressed and frustrated at work, but only very slightly to feeling successful. Of the three questions we asked about job pressure (working hard, working fast, having too little time to get everything done), only one is related to feelings of success at work: Employed parents who don't have enough time to get everything done at work feel less successful at work than other parents.

▼ **Focus at work and feeling successful** When parents talk about feeling successful, they talk about being focused. For example, a parent said:

I feel I have had a good day when I can really pay attention to my work, I'm not rushing, jumping over details that I should remember. When I have a day where I can't focus, the concept of "losing it" has real meaning.

The statistical findings are as strong as parents' statements. When parents can focus, without undue interruption, without being thrown task after task after task, they feel much more successful: 55 percent of those who never have difficulty focusing on their work feel very successful compared with 24 percent who very often experience difficulty in focusing.

▼ **Job quality and feeling successful** All of the measures of job quality are significantly linked with feeling successful at work. Forty-two percent of employed parents, for example, who strongly agree that they have a say in what happens on their job feel very successful compared with 14 percent who strongly disagree.

▼ **Support at work and feeling successful** Our relationships at work are very influential in our feelings of success and accomplishment. Obviously, supervisors are important, but so too are

PREDICTING SUCCESS AT WORK

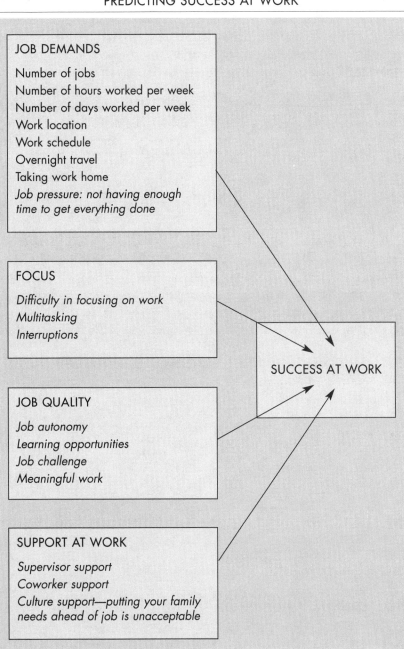

JOB DEMANDS

Number of jobs
Number of hours worked per week
Number of days worked per week
Work location
Work schedule
Overnight travel
Taking work home
*Job pressure: not having enough
time to get everything done*

FOCUS

*Difficulty in focusing on work
Multitasking
Interruptions*

JOB QUALITY

*Job autonomy
Learning opportunities
Job challenge
Meaningful work*

SUPPORT AT WORK

*Supervisor support
Coworker support
Culture support—putting your family
needs ahead of job is unacceptable*

SUCCESS AT WORK

coworkers. When employed parents look forward to being with their coworkers and feel a part of the group they work with, they have much higher odds of feeling successful. The supportiveness of the workplace culture also makes a difference but seems to have a less powerful impact than that of the people we work with day in and day out.

Our findings about feeling successful are summarized on page 129 with statistically significant findings in italics. Take a minute to reflect on when you feel successful at work. What happens to elicit these feelings? What makes those times different from the moments when you feel burned out and stressed?

YES, THERE IS SOMETHING ABOUT WORK

As this model shows, work does affect us: Work can make us feel on top of the world or on the bottom; it can lead to feelings of stress or satisfaction, or feelings of being overwhelmed or supported. It is these feelings that have been masked, covered up by the decades-old question of whether or not mothers should work. It is not *that* we work, but *how* we work that makes a difference in the kind of person who goes home to children.

But does work itself—the actual conditions of our jobs and work-places—affect how we parent? To begin to answer that question, we'll explore family life today.

There's Something About Family Life, Too

recently attended a small meeting to brief a high-level representative of the federal government on trends in family life today. In attendance were a dozen women selected as seismographers of the current cultural terrain. The first question was asked of a prominent book editor: "You read many, many manuscripts. Writers are often the first to sense a change. What are you hearing from writers?"

The book editor spoke of a sense of isolation, an aloneness, a longing for community. So did an artist. So did the executive director of a theatrical company. A social scientist spoke of the numbers of young boys who are "drugged" on Ritalin. A doctor spoke of the number of adolescent girls on Prozac—one quarter of her niece's class in school, she estimated.

Reasons for this malaise were proposed: straitjacket views of masculinity and femininity that are pressed onto boys and girls by families and the larger society; the high-stress life that children today lead; the fact that people are willing to nurture others but not themselves, in effect depleting their ability to nurture others; and a society in which "drive-by parenting" is the norm.

This is not the first meeting that I have attended in which the ills of children are discussed. Nor will it be the last by a long shot. But it was unique in that participants didn't hold parents completely hostage for the problems of children. Instead, they saw these problems as stemming from families *as well as* from societal attitudes and the loss of community. Many of the other meetings I attend lay the problems of kids solely at the feet of their so-called drive-by parents—a concept that doesn't really jibe with our findings.

There is little dispute within the public at large that kids are in trouble. The public, including those with and without children of their own as well as with and without everyday contact with kids, have a very negative view of teenagers—a view that is reinforced by the senseless violence in schools and on the streets today. This is perhaps not surprising, but what is surprising is that most also see younger children in negative terms as well: "lacking in discipline and being rude or spoiled." As one father said, "It's 'I want, I want, I want.' "[1]

The root cause of these problems, according to many, is that parents have not inculcated kids with strong enough values. We heard similar comments in our one-on-one interviews. A father who coaches at a local high school told us about the consequences of the lack of parental guidance he sees:

> *No respect and no responsibilities. I don't blame kids, I blame the way we have got so engrossed with the almighty dollar. Parents work and think that they are really helping their kids by giving them things. Parents for some reason have gotten off track and they think that material things are going to make up for not being there. Kids don't respect things because they don't have a lot of guidance at home. They're raising themselves.*

A mother expands on this reasoning:

> *They're spoiled because people in my age group have more high-powered jobs—they are making more money than their parents ever made. They're able to provide, and they feel they should provide kids with material things . . . which I feel is wrong. They should be spending time with their child, talking with their child. I don't think there's anything wrong in trying to do the best for your kids, but the best for your kids isn't always material. The best for your kids is giving them you.*

Another mother adds:

> *Many parents feel so guilty about working that they are afraid to discipline their children.*

HOW DO EMPLOYED PARENTS SEE THEMSELVES?

If the public blames parents for the shortcomings of children, how do employed parents judge themselves? We asked employed parents with a child birth through 18 to grade themselves on the same set of parenting skills that children used to judge their parents (see Chapter 2).

Although the public doesn't feel that parents raise their children with good values, most employed mothers give themselves very high marks for doing so—82.5 percent give themselves an A, only 1 percent give themselves a C, and no one gives herself a lower grade than that.

In fact, more than three quarters of this representative sample of employed mothers give themselves an A for making their child feel important and loved (87 percent), being there for their child when he or she is sick (87 percent), raising their child with good values (82.5 percent), encouraging their child to want to learn and to enjoy learning (76 percent), and being someone whom their child can go to when upset (76 percent). At the other end of the spectrum, a strikingly low 15 percent give themselves an A for controlling their temper when their child does something that makes them angry—the only item that dropped below 50 percent for mothers, and quite a precipitous drop!

Clearly, most employed mothers don't see themselves as completely responsible for the problems of today's kids—perhaps "other parents" but not them.

Employed fathers are somewhat harder on themselves than employed mothers. In nine of the twelve parenting skills, fathers give themselves significantly lower marks than mothers, though the magnitude of difference between mothers and fathers is typically not huge.[2]

Less than 50 percent of fathers give themselves an A for knowing what is really going on in their child's life (47 percent), being involved with their child's school or child care (47 percent), spending time talking with their child (43 percent), establishing family routines and traditions for their child (42.5 percent), and controlling their temper when their child does something that makes them angry (23 percent).

5.1

EMPLOYED MOTHERS WITH A CHILD BIRTH THROUGH 18: VIEWS OF THEMSELVES

For the following statements, please tell me how you would grade YOURSELF on . . .

	A	B	C	D	F
Making your child feel important and loved?	87%	12%	1%	0%	0%
Being there for your child when he/she is sick?	87	11	1.5	0	0
Raising your child with good values?	82.5	17	1	0	0
Encouraging your child to want to learn and to enjoy learning?	76	21	3	0	0
Being someone your child can go to when he/she is upset?	76	20	2.5	1	0
Being able to attend important events in your child's life?	73	22	3	1	0
Appreciating your child for who he or she is?	69	28	2	0	0
Knowing what is really going on in your child's life?	66	26	7	1	0
Being involved in what is happening to your child at school or child care?	64	28	7	0	0
Spending time talking with your child?	58.5	37	5	0	0
Establishing family routines and traditions for your child?	56	32	10	1.5	0
Controlling your temper when your child does something that makes you angry?	15	48	31.5	3	1

5.2

EMPLOYED FATHERS WITH A CHILD BIRTH THROUGH 18: VIEWS OF THEMSELVES

For the following statements, please tell me how you would grade YOURSELF on . . .

	A	B	C	D	F
Raising your child with good values?	74%	23%	2%	0%	0%
Making your child feel important and loved?	72	25	2	0	0
Encouraging your child to want to learn and to enjoy learning?	69	28	2	1	0
Appreciating your child for who he/she is?	64.5	31	4	0	0
Being there for your child when he/she is sick?	64	26	9	0	1
Being someone your child can go to when he/she is upset?	62	27	7	2	0
Being able to attend important events in your child's life?	60	29	8	1	1
Knowing what is really going on in your child's life?	47	39	12	1	0
Being involved in what is happening to your child at school or child care?	47	34	12	3	.5
Spending time talking with your child?	43	42	12	2	1
Establishing family routines and traditions for your child?	42.5	41	13	3	0
Controlling your temper when your child does something that makes you angry?	23	43	28	4.5	1

HOW DO PARENTS AND CHILDREN COMPARE ON GRADES GIVEN TO PARENTS?

"Of course, parents—especially mothers—give themselves high marks on such attributes an instilling good values," one could say. As parents, we want to believe that we are doing a good job. So the obvious question is, How do mothers' and fathers' grades compare to the grades that children give to their parents? Although kids are certainly not objective either, they have less psychological motivation to inflate grades for parenting skills than their parents do.

In compiling the tables, I was struck by how large some of the variations are. For example, very few mothers and fathers give themselves less than a C compared with sometimes double-digit percentages of children who give their parents a D or F.

So we ran tests of statistical significance, comparing the grades that children give their mothers and fathers with the grades that parents with a child the same age give themselves.[3]

Comparing children's and mothers' grades

First we look at teenagers and their mothers. We found that all of the comparisons for children 13 through 18 years of age and mothers with a child aged 13 through 18 differed significantly *except* mothers' and children's assessments of the mother's controlling her temper when the child does something that makes the mother angry and the mother's being there for the child when the child is sick. Otherwise, the differences tend to be quite large.

I'm sure you know where this is headed: Mothers of teenagers give themselves higher marks than the teenagers give their mothers! For example, 82 percent of mothers give themselves an A on making their child feel important and loved compared with 64 percent of teenage children. Similarly, 74 percent of mothers give themselves an A on being someone their child can go to when upset compared with 43 percent of children. And 54 percent of mothers give themselves an A on knowing what is really going on in their child's life compared with 32 percent of children. On many of these parenting skills, some children give their mothers a D or F, whereas almost no mothers give themselves grades that low.

What about values? Since the public thinks that parents are not instilling values in their children, how do teenage children think mothers are doing? Pretty well. Eighty-four percent of mothers give themselves an A and 75 percent of teenagers give their mother an A. On the other hand, 10 percent of teenagers give their mothers a C or lower compared with 1 percent of mothers of a teenager. And no mothers of a teenager give themselves a grade lower than a C! Some parents, but by no means most, are failing their children in this area.

When we compare mothers with a child 8 through 12 years old and children of this age on how mothers are graded, we find far fewer differences. In fact, there are only two: knowing what is really going on in the child's life and establishing family routines and traditions.

Does that mean that mothers are more competent when their children are younger or that teenagers are tougher critics? Our analyses reveal that mothers don't differ in their assessments of their own parenting competence when they have older and younger children; thus it seems that teenagers are tougher critics.

It makes sense that older children are more critical. The parenting younger children receive is the only parenting they really know, and that is less true for older children. Not only do teenagers have more experience with the parenting styles of their friends' parents, but they also have the ability to think more abstractly and to take multiple perspectives. Furthermore, many are trying to distance themselves from their parents. Yet, this explanation begs the question of whether mothers' (and possibly fathers') parenting changes with older children, in which case teenagers might be somewhat realistic in their assessments. These issues would be fascinating to explore.

Comparing children's and fathers' grades

Since fathers give themselves lower marks than mothers, I wondered, Is there a greater alignment between their views and the views of children? Yes, to a degree. Of the twelve parenting skills we assessed, there are statistically significant differences between teenagers' assessments of their fathers and fathers' self-assessments on five parenting skills: making the child feel important and loved, being someone the child can go to when he or she is upset, knowing what is really going on in the child's life, encouraging the child to want to learn and to enjoy learning, and being involved with what is happening to the child in school. By contrast, teenagers and mothers differ on fully ten of twelve parenting skills.

For three grades, fathers give themselves *considerably* higher marks than teenagers do: knowing what's really going on in their child's life, being involved with what is happening with the child in school, and being someone the child can go to when upset. For example, 50 percent of fathers of a teenager give themselves an A for being someone their child can go to when he or she is upset compared with 37 percent of teenagers.

When we compared fathers of a child 8 through 12 years old with children of the same ages, we found a difference on only one of the eight items on which children of this age graded their parents: appreciating the child for who he or she is. There, interestingly, the pattern is reversed, with 82 percent of children giving their fathers an A compared with 52 percent of fathers.

Why is there a larger disparity between children's and mothers' assessments than between fathers' and children's? Do mothers tie their identity and self-esteem more closely to how good a parent they are? Perhaps mothers *need* to see themselves as competent? Are fathers more realistic about what they are good at and what they aren't?

We will have to reserve these questions for another study. However, we can probe more deeply into mothers' and fathers' family lives, asking: Under what circumstances are employed mothers and fathers more likely to give themselves higher marks as parents? It turns out that the conceptual model that I began to develop in Chapter 4 plays a pivotal role in helping us answer this question.

FAMILY LIFE TODAY: ELABORATING A NEW MODEL OF WORK AND FAMILY

Family demands

Just as work has demands, so too does family life for employed parents with a child birth through 18:

> I walk in the door and the children are on top of me. The little one needs one thing, the older one needs something else. I sit down on the floor and they are literally on top of me, wanting to tell me what has happened, wanting to crowd each other out.
>
> MOTHER OF A TODDLER AND A PRESCHOOLER

> Dinner is over, the dishes are done, the kids are settled into doing homework, and I sit down for the first time all day to do something for myself—like read the paper. Not more than two seconds pass and chaos ensues. The kids get into a fight, there is a crisis with the homework, the dog throws up. It is always something.
>
> FATHER WITH TWO SCHOOL-AGE CHILDREN

I used to think that life would calm down when my kids were older but it just hasn't happened that way. Maybe I'm not putting food in their mouths anymore, but now I am running around, taking them to buy the shoes they need for gym, to their friend's house, to the school play at night. I mostly love doing it, but there are times when I'm living in a three-ring circus.

MOTHER WITH A TEENAGER AND AN ELEMENTARY SCHOOL–AGE CHILD

I'm cooking pasta with one hand and I am feeding the baby with the other and the telephone's ringing and you know sometimes I just feel like we have taken on too much.

MOTHER WITH AN 8-YEAR-OLD DAUGHTER AND AN INFANT

The following are the components of *family demands*:

▼ **Spouse employment** There is a refrain I have heard (and repeated) again and again. When there is too much to do, too much pressure, too little time or energy, people (both men and women) say, "What I *really* need is a wife at home." This domestic paragon would care for children, shop for groceries, do laundry, help with homework, be there when the repair person comes, and so forth. The result, we imagine, would be a less chaotic, a more peaceful family life—in other words, fewer family demands on working parents.

FAMILY DEMANDS
Spouse employment
Number of hours spouse works per week
Number of children
Age of the youngest child
Time with the child
Activities with the child

How many employed parents do have a "spouse" at home? Certainly not many employed mothers—only 1.5 percent. By comparison, more than one in four—26 percent—of employed fathers have a spouse who is not employed. Interestingly, parents with more education or higher household incomes are no more likely to have a nonemployed spouse than are employed parents with less education or lower household incomes.

▼ **Number of hours spouse works per week** The number of hours that the spouse works can also affect how we experience the demands of family life. If one's spouse works very, very long hours, he or she might offer less help around the house than the spouse who works fewer hours and is potentially more available to help out.

As would be expected, employed mothers have spouses who work much longer hours than employed fathers do. For example, 27.5 percent of mothers have spouses who work more than 50 hours a week compared with 4 percent of fathers.

5.3	Employed Parents with a Child Birth Through 18: All Paid and Unpaid Hours Worked by Spouse Each Week		
	Fathers	Mothers	Total
Less than 35 hours	30%	8%	20%
35–40 hours	50	35	43
41–50 hours	16	30	22
More than 50 hours	4	27.5	15

Significance: *** = $p < .0001$.

In families with lower household incomes, employed parents have spouses who work fewer hours. Not a surprise.

▼ | **Number of children** Why is it that the old woman who lived in a shoe comes to mind? Undoubtedly because she had "so many children, she didn't know what to do." With more children presumably comes an increase in the demands of family life.

Employed fathers have more children than employed mothers. (By our definition, this means that they live with these children at least half the time.) For example, 29.5 percent of fathers have three or more children compared with 18.5 percent of mothers.

Of all of the demographic factors we looked at—level of education, household income, age of children, gender of children, and so forth—only one is related to the number of children: Single parents have fewer children than parents who are married.

▼ | **Age of the youngest child** When a colleague, Diane Hughes, and I conducted a study of work and family life at the pharmaceutical company Merck years ago, we found that parents with younger children were more stressed. So for this study, we include the age of the youngest child in our construct of family demands. Our analyses reveal that employed fathers have younger children on average than employed mothers.

▼ | **Time with the child** As you may recall from Chapter 3, the amount of time spent with children *and* what happens in that time affect children. Now let's look at which characteristics of parents are related to how much time they spend with their children.

As I discussed at length in Chapter 3, mothers spend more time with their child from birth through the age of 18 than fathers. For example, more than twice as many mothers (33 percent) spend 4.5 hours or more on workdays with their child as fathers (15 percent).

Household income matters, too. Parents whose household income is $25,000 or less spend more time with their child than parents whose household income is $75,000 or more: Three times more parents (35 percent) from this lower-income group spend 4.5 hours or more with their child on workdays compared with the higher-income group (11 percent). Families from lower-income households also work fewer hours on average so perhaps they have more time to be with their child—an assumption we will test later in this chapter.

As I noted in Chapter 3, parents spend much more time with a younger child than with an older child. In addition, mothers spend more time with their daughters than their sons on workdays, but equal amounts of time on nonworkdays, and fathers spend equal amounts of time with their daughters and their sons on workdays and nonworkdays.

Does the amount of time that parents spend working affect the amount of time they spend with their child? I was asked this question recently by a *Newsweek* magazine editor, and it is an important question. Common sense would suggest that parents who work longer hours would spend less time with their children. But, in fact, I discovered that on this issue common sense appears wrong. The total number of hours mothers and fathers work per week is *not* related to the amount of time they report spending with their child on workdays or on nonworkdays.

Because this is an unexpected finding, I decided to test it further, using information from children. We found that fathers' working hours have no bearing on the amount of time children report spending with them. However, the story changes when it comes to mothers. Children whose mothers work full-time report spending less time with them on workdays—but not on nonworkdays—compared with children whose mothers work less than full-time.

Are mothers exaggerating? Or was the way we asked children to report on their parents' work time—as full-time, part-time, or less than part-time work—too general?[4] I wish I knew. But even with this discrepancy, it appears that by children's account, many parents are spending considerable time with them: 56 percent of children spend 3 hours or more with their fathers and 68 percent spend 3 hours or more with their mothers on workdays. For the majority, this is hardly "drive-by parenting." This finding leads me to suspect that many parents are begging, borrowing, and stealing time from everywhere else—particularly from time for themselves—to spend with their children.

Simply talking about hours spent with children overlooks the strong and conflicted feelings most of us have about time. Our fantasy of family time is of being rested, being together, escaping from the pressures of scheduling, and feeling spontaneous. In reality, we find that there is never enough time; children are making one demand after another; and we are sacrificing our own needs for the sake of the children. Because of these contradictions, Kerry J. Daly of the University of Guelph in Canada compares the way we live family time to the way we videotape a wedding: We are so preoccupied with creating memories that we miss the present. In addition, many of us live with chronic guilt: We feel we are failing our children because there is never enough time. Yet, we are unwilling to give up or to try to reconcile the discrepancies between our fantasies and realities and thus spend time "managing guilt" rather than trying to get rid of it.[5]

Daly's analyses fit well with the theory I developed in *The Six Stages of Parenthood*. From extensive interviews with parents over the course of parenthood, I found that problems occur when there is a gulf between our expectations and reality. We can either stay stuck (as Kerry Daly is arguing many of us are) or can attempt to change. I found that growth results from reconciling expectations with reality, either by making the expectation more realistic or by changing ourselves to live up to the expectations. I saw—and see—guilt as initially a positive force, telling us that there is a conflict between what we expect and what is actually happening. If we don't heed the warning signs, if we don't try to reconcile our fantasies and realities, then guilt can fester and begin to eat us up. But if we address the guilt and change accordingly, we are being much more "intentional" as parents.[6]

▼ | **Activities with the child** Time, as I said in Chapter 3, includes both the amount of time we spend together *and* what we do when we are together. The activities we engage in with our child are another component of family demands. Since we have explored these activities at length in Chapter 3, here we simply look at which parents with kids from birth through 18 are more likely to report engaging in activities with their child.

Eating a meal together Parents eat meals more frequently with a child who is younger than with a child who is older. None of the other demographic factors we looked at—such as the household income or the gender of the parent and the gender of the child—is significant.

Playing and exercising together Parents play and exercise more frequently with a younger child than with an older one. Fathers play or exercise more frequently with a son than a daughter, whereas fathers and mothers play and exercise with a daughter with equal frequency.

Doing homework together Mothers are more likely to do homework with their child—both sons and daughters—than fathers are. Parents from lower-income households do homework with their child more often than their higher-income counterparts. Finally, parents are more likely to be involved with homework with younger school-age children than older school-age children, including teenagers.

Watching television together Mothers and fathers say that they watch television with their child with equal frequency. Looking a bit further, however, we find that mothers watch television more often with a daughter than fathers do, though mothers and fathers watch television with a son equally often. There are also educational and income differences in the parents who report watching a lot of television with their child. For example, 45 percent of parents with a high school or lower level of education watch television with their child every day compared with 24 percent of parents with a 4-year or higher degree. Likewise, 59 percent of parents in households with incomes of $25,000 or less watch television every day with their child, whereas 28 percent of parents with household incomes of $75,000 or more do. Parents also watch more television with a younger child than with an older child.

Putting the results together. What is particularly interesting about this set of results is not just what is significant but what is *not* significant. For instance, there are no differences between single parents and married parents in how often they are involved with their child in these four activities. Furthermore, fathers in households in which the mother is employed and those in which the mother is not employed do not differ in how often they participate in activities with their child.

Focus on one's child

As was the case for our conceptual model of work, the second component of our model for family life is *focus*.

FOCUS ON ONE'S CHILD

Repeatedly, parents told us stories of how successful they felt when they could really focus on their child.

> *Being there for your kids is emotionally and mentally—it doesn't have to be physical. There was a time when the joke at the dinner table was "Earth to Mom, Earth to Mom," because I would be physically sitting there but mentally somewhere else. Then the issue became "I will focus on you, I do want to be here for you." I think I started just trying to be mentally more alert and trying to look more into them and say, "I'm here, this is our time."*
>
> MOTHER OF TWO TEENAGE CHILDREN

> *I feel good when I can focus on my kids and I can feel like I am present and in the present tense and not always kind of figuring out the next transition . . . when I can be creative and I can encourage their creativity, rather than thinking about how to get from one point to another like [from] meal to bed time.*
>
> MOTHER OF AN 8-YEAR-OLD DAUGHTER AND INFANT SON

Sometimes it is not easy for parents to focus on their children. Many tell stories about these more difficult times.

> *When I'm sitting there with [my son] and we could be watching cartoons or something or we could just be playing a game of tic-tac-toe and I'm already thinking, "What do I have to do next?" I'm not there, you know? I'm not focused on him. I'm just thinking, "Okay, what do I have to do? I have to start cooking in ten minutes or twenty minutes or I have to iron school clothes for him." My mind is just not there.*
>
> MOTHER OF A SON, AGE 8

> *Often at night I feel [that when I'm] putting them to bed they need sort of a long process of winding down. Often that's when my son wants to talk to me and I have that feeling: I just can't*

wait to be by myself. What I want them to do is just go to bed. And so I'm not there for them when they need me and when it's most conducive for them . . . I'm rushing them, "Brush your teeth!"

MOTHER OF SON AND DAUGHTER, AGES 8 AND 9

Others speak of the conscious effort it takes to break through the barriers to concentrate actively on their children.

I'll ask Thomas to get something out and we'll play it together. Sometimes he'll say, "You're not really playing with me," and it's maybe true. I may be lying on the floor and I may have built my portion of the road and think, "Well, let's let him carry this scenario out and finish the road." He'll get into it, but he'll look up sometime and say, "Come on, play with me!"

MOTHER OF TWO CHILDREN

I'm asking the questions and he's willing to give me the answers and he starts smiling right away and he wants to talk more, so it forces me to sit there because I'm asking the questions and he's going to talk to me. So that works, but it takes conditioning myself, telling myself, "If I don't do this my son is going to grow away from me. I'm going to be here for him physically but we're not going to be close." And I do want my son and myself to be very close.

MOTHER OF 8-YEAR-OLD BOY

We asked parents, "How easy or difficult is it for you really to focus on your child when you are together—very easy, somewhat easy, somewhat difficult, or very difficult?"

The majority of parents (62 percent) say that it is very easy. Another 31 percent say that it is somewhat easy; 6 percent say that it is somewhat difficult; and 1 percent say that it is very difficult. Fathers and mothers, parents from lower- and higher-income households, parents with older and younger children, all find it equally easy or difficult to focus on their child.

I was interested in children's perceptions, so we asked children in the seventh through twelfth grades, "How easy or difficult is it for your mother—and your father—really to focus on you when you are together?" Considering how often we find discrepancies between children's and parents' realities, it is interesting that there are none here. Children, mothers, and fathers agree on focus. It is especially interesting when we consider how important the capacity to focus turns out to be—both at work and at home.

Parenting autonomy

As I noted in Chapter 4, studies show that when employees have some control or autonomy in their jobs, they are healthier and more committed.[7] Believe it or not, the same has also been found to be true of basic household chores![8]

I wondered whether there would be similar findings in terms of child rearing. Would parents who feel that they can raise their

> **PARENTING AUTONOMY**
>
> Raising one's child as one wants to

children the way they want to (that is, they have autonomy) feel that they fare better as parents? More than that, I wondered how many parents feel that they have constraints on how they raise their children. So I include *parenting autonomy* in this model.

Parents were asked how strongly they agreed or disagreed with the statement "I feel like I can raise my child the way I want to." Overall, 61 percent strongly agree with this statement, 30 percent somewhat agree, 5.5 percent somewhat disagree, and 3 percent strongly disagree.

In looking at these responses, I wonder whether the glass is half empty or half full. Is it remarkable that three in five parents can raise their child they way they want to? Or is it remarkable that two in five parents have some to strong ambivalence about their autonomy in raising their child?

I also wondered which parents have more or less autonomy. For example, do parents of older children feel that they are less able to raise their children as they wish because of the pressures of the teen environment? Do lower-income parents feel less control because they may live in neighborhoods where they feel their child is being led astray by others? Do single parents dislike and discredit the influence of the child's other parent? Our demographic analyses provide no clues. Rich and poor, fathers and mothers, single parents and married parents, better- and less well-educated parents, look the same when it comes to parenting autonomy.

Support at home

I include parenting *support at home* in the conceptual model because having a supportive workplace environment is a powerful predictor of employees' well-being and even physical health and because research on family life likewise finds that what is called *social support* is a powerful predictor of the well-being of family members. I define support at home as support from family and friends when a problem with one's child arises, comfortableness about turning to others when such a problem arises, sharing of child-related responsibilities with one's spouse or partner, and the impact of nonparental child care on the child.

SUPPORT AT HOME
Support from family and friends
Comfort in seeking support
Sharing the care of the child
Impact of nonparental child care on the child

Support from family and friends Studies have found that when employees have informal or formal help from family and friends, they are less prey to feelings of work-family stress and are in better shape physically and psychologically. Moreover, the support we receive at home makes a difference in how easily we recover from a stressful day at work—no surprise.[9]

Researchers have further differentiated among the types of help people receive—such as practical help with the things we have to do like cleaning the house, appraisal help with figuring out what is bothering us, informational help with resources that might be useful, and emotional help and understanding.[10]

When my children were young, I always defined support as the "middle of the night test." If I felt I had someone I could call anytime, even in the middle of the night, and ask for help with my children and the response would be "Sure," no questions asked, then I would feel really comfortable and safe. Thus, I feel that the most pertinent overall question to ask about support is to discern whether parents have access to support when a problem with a child arises. In fact, the stories that have survived in my community from the days when we had young children are just those stories: The times when someone called a neighbor with an emergency and was unconditionally helped or the times when someone called a neighbor with an emergency and was turned away for a silly reason (particularly in retrospect). We retell those stories now and we laugh, but we didn't always then.

We asked parents how strongly they agreed or disagreed with the statement "I have the support I need from my family and friends when I have a problem with my child."

Just over two thirds of employed parents (67 percent) strongly agree that they have support when they have a problem with their child, and only 7.5 percent disagree either somewhat or strongly that they have ready support if they need it.

▼ | **Comfort in seeking support.** Studies have also found that help can be positive and negative. It can come with strings attached ("You really owe me now") or can be free, so to speak.[11] In my community, we still tell stories now of the people whom we asked for help—like having a child over so the parents could go out or go shopping—and who then subtly punished us for weeks. Thus, the second statement we asked parents to evaluate was "I feel comfortable turning to my family and friends when I have a problem with my child."

Somewhat fewer parents (57 percent) strongly agree that they feel comfortable asking for help from their family or friends. In fact, 13 percent indicate that they are not comfortable turning to others.

The only demographic difference that emerged is that parents of an older child feel less comfortable turning to others when problems with their child arise. For example, 51.5 percent of parents with a child 13 through 18 years old strongly agree that they feel okay about turning to their family or friends for help compared with 69 percent of parents with a child birth to 3 years old. This is an unfortunate finding. Problems are often more troublesome in the teenage years. I wonder whether we don't want to admit that we have problems (perhaps because we feel that we might be blamed for them); whether we sense the societal negativity about kids this age; or whether we have less access to support because we are busier at this point in our lives and the kids are often traveling in a separate world as well.

I had a formative experience about the barriers to asking for and receiving help when my daughter began high school. The senior boys were pursuing the ninth-grade girls, asking them to parties at New York City clubs where they had to pay a hefty price to get in (with the senior boys getting a cut of the profits). Fearful of not being "in," the girls wanted to go to the parties and pressured their parents relentlessly because "everyone else is going." Few of the parents knew each other because it was a new school for most of us. One of the parents tried to get the school to do something about this issue. The school refused because "the parties are not happening on school time." This parent argued—unsuccessfully—that the girls were being "extorted" on school time, but the school had "more important issues to deal with." Finally, one of the parents invited the other parents to her house so we could meet each other. At that event, we decided to hang tough and refuse to let our daughters (and sons) go to the parties. We also exchanged phone numbers so we could call for mutual reinforcement if the kids upped the pressure. Of course, the kids did, but we hung tough.

More than the fact that we finally succeeded in stopping the senior boys from taking financial advantage of the freshman girls and we prevented our children (at least temporarily) from going to parties with drinking and drugs, we all felt great relief in knowing that we could turn to each other. Rather than seeing my daughter's friends' parents as "those other parents," presumably too self-absorbed to pay attention to whether their children went to clubs, I learned that most were just like me—struggling to raise a teenage child in the right way.

5.4

Employed Parents with a Child Birth Through 18: Support from Family and Friends				
	Strongly agree	Somewhat agree	Somewhat disagree	Strongly disagree
I have the support I need from family and friends when I have a problem with my child.	67%	26%	5%	2.5%
I feel comfortable turning to my family and friends when I have a problem with my child.	57	30	8.5	4.5

▼ **Sharing the care of the child** I include sharing the care of the child in this conceptual model. Not surprisingly, many studies find that mothers spend more time and take greater responsibility than fathers.[12] Although our 1997 National Study of the Changing Workforce found that fathers in dual-earner households have increased the amount of time they spend doing things with and caring for their children over the past 20 years, both fathers and mothers—especially mothers—want their spouse to do more.[13]

Many studies indicate that sharing the care is in the eyes of the beholder.[14] One study expands the notion of equity to include the perception of fairness to one's spouse. They found that mothers are least depressed when they feel the division of labor is fair to both them *and* their husbands and most depressed when they perceive the division as very unfair to them *or* to their husbands. Control or discretion over the tasks and timing of household work is another factor.[15]

Over the years, the issue of who cares for the children has been an ongoing hot topic in the seminars I have conducted for employed parents. The scenario doesn't seem to change much. One or more mothers will say that they want and really need more help from their husbands. The agitation of fathers begins to be palpable. One will finally speak out, saying that he tries to help more, but that he always gets criticized for doing things the wrong way:

> *I don't give the kids the right food. I don't put them in the right clothes. I don't handle their arguments in the right way. I want to be with my kids but when I get criticized, I also want to quit.*

Mothers are often the gatekeepers to fathers' involvement with their children, saying, "Help me. Ooops. You aren't helping me in the right way." Yet some of mothers' criticisms may well be justified:

> *I have asked my husband a million times not to give the kids dessert before dinner because it makes the kids wild and crazy and I have to pick up the pieces when they get that way. Try as I might, he still falls for their pleas for having cookies while they are waiting for dinner.*

Sometimes, however, mothers criticize fathers just because they are doing things differently—not wrong, simply not the way we would do them. That can feel threatening to the sense of order we are trying to create in our homes. It can also feel threatening when deep in our hearts, we're not sure whether we are doing things right ourselves. Sharing the care of children can become a battlefield, or it can be a source of support.

Not surprisingly, employed mothers in this study are more likely to have the responsibility for taking care of the children. For example, 52 percent of mothers say that they have "most of the responsibility" compared with 4 percent of fathers.

5.5

Employed Parents with a Child Birth Through 18: Sharing Child-Related Responsibilities		
How are child-related responsibilities shared with your spouse/partner in your household?	Fathers	Mothers
They are shared about equally.	55%	47%
I have most of the responsibility.	4	52
My spouse/partner has most of the responsibility.	40	1

Significance: *** = p < .0001.

Since the parents in the analyses include both those in traditional and those in dual-earner families, we wondered how parents view care in dual-earner families. We found that fathers say that responsibility for the care of children is fully shared more frequently (62 percent) than mothers (47 percent). A mother we interviewed put it this way:

> My husband thinks we are sharing if he takes the girls to a birthday party and I pick them up. But who bought the party dresses? And who picked out the presents? And who made the play dates so they would be invited to the party in the first place?

5.6

Employed Parents with a Child Birth Through 18: in Dual-Earner Families: Sharing Child-Related Responsibilities		
How are child-related responsibilities shared with your spouse/partner in your household?	Fathers	Mothers
They are shared about equally.	62%	47%
I have most of the responsibility.	4	52
My spouse/partner has most of the responsibility.	34	1

Significance: *** = p < .0001.

Still, it is remarkable that 47 percent—nearly half—of mothers in dual-earner families report that they share child care about equally with their spouses or partners!

▼ **Impact of nonparental child care on the child** I define child care as another form of support for today's families, though it can also be an issue that is conflict-laden. Our feelings about our child care providers are complex. As another woman put it, you are cursed if you find good child care and cursed if you don't:

> *If we find fabulous child care that we love, it means that (a) we're good parents, but (b) we can be easily replaced. We are expendable. If the child care is bad, it (a) adds to our stress, but (b) proves our necessity.*

Avoiding a clear-eyed assessment of our child care situation becomes a means for coping with this ambivalence. A mother explains:

> *I think that parents who are working because they choose to feel guilty because they feel in the back of their mind, "Well, should I be staying home? Am I being selfish to be working?" Parents who have no choice feel "I have no choice but to leave you, and I have to think that you're going to be okay. Otherwise, I'm not going to be okay." Parents have a very hard time dealing with the guilt. And I think that one of the ways you deal with the guilt is that you just don't focus in on this.*

I was sitting in the office of a news reporter of a large metropolitan paper. She began to tell me about the string of failed child care arrangements she had made for her child. One provider had been fired. Another had left unexpectedly. Her daughter had hated still another. Although she could easily admit problems with child care in her daughter's *past*, she couldn't quite bring herself to say something bad about her current provider. After all, she was leaving her child with this person. So she said, "She's better than some of the others." But her face belied her claims. It was no longer a competition; she felt somewhat trapped in a relationship gone sour. After all, her daughter had been through a revolving door of one person after another. So this mother had resigned herself to the "not great/not terrible" status quo.

After my many years of studying this issue, I can now tell quite quickly when child care is working for the child and the family. I was in a living room in the Northwest. A mother was telling me about her child care. "She's family," she said. It was all she had to say. I knew it was right. Her daughter echoed the same feeling. The person had become part of their kith and kin system. How different from the story of the newspaper editor! Sitting in that living room, I recalled a drawing that my daughter had made when she was little. She drew a picture of our family: her mother (me), her father, her brother, and Joni Weber—the neighbor who had cared for her for many years. Joni was very tall in this picture, she was smiling, and she was holding hands with the rest of our family.

The relationship between the parent and the child care provider begins with normal feelings of competition. It is hard to share the care of a child, particularly a young child. When I ran a parent cooperative child care center at Bank Street College years ago, I used to call it the "6-week syndrome" (though there is nothing really magical about 6 weeks). I told the staff at the beginning of the year, "In about 6 weeks, the parents will begin to complain about you and you will begin to complain about the parents. That means that you are getting attached to the child and this attachment stirs up feelings of normal tension and jealousy."

I can tell, however, when the parent and the provider have moved beyond these normal feelings. They talk about child care as "a new extended family."[16] And what if child care isn't working right? We often resist doing something about it because it means putting our children through a change. It means unearthing all of those feelings of distrust, of competition, of guilt, of ambivalence all over again.

Children, too, can be reluctant to tell us that child care isn't working. I was in a child's bedroom in Los Angeles, sitting at the foot of her bed, talking with her and her sister, when one of the girls confided in me that they didn't like their baby-sitter. I asked them whether they had told their mother or father about this, and they both chorused, "No." "Why not?" I asked. "Because the next one might be worse." Likewise, a 10-year-old boy told me that he hadn't told his parents about some of the things his family child care provider had done (such as leaving him in charge of the babies while she ran errands) because he didn't want to upset his parents. They were so proud that they were using a "good" child care provider.

So, how to ask parents about child care and get a useful answer? We can ask parents to assess the impact of the nonparental child care on their child. This type of question gets beyond the barricades we erect when thinking about our children's care. If we feel that the child care provider is good for our children, we are more likely to have incorporated this person into our "new extended family."

Most parents with children from birth through 18 years of age see the impact of child care as positive: 27.5 percent as very positive and another 45 percent as somewhat positive. On the other hand, 2.5 percent see the impact as very negative and 20.5 percent as somewhat negative, with 5 percent reporting that the impact was neutral. So this question does get at the real variations in parents' experience with child care.

Parents with very young children feel more positive. For example, 31 percent of parents with a child from birth through 3 years old say that the impact of child care is very positive compared with 19 percent of parents with children 13 through 18 years old. Does this mean that parents of older children can finally admit that the child care they have used is not great? That's possible, given the fact that most studies find that child care in this country is uneven at best and typically mediocre in quality.[17] Or perhaps parents of older children know more about the realities of their child's care because older children are more likely to voice complaints to their parents.

Whatever interpretation is true (and there is probably truth in all of them), in subsequent research I'd like to use the insight gleaned from the one-on-one interviews conducted for this book and ask parents whether the child care provider or teacher feels like family. It is a question you can ask yourselves.

Because we also asked teenage children the same question about child care, we are able to make comparisons between children 13 through 18 years old and parents with a child the same age. Interestingly, children see their child care in a more positive light than their parents do.

5.7

Employed Parents and Children with Employed Parents: Impact of Nonparental Child Care on Child's Development		
What kind of effect has the care you have (your child has) received by people other than (the) your parents had on your (your child's) overall development?	Parents with a child 13 through 18	Children 13 through 18
Very negative	1.5%	3%
Somewhat negative	28.5	5.5
Somewhat positive	50	42
Very positive	20	50

Significance: *** = p < .0001.

TESTING OUR MODEL OF WORK AND FAMILY

Looking at the Grades We Give Ourselves

To test our model once again, we look at how these four features of family life—demands, focus, autonomy, and support—are linked to the grades we give ourselves in parenting, our stress and success in parenting, and our child's well-being.

It turns out that several aspects of home life are linked—again and again—to better grades on each of the twelve parenting skills:

▼ FAMILY DEMANDS: The more time that parents spend with their child on workdays and nonworkdays, the higher the grades they give themselves. Also the more often they engage in activities with their child, the higher the grades they give themselves.

▼ FOCUS: The easier parents report that it is to focus on their child, the higher the grades they give themselves.

▼ AUTONOMY: Parents who can raise their child the way they want to give themselves higher grades than parents who don't feel they can do so.

▼ SUPPORT: Parents who feel that they have friends and family they can turn to give themselves higher grades than parents who do not have this support system. Parents who either take more responsibility for the care of their child or share the care about equally with their spouse give themselves higher grades. And parents who see the nonparental child care they have used as "very" positive for their child give themselves higher grades than those who don't have this feeling.

The italicized items in the diagram on page 156 illustrate those factors that were repeatedly linked to parents' giving themselves higher grades in parenting skills:

The importance of being an intentional parent

Since work demands are typically seen as negative, I had likewise cast family demands in negative terms. Our findings indicate, however, that some family demands are in fact quite positive—those that involve putting time and energy, and more intention, into parenting.

If I were looking for a unifying theme to tie these findings together, I would call it *intentional parenting*. Parents who put more into being a parent—by spending more time with their child, doing more together,

PREDICTING PARENTS' POSITIVE VIEWS OF THEMSELVES

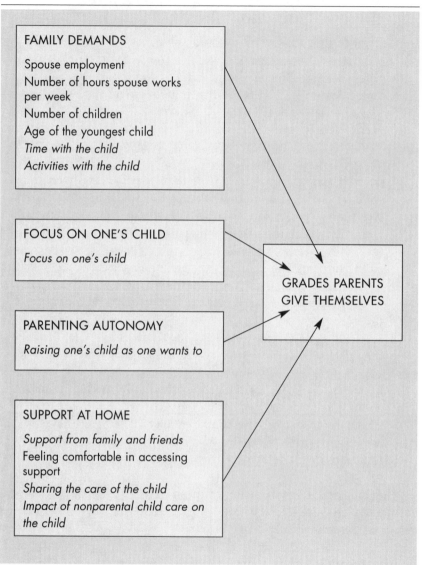

FAMILY DEMANDS

Spouse employment
Number of hours spouse works
per week
Number of children
Age of the youngest child
Time with the child
Activities with the child

FOCUS ON ONE'S CHILD

Focus on one's child

PARENTING AUTONOMY

Raising one's child as one wants to

SUPPORT AT HOME

Support from family and friends
Feeling comfortable in accessing
support
Sharing the care of the child
*Impact of nonparental child care on
the child*

**GRADES PARENTS
GIVE THEMSELVES**

paying attention to or focusing on their child when together, raising this child in the way that they want to, and setting up a system of support to back themselves up—obviously feel better about the kind of job they are doing as parents. As the former governor of West Virginia, Gaston Caperton, says, "They don't build statues to people who say, 'It won't work.'" This is as true of family life as it is of public service.

These findings recall an earlier study I conducted with several colleagues on family child care and relative care. We found that providers who were more "intentional" about providing child care did the best job (they wanted to be child care providers, they thought ahead about what they were going to do with the children, they sought out others who could help them, and they also sought out opportunities to learn more about children and their development).[18] Intentionality is a very useful concept for parenting as well.

▼ **What's not significant?** It is important to note that some of the factors I expected to be significant are not. For example, having an employed spouse is only significant once: Employees with a spouse who is not employed give themselves better marks for controlling their tempers. Likewise, the number of hours the spouse works is significant only twice: Parents with a spouse who works longer hours give themselves higher marks on making the child feel important and loved and spending time talking with their child than parents with a spouse who works fewer hours. Perhaps if one's spouse is away more, the other parent is more "intentional."

The perceived impact of child care is interesting. Parents who see the impact of child care as "very positive" give themselves much higher marks than those who see the impact as "somewhat positive." My assumption is that parents who feel that the impact is very positive have found child care arrangements that become like "an extended family" and they feel good about themselves for this accomplishment. Parents who say that the impact of their child care is "somewhat positive" probably haven't quite faced up to their own ambivalence about their child care arrangements, and this ambivalence may rebound on the way they judge their parenting competence.

You can use these findings to take stock of your own family life. How would you have answered the questions about the demands of family life; your capacity to focus on your child; the autonomy you have in raising your child as you wish; the support you receive from family, friends, your spouse or partner if you have one; and the nonparental child care you have used? What's within your ability to change and what cannot be changed?

Stress in caring for one's child

The second outcome we assessed is stress in caring for one's child. This question parallels the question we asked about stress at work. We asked employed parents with a child birth through 18, "In a typical workweek, how much stress do you experience in caring for your child—a great deal, a moderate amount, very little, or none at all?"

Only 6 percent of employed parents report feeling a great deal of stress in caring for their child; twice as many—13 percent—report none at all. In the middle of the continuum 36 percent report a moderate amount of stress and 45.5 percent report that they experience very little. Since none of the demographic factors we looked at (mothers versus fathers, educational level of parent, household income, or the age or gender of the child) makes a difference, it seems that stress in caring for one's child is related to other factors than family demographics.

▼ **Are parents more stressed when working or when parenting their child?** In looking at these findings, I was immediately impressed by the large differences between stress at work and stress in caring for one's child. For example, 24 percent of parents experience a large amount of stress at work compared to 6 percent who experience a great deal of stress in parenting their child. That's four times as many parents who feel very stressed at work—a significant difference.

5.8 ══════════════════════════════════════

**Employed Parents with a Child Birth Through 18:
Stress in Caring for One's Child and Stress at Work**

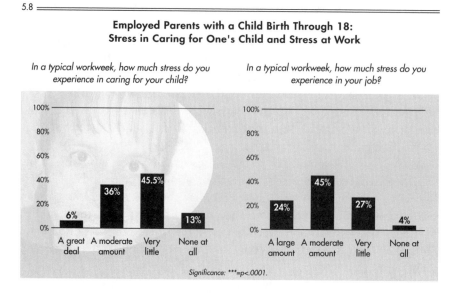

In a typical workweek, how much stress do you experience in caring for your child?

In a typical workweek, how much stress do you experience in your job?

Significance: ***=p<.0001.

In *The Time Bind,* Arlie Hochschild argues that parents go to work to escape the pressures of parenting. Our findings seem to indicate that parents *report* that stress is higher at work than at home.[19]

Under what conditions are parents more likely to feel stressed in caring for their child?

When we tested our model, we found that demands, focus, autonomy, and support are all linked to parents' feelings of stress in caring for their child in the following ways (see diagram on page 160):

▼ FAMILY DEMANDS: The more often parents eat meals, play with, and exercise with their child, the less stress they experience in caring for that child.

▼ FOCUS: The easier parents report that it is to focus on their child, the less stress they report.

▼ PARENTING AUTONOMY: Parents who can raise their child the way they want to feel less stress in caring for that child.

▼ SUPPORT: Parents who feel that they have friends and family they can turn to and who feel comfortable in accessing that support experience less stress than parents who do not have this support system. Parents who see the nonparental child care they have used as positive for their child report lower levels of stress than parents who don't have this feeling.

We also looked at parental frustration in caring for the child, and the results were very similar to those pertaining to stress in caring for the child.

Success in parenting

Just as we asked about success on the job, we asked parents about their feelings of success at home: "Overall, how often do you feel successful as a parent—very often, often, sometimes, rarely, or never?"

Forty-four percent of parents say that they feel successful as a parent "very often," and another 36.5 percent say that they feel successful "often." Virtually no one says that he or she feels successful rarely (1 percent) or never (0 percent). The only significant demographic predictor is the age of the child: Parents with a younger child feel more successful than those with an older child.

▼ **Do parents feel more successful at work or as parents?** It is a central thesis of Arlie Hochschild's *The Time Bind* that parents experience more success at work than at home.[20] It is certainly true that the markers of success are clearer at work than at home: There are no performance reviews at home, no merit raises. Very few people

PREDICTING STRESS IN CARING FOR ONE'S CHILD

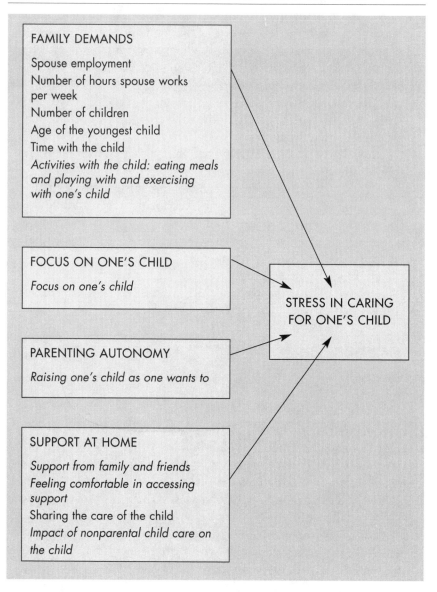

FAMILY DEMANDS

Spouse employment
Number of hours spouse works
per week
Number of children
Age of the youngest child
Time with the child
*Activities with the child: eating meals
and playing with and exercising
with one's child*

FOCUS ON ONE'S CHILD

Focus on one's child

PARENTING AUTONOMY

Raising one's child as one wants to

SUPPORT AT HOME

*Support from family and friends
Feeling comfortable in accessing
support*
Sharing the care of the child
*Impact of nonparental child care on
the child*

**STRESS IN CARING
FOR ONE'S CHILD**

at home stop and say, "You're doing a great job." Or "You deserve a break today." A mother of three says:

> *At home, it is hard for me sometimes, 'cause I don't feel that you get a lot of feedback. And I feel sometimes with the children, [I am mainly] focusing on the negative. It's what we didn't do. Some-*

times that can be very, very difficult. You have to be able to come out of that and say, this is just the kids and you know you're doing the best you can and you can't always please them.

The tasks at home can seem more amorphous and never-ending than those at work for some parents. Yet there is nothing in the world more gratifying than a child's smile, than the handwritten, misspelled notes we get saying they love us; the drawings they make for us; or the secrets they confide in us.

In comparing parents' ratings of how frequently they feel successful in parenting and at work, we find that the home ratings are significantly higher. Although we didn't find differences between mothers and fathers, some research has found that men are happiest at home and women are happiest outside the home.[21]

How might Arlie Hochschild react to this finding? I also suspect that she would argue that although employed parents profess feeling successful as parents, they "vote with their feet" (meaning that their actions speak louder than their words) by *choosing* to spend more time at work away from their children. We all know that many parents don't take advantage of flexibility when it is offered and don't reduce hours when that is seemingly possible. Why are parents doing this?

On one hand, I think that there is a great deal of pressure to work long and hard in today's downsized workplace, where many parents worry about losing their jobs. On the other hand, we find that the number of hours parents work doesn't fully determine the number of hours they spend with their children. So despite long hours of work, many

5.9

Employed Parents with a Child Birth Through 18: Success in Parenting and at Work

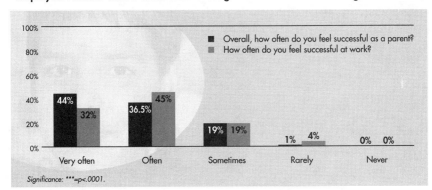

Significance: ***=p<.0001.

parents seem to be doing all that they can to be with their children. Of course, some parents are escaping home and hearth, but this study indicates that most aren't and that they feel more success as parents than they do on the job.

Under what conditions are parents more likely to feel successful as parents?

Our findings reveal the following patterns (see diagram on page 163):

▼ FAMILY DEMANDS: Parents whose child is younger, who participate in more activities with their child, and who spend more time with their child on workdays and nonworkdays feel more successful than other parents.

▼ FOCUS: The easier parents report that it is to focus on their child, the higher the level of success they report.

▼ AUTONOMY: Parents who can raise their child as they want to feel more successful as parents.

▼ SUPPORT: Parents who feel that they have friends and family they can turn to and who feel comfortable in accessing that support experience more success than parents who do not have this support system. Parents who either share the care of their child with their spouse or take more of the responsibility and who view the nonparental child care they have used as very positive feel more successful as parents.

Children's behavior problems

In the final analysis, it is how our children are doing that counts: Are they developing well or are they having problems? To measure this construct, we used the Behavior Problem Index.[22] This measure consists of six statements that parents with a child from ages 4 through 11 were asked to respond to by indicating how well each of the statements describes their child—Is this often true, sometimes true, or not true at all?

How are the children of employed parents faring today? Here's what we learned.

▼ **Is unhappy, sad, or depressed** Although only 1 percent of employed parents say that it is often true that their child is unhappy, sad, or depressed, 27 percent say this is sometimes true. Older children are more prone to these unhappy feelings than younger children. More than one third of parents with a child 8 through

PREDICTING SUCCESS IN PARENTING

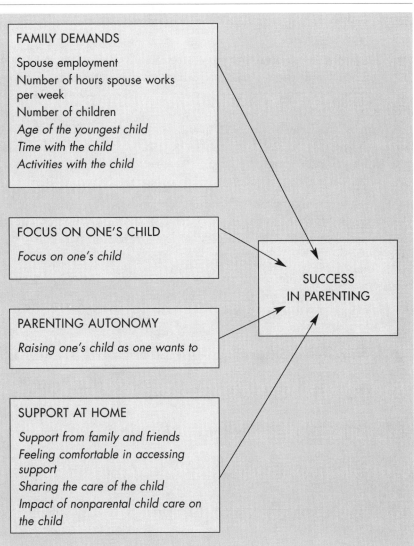

11 years old (35 percent) report that it is sometimes true that their child is sad or depressed compared with 19 percent of parents with a child 4 through 7 years old.

▼ **Does not get along with other children** Similar proportions of parents say that their child does not get along with others as say that their child is unhappy, sad, or depressed—2.5 percent say this is often true and 20 percent say that it is sometimes true. None of the demographic factors we looked at was related to how well the child gets along with other children.

▼ **Cannot concentrate or pay attention for long** More parents report that their child has difficulty concentrating or paying attention than report problems on getting along with other children or feeling unhappy, sad, or depressed. Thirty-eight percent say that this is sometimes true of their child, and 7.5 percent say it is often true. Although one might expect parents of boys to say this more often than parents of girls, this is not the case.

▼ **Feels worthless or inferior** Not many parents have a child whom they see as feeling worthless or inferior: One percent say this is often true and 14 percent say it is sometimes true.

▼ **Acts too young for his or her age** Four percent of parents say that it is often true that their child acts too young for his or her age and 18 percent say that it is sometimes true.

▼ **Is nervous, high-strung, or tense** Of parents asked about their child's being nervous, high-strung, or tense, 6 percent say that this is often true and 21 percent say it is sometimes true.

Under what conditions are parents more likely to have a child with a behavior problem?

Applying the model I've developed in this chapter, the following patterns emerged as shown in the diagram on page 166:

▼ FAMILY DEMANDS: Parents who spend more time with their child on weekdays are less likely to have a child who is unhappy, sad, or depressed, or nervous and high-strung. Parents who spend more time with their child on nonworkdays are less likely to have a child who is unhappy or feels worthless. Parents who eat meals with their child more often are less likely to have a child who is unhappy, who has trouble concentrating, or who is nervous and high-strung. Parents who play or exercise with their child more often are less likely to have a child who is unhappy, does not get along with other children, feels worthless, or is nervous and high-strung.

▼ FOCUS: Parents who feel that it is easier to focus on their child are less likely to have a child who feels unhappy, is unable to concentrate and pay attention, or is nervous and high-strung.

▼ AUTONOMY: Parents who can raise their child the way they want to are less likely to have a child who is unhappy, has trouble getting along with other children, is unable to concentrate, acts young for his or her age, or is nervous and high-strung.

▼ SUPPORT: Parents who feel that they have friends and family to whom they can turn are less likely to have a child who is unhappy and depressed, has trouble getting along with other children, feels worthless, or is nervous and high-strung. Parents who share the care of their child equally are less likely to have a child who has trouble concentrating. Finally, parents who see the nonparental child care they have used as very positive are less likely to have a child who is unhappy and depressed, feels worthless, or is nervous and high-strung.

There are several observations that I want to make about these findings. First, it is important to take note of what's missing. Some of the expected aspects of family life never appear. For example, whether a parent comes from a household in which both spouses work or only one works does not make a difference. Neither does it matter whether the parent is single or married or rich or poor.

The second observation has to do with the proverbial chicken-and-egg debate. Do parents who can focus on their child have a child with fewer behavioral problems, or is it easier for parents to focus on a child who has fewer behavioral problems? Some clues to the answer to this question come from the NICHD study of early child care. These researchers found that parents were just as likely to be warm and responsive with a child who was fussy and difficult to soothe as a child who had an easygoing temperament.[23] So perhaps parents who can focus on their child will have a child with fewer behavior problems, and that encourages parents to continue their focus, et cetera. These are questions for future studies.

The issue of causal direction arises when we consider parenting autonomy. Does a parent's having less autonomy result in a child's having fewer behavior problems or does having a child with problems lead parents to feel less in control? This is somewhat of a needless "tail to chase." Suffice it to say that parents with a child who exhibited behavior problems would probably fare better if they felt they had more autonomy.

PREDICTING CHILD BEHAVIOR PROBLEMS

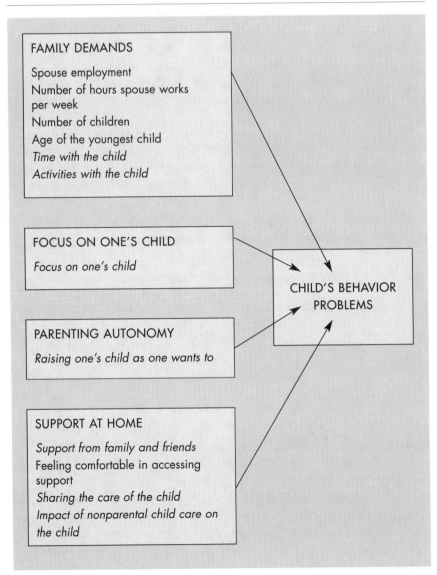

I was especially struck by the importance of social support. Having friends to turn to really does help in parenting. Once again, it is impossible to untangle the causal path. Parents who have a child with behavior problems may receive less support because their problems overburden others. If so, this would be a troubling finding, since these parents probably need more support from others.

WHAT MATTERS? INTENTIONAL PARENTING *AND* THE SUPPORT OF OTHERS

Just as there is something about work life that makes a difference in how stressed or successful we feel, there is something about family life, too. Although the general public worries about the problems of kids these days, our data reveal that most employed parents are not drive-by parents. And although the public at large lays the blame for the problems children face squarely on the shoulders of their parents, we see it is more complex than that. There are traits within ourselves—our *personal resources*—that can make a difference: Being a more intentional parent, having the capacity to focus on our children, and having the autonomy to raise our children the way we want to are important, time and time again. In addition, there are *external resources* outside the family that matter, too—including the support of family and friends, and child care that is seen as good for the child's development. We *can* make a difference, and others can help us do so as well. So once again, it is not either/or—either the family or the community—that is responsible for how our children fare. *Both* make a difference.

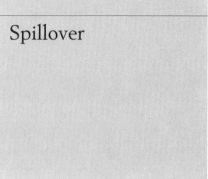

Spillover

ork matters. Family life matters. But how do they fit together? Until recently, work and family life were seen as separate spheres, so there was no need to address this question. And the connections between these two major aspects of our existence remained vague and obscure.

Then, work and family came to be seen as distinct, but linked by what is typically called *work-family interference*. Chaya Piotrkowski at Fordham University has delineated two types of interference: structural and psychological. *Structural interference* occurs when work demands make it difficult or impossible to meet family demands, or vice versa. *Psychological interference* occurs when experiences in one aspect of our lives—work or family—have negative psychological effects in the other, such as increasing our level of stress, putting us in a bad mood, making us depressed, or reducing our energy level.[1]

The dynamic connections between work and family have been described by researchers as *spillover.* It has always interested me that we settled on a water analogy to articulate these connections. The image is of water rising and rising until it spills over its banks and floods.

Spillover was a common theme in our interviews—but with a twist. I asked a parent what she thought were the crucial issues in managing work and family life. This mother of three said:

> *I think that there is enough guilt when you can't be there [with
> your kids], but when you're there and you are so totally stressed
> that you can't focus, that's worse.*

I said, "You're there physically but not—" "not there psychologically," she finished the sentence. Then she continued:

> *When you are already stressed out by work and then you've got
> to deal with three screaming kids and you can't get them to do
> what you want . . . and they are just behaving like kids. Your tol-
> erance level for it is much lower.*

When I used the word *spillover* to describe the situation, she noted:

> *It is not only spillover, it is spill in. There's a bucket of stress, but
> now you have more stress. It's not this kind of stress and that
> kind of stress. It is a blending.*

I agree with this mother's implicit criticism of how spillover typically has been defined in research. It has been assumed that work and family are distinct but linked. For this mother, however, there is a blending: Work stress spills into home life, but the stresses of home are also present in the mix. Together, they make a more potent brew than either makes alone.

Another problem with the typical definition of spillover has been its focus on conflict. Work and family are seen as doing battle with each other. In reality, both home life and work life can also be enjoyable and rewarding, creating positive spillover from one domain to the other. However, we have paid much less attention to the ways that work and family complement and strengthen each other—to the positive synergy between the two.

HOW DOES SPILLOVER AFFECT US AS ADULTS?

In addition, much of the existing research has relied on pencil-and-paper measures of what is going on in our lives at one point in time, applying static measurement to what is a dynamic process in constant flux. Ask a parent how things are going today and you might get a very different response from what you would have heard last month or even last week. But in the last few years, there have been some new and more comprehensive approaches to investigating spillover.

Where are men and women the happiest—at work or at home?

In 1994, Reed Larson at the University of Illinois and his colleagues Maryse Richards and Maureen Perry-Jenkins selected an ingenious way to assess the daily emotional experiences of mothers and fathers moment to moment at work and at home. The participants in their study—employed fathers and employed and nonemployed mothers in fifty-five families—carried pagers for 1 week. Whenever they were signaled, at random times between 7:30 A.M. and 9:30 P.M., they filled out a form that asked what they were doing at the time and how they felt about it. They also were asked about how much choice they had in doing the particular activity and, if they were in the company of others, how friendly or unfriendly these other people were.[2]

Larson and his colleagues found that mothers are happier at work and/or outside the home, and fathers are happier at home. This is true even of nonemployed mothers. Mothers are unhappier than fathers when doing housework and caring for children. One cause of these differences is choice. Mothers feel that they have less choice about doing housework and child care, whereas fathers view these activities as more discretionary. In addition, these researchers and others have found that men and women do different tasks at home. Men's chores tend to be "one-off" tasks, such as fixing something that's broken, or more voluntary tasks such as outdoor work, whereas women's tasks tend to be necessary, daily, and repetitive, recurring day after day, like washing dishes or doing laundry.

This study also found that women are unhappier than men at home when they are socializing and using media (like watching television). The researchers suggest that women are less able to draw a line between their responsibilities and so-called leisure in their own homes. Their feelings of obligation "spill over." They feel "on call" all the time.

So what about work? Why aren't men as happy as women at work? It isn't that they work harder. In fact, this study and others have found that women spend more time actually working while on the job than men do. It comes down to choice for men, too. Men report having less choice than women do at work; furthermore, those men who feel that they have the least choice are the unhappiest. The authors speculate that "because of their provider role, men have less discretion to quit."[3]

And women at work? Choice at work is less important to their moods. But feeling rushed and hurried is—women who feel hurried at work aren't as happy. The friendliness of the work situation also matters to women.

Summing up men's and women's experiences at work and at home, the study finds they are equally happy overall. But isn't it fascinating that each feels *least* happy in his or her traditional role and *most* happy in the spouse's traditional domain?

How do feelings of distress spill over?

These findings about our emotional life at work and at home gave rise to another question: Do our feelings at work carry over to our feelings at home, or vice versa? To address this question, David Almeida of the University of Arizona and Ronald Kessler of Harvard University asked 166 couples (including those with wives who were employed and not employed) to keep time diaries of their emotions and track daily stressors over a 42-day period. Their focus was on feelings of distress.

They found that wives are more likely to report having some distress during any given day and are also more likely to report feeling very distressed. Although wives are more likely to become upset and distressed, they are no more likely to remain distressed than their husbands.

Why do wives get more upset? For very good cause. They have more stressful things happening in their lives: They take greater responsibility for the kids, the house, the laundry, the meals. When the number of stressors affecting men and women is held constant by a statistical procedure, men and women do not differ in whether or not a day becomes "a high-stress day." But they do differ in other ways. Women are less likely than their husbands to *stay* stressed over consecutive days.

The authors speculate that this finding may relate to the different things that upset men and women. Women tend to get more upset by arguments with other people and by the immediate demands that others make of them, whereas men get more upset by work and financial problems. "Perhaps wives cannot stay distressed because this interferes with the care they need to provide to others . . . [whereas husbands] may have a tendency to disengage from others."[4]

Can good moods spill over as well as bad moods?

Kevin J. Williams and George Alliger of the State University of New York at Albany expanded the scope of these studies of spillover by looking at good feelings as well as negative feelings.[5] They assigned preprogrammed watches to a group of forty-one full-time employed parents. The parents in the study were signaled at random times from 7:30 A.M. to 9:30 P.M. over a 7-day period; at these times they stopped what they were doing and filled out a brief questionnaire asking about the following:

▼ The *activities*[6] they were engaged in (job-related activities or fam-
ily-related activities such as caring for children, eating, playing)

▼ The *demands of the task* (i.e., whether they were rushed or hurried, challenged, working hard, and putting forth effort)

▼ Their *personal control* (the degree of choice over when and how
to complete an activity and the degree of personal control over
the activity)

▼ Their *progress toward meeting their goals*

▼ Their *mood* (elation, fatigue, distress, and calmness)

▼ The extent to which they were *juggling* different activities at
the same time

At the end of the day, participants completed another questionnaire,
which assessed their *work-family conflict* for the day and *their involvement and satisfaction with their work and family roles* that day.

Among the findings:

▼ When parents are juggling (their task has been interrupted in
the past 30 minutes, causing them to manage two or more tasks
at the same time), they are more distressed and less calm.

▼ When the demands of the tasks are higher, parents are more
distressed, less calm, and more fatigued.

▼ When they feel more in control of the tasks they are doing, parents are calmer and less distressed. And when they are making
progress toward their goals, they are also calmer.

▼ When parents are trying to manage work and family tasks *at
work*, they feel more negative. But when they are trying to manage work and family tasks *at home*, there is no impact on their
mood. As the researchers state, "This finding implies that
although family intrusions into work adversely affect mood,
work intrusions into family do not."[7]

▼ Unpleasant moods spill over from work to family and from
family to work, but pleasant moods do not. There is little
spillover of good feelings from one part of our life to another.

▼ Women are more likely than men to have their negative feelings at work carry over into their home life and their negative
feelings at home carry over into work.

These results have important implications for the way we manage
work and family. First, certain features of our lives at work and at home—
demands, autonomy (which they call control), and a lack of focus (which

they term *juggling*)—affect our moods. My study for *Ask the Children* found these same factors to be important, and they are included in the model of work and family life discussed in Chapters 4 and 5. Second, the moods we experience while we are working seem more durable and more likely to spill over into our moods at home than our moods from home are to spill into our work situation. Third, negative moods move across boundaries of work and home, but positive moods have little spillover.[8]

Does the study mean that our positive moods don't matter? No, as we will see later in this chapter. In addition, in Chapter 9, I will show that children are more likely to want to be like us, to model themselves on us as parents, when they hear about the good things about our jobs and when they feel we like our work. Thus, I find that positive spillover can benefit our children.

HOW DOES SPILLOVER AFFECT HOW WE PARENT?

When parents feel frustrated, angry, or distressed at work, they can be more punitive or harsh with their children.[9] Over the past decade, Rena Repetti at the University of California at Los Angeles has been investigating this kind of spillover.

How do fathers respond to their children on stressful days?

One study was conducted with fathers who were air traffic controllers (ATCs). This is a fascinating profession to study because the stress factors at work can be objectively measured. These include the weather conditions (especially visibility) and the volume of air traffic. Over a 6-month period, Repetti followed fifteen ATCs who were fathers with a child between 4 and 10 years old. On 3 consecutive days, each ATC filled out a survey at night that assessed his perceptions of the workload that day, interactions with coworkers, and interactions after work with one of his children.[10]

Repetti found that on days when fathers *perceived* that their work was more demanding (busy, difficult weather conditions), they tended to withdraw from their child. Moreover, Repetti found a connection between the fathers' perceptions and the objectively measured stressful conditions at work: When the visibility at the airport was lower (as reported by the National Climatic Data Center), fathers were more emotionally withdrawn—they expressed less affection and described less warmth and closeness with their child. They also expressed fewer negative feelings such as anger and tension.

Work also affects men's relationships with their wives. On days when the workload was *seen* as higher, the ATCs were more likely to withdraw from their wives. This makes sense: Withdrawing may help people who are upset gain the time and space they need to calm down.[11]

Repetti also looked at the social climate at work, comparing fathers' perceptions with descriptions of the social climate provided by other ATCs who worked on the same team (or work group). She found that when coworkers described a more difficult atmosphere at work, fathers reported more negativity in their relationship with their child after work, such as *less* affection, laughing, and playing together and *more* feelings of hostility, tension, and disappointment.[12]

How do mothers respond to their children on stressful days?

Do mothers behave in the same way when work is stressful? Rena Repetti and her colleague Jenifer Wood conducted a study of 30 mothers with preschool-age children for 5 consecutive weekdays. At the end of the workday, mothers filled out a questionnaire assessing their day at work, particularly their workload and their negative interactions with coworkers and supervisors. Then, 13 mother-child pairs were videotaped for a 10-minute reunion period at pickup time at a child care center.[13]

Through painstaking analysis of these videotapes, the researchers found that mothers are more withdrawn on days when they feel their workload is higher and the stress among coworkers is more pronounced. After these difficult days at work, the mothers initially pay less attention to their child and appear less warm and caring. So women, like men, seem to pull back after a difficult day at work.

Do children "get it" when their parents are stressed?

The fascinating aspect of this reunion study is that children seem to "get it" very quickly. They seem to know that their mothers are not acting the way that they usually do. Although we sometimes suspect that our children respond to those days when we are upset by doing everything in their power to make things worse, that's not what this study showed. In fact, the children in this study were less likely to whine, demand, and argue when their mother pulled back. As Repetti and Wood state, it is almost as if children are on "their best behaviors" when their mothers have one of those days.

In addition, children seemed to try to reach out to their mothers when they were more withdrawn than usual. They made statements like "Look what I did." Or they tried to make their mothers laugh by being funny or cute. At the same time, the children appeared to the observers to be more anxious, less happy, and less affectionate.

Mothers who were distressed in the first part of the reunion period responded in turn. They warmed up, talking to their child, becoming more affectionate. Thus, the children's behavior helped to shape how mothers behaved.

These findings remind me of the videotapes of attachment relationships made by the pediatrician Berry Brazelton and his colleague Ed Tronick at Harvard University showing the exquisitely intricate interaction between baby and parent (as discussed in Chapter 2). Typically, the child will do something and the adult will respond, matching the baby in tone and in intensity. When the experimenter tells the parent to "freeze," to stop responding, to go blank, the baby does everything he or she can to reengage the parent—coos, makes engaging sounds, flails his or her arms toward the parent. It is apparent from the Repetti study that the parent-child dance—this synchronized give and take that begins in infancy and builds the parent-child attachment relationship—continues into the preschool years and undoubtedly beyond.

So do children "get it" when their parents are distressed? Our one-on-one interviews with children indicate they do. Virtually every child we interviewed gave detailed accounts of how he or she responded when it was "one of those days." One teenage boy says:

> *You can tell when my dad's upset when he's had a really stressful day. He looks like he is really ready to blow.*

This teenager, like many other children, seems to know what is causing the stress. For example, he says:

> *If things don't work out, [my dad] doesn't draw a paycheck.*

And he, like many other children, has techniques for managing these situations:

> *That's when you go upstairs and start studying.*

Older children can empathize with their parents. A teenage girl says:

> *When you are in a bad mood, you don't want to do anything but sulk. So if [my parents] have had a bad day, I just leave them alone. When I am in a bad mood, I don't want to be bothered. So I give them time to cool down. Usually their moods will change after a while.*

Rena Repetti has come to a somewhat different conclusion than we did in our interviews with children. In one of her most recent studies, she studied fifty-three dual-earner families and twenty-eight single-mother families with a child in the fifth or sixth grade. For 5 consecutive days, before leaving work the parents filled out a form rating their interactions with supervisors and coworkers. Before going to bed at night, parents and children completed a form in which they described their interactions with each other for that evening. These items asked how involved, affectionate, and friendly the parent was that evening.

Fathers reported that they were less responsive and more withdrawn with their child on days when they had tense encounters with coworkers and supervisors. The children's descriptions of their fathers supported the fathers' claims of withdrawal. Fathers also said that they were more irritable, but children didn't seem to notice this behavior.

Findings for the mothers are particularly surprising. Mothers reported that they were *more* responsive, playful, and involved with their child when they had a really bad day at work. The children's descriptions of their mothers supported this assertion as well.[14]

How can we reconcile these finding with those from our interviews? Are mothers recovering quickly—so that by the end of the day, the child and the mother remember the good moments, not the bad ones? Are mothers compensating for a bad day at work by plunging into their relationship with their child and savoring the time they have together? Are these findings a function of the particular group Repetti studied (upper middle class) or the age of the child (preadolescent), or the work situation (the mothers were less involved in their careers than the fathers)?

We certainly heard from mothers about their making a concerted effort to *be with* their child, no matter what kind of day they had. A recently widowed mother with a teenager reports:

> *You come home and you're exhausted, you're tired, and you have certain chores that you have to do. I was always very much aware that I had to give my daughter time, so somehow you have*

to put the job in perspective. It's not that you want to shortchange the job, but you have to make sure that you save, that you maintain some [of your time and energy] for your home life.

But we also heard from parents that their children could detect a bad day:

[My children] want to know that I'm one hundred percent there. But I can't always be there because I'm bothered about something or frustrated and I think that is hard for them. I think probably they can assess pretty fast that I'm not in a great mood and they probably just go off by themselves or something until they know that I've come out of it. I sit at a table and then I regroup.

In fact, one mother says that after a "pretty hectic day" when she came home "stressed" her child wrote her a note to calm down.

I don't remember ranting and raving at her but I guess [from] my movements—I was moving pretty fast—and the look on my face, she just picked up on it. She went off, wrote this little thing, came back, and put it on my desk.

It said, "Hey, Mom! Stressed? Take a few whacks and then take another shot at it. Love ya, Jade."

When I saw it, it was like "Whoa." I was floored. I kind of sat down and took a few breaths.

It is clear that there remains a great deal to learn about spillover. The large-scale surveys of parents and children we conducted shed further light on these issues.

HOW OFTEN DOES PARENTS' WORK INTERFERE WITH THEIR PARENTING?

We asked employed parents with a child birth through 18 years the following questions to define and identify work interference: "During the past 3 months, how often did you . . .

▼ think about your work when you were with your child?"
▼ worry about your work when you were with your child?"
▼ have your child wait to be with you because of your work?"

▼ get interrupted by the demands of work when you were with your child?"

6.1

**Employed Parents with a Child
Birth Through 18: Thinking About Work
When with Their Child**

*During the past 3 months, how often did you think
about your work when you were with your child?*

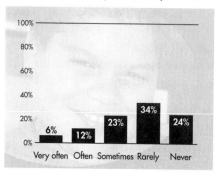

			34%	
Very often	Often	Sometimes	Rarely	Never
6%	12%	23%	34%	24%

How often do parents think about their work when they are with their child?

Over a 3-month period, we found that 18 percent of parents think about their work often or very often when they are with their child. Another 23 percent report that they sometimes think about their work. Taken together, 41 percent think about work at least some of the time. One parent who is an accountant said:

> *I think that I often am not really with [my children] when I am with them. I feel like I can't wait for them to go to bed sometimes at night because I need to get something done for [a client] right away. Sometimes I feel like I have dead weights around my ankles and I can't move. There's nowhere I can go [until they go to sleep].*

Given how pressured work has become, it is evident that many parents (at least three in five, according to this study) seem to be making a concerted effort *not* to let the considerable pressures of work invade the time they have with their child. One mother, who is very conscious that her time with her school-age son is fleeting, has deliberate techniques for staying focused on her child:

> *When I sit down [with him], I try not to be antsy. If I find myself thinking about other things, I just try to keep my mind here instead of drifting off. Kind of like when you say a prayer, you start thinking of other things than what you're praying about.*

How often do children say that their parents think about work when they are with them?

Do kids agree with parents' assessments of themselves? Often, parents and children see the world quite differently. Remember how divergent kids' and parents' perceptions are of how often they share activities such as meals, homework, and exercise. So it stands to reason this might be the case again.

We asked children in the seventh through twelfth grades the same question we asked parents—to assess how often their mothers and their fathers think about work when they are together. Surprisingly, there are *no* differences in children's assessments of their mothers and fathers and the self-assessments made by mothers and fathers with children of the same ages.

How often do parents worry about work when they are with their child?

Fewer parents say that they have worried about work over the past 3 months when they are with their child than say they think about work: Ten percent say that they worry about work often or very often, and another 19 percent say they worry sometimes; 71 percent say they rarely or never worry.

How often do children say that their parents worry about work when they are with them?

This is an interesting question since, as we will see in Chapter 8, many children worry about *us*. But do children see *us* worrying about work when we are with them? Not much. There are no differences between the assessments of seventh- through twelfth-grade children of their mothers and fathers and the assessment of fathers and mothers with a child of the same age.

How often do parents have their child wait because of work?

A mother who is an executive thinks back to when her children were young. One of her most poignant memories is telling her children to wait:

> *I remember saying to [my daughter] when she was very young, "Just a minute" a lot.*

In fact, only 3 percent of parents say that they have their child wait very often, another 10 percent say that they do so often, and 25 percent say sometimes. Taken together, 38 percent of parents ask their child to wait at least sometimes; 62 percent rarely or never make their children wait because of work.

How often do children say they have to wait to be with their parents because of work?

This teenager remembers waiting for her mother:

> *It was really kind of annoying for our whole family that we would go on vacation and since she was in charge of her office, she would always have to call the office and make sure that everything was all right and that there were no major issues. I remember having to stop at truck stops so she could call in.*

Her father recalls keeping her and her brother waiting when it was his turn to carpool:

> *I didn't leave enough time to get there from work or I tried to finish something and got caught in traffic.*

For how many of us does this have the ring of truth? But this father felt it wasn't such a big deal to his children:

> *I think the children's attitude was "Well, don't feel guilty about it. Just BE here on time!"*

Children do not report having to wait very often. As we have found thus far, there are no differences between mothers' and fathers' assessments of how often they ask their seventh- through twelfth-grade child to wait because of work and seventh- through twelfth-grade children's assessments of their own mothers and fathers.

How often do parents get interrupted by work demands when they are with their child?

Over a 3-month period, only 5 percent of parents get interrupted by work demands very often or often when they are with their child, and another 13 percent say that work interruptions occur sometimes. Fully 82 percent state that this happens rarely or never.

One of the questions we asked parents in our one-on-one interviews was to recall how their own parents' work affected them, in hope of discerning what the more lasting effect of parents' work on children might be. Those parents who remembered work as always interrupting the time they had with their parents had some sad memories. One mother whose father was a veterinarian had the double bind of not really being able to get angry at her father because he was saving animals' lives:

I think intellectually as a child I knew that if a dog was run over on Thanksgiving Day, you just couldn't let it die. But did that make me happy? Of course you couldn't ask a dying dog to wait until you finished your turkey dinner. So therefore you feel even more guilty when you feel like that's intruding on family life. You are probably less inclined as a child to speak up and say "Hey. What about me?"

All you wanted to do was have dinner or play a game or have him help you with your homework. I sometimes would say, "Couldn't we have just one dinner without having the phone ring?"

How often do children say that their parents' work interrupts them when they are together?
Although the children and parents in my study are not in the same families, it again appears that parents with a child in the seventh through twelfth grades and children of the same age report the same realities: Work interruptions are rare. There are no differences between mothers' and fathers' assessments of how often work interrupts their time with their child and children's assessments of work interruptions.

WHICH PARENTS EXPERIENCE MORE WORK-FAMILY INTERFERENCE?

As the next step in figuring out which aspects of our work and family life affect us most powerfully as parents, we added our findings about work interference to our work-family model.[15] We combined the ways that work interferes with parenting in one scale. Then, to see which parents are more likely to experience work interference with parenting, we looked at the following groups of potential predictors:

▼ Personal characteristics and priorities
▼ Parenting characteristics and support
▼ Job time demands
▼ Stresses and strains on the job
▼ Job quality
▼ Workplace support

We found that those parents most likely to experience negative interference of work on parenting:

▼ *put a higher priority on work than family.*

▼ *are* more likely to be *managers or professionals.*

▼ *have less parenting support* at home from their family and friends when their child has a problem.

▼ work more hours per week, work more days per week, and do work at home before and after the regular workday more often—that is, *have jobs that demand more time.*

▼ don't have enough time to get everything done at work; find it more difficult to focus at work; and experience more stress and frustration at work—that is, *experience more stresses and strains on the job.*

▼ have more job autonomy; have more challenge in their jobs; and are less satisfied with their opportunities to learn on the job—that is, *have better- and worse-quality jobs.*

▼ *do not have a supervisor.*

What's important about these findings?

What strikes me immediately about these findings is that they represent, almost to a tee, all the ways that work has changed over the past 20 years: Parents are working more hours, parents are taking work home more often, and parents feel that they are under more time pressure.[16] In addition, the issues of focus, multitasking, and work interruptions have come front and center in this age of downsizing when fewer people do the same amount of work; in the 24-hour global economy, when more of us are being called on to meet customers' needs for longer hours; and as technology makes us instantly accessible, wherever we are.

Our 20-year comparison between the Department of Labor's Quality of Employment Survey and our 1997 National Study of the Changing Workforce also shows that job autonomy has increased since 1977, as have job challenges that require employees to keep learning and be creative. These aspects of work increase our commitment and loyalty to our employers and our satisfaction with our jobs, but they also seem to have the unintended consequence of seeping into our family lives as well, reducing the amount of time and energy we have for parenting Thus, having a "better job"—given all the challenges that go with it—can be a mixed blessing.[17]

Our finding that the parents who experience more interference are those who put work first is crucially important. Although the workplace has changed in ways that can indeed carve into our relationships with our children, in the final analysis it is our choice: Do we place a higher priority on work or on family?

What's missing from these findings?

Just as I was struck by what is present in these findings, I was equally interested by what's missing. Since so much of the debate about work and family life focuses on mothers, it is fascinating that there is no difference between mothers' and fathers' reports of work's interfering with their parenting. Likewise, since so much of the debate revolves around family structure and family type, it is interesting that the type of family we live in (families with and without working mothers; married parents or single parents) has no connection to whether our jobs interfere with our parenting. Presumably, having a spouse at home would free us to become more wrapped up in our jobs, but that doesn't seem to be the case. It is fascinating—and important—to find that parents are taking responsibility for their own relationships with their child, regardless of the type of families they live in.

Finally, I was fascinated to find that a supportive supervisor and a family-friendly workplace don't affect whether work interferes with parenting. Parents in family-friendly workplaces and with supportive supervisors and those without are equally likely to report that work interferes with parenting. Interestingly, support at home from family and friends *does* make a difference. Perhaps addressing work interference is beyond the reach of a family-friendly workplace and a supportive supervisor.

HOW OFTEN DO PARENTS' JOBS SPILL OVER INTO THEIR RELATIONSHIP WITH THEIR CHILD IN NEGATIVE WAYS?

Spillover has been defined primarily as negative emotional spillover: "a process whereby feelings of frustration, anger, or disappointment at work lead to the expression of greater irritability and impatience or more power assertion at home."[18] In order to assess *negative job-to-parenting spillover*, we asked employed parents with a child birth through 18 years, "During the past 3 months, how often . . .

▼ have you *not* had the energy to do things with your child because of your job?"

▼ have you *not* been in as good a mood as you would like to be
with your child because of your job?"

▼ has your job kept you from doing as good a job in parenting
your child as you would like?"

How often do parents not have energy to do things with their child because of their job?

Lack of energy to parent is certainly an issue that we heard about from
parents. A single mother with an 8-year-old child recounts how this
feels:

> *With kids, you have to BE in it with them, you have to feel
> their emotions. When they come to you and they say some-
> thing to you, they want you to KNOW how it feels. And I'm
> listening to [my son], but it just always seems like, I'm tired.
> Not that I'm not concerned. I am. But sometimes I'm just so
> exhausted.*

So how often does this happen, according to parents?

Almost one in seven employed parents (14 percent) says that over
the past 3 months, he or she often or very often has not had the energy
to do things with his or her child because of the job. If one includes
"sometimes," the number of parents feeling depleted rises to 46 percent—almost half of all employed parents. In contrast, 54 percent of
parents rarely or never feel depleted of energy.

Do children agree?

Children in the seventh through twelfth grades were asked the same
questions, and their answers were compared with those of parents with
a child of the same age. And yes, children agree. In fact, children are concerned about their parents. When children are asked why they worry
about their parents (and an astounding two thirds of children with
employed parents are worried at least some of the time), the third most
frequent reason they cite is that their parents are tired (see Chapter 8).
In addition, among the top four wishes to change the way their parents'
work affects their family life, children wish that their parents would be
less tired by work (see Chapter 3).

How often are parents *not* in a good mood with their child because of their job?

Parents were asked, "During the past 3 months, how often have you *not* been in as good a mood as you would like to be with your child because of your job?"

Fifteen percent of parents feel that their mood with their child suffers often or very often because of their job. If we include the parents who say they sometimes experience this situation, the figure rises to 45 percent. On the other hand, more than half of all parents—55 percent—say that this happens to them rarely or never, so it's close to a fifty-fifty split.

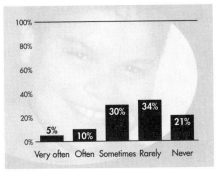

6.2

Employed Parents with a Child Birth Through 18: Not in as Good a Mood with Child Because of Job

During the past 3 months, how often have you not been in as good a mood as you would like to be with your child because of your job?

Very often 5% · Often 10% · Sometimes 30% · Rarely 34% · Never 21%

Do children agree?

Here, we find differences for the first time. Both mothers and fathers report more negative mood spillover from work to parenting than children in the seventh through twelfth grades do. For example, 20 percent of fathers say they "never" experience negative mood spillover compared with 40 percent of children who say their fathers never experience this. Seventeen percent of mothers say they never experience this kind of spillover compared with 36 percent of children who report their mothers never experience this kind of spillover.

Do these differences between parents and children occur because parents control their moods, that is, disguise their moods or recover quickly (as the videotaped reunions observed by Rena Repetti suggest)? A woman who is a writer explains:

> *I can have a bad day at work and feel it spilling over, but my actual action may not show that and my child may not perceive it. Isn't that what's called maturity? My feelings don't always have to dictate my behavior.*

How often do parents feel that their job has kept them from doing as good a job in parenting as they would like?

This is the ultimate question—in a sense the summary question: "During the past 3 months, how often has your job kept you from doing as good a job in parenting as you would like?" As Stewart Friedman and Jeffrey Greenhaus find in their seminal study of business school graduates, a very serious problem is the *psychological* interference of work and family life.[19] Since it is likewise my contention that it is not *that* we work, but *how* we work that affects us as parents, this question is intended to probe parents' feelings on this score.

Twelve percent of employed parents feel that their job makes them poorer parents than they want to be often or very often. About one out of four (24 percent) feels that this happens sometimes.

6.3

Employed Parents with a Child Birth Through 18: Job Keeps Parents from Doing a Good Job as Parents

During the past 3 months, how often has your job kept you from doing as good a job in parenting your child as you would like?

Very often 3% Often 9% Sometimes 24% Rarely 30% Never 34%

So more than one third of all employed parents (36 percent) believe that their job negatively affects their parenting competence on a somewhat regular basis. We did not ask children this question.

HOW OFTEN DO PARENTS' JOBS SPILL OVER INTO RELATIONSHIPS WITH THEIR CHILD IN POSITIVE WAYS?

At the Families and Work Institute, Arlene Johnson and I have long taken the position that work can have positive as well as negative effects on family. Although previous studies have not found much in the way of positive spillover from work into parenting,[20] I wanted to know parents' views. We asked employed parents, with a child birth through 18 years, "During the past 3 months, how often . . .

▼ have you had *more* energy to do things with your child because of your job?"

▼ have you been in a *good* mood with your child because of your job?"

How often do parents have *more* energy to do things with their child because of their job?

Since some other researchers have previously found more negative than positive spillover, it is interesting that in parents' views, they are just as likely to have more energy at home because of their work as to have less energy: Seventeen percent say that they have had more energy often or very often, and another 26 percent say sometimes.

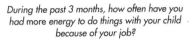

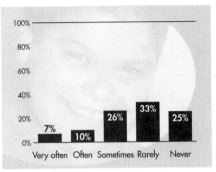

Employed Parents with a Child Birth Through 18: Have More Energy for Child Because of Job

During the past 3 months, how often have you had more energy to do things with your child because of your job?

Do children agree?

Children in the seventh through twelfth grades were asked the same question with regard to their mothers and their fathers, enabling us to make comparisons with parents who have a child of the same age. We find that there are no differences in the assessments of children and of parents.

How often are parents in a *good* mood with their child because of their job?

Remember that the study monitoring parents' moods over the course of several days found that bad moods tend to spill over and good moods do not.[21] I was interested in parents' *perceptions* of positive mood spillover. In our open-ended interviews, parents told us that if they are feeling good about work, they carry those feelings home:

> *If I have had a particularly good day—a meeting has gone well, someone has appreciated my work, I've won a contract that I was after—I come tripping in the door.*

Thus, in our survey we asked parents, "During the past 3 months, how often have you been in a good mood with your child because of your job?" Contrary to the findings of other research conducted on small, nonrepresentative samples or observational studies, the Ask the Children survey of a large and representative sample of employed parents

6.5

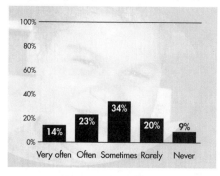

**Employed Parents with a Child
Birth Through 18: In a Good Mood
with Child Because of Job**

*During the past 3 months, how often have you been
in a good mood with your child because of your job?*

100%

80%

60%

40%

34%

20%   23%   20%

14%   9%

0%

Very often Often Sometimes Rarely Never

finds that parents themselves *report* that good moods from work spill over to home more often than bad moods do. For example, 37 percent report being in a good mood at home because of their jobs often or very often compared with 15 percent who say that their moods suffer often or very often because of work. In fact, only 29 percent of employed parents rarely or never experience good moods spilling over.

Do children agree?

As with negative moods, I find a discrepancy between parents and children when it comes to assessing positive moods. Children are far less likely to say that their mothers or fathers are in a good mood with them *because of their jobs* than parents are. For example, four times more fathers (20 percent) than children (5 percent) say that fathers have been in a good mood with their child because of their job very often. The level of magnitude is lower for mothers and children but still exists: Eleven percent of mothers say that they are very often in a good mood with their child because of their jobs compared with 6 percent of children.

Perhaps kids don't see the good moods as much because parents may come home happy but whatever they face as soon as they open their front doors may sweep those good feelings away. As one parent says:

> If I am met at the door by one kid telling me something awful that the other one did, my husband is peeved that the car needs an expensive repair, the dog is throwing up because one of the kids fed her something sickening, and another kid is wailing about a homework assignment—it's hard to hold on to that good mood.

Or perhaps children are simply less attuned to our moods—positive or negative. Moreover, maybe children are less able to discern (possibly because we don't say so) that *it is work* that has put us in a bad or good mood. So they see that we're in a good mood, but they don't connect it with work.

In contrast, virtually all of the children we interviewed in person told us how they play detective to figure out their parents' mood and energy level. The following statement was typical of children's comments when we interviewed them in person:

> My mom—she's very expressional. If she comes and picks me up from the baby-sitter's and says "Come on, just hurry up, I really want to get home," I know that she's had a really bad day. My dad keeps everything inside. He's not very talkative. But I can tell by the expression on his face.
>
> 9-YEAR-OLD GIRL

Our survey findings also reveal that children are worried about stressed-out parents and wish that their parents would be less stressed. So, I conclude that these differences are of degree rather than of substance. In other words, children see moods spilling over *less frequently* than parents, but it still happens: Thirty-six percent of children say that their mothers and 31 percent say that their fathers are not in a good mood with them because of work at least some of the time that they are together. And 13 percent say this happens with their mothers and 11 percent say this happens with their fathers often or very often.

WHICH PARENTS EXPERIENCE MORE NEGATIVE SPILLOVER FROM THEIR JOBS?

Work spills over into parenting in *negative* ways more often when parents:

▼ *place a higher priority on work than their family life.*

▼ take less responsibility for the care of their child; have less support at home from family and friends when there is a problem with their child or feel less comfortable accessing this support; feel that the nonparental child care they have used has had more of a negative impact on their child; and feel less free to raise their child the way they want—that is, *have less parenting support and autonomy.*

▼ work more days per week—that is, *have jobs that demand more time.*

▼ feel they don't have enough time to get everything done at work; find it more difficult to focus at work; and experience more stress and frustration at work—that is, *experience more stresses and strains on the job*.

▼ have less job autonomy; feel that their work is less meaningful; and are less satisfied with their learning opportunities on the job—that is, *have worse-quality jobs*.

▼ have less supervisor support, less coworker support, and less family-friendly workplaces—that is, *have less workplace support*.

As we continue to find, the aspects of work that are significant are lack of support, less autonomy, and more demands. Lack of support and less parenting autonomy are important at home, too. As with negative interference from work, it comes down to our priorities: Parents who put work first experience more negative spillover at home.

It is interesting that some of the aspects of our lives that people would expect to make a difference—such as whether or not we are in a single-parent family, or whether we are in a dual-earner family or one in which the mother stays at home to care for the child—don't matter.

Even the gender of the parent doesn't matter, according to these assessments by parents. Whereas smaller-scale observational studies of nonrepresentative groups of parents have found differences between fathers and mothers, we don't find differences in fathers' and mothers' *perceptions* of negative spillover or *reports* of work interference in our large-scale survey. What do you think—from your own experience?

WHICH PARENTS EXPERIENCE MORE POSITIVE SPILLOVER FROM WORK TO PARENTING?

When we look at the *positive* spillover from work to parenting (we have more energy, we are in better moods with our child because of our jobs), we find that it works in somewhat of an opposite way but that many of the same aspects of our lives come to the fore. Parents who experience more positive spillover:

▼ *are married*.

▼ have more support from family and friends when there is a problem with their child; feel more comfortable accessing this support; and have more autonomy to raise their child the way that they wish—that is, *have more parenting support*.

▼ work more days per week—that is, *have jobs that demand more time*.

▼ experience less stress and frustration at work—that is, *experience fewer stresses and strains on the job*.

▼ have more job autonomy; feel their jobs are more meaningful; are more satisfied with their opportunities to learn on the job; and are challenged to keep learning and be creative on the job—that is, *have better-quality jobs*.

▼ have more supportive supervisors and better coworker support—that is, *more workplace support*.

The fact that working more days makes a positive difference seems contradictory. One would expect parents who work more days to be more burned out. I think the explanation lies in the fact that many of us who work more tend to like our jobs more, so it stands to reason that work might be related to parenting in positive ways as well as negative ways. But is there a breaking point? Is there a limit to the number of days and hours we can work without experiencing more negative than positive spillover? Probably there is, but this threshold might differ for each of us. What's too much for you might not be too much for me, or vice versa.

Another interesting finding is that although having a supportive supervisor and having a family-friendly workplace don't seem to affect the degree to which work interferes with parenting, they *do* affect our moods and our energy levels with our child—in both positive and negative ways. Perhaps this is because work interference with parenting is more a matter of how we *as individuals* handle competing demands (thinking about work, worrying about work, getting interrupted by work, and asking our child to wait because of work). Thus it might be beyond the reach of family-friendliness in the workplace and supportive supervisors, whereas the moods and energy level that we bring home from work would clearly be influenced by the support we receive for parenting at work.

Finally, I want to note that some of the factors associated with work interference with parenting follow the trend lines of current business change, such as giving workers more autonomy and more challenging jobs. This trend may create a win/lose situation—a win for employers and even for employees, but a loss for the family. Paradoxically, these same factors (autonomy and job challenge) are also associated with more positive spillover, creating a win/win situation for both the employer and the family. One critical difference in these two scenarios rests with the values of the parent: Parents who *put work first* experience more work interference and more negative spillover. To quote Stewart Friedman at the Wharton School of the University of Pennsylvania: "The more our core values are bound to the family, the more likely we are to feel we are doing a better job as parents."[22]

HOW OFTEN DO PARENTS' RESPONSIBILITIES FOR THEIR CHILDREN SPILL OVER INTO WORK IN NEGATIVE WAYS?

Now we switch directions and look at spillover from the family into work. The concept of family-friendly assistance at the workplace has been predicated on spillover that moves from home to work—that is, family problems that spill over into work, affecting our job performance in negative ways. I wanted to assess how often—and under what circumstances—this occurs. We again asked a similar set of questions, but with a *parenting-to-work focus:*[23] We asked employed parents with a child birth through 18 years, "During the past 3 months, how often . . .

- ▼ have you had *less* energy to do your job because of your children?"
- ▼ have you *not* been in as good a mood at work as you would like because of your children?"
- ▼ have your children kept you from doing as good a job at work as you would like?"
- ▼ have your children kept you from concentrating on your job?"

How often have parents had less energy to do their job because of their children?
Almost one in seven employed parents (14 percent) says that over the past 3 months, he or she has had less energy to do the job because of his or her children often or very often. If one includes "sometimes," the number of parents feeling depleted of energy goes up to 30.5 percent—nearly one third of all employed parents.

How often have parents not been in a good mood at work because of their children?
Relatively few parents (8 percent) report that they have not been in as good a mood at work as they would like because of their children often or very often. In fact, almost three in four parents (73 percent) say that this happens rarely or never.

How often have children kept parents from doing a good job at work?

The story that continues to emerge as I look at these findings is that parents do not feel their children impede them very much at work. Only 5.5 percent of parents say that this happens often or very often. Fully 44 percent say that this never happens.

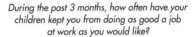

Employed Parents with a Child Birth Through 18: Children Keep Parents from Doing a Good Job at Work

During the past 3 months, how often have your children kept you from doing as good a job at work as you would like?

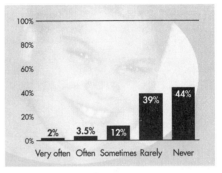

How often do children keep parents from concentrating on their job?

The answer is rarely or never, according to 76 percent. Conversely, only 7 percent say that in the last 3 months, their children have kept them from concentrating on their job often or very often, whereas 17 percent say sometimes.

Since parents report such a low level of spillover from parenting to work, does this mean that family-friendly assistance from employers is not really necessary? Of course not. For one thing, this study assessed the spillover of mood and energy from parenting to work, not the *practical* difficulties of managing work and family life, such as having child care arrangements that fall apart, with an impact on whether an employee can go to work in the first place and perform well in the second place. For another, when we looked at spillover from work to parenting, we saw that family-friendly assistance does provide real support for parenting. The findings from this study call for reframing our conception of how parenting responsibilities affect us on the job, as we will see even more powerfully when we turn to the topic of positive spillover.

HOW OFTEN DO PARENTS' RESPONSIBILITIES FOR THEIR CHILDREN SPILL OVER INTO WORK IN POSITIVE WAYS?

Since we find that few parents report that their children affect them negatively at work, now we look at *positive* spillover and ask, "During the past 3 months, how often . . .

▼ have you had *more* energy to do your job because of your children?"

▼ have you been in a *good* mood at work because of your children?"

How often have parents had more energy to do their job because of their children?

More than twice as many parents say that their children give them more energy to do their jobs often or very often (34 percent) as say that their children deplete them of energy to do their jobs (14 percent). If one adds the "sometimes" responses, then 59 percent of parents say that their children give them more energy to do their jobs at least some of the time. This is certainly different from the perspective commonly held by businesses that children are a distraction, and even detract from work. Even if social desirability is at work here (people saying what they think interviewers will approve of), the wide disparity between the number of parents who report a lack of energy at work due to children and those reporting more energy at work due to children is too large not to be taken very seriously.

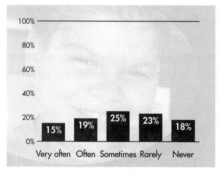

6.7

Employed Parents with a Child Birth Through 18: Have More Energy for Job Because of Children

During the past 3 months, how often have you had more energy to do your job because of your children?

- Very often: 15%
- Often: 19%
- Sometimes: 25%
- Rarely: 23%
- Never: 18%

In our 1992 National Study of the Changing Workforce, we found that supervisors who have child care responsibilities and/or working spouses are seen as better bosses by the people they supervise than other supervisors. Perhaps the finding here that children energize us helps explain why having children may make us better bosses. I have certainly experienced these feelings myself. For example, just as I was writing this section of the book, my son came in and we ended up fooling around with our dogs together. When I returned to writing and to responding to the calls from my office, I did so with renewed and heightened energy.

How often have parents been in a good mood at work because of their children?

Fully 71 percent of employed parents say that they have been in a good mood at work because of their children often or very often, compared with only 7 percent of parents who say that they have rarely or *never* been in a good mood at work often or very often because of their children. In other words, parents are *much* more likely to be in a good mood at work than a bad mood because of their children. The discourse on working parents in the United States has completely ignored this possibility. In fact, I am frequently distressed by how often the word *problem* is attached to anything related to children and work: "the child care problem," "the sick child problem." In con-

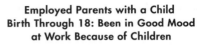

Employed Parents with a Child Birth Through 18: Been in Good Mood at Work Because of Children

During the past 3 months, how often have you been in a good mood at work because of your children?

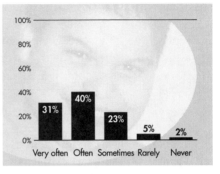

trast, there is public discussion in Europe about considering the competence gained from parenting as a valuable asset to be put in the mix when employers make hiring decisions.[24]

WHICH PARENTS EXPERIENCE WHICH TYPES OF PARENTING-TO-WORK SPILLOVER?

The employed parents most likely to say that their children affect them in *negative* ways at work:

▼ *put a higher priority on work than on family life.*
▼ have less support from their families and friends when there is a problem with their child; rate the impact of the nonparental child care they have used as more negative; and feel that they have less autonomy to raise their child the way they want to—that is, *have less parenting support and autonomy.*
▼ feel that they don't have enough time to get everything done at work; have a harder time focusing at work; and experience more stress and frustration at work—that is, *experience more stresses and strains on the job.*
▼ feel that their work is less meaningful—that is, *have lower-quality jobs.*
▼ don't have an immediate supervisor; work in a less family-friendly workplace—that is, *have less workplace support.*

In contrast, we find that the parents who experience more positive spillover from parenting to work:

▼ *are fathers.*
▼ *put a higher priority on family.*
▼ have more support from family and friends when there is a problem with their child; feel comfortable accessing this support; feel that the nonparental child care they have used is more positive; and feel that they have more autonomy in the way they raise their child—that is, *have more parenting support and autonomy.*
▼ work more days per week—that is, *have jobs that demand more time.*
▼ feel that they can focus on their work; experience less stress and frustration at work—that is, *experience fewer stresses and strains on the job.*
▼ have more autonomy at work; have more meaningful jobs; are more satisfied with their learning opportunities on the job; and experience more challenge in their jobs—that is, *have better-quality jobs.*
▼ have more coworker support and work in a more family-friendly workplace—that is, *have more workplace support.*

Once again, the same conditions that we have been examining as critical factors in work and family life rise to the top, such as the quality of our jobs and the amount of autonomy and support we have. The same factors that affect our work life also affect our family life.

It is interesting that employed fathers experience more positive spillover from parenting to work. This is similar to the finding of other research that shows that fathers are happier in their less traditional role: being at home.

These findings continue to reinforce the point that I have been making throughout the book: the wisdom of the both/and approach rather than an either/or one. As I concluded in Chapter 5, the parents who cope most positively with work and family demands have both *personal resources* (they can raise their child the way they want to; they make family their priority) and *external resources* (the support of others). These are the parents who both are *intentional* and who have the *support* for being so!

WHAT'S THE BOTTOM LINE?

When we compare job-to-parenting spillover and parenting-to-job spillover, here's what we find:

▼ Jobs are more likely to reduce our energy for parenting than children are to reduce our energy for performing our jobs.

▼ Conversely, children are more likely to increase our energy for our work than our jobs are to increase our energy for parenting.

▼ Jobs are more likely to have a negative impact on our moods with our child than our children are to have negative impact on our moods at work.

▼ Conversely, children are more likely to improve our moods on the job than our jobs are to improve our moods with our child.

▼ Jobs are more likely to have a negative impact on our performance as parents than children are to have a negative impact on our performance at work.

If these results sound more like tongue twisters than research findings, I'll use a variation on a phrase adapted from a Clinton campaign mantra about the economy: "It's the job, stupid!" Jobs deplete us for parenting far more than parenting depletes us for our work. Yet, the business case has historically been made on the opposite assumption—children have been seen as drains on our productivity. The case for business's becoming family-friendly thus needs to be reframed: Business must recognize that children are assets rather than deficits. Moreover, since the Families and Work Institute's National Study of the Changing Workforce also finds that good-quality jobs, supportive workplaces, and reasonable job demands all are associated with indicators of productivity,[25] we ultimately have the possibility of a win/win proposition. Rather than seeing life off the job and on the job in opposition, the evidence points to mutual benefit: A happy parent is a better worker; efforts to improve workplaces can—for the most part—also help us be the kind of parents we would like to be!

How Do Work and Family Life Affect Us as Parents?

have spent many years trying to understand how work and family life affect us as parents. I have conducted numerous studies of work-family life over the years. I have convened groups of leading researchers to share what they have learned. I have culled through hundreds and hundreds of papers written by other researchers. I have traveled across the country interviewing parents and their children. Most recently, I have undertaken this nationally representative survey of more than 1,000 children and more than 600 employed mothers and fathers and have pored over the findings to extract the story they tell. With the final results in, it was time to go back to the source—to talk to parents and children, to share these findings, and again to listen.

With the help of a colleague, I brought together a group of parents and children: 4 employed fathers, 5 employed mothers, and 7 children, ages 8 through 15.

As the parents and children assembled, there was some visible tension about having this discussion in front of each other because, as became immediately clear, these families—like most families everywhere—had not talked *intentionally* about these issues before. I began by asking the children a question that we had asked the children in our survey: "If you were granted one wish to change the way that your mothers' or your fathers' work affects your life, what would that wish be?"

A girl said:

> *When I was younger, I wished they could go on more field trips with me.*

A boy said:

> *When I go home from school, sometimes I would like to be able to talk to someone.*

And another girl added that her mother's work-related calls bothered her:

> *When my mom is on the phone, I don't really get to talk to her.*

A boy also talked about Monday nights:

> *On Mondays I don't usually eat a good dinner because I have to cook.*

The children were talking about their feelings with a small *f*—they were talking about *details* of their lives that they might like to change (not the "big picture" wishes we found in the survey). In contrast, the parents—when asked to guess what children would wish—talked about children's feelings with a capital *F*:

> *Kids want their mothers to be home.*

Although the children were talking about both mothers and fathers, the parents veered straight to mothers: "Kids want their *mothers* to be home."

I asked another question: "Can you tell what kind of day your parents have had at work?" One of the boys was the first to answer:

> *I can tell what kind of day my parents have had. Sometimes if they come home and they are mad, they tell me to be quiet or go away. They don't want to talk. They want to be by themselves. If I ask them a question, I mean they hear me but it's not like they*

really want to hear me. On a good day, they come home and they
are happy.

Noting what kind of day your parents have had is strategic, he said, because you have to pick the right moments to ask for something you want.

A teenage girl preferred her parents to be neither too happy nor too burned out:

> *When they are in a good mood, they ask a million questions when*
> *they get home. When they aren't in a good mood, they don't talk.*
> *I am not sure I like it either way. I like it in the middle.*

Why?

> *If I've had a bad day, I don't want to talk. I am older. There are*
> *more things that happen to you [when you are older] and some-*
> *times you don't want to talk.*

Again, the children were talking about everyday normal feelings, of reading their parents' moods, and of the match between their own moods and those of their parents—something that all kids do. But again, when the parents spoke, the conversation veered back to working *mothers*. One mother justified her working:

> *My daughter shares with a lot of people how proud she is of what*
> *I do and that makes me feel really good.*

Another mother described her feelings about her work life/home life as a perpetual roller coaster:

> *I have a 19-year-old daughter and a 15-year-old daughter and*
> *I have been doing this for a very long time. From day one. And*
> *sometimes I feel like the walking wounded and sometimes I feel*
> *completely heroic. Other days I think that I am completely out of*
> *my mind that I have gone at this pace. Who am I to be [work-*
> *ing] when she is home for two days sick and I only stay home for*
> *one of them?*

In response her daughter looked at her quizzically and said:

> *On days when I am sick, I am upset but I can deal.*

What is going on? Why is this group of employed fathers and mothers—in which some of mothers have worked for years, even from "day one"—continuing to question whether mothers are doing the right thing by working? Of course, there are many reasons:

▼ **There are societal expectations and pressures.**

As one mother put it:

> *There is conflict between having this idealized vision of what a great job is and having this idealized vision of what being a great parent is. And the higher the bar gets raised on either of those fronts, the more difficult it is to meet those expectations.*

A father added:

> *The bar gets set so high that you could take the rest of your life off trying to fill these expectations.*

He continued:

> *That's all a part of [the] better, smarter, earlier, faster [mind-set] that permeates all parts of our society.*

For most of the mothers, these expectations continue to mean that if you are "going to have it all" (i.e., work), then you are going to have to "do it all." Studies by the Families and Work Institute have shown that the meaning of "do it all" has changed somewhat over the past two decades, as many parents have given up on having a perfect house and fathers have begun to contribute more to family work. Nevertheless, both parents feel the pressure to prove that their family decisions are benefiting, or at least not harming, their children.

▼ **Some of these parents didn't have working mothers themselves, so they have not internalized the idea that it might be okay.**

I think about my own experience growing up. I mean nobody's mother worked.

▼ **It is an era of self-conscious parenting, with advice—sometimes contradictory advice—from all corners.**

The bookstore has four shelves of books for parents.

▼ **Parents' family or community may not support mothers' working.**

Parents talked about the pressure to participate at school. They talked about teachers ("working mothers themselves!") who made life difficult by scheduling school activities when the mothers (note: they said mothers) could not participate. They talked about mothers and mothers-in-law who were blind to their working:

It took a long time for [my mother-in-law] to be proud of what I did. She wouldn't even talk about it. My job didn't exist. Only [my husband's] job existed.

This mother felt so troubled by these pressures that:

I feel I need to prove that my kids are okay even though I may not be home [all day].

Like a compass needle always drawn to magnetic north, no matter what the topic, the conversation returned time and time again to the issue of whether employed mothers were doing the right thing. Asked for concluding remarks, a father said:

We just don't know yet what impact our working has had on this generation. This is a brand-new thing. Twenty years from now we will have a better idea.

A mother added:

I hope my kids don't [ultimately] feel bad that I worked.

This question to a greater or lesser degree preoccupies employed parents throughout the country. Asking parents about their attitudes—as we did for this study—reveals this truth. So does the television news that comes on while I am writing this chapter. The teaser for the late night news all evening was "Good news for mothers: A new study shows that their working doesn't hurt their children." Yet this study also included fathers—a fact overlooked by the media.[1] And this study is hardly news, albeit well designed and more longitudinal than most. As we noted in Chapters 1 and 2, for the past 20 to 30 years there have been similar studies with similar findings.

Do I think that it is wrong for parents to question? No. These parents reveal that they really care by asking again and again whether mothers are doing the right thing. As one father put it, we are living in a transitional period (though history would indicate that, for the most part, mothers have always worked).[2] And according to one mother, the fact that people are living different kinds of lives "has created a lot of good questions." She continued:

> I think that they are good questions. And a lot of us have arrived at some good answers. But it is my hope that my daughters have a different kind of experience.

Although I don't think that it is wrong to question, I do think that these mothers and fathers are stuck in the wrong question. It's part of our ongoing tendency to see this issue through an either/or perspective. These mothers *are* working, by choice and by necessity. So the question ought to shift from should *mothers* work to how do *mothers' and fathers'* jobs affect them and thereby their children?

It is my hope that adding children's voices to this national conversation will help us become unstuck and shift our focus. When asked for concluding remarks, one boy said:

> How a kid grows up has to do with personality—what you want to do, who you are. I think that parenting helps. It makes it better or worse.

He brought the group to laughter by adding:

> Parents can *give you all of these problems that put you on a talk show.*

But this child had other lessons:

> *If you are trying as a parent, if you are leading by example, if you are following what you preach, then your kids will turn out pretty good. Some people are going to be a little bit better parents than others. [Mothers'] working isn't the main problem.*

He also noted that parents can use working as a catchall explanation allowing them to avoid or deny a more clear-eyed assessment of their children's problems:

> *Working is used as an excuse. "Oh, I am working." Working does change things somewhat. But some parents are saying that the reason my kid has these problems is because I wasn't able to be home.*

His father summarized:

> *He is saying that some parents are using working as an excuse for not taking the responsibility for a child's bad actions. It has nothing to do with the [fact that] parents work.*

So what does it have to do with? To address that question, we conducted a final set of analyses.[3]

PUTTING IT ALL TOGETHER

We've been exploring several questions: How do work and family life flow together? How do work and family life affect us as parents? How does our parenting affect our children's development? And how does all of this affect us, in turn, back at work?

I used a water analogy to describe spillover in Chapter 6, and I will continue to use it to describe the full work-family conceptual model we've developed. Here, we will test the model against our empirical data.

Think of work and family life as forming a circle of moving water—a stream with currents that diverge and converge as the water circulates. Think of the supports we have in our lives—our families, our friends at home and at work, and our communities—as forming the streambed, shaping the flow for better or for worse. At times, the water moves smoothly; at times it is turbulent, broken by rocks that jut out.

A Model of Work and Family Life

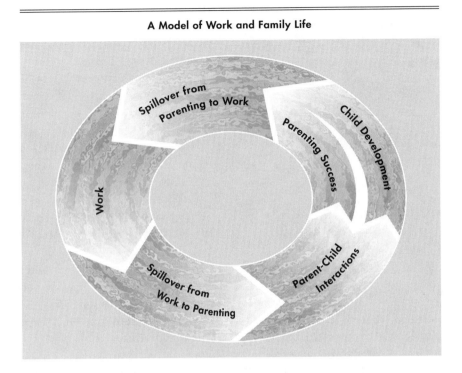

Let's think of ourselves as navigating the stream. To steer through these waters, we need to understand the many outside forces affecting our passage—some of which are beyond our control; others of which are not. And we need to know ourselves: our life priorities and where we really want to go. We are at the helm, with at least some control over the course of our voyage.

TRACING THE FLOW FROM WORK TO SPILLOVER

The University of Massachusetts study that was the media story of the week showing that "a mother's employment outside the home has no significant negative effect on her children" quickly moved into the talk radio realm, where it was met with doubt, questions, even hostility. Interestingly, this study was never intended to pit working mothers against mothers at home. In fact, the comments of the principal investigator, Lisa Harvey, on the press release were "I think that this [study] suggests that there is not one right way of doing things for all families. For some families it may be best for both parents to be

A Model of Work and Family Life

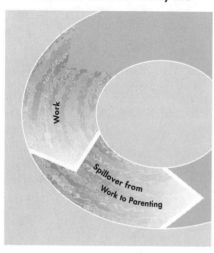

employed and for some families it may be best for one parent to stay home."[4] Why do such findings stir up such strong public opinion? First, because they raise an issue that is not settled in the minds of many parents, whether or not the mother in the family is employed. And second, because employed parents know intuitively that their work does have some impact on their children.

In my view, the studies to date have not been looking at parental work fully. Like the University of Massachusetts study, most studies have assessed such factors as when the mother returned to work after childbirth, how much time the mother worked, and whether the working was continuous. Most have not looked at the *conditions* of the mothers' and fathers' jobs.

In the Ask the Children study we have identified many of the conditions at work that spill over, affecting how we steer a course in the stream of work and family life.

- ▼ *Jobs that demand more time*: the number of hours we work, the days we work, the nights we travel, and the amount of time we work at home before and after work.
- ▼ *Stresses and strains on the job*: our ability to focus, the feeling that we don't have enough time to get everything done, and the stress and frustration at work.
- ▼ The *quality of our jobs*: the autonomy we have at work, the meaningfulness of our jobs, the satisfaction we have with our learning opportunities, and the challenge we experience on the job.
- ▼ The *workplace support* we have: support from supervisors, coworkers, and the family-friendliness of the workplace culture.

These currents flowing from our lives at work interact in many ways—sometimes reinforcing one another, sometimes counteracting each other, always interacting with who we are and who we want to be.

These currents spill over, interfering with our parenting, affecting our moods and energy levels in positive and negative ways.

TRACING THE FLOW FROM SPILLOVER TO PARENT-CHILD INTERACTION

Can spillover from work actually affect our interactions with our children? One of the fathers in the group I met with feels strongly that it can:

> I feel very caught up with the system and the stress that comes from the system. I have mentioned to [my wife] that something must be wrong because I feel that the weeks go by and the weeks go by and the years go by and I feel like I don't really have control.
>
> I am waiting for that one day when maybe someone will walk into my office and say that we are going to let you go. Okay, now I have to confront all of those issues that I have been pushing aside because I get up at 5 in the morning to go to work and I don't really walk into the house until 8. And then it's Friday. And then it's the weekend stuff and then it's Monday again. That's the life. It just rolls and rolls and rolls. There is something wrong with this.

Another father challenged him:

> It may be that all of this guilt has no relevance at all on how your kids turn out. If you go to work at 10 and come home at 3, you may have the same kind of child 20 years hence.

And the father answered:

> That's true, because I have no idea of the future, but it must have an impact on my children because it has an impact on me. So if it has an impact on me, it has an impact on them.

We can test these two fathers' differing assumptions: Does spillover from work affect our interactions with our children?

In earlier chapters we've discussed what studies find is the crux of positive parent-child interaction. First, it's whether the child is cared for and loved. Second, it's whether the child is responded to by an adult who can read the child's cues and clues, can understand what the child is trying to say, then engage in a give-and-take conversation or interaction, back and forth, back and forth. In other words, it is communication, whether verbal or nonverbal, in which there are real listening, understanding, and response.

In this study, we looked at four facets of parent-child interactions that I hypothesized make it more likely that there will be a warm and responsive relationship.

1. Spending time together

To engage in that enriching give and take, there has to be time. A mother in this group said:

> Just because you are at home, [doesn't mean that] you are going to have quality experiences with your kids. The odds do increase with the amount of time that you spend. There is always that unsuspected moment when you are just hanging out that all of a sudden you have a good conversation. And the more that you are around, the more you might have that kind of conversation.

A father responded strongly:

> I agree. Just don't call it quality time!

From these parents' comments, it appears that they are just as eager as I am to banish the notion of quality time. "Quality time" has become an unattainable goal, even a burdensome one. It's as if we are supposed to be having a certain ratio of fabulous experiences per hours spent with our children. It's as if there is no room in this scenario for just being together—much less for the difficult moments, the upsets, the annoyances, and the anger that are a part of family life. Sometimes when I hear parents in the seminars I conduct talk about quality time, I begin to picture angels singing and violins playing—that's how unrealistic the expectations are. The notion of quality time has replaced the notion "And they got married and lived happily ever after." But when we add children's voices to this discussion, the clues children give us indicate that we can begin to move away from the idea of quality time. I suggest that we use *hang-around time*. These are words that parents use. For example:

Some of the moments I remember most were the breakfasts my mom and I used to have on Saturday mornings or fixing dinner together at night. We would just hang around together. The size of the dinner salads I made were in direct proportion to the amount of "stuff" I had to tell my mom about the events of my day.

2. Spending unrushed time

All of the parents and children in this group talked about the fast pace of life today, not only for adults for also for children who have activities after school and interests they pursue. As one of the mothers put it:

To have a hectic life is a given.

The children, however, differentiated between following a schedule and feeling rushed. One child talked about the schedule for morning showers in her house. It was a highly organized schedule, but it didn't feel rushed because everyone knew the so-called rules. Another child told of getting breakfast down to a 6-minute science so he could sleep as late as possible. He was moving quickly but he didn't feel rushed because the choice to sleep a bit later was his. This differentiation is key. We don't have to drop everything to have unrushed times with our children—nor could we. We just need to be mindful of having some time when "we are going with the flow."

Most of the families in this group had established rituals to provide unrushed time. For example, one father had a routine in which his oldest daughter dropped him off at the train so she could take the car:

We got to ride in the car together—we had a good time in the car. We could say a few nice words to each other and start the day in the right way.

For other families, it was the ritual of having a special dinner together on a regular basis:

Every Friday night, we have a TV dinner. We have trays in the family room. We don't go out. Before we watch TV, we all go around the room and say what we are grateful for. And just that little moment gives us time to regroup. Monday through Friday, every morning is going to be dreadful but at least we have Friday nights.

Another family also had a Friday night dinner ritual, in which each member in turn talked about the best part and the worst part of his or her week.

Is there a magic amount of unrushed time that is necessary? No, there is no magic number that is right for all families, but there is probably an amount that is right for your family and for mine. And we can usually tell when it is getting off kilter: when, in the words of one of the children, there is not enough "mellow time."

3. Spending focused time

Spending some mellow time together becomes the catalyst for focused time. As I've said in previous chapters, it is fascinating to me how often parents use the word *focus* when they describe a real connection with their children. Listen for it. I am sure that you will hear it as I did again and again over the years I spent researching and writing this book. And I certainly see it in the research literature on the guideposts for healthy child development.

What is focused time? It is the time that we spend communicating and connecting. I recently heard a speech about the brain development of young children in which it was assumed that stimulating brain development involved providing black and white mobiles for a baby to look at, toys for the baby to reach for or explore, even sheets of colored paper for the baby to crawl on. This speaker missed the main point about all development. It is through *relationships* that babies learn. Instead of showing the baby a mobile with shapes that look like faces, parents and other care givers will do a lot better to face the child, imitate his or her "dadadadada," bang the table when the baby bangs the table, smile when the baby smiles, and turn away when the baby has had enough.

The fields of developmental psychology and neurobiology have scientific language to describe this interaction. Peter Fonagy of the University College of London talks about the ability of the parent to think about (reflect on) the child's *state of mind* as well as his or her own state of mind. The parent attempts to understand the child's feelings, thoughts, intentions, beliefs, perceptions, and memories. Children who are understood in turn learn to understand other people. Allan Schore and Daniel Siegel, both of the University of California at Los Angeles, talk about *attuned* and *contingent communication*—in which the parent reacts directly as a function of what his or her child says or does, and vice versa.[5]

There is a danger that the notion of focused time will replace that of quality time and become just another "rock in the knapsack of shoulds" that parents carry on their backs. Focused time involves the give-and-take of interaction. It is different from quality time because it isn't always a happy time. It is just as likely to involve resolving a difficult problem or conflict in the family as it is to be having a happy conversation.

There is also the danger with focused time that parents will think that there are a magic number of "focused minutes" that they should have with their child each day. Despite these dangers, I think that the notion of focused time is crucial and must be stressed.

The parents in my group set the stage for this kind of connection to happen. One father talked about the importance of spending time alone with each child whether by chance or by design:

> *Our kids love it when one of the kids is out of the house. The other one loses interest in the TV and plops in the middle of the kitchen or whatever room you happen to be in and they can demand that time when there is no competition from the sibling.*

Parents also have to clear the deck emotionally so they can be "open to those moments":

> *You know those moments and you take advantage of them.*

The children in this group were very attuned to when their parents were "there but not there." According to an 11-year-old,

> *You can tell because you get a short and simple answer.*

In our one-on-one interviews with children, they told us that they would put their hands on their parents' faces and tell them to "tune in, please." My favorite technique was described by a parent, who reported that her child would say, "Earth to Mom, Earth to Mom." Still another asked her father to repeat to her what she had just said to see whether he was really listening.

One of the boys in our group didn't think the latter was a very good idea because some parents are very good at parroting back words, even though they haven't really been listening. This child had a listening test:

> *When my parents aren't paying attention, then I will say outra-*
> *geous things (like goldfish on the grass) in the middle of a sen-*
> *tence just to test if they are really listening.*

The children understood that their parents might be preoccupied.
And although they might not like to wait for attention, they typically
understood:

> *When I was sick, my mother stayed home with me but she had*
> *to get work done. I understand. Sometimes it is kind of frustrat-*
> *ing because you want to talk and she will say, "You can't talk*
> *because I have to get some work done." She is there but you can't*
> *talk to her. But I understand.*

This child suggested that parents set aside times when they don't
want to be interrupted and times when interruptions are okay and, in
fact, told of a child whose mother used that technique successfully. The
others agreed: They didn't mind waiting, but they liked clarity so that
"Just a minute" didn't multiply into many minutes, even hours.

The key, according to one of the girls, is the parent's intention:

> *I think that something that goes on with kids is "Wouldn't you*
> *rather be with me than do this other thing?" I want my mom to*
> *like her job but not more than she loves me.*

I'd say this goes for dads, too. Focused time is important.

4. Spending nonstressful time

The fourth kind of time that is important is nonstressful time. We all
need time with our children that is relaxed and not pressured. Does this
mean that there is no room for conflict or stress? Not at all. There will
be stress in parenting, but it's better if we can deal with the stress constructively rather than denying it or blaming ourselves for it.

In fact, I think that one of the best gifts parents can give their children is to teach them how to deal with stress constructively. Here's an
example. Rather than wishing that siblings wouldn't fight ("Just go
away"), rather than denying the siblings' feelings of anger toward each
other ("You really love your sister"), or rather than putting children
down ("You are an awful person for fighting with your brother"), parents would do well to teach their children how to negotiate with each
other without being hurtful.

A Model of Work and Family Life

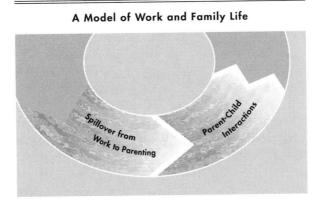

Do interference and spillover from work affect the types of interactions we've just discussed?

As an example, let's look at focused interactions. We find that:

▼ parents who experience more interference and more negative spillover from work have less focused interactions with their child.

Interestingly, negative spillover is slightly reduced for parents who experience some positive spillover from work to parenting. It is also slightly reduced for parents who feel that they have meaningful work and the support of their coworkers. But negative spillover is almost *swept away* for parents who:

▼ can raise their child the way they wish.
▼ have friends and family they can turn to when they have a problem with their child and feel comfortable accessing that support.
▼ feel that the nonparental child care they have used is good for their child.
▼ have employed spouses who share the care of their child more equally.

Let's take two other examples: rushed interaction and stressed interactions with our child.

▼ Parents who experience more negative spillover and more interference from work are more likely to feel rushed and stressed with their child.

▼ When work is given more priority than family life, negative spillover and interference lead to even more stressed and rushed interactions between parents and children.

▼ Positive factors at work and at home (such as support and autonomy) do little to reduce the negative impact of spillover on parent-child interactions.

TRACING THE FLOW FROM PARENT-CHILD INTERACTIONS TO FEELINGS OF SUCCESS

As we continue to follow the process we are mapping, we find that parents who spend more time with their child and who have more unrushed time, more focused time, and more nonstressful time feel much more successful as parents. The statistical relationships are very strong!

In addition, four characteristics of life off the job make us feel more successful:

▼ having nonparental child care arrangements that we see as being good for our child.

▼ having friends and family we can turn to when we have a problem with our child.

▼ feeling comfortable turning to those friends and family for support.

▼ feeling free to raise our child the way we want to.

One factor makes us feel less successful as parents:

▼ putting a higher priority on work than on family life.

Again, our priorities are at the helm.

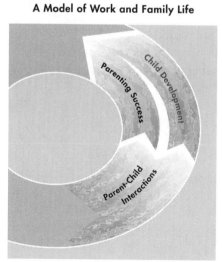

A Model of Work and Family Life

TRACING THE FLOW FROM PARENT-CHILD INTERACTIONS TO BEHAVIOR PROBLEMS

To what extent do the interactions we have with our children affect their development? The parents whom I brought together vacillated about the extent of their impact on their children. At times, they talked about having a profound impact, almost as if they molded their children like pieces of clay. At other times, they talked as if their children were simply the product of genes.

> *You look at the people who grew up in the 1930s whose parents were working and getting paid by piecework in sweatshops and their kids went on to City College and became Nobel Prize winners.*

Rather than being an either/or proposition, both views are true. Who a child becomes is a product of the *inextricable* interaction of his or her genetic endowment with experience. It is nature *and* nurture.

When we assess how parents' interactions with their children are linked with child behavior problems, we find a *very* strong connection. Parents who spend less time with their children and who have more rushed, more stressful, and less focused interactions with them are more likely to have children who:

▼ are unhappy, sad, or depressed.
▼ don't get along with other children.
▼ have trouble concentrating or paying attention for long periods.
▼ feel worthless or inferior.
▼ act too young for their age.
▼ are nervous, high-strung, or tense.

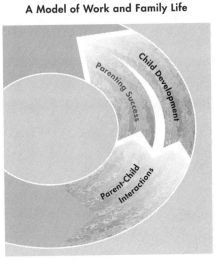

A Model of Work and Family Life

Parenting Success
Child Development
Parent-Child Interactions

Returning to the analogy of the stream, it is as if at this point, there is only one major current that makes a difference—the interactions parents have with their child. It is to be noted that we didn't measure other factors that are known to matter, such as the influence of the peer group.

TRACING THE FLOW FROM FEELINGS OF SUCCESS AND CHILDREN'S BEHAVIOR TO SPILLOVER FROM PARENTING TO WORK

As we continue to follow the work-family flow in our analyses, we now consider spillover from parenting to work.

Spillover from work to parenting has been an important undercurrent throughout the stream, and it reasserts itself strongly here. However, it is not negative spillover, but *positive* spillover, that makes itself powerfully felt.

▼ Parents who experience positive spillover from work to parenting, who feel successful as parents and believe that their child is developing well, reinvest this positive energy in work.

There is a crucial message to employers in this finding: The positive things that happen to us as a result of our jobs and the positive things that happen to us at home *both* contribute to an increased investment in work. Whereas some employers may see family life as beside the point, it is anything but that. Good experiences at work flow into good experiences at home, which pay dividends back at work.

My friend Bea Romer, the wife of the former governor of Colorado,

A Model of Work and Family Life

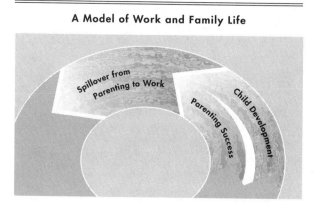

Roy Romer, said it best: "My husband always made better decisions for the state when he had played with his grandchildren over the weekend."[6]

A Model of Work and Family Life

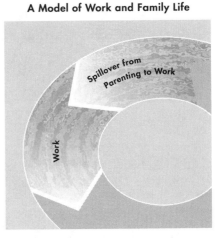

TRACING THE FLOW FROM SPILLOVER FROM PARENTING TO WORK BACK TO WORK

Now we return full circle, back to work.

We find that parents who say that they are in a worse mood at work, have less energy for their jobs, have more trouble concentrating at work, and produce lower-quality work—all because of their children—feel far more unsuccessful at work and dislike their work more. Conversely, parents who say that their children give them more energy and put them in better moods at work are far more likely to feel successful at work and to like their jobs more. So, the flow goes round and round: from work to family to work to family to work.

Because statistical analyses can seem abstract and hypothetical, let's look at the model we have developed through the story of one family.

AN EXAMPLE: THE SANDERSON FAMILY[7]

By any standard, Cathy and Fred Sanderson have demanding full-time jobs, although Fred recently has increased the intensity of his job at the same time that Cathy has decreased that of hers.

For a decade, Cathy headed a small national company. She headed out on the 7:09 train every morning to the city, to a company where she sometimes "felt like the mother" dealing with ongoing employee strife. Although she was in charge, she felt as if her schedule ran her. And though she controlled the budget, she was always worrying about bringing in money. A couple of years ago, on a family vacation on top of a mountain in Maine, they met another family who asked aloud what Cathy and Fred had been asking themselves.

> *This woman said to me, "Have you accomplished anything?"*
> *Without a moment's pause, my daughter answered, "No."*

Cathy believed in the kind of work she did, but this particular job clearly was draining her. She was especially shaken by her daughter's response. Many of the conditions of Cathy's job were ones we have found lead to burnout. That "mountaintop" experience turned Cathy's latent desire to find another job into an active search. She began to look for a job that was closer to home, that was more connected to her community, and that was more meaningful and less stressful. The job she found was heading a much smaller organization in the same field, but one that was 5 minutes from her house. As she was looking for a new job, Fred, who worked at a national social service organization, changed his job assignment, increasing his travel to 2 or 3 days a week and was less available to the family.

Cathy describes how her work demands used to interfere with parenting her two children, Maria, now 18, and Ben, now 15:

> *Certainly with the structure of a commuting job there were times*
> *I would say I would be home at a certain time and then [would*
> *call] to say that I was taking the next train and the question*
> *would be: "Should we wait to have dinner with you?"*

Work responsibilities weighed heavily on Cathy and there was inevitable negative spillover of job stress to home:

> *The children ask you if you had a bad day at work, and then*
> *they say, "Don't take it out on us." One of the problems of being*
> *the boss is that everybody else was being accommodated because*
> *that was important. I never yelled at anybody at work—for ten*
> *years I never yelled at anybody, but I yelled at my kids, and I*
> *would question that. It is not fair.*

Everyone in the family acknowledged that Fred's work has been less stressful than Cathy's. Even when he was "tired, anxious, or short with the kids," his job caused less distress. Maria reflects on how her parents came home from work:

> *My mom would have headaches all the time. They both used to*
> *spend a ton of time on the phone and [over]react to little*

things—it was just like the little things would [make them] flip on occasion.

At times, Maria and Ben also experienced this situation as not right. They would say, "It's not fair to take it out on us." At other times, Maria would leave her parents alone and wait to share her concerns: "I'll talk about it when you are not as stressed." Like many children of working parents, Maria tried to alleviate the situation, though she recognized her limitations:

> *I understand their jobs but I can't really help them. They can help me with my schoolwork because they have already been through high school, but [there's] not that much I can do for them in terms of work because I haven't been through that. I can do stuff at home, like cooking dinner. I can't really take any of the actual work pressure off them, but I can take the home pressure off.*

Ben, too, found a way to reduce stress on his parents: by living up to their expectations and not giving them cause to be concerned about him:

> *I don't think I need to take care of them. It's more like not putting a lot of stress on them, making it easier for them to be a parent, trying to be really good so that they don't have to yell at me or anything. I don't think it stresses them out to hear my problems as long as they don't have to worry about having to tell me what not to do.*

Did this pressure and stress harm the children? Not in a profound way. Both Maria and Ben are articulate, caring children. Why have their parents' work lives had less of an impact than they might have? Because, as our study finds, a positive home life and intentional parenting can reduce stress. Cathy says:

> *We have made it a point to think about our relationship with our kids and put it first.*

In addition, the Sandersons live in a close-knit, supportive community that includes their neighbors and friends. Both are very involved with their religious community, which they see as providing support and time to reflect. Cathy says:

> *The purpose of the Sabbath is to separate the workweek from the Sabbath. The word means to separate. The notion is that in order to be healthy, you have to have a break from anything that is work in order to restore yourself.*

The Sanderson family also believes in creating and sticking to key rituals and traditions, and these have served as antidotes to stress. Throughout their children's lives, they have intentionally maintained the sanctity of the dinner hour. They do not watch TV or answer the phone; they talk about the events of the day, focusing especially on Maria and Ben. Fred, the father, describes the ritual that has become very important in his family:

> *It goes one kid and then the other kid, and they take turns. I don't exactly keep track of who [goes] first, but one and then the other does a report of a school day, period by period, what happened after school. We listen to them and they talk. We ask them questions. We probe for more details. We tell other parents that their children are doing this or that, and those parents have no idea.*

Cathy and Fred used to include their own work-related matters in their dinnertime conversation, much as their own parents had. Now they have made a conscious decision not to talk about their work during dinnertime. Cathy explains:

> *I realized after a while that mostly what the children were hearing about was the frustrations. I tried to change that so they could hear about the good stuff, but I think it is easy to fall into just reporting on the problem and I do not think that is a good message for the kids.*

Maria and Ben value this family time. Maria, especially, appreciates the trust that she and her parents have and recognizes its foundation in their being able to talk with one another:

> *I never really understood the concept of not telling my parents something, because for me, you just did. They asked what you did in school and you just said it. When I got into middle school and I started having things that were like secrets from my friends, I guess I tested out my parents and they didn't tell any-*

one. They tell me secrets and tell me not to tell people. And so if your parents tell you things, then you can begin feeling comfortable telling them.

Maria doesn't question whether or not her parents should work, and neither do her parents. Rather, Maria thinks they feel guilty about how much work they do or about missing out on their children's activities. She accepts some responsibility for their guilt:

I say, "Well, why didn't you come today to my field hockey game?" I usually make them feel guilty. And then either they say, "Well, we really can't do anything about it," or "We'll try to make this many games," or "We'll come to the next one." A lot of times they make me feel guilty back. It's like this guilt game and it doesn't really lead anywhere.

Like any child with parents in any circumstances, Maria knows how to push the buttons that get the results she wants.

It's just like if you really want something, then sometimes you can make your parents feel guilty and you'll get it. But it doesn't always work.

The moments that mean the most to Cathy are the moments when she is really connecting with her children.

Now [that they are older], it is being available to them on their terms. Being around when they have a question. Being able to talk through a problem with them. Just being there when they are upset.

Her daughter concurs about the best times:

They are the times you spend with your parents and talk about issues and things that are happening in your life, I guess. Like one of my friends said she could not go out because her parents were spending some "quality time" with her and what they were going to do was watch movies. So I really didn't feel that was quality time, since she was not talking to her parents.

In describing the relationship between work and family life, Cathy says:

> *The point is you don't have to only pay attention to work or to the family. Not one or the other. You have to pay attention to the combination, to the choices you are making at all times.*

Her priority on the family is clear, but for her, there are inherent differences in the nature of work and the nature of family that make it difficult to manage them:

> *My work is both more compelling and more predictable in some ways. There is more structure to it. You have rules of behavior. Even when you are working with your kid on something like a school project or an essay, there is an emotional content to it that requires a lot of time, attention, patience, and resilience of you as a parent. You feel it more intensely and it is a more demanding relationship. There is more at stake.*

Fred also sees his work and family life as requiring constant decisions. He has a job that could consume him:

> *I could spend 24 hours a day, 7 days a week doing work, and still not put in all the time that needs to be put in to accomplish what I want to accomplish.*

But so could family life:

> *There are times I feel like either I should be spending more time with my family or more time at work. And there certainly is a tension there. And the answer is about how you divide your time and often it's not clear.*
>
> *A lot of it has to do with the demands of others. At work, it's getting back to people who are expecting information from me because they need to do something tomorrow. At home, there are the members of my family who need or want time with me and who I want to spend time with. The demands of work and family are equally compelling, though at one time or another, the demands from one side or another may be stronger.*
>
> *I feel very torn about it. You know you can't do everything, and there are some times that I just want to sit down and watch a basketball game or read a book. Sometimes I'm able to do it, but a lot of times I can't. I just feel it's really hard and I feel there*

are a lot of demands that I place on myself as well. So I really feel like it's a constant struggle to do well in all these arenas and to enjoy things you like to do by yourself as well.

NAVIGATING: A NEW CONCEPT

What is the right word to describe the interconnection, the harmony and disharmony, between work and family life that families experience—like the ones we've interviewed?

Most talk about "balancing." In some ways, *balancing* is a good word because it describes a process of continual motion, in which the challenge is to find the right equilibrium. And it describes two sides—work and family—that are different but linked in many ways. But in other ways, *balancing* is not a good word. It implies the either/or connection that I've been saying is not accurate, assuming that if you give to work you take away from family life.[8] Furthermore, although work and family are separate and some boundaries are obviously necessary, these boundaries have been blurring, particularly with the advent of technology that has brought work into our homes, creating what Bob Johansen, president of the Institute For The Future, has called the "everytime, everyplace workplace." Moreover, as our study shows, work flows into family and back into work again. Finally, balancing implies individual responsibility for solutions,[9] but as a parent in our group said, the community, the company, and the society all bear some responsibility as well.

The other word that is commonly used is *juggling*. But *juggling* sends the message that there are too many balls in the air; that only someone with consummate skill (a trained juggler) can manage. Otherwise all of these balls will fall to the ground, perhaps breaking, certainly scattering.

People who study work and family have been advocating the word *integrating*. Their point is that we have moved beyond the period in which we see work and family as separate spheres, linked by conflict or interference. This is true, but, as our study shows, the spillover from work to family and from family to work can be both positive and negative. We can't erase the negative aspects of managing work and family responsibilities any more than we should ignore the positive ones.

So it was time to look for a new word. I began by looking in the dictionary. I would look up one word and that would lead to another word and another. I created a folder called "The Word." I began to carry my list with me everywhere so that if someone said the right word, I would be able to write it down immediately. In fact, the *New York Times* profiled me for a regular feature in the Sunday Money and Business section on business leaders who describe what's in their briefcases, purses, or offices. I mentioned my list of words, and in response, I got a number of suggestions, including an offer from *Parenting* magazine to ask their readers for the right word. This was followed by a piece by the Newark *Star-Ledger* columnist Dory Devlin that described my search for the right word.

The parents who wrote in response to the *Parenting* magazine query echoed my assessment of why *balancing* doesn't work. One said that balance implies an "equal division of time and energy." What is needed is a word that frees parents up "to give thought to what's an appropriate level of investment at the time."

Since I was using a water analogy throughout the book, I spent a day by the beach writing down all of the words that came to mind. I asked my friend who is a consummate crossword puzzle and Scrabble pro for advice. I emailed my college roommate, who is very clever with words and slogans. She offered a number of interesting possibilities, like *concentrance* (a combination of *concentrate* and *balance*) and *synchrance*.

I also called on a number of experts. Still in pursuit of a water analogy, I asked William Ryan, the coauthor of *Noah's Flood* and a senior scientist at Lamont-Doherty Earth Observatory of Columbia University. I asked Edwin Nichols, a psychologist who studies the philosophical aspects of cultural difference; he has looked at the fact that the predominant logic system in the Euro-American culture is dichotomous (either/or), whereas diunital (the union of opposites) or other logics are used in various other cultures. He suggested the notion of *systemic convergence*: flowing and joining together. The mathematician Keith Devlin, dean of the School of Science, Saint Mary's College of California, suggested *concordance*: "Physicists use it to describe the way two systems (mechanical, electronic, or whatever) often tend to come into agreement or synchrony." I talked with Mark Morris, chairman of Bates North America, who suggested *confluence, congruence*, and *weaving*, among others. The management expert Phil Mirvis suggested *synthesize*. Paul Saffo at the Institute For The Future suggested *resilience*.

In all, I collected more than four dozen words: *orchestrating, coordinating, attuning, synchronizing, regulating, aligning, fitting*—to name a few others. And still the search continued. Then, late one afternoon, as Terry Bond of the Families and Work Institute and I were talking about the analyses for this chapter, the right word hit: *navigating*.

Navigating works because it is an ongoing process, not an ideal state. It works because it acknowledges the fluid interchanges among individual, work, family, and community rather than treating them as separate spheres. *Navigating* works because there are many forces and factors that combine to buffet or protect us. It works because to stay our course and maintain an even keel, we need to be well attuned to the environment around us. *Navigating* works because we are not expected to do it alone. But it really works because we ultimately set the course we want to follow. *Navigating* is the best descriptor of what we learned in our research journey.

In the course of searching for the right word, I came upon a passage in the *Tao Te Ching* that says what we found in another way:

In work, do what you enjoy.
In family life, be completely present.[10]

What Are We Teaching Children About Work and Family Life?

or as long as I can remember, adults have been asking children what they want to do when they grow up. The answers are often cute. Or funny. Recently, Ellen Ruppel Shell, a writer at *Parents* magazine set out to find out what parents are teaching children about their own work. After interviewing countless parents, she was surprised by what she heard—or in this case, didn't hear: Few parents seem to be *intentionally* telling children about their work. "They are too young," "They wouldn't understand," "I'm not sure; I haven't thought about it," parents explained.

A man who attended a recent speech I gave had a different response: "Whenever I try to tell my son about what interests me, what challenges me, what excites me about my work, I get the feeling that he isn't interested."

Isn't interested? I asked some children whether their parents told them about their work. Some said yes. One—whose father is an artist—said, "I can see his work in action." Another—whose father is in mortgage banking—said no. Why not? "He thinks I wouldn't understand what he does. It makes me furious."

I remember many years ago when I was teaching, and the 4-year-olds in my class used to "play" office. They would fill up bags with papers and carry them to the pretend "office," then turn around and carry them back to the pretend "home" again (a pretty realistic depiction of office life!). Fred Rogers of *Mister Rogers' Neighborhood* told me how as "little Freddie Rogers," he reported to his classmates that his father "goes to the office and does nothing." As he put it, "He wasn't a fireman; he wasn't a policeman; he wasn't directing traffic; he wasn't putting thermometers into children's mouths. So I thought he did nothing."[1] He also told me a story about Yo-Yo Ma, the well-known cellist. According to Fred Rogers, Yo-Yo Ma's son thought that he worked at the airport because this child would often go in the car to drop off his father or pick him up there. One child we spoke to thought her father—an international financier—threw around paper airplanes because that's what he did whenever she visited him at the office. And a man I spoke to said:

> *I took my nephew to work one day. At the end of the day, he asked me how much money I earned. I told him. He was astounded. He said, "You make that much money just for talking on the phone all day!"*

Children may not understand what we do. Explaining to a young child that an office worker does more than talk on the phone or a writer does more than play with a computer can be a challenge. Children also may not be interested. They want to tell us about what's going on with their lives and may be less enchanted by ours.

But I suspect that there is another reason why some of us may not be *intentionally* talking with our children about what we do. I suspect that it hearkens back to our ambivalence about working and about the impact of our work on our children. In fact, only 32 percent of employed parents describe the impact of their working on their child as "very positive," and the remainder of parents have a decidedly mixed assessment—with 12 percent putting their vote on the negative side of the ballot.

Moreover, we heard parents say repeatedly that "*other* parents" don't have the ambivalence they do:

From a mother:

> *Fathers have always worked so they don't obsess about it in the same way that mothers do.*

8.1

Employed Parents with a Child from Birth Through 18: Impact of Working on Their Child

Would you describe the impact that your working has had on your child as...

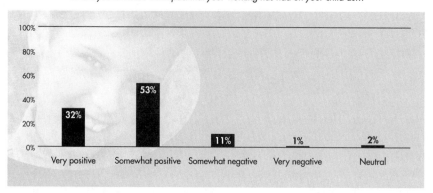

From a white person:

> *Working has been a "given" in so many other [racial] groups so they're probably used to it.*

And from a person who chooses to work:

> *If you HAVE to work, you don't worry about it. Sometimes I wish I had to work, that I didn't have a choice. It would be easier.*

In fact, these assumptions don't hold water. Rich and poor, black, white, and brown, fathers and mothers alike—all are equally likely to share similar ambivalence about the impact of their working on their child.

It makes sense that our ambivalence plays a role in how intentionally we talk to our children about work. If we say that we are leaving our children for something we love, it can feel like a breach of the parent-child bond; it can feel competitive. Ellen Rubell Shell concluded that she dodged her child's questions about work because she felt that talking about work would compromise the centrality of her relationship with her daughter. She didn't want her child to think that something else in her life was important.[2]

I have found that we may not talk *with* our children about what we do and the way we feel about our work, but we definitely talk about it *around* them. And—particularly if something is troubling us—the children are listening.

When I interviewed children years ago for the Family Study, I was impressed by how many children seemed to know what was going on with their parents at work. They knew that their mother's boss was capricious. They knew that their father was late in meeting a deadline. They knew what was causing their parents to be stressed. And many seemed to know these things whether their parents told them or not. Consider your own childhood. I bet you, too, have some stories to tell about what was going on in your parents' lives.

When you think about this, it makes sense. To survive, babies learn to be sensitive and responsive to their parents' facial expressions and tone of voice. Parents provide security, so babies are constantly checking in to be sure that they are safe. Children continue to do this as they get older. The better they are at reading faces and places, the safer they are likely to feel (and be).

I have often thought of children as detectives. Surrounded by information, some overt, some hidden, they continually sift through clues to try to understand their family lives. They listen, they watch, they ask questions, or they look uninterested (in effect, going undercover) while they are, in fact, paying acute attention.

At a 1998 speech, Arlie Hochschild, author of *The Time Bind*, described children as "eavesdroppers," engaged in a research project, "living in a glimpsed world."[3] They are actively trying to make sense of their world and their place in it, including how their parents' work affects their parents and thereby the family.

What, then, do children know about our work?

WHAT DO CHILDREN KNOW ABOUT THE *KIND OF WORK* WE DO?

Since work has traditionally been seen as the province of fathers, it is interesting that children know more about the kind of work their mothers do than what their fathers do. Though these differences aren't huge, they are statistically significant. Among children 8 through 18 years old, 66 percent know "a lot" about their mothers' work compared with 54 percent who know "a lot" about their fathers' work.

Parents are surprised to learn this. Moreover, neither mothers nor fathers seem to have thought much about the fact that they are providing children with a picture of the world of work and that their characterization of work may affect how children think about their own jobs or careers in the future.

How are children learning about their parents' work? Some children have direct knowledge from personal visits to their parents' workplaces. A 13-year-old girl talks about her office visits:

> I've been to my dad's office a couple of times when I didn't have school. They have meetings. My dad works on the computer and he helps people. He knows the most about computers and if something breaks, they'll call him up and he'll fix it.

Another teenage girl knows about her parents' work from spending time with them and from listening to conversations:

> I know what [my mom] does, 'cause when I go to work with her, I just basically see everything. And with my dad, I listen. I know he puts medicine in people to make them go to sleep.

Unfortunately, some children have little knowledge of their parents' work because of a lack of communication in the home. A 13-year-old girl says of her mother's work:

> I don't really know what [my mother] does. I just know that she types, and that's all I really know.

And of her stepfather:

> I ask [my stepfather] all the time and he's like, "Why do you always ask me?" I don't really know where he works at. He works at this building, and it's like for food and stuff. And they have like cups and silverware and stuff. And I ask like, "Do y'all box it or something like that?" And he's like, "No," 'cause he's like the assistant manager or something. And I go, "That's nice. You just have to tell me what you do because if somebody asks me I'm not going to know."

We found that children who believe that their families are in good economic health—that they have enough money to buy the things they need and can afford special things—know more about their fathers' work than children in families who see their families' economic situation as more precarious. Perhaps fathers who feel successful as economic providers share more about the kind of work they do than fathers who feel less successful. Furthermore, sons know more about their fathers' work than daughters do. In terms of mothers' work, there is no difference between what boys and girls know, but interestingly, younger children (8 through 12 years old) report knowing more than older children (13 through 18 years old).

In another study, Chaya Piotrkowski of Fordham University and her colleague Evan Stark found that children are most knowledgeable about the concrete aspects of their parents' jobs (job loss, the physical environment at work, the extent to which their parent must work hard) and less knowledgeable about the more abstract conditions (the parents' social relations at work, the parents' job control). Nevertheless, they are pretty good judges of whether their parents are satisfied with their jobs.[4]

In our study, we also found that children are more likely to speak to or visit their mothers than their fathers at work: Nine percent of children have no contact with their mothers at work compared with 18 percent who have no contact with their fathers.

For those children who do speak to or visit their parents at work, we asked whether their parents feel like the same or different people. This observation came from one adult, recalling her own childhood:

> My mother had this different voice, her "work voice." It was a stronger voice, a more serious voice. I was always mystified by that voice. Then one day I was making a work call from home and my husband commented that my voice had changed. I guess I have "become" my mother.

Almost three quarters of children who have contact with their parents at work (73 percent) report that their father and mother seem like the same person as they are at home. Twenty-one percent say that they seem like somewhat different people and 6 percent say they are "very different." Although one might expect children to respond in different ways for mothers and for fathers, they do not.

On the other hand, younger children 8 through 12 years old are four times more likely to feel that their mothers are very different in these two roles (21 percent) than older children 13 through 18 years old (5 percent). Perhaps older children are more accustomed to knowing their mothers as individuals—apart from their mothering role—than younger children are. These age differences do not appear in children's perceptions of their fathers.

WHAT ARE CHILDREN LEARNING ABOUT *HOW WE FEEL* ABOUT WORK?

Since I suspect that we are not talking *intentionally* about work to our kids because we don't want to set up a contest between our jobs and our children, I wondered whether we disguise our feeling about work. Do we say, "I wish I didn't have to go," "I wouldn't go if I didn't have to"? Beyond that, I wondered, Do children think that we like our work?

In our one-on-one interviews, we heard from children who thought their parents hated their work and others who thought their parents liked their work:

> *I know my dad wants to work because when he was a child he wanted to learn things for science and be a scientist. He works with cells. So he wanted to make new experiments and he thought it was fun—well, not fun but kind of interesting.*
>
> 10-YEAR-OLD BOY

Interestingly, only about two in five children (41 percent) think that their parents like their work a lot. Another 45 percent think that their parents like their work "somewhat," 10 percent say "very little," and 4 percent say "not at all." Children who see their families as having more than enough money to buy the things they need are more likely to think their fathers and their mothers like their work. Younger children are also more likely to think that their parents like their work than older children.

Do older children, therefore, have a more realistic perspective? No— if you take parents' opinions into account. In contrast to what children say, more than three in five employed mothers and fathers with a child from birth through 18 years old (62.5 percent) say that they like their work a lot.

When we compared the views of parents with a child 8 through 18 years old with the views of children of the same age, we found remarkable differences. For example, 60 percent of fathers say they like their work a lot compared with 41 percent of children who say so of their fathers. And 69 percent of mothers say they like their work a lot compared with 42 percent of children who say so of their mothers. These represent differences of 19 through 27 percentage points!

8.2

Comparison of Employed Parents and Children with Employed Parents: How Much Parents Like Work

To what extent do you like your work?/ Do you think your mother/father likes his/her work?	Father with child 8 through 18	Child 8 through 18 about father	Mother with child 8 through 18	Child 8 through 18 about mother
A lot	60%	41%	69%	42%
Somewhat	35	46	24	43.5
Very little	4	10	7	11
Not at all	1	4	0	4

Significance: *** = p <.0001.   *** = p <.0001.

We had also asked parents to *guess*, "To what extent does your child think you like your work?" When we compared fathers' guesses with children's views of how much their fathers like their work, we find that fathers assume that their child's opinion will closely parallel their own. This reminds me of a cartoon in which a father looks at his child and sees himself. However, when we make the similar comparisons of mothers and children, we see that mothers are less likely to expect that their child's opinion will parallel their own.

8.3

Comparison of Employed Parents and Children with Employed Parents: Parents' Assumptions and Children's Feelings About Parents' Liking Work

To what extent does your child think you like work?/ Do you think your mother/father likes his/her work?	Father with child 8 through 18	Child 8 through 18 about father	Mother with child 8 through 18	Child 8 through 18 about mother
A lot	61.5%	41%	59%	42%
Somewhat	33	46	30	43.5
Very little	4	10	9	11
Not at all	2	4	2	1

Significance: *** = p <.0001.   ** = p <.001.

These findings make it clear that mothers and fathers are not adequately communicating how much they like their work. It is understandably hard to say that we are leaving our child for something we enjoy and conversely much easier to say that we are only working because we "have to" or because we need money to pay for things for our kids. But the by-product of such behavior is that we are not fully teaching our children about the world of work, particularly that we can care about what we do to earn a living. Our interviews with children make it clear that children think it's positive for us to care a great deal about our jobs, just as long as these feelings don't eclipse our feelings for them.

WHAT DO CHILDREN THINK IS MOST IMPORTANT ABOUT OUR WORK?

I suspect that children would answer that money is the most important aspect of our work. Recall from Chapter 3 that when children were asked, "If you were granted one wish to change the way that your mother's/father's work affects your life, what would that wish be?" 23 percent (the highest proportion) wished that their mothers and their fathers would make more money.

Other evidence of the emphasis children put on money comes from the answers of children in the seventh through twelfth grades to the questions "What is the best thing about having a working father?" and "What is the best thing about having a working mother?" Money leads children's lists by a long way.

Several years ago, a study conducted by the Families and Work Institute made headlines because we found that women are now defining themselves as economic providers. In another study, we also found that women provide substantial economic support for their families: In dual-earner families with children, fathers contribute 63 percent of the couples' earnings and mothers contribute 37 percent. Now it appears clear that, although we continue to debate the benefits of maternal employment in political and policy circles, children accept their mothers as important economic providers as well as their fathers.[5]

8.4

Children in the Seventh through Twelfth Grades with Employed Parents: Best Thing About Having a Working Father/Mother

What is the best thing about having a working father/mother?	
My father/mother can buy things I need.	38%
My father/mother is able to buy me special things.	22
My father's/mother's work helps people.	12
I get to learn about the world of work.	3
I get to learn things that other kids do not learn.	3
I get to make friends.	1
I get to go to interesting places.	2
I get to help out with her/his work.	2
Other	8
Nothing	9.5

Although it is impressive that 12 percent of the children say that the one best thing about their mothers'/fathers' work is that it helps people, this figure pales beside the 60 percent of children who focus on money. In addition, only 3 percent of children say that they get to learn about the world of work.

When we don't share our feelings about work constructively, we are missing a chance to help frame our children's views about their own work in the future. The work-family researchers Chaya Piotrkowski of Fordham University and Evan Stark have found that a number of adults formed ideas about work when they were children and "they attribute decisions about their occupational lives to these early impressions" of their parents' work. They call parents' work experiences a "living laboratory" for children.[6]

Whenever I have the opportunity, I ask young adults about their best and worst memories of their own employed parents and how these experiences have affected their feeling about their own careers or jobs. Young adults mention their gratefulness to their parents for the sacrifices their parents have made for them and express their pride in seeing their parents in their work roles. They also mention their pain when a parent didn't pick them up from school as expected, didn't show up for an important event, made them wait for hours, was stressed out from dealing with irresponsible people at work, was too exhausted to pay attention to them, or was angry because of the tension at work. Almost inevitably these adults concede that their early experiences with their parents' work "hold much impact throughout life."

Are we "protecting" our children from the notion of work?

How we present our work to our children also has its roots in our images of childhood, particularly whether we see children as vulnerable and in need of protection from the outside world or as strong and capable of coping with difficulties. According to Arlene Skolnick of the University of California at Berkeley, our views of children have swung back and forth between these two poles. "One of the recurring themes of the growing literature on the history of the family is how ideas about children taken for granted in one era come to be regarded as false by the next." In medieval times, children were seen as "miniature adults" in paintings and other representations of them. This view was replaced by Calvinism's idea of the child as the demonic child, then by the image of the "noble savage" in the late eighteenth century. In the Victorian era childhood was a "never-never land of fun and games," but in America, this happy view coexisted with the Puritan image of the demonic child. Then, with the advent of Freudian theory and developmental psychology, children became defined by their "place on a staircase of development," by their ages and stages. As they grow, they move from vulnerability to competence.[7]

The child's role in the economic survival of the family has also undergone change. In the early days of this country, children were seen as necessary for family survival. They were needed to help till the fields, plant the seeds, harvest the crops, make clothes, cook, and watch over the smaller children. Until child labor laws were enacted in the 1920s and 1930s, a number of children worked grueling hours in dismal industrial situations.

Now that children are no longer integral partners in their family's economic enterprise, they have become priceless—parents scrimp and save for them and spend a great deal of money to raise them. Viviana Zelizer of Princeton University asks, "How did the social valuation of children change so dramatically within a relatively short period of time? Why did the sentimental value of children's lives increase just when their contribution to the household disappeared?"[8]

Diane Ehrensaft at the Wright Institute in Berkeley, California, argues that there is a new conception of the child that is an amalgam of various images from the past. She calls the child of today the "kinder-dult," born of the tension that parents face in managing work and family life. She feels that we have conceived a double image of a child who is half miniature, competent adult; half innocent, vulnerable cherub.[9]

Our generation was born to feel that our horizons were limitless, that we should be "all that we can be." But as adults we see schools where children harm other children; we live in a world of drive-by shootings and "stranger danger." We also see a world where the prices of success and failure are high, where it's "winner take all." So we simultaneously want to push our children to perform (to be "all that *they* can be") and to protect them.

In addition, we feel guilty that we can't be with our children more. Guilt can lead us to overcompensate, according to Ehrensaft. We figuratively say to our children, "I ask so much of you in my absence, how can I ask anything of you in my presence?" She feels that both fathers and mothers are drill sergeants by day and fairy godparents by night. We both pressure and coddle our children.

To the extent that this split image actually exists, it can be dysfunctional. In fact, Ehrensaft calls for creating a more integrated image of children today. I think that it is our fundamental *ambivalence* about our vulnerable children/our competent children—how well they are faring and how well we are caring for them when we work—that colors the way we present our work to our children.

Operating in the shadow of ambivalence, we tend not to be aware that we are teaching children about work, whether we intend to or not. I am reminded of how we talked with children (or, more accurately, talked *around* children) about the Gulf War. Many parents I spoke to for several television shows on the topic (granted it was a very limited group) didn't think that their children were paying attention when they talked about the war to other adults. They also didn't think that the children were tuned in to the nonstop television coverage of the war blaring the latest news from the front. I found, however, that many children were paying acute attention. Always detectives, they were trying to figure out where the Gulf is ("Near New Jersey," said one child). Trying to figure out whether they were safe ("Bombs could hit us," a child said). Trying to figure out whether their parents were going to be sent to war. Because they sensed their parents' tension, some of the children I interviewed did not ask their parents directly about what was happening. One wonders whether this dynamic would also hinder children's asking their stressed-out parents about their work.

Children do seem attuned to our tensions about work. Yet, as many times as I have told the story about the child who knew her mother's boss was asking her to do inappropriate tasks or the child who knew that his father was supposed to train someone who was a jerk, I have always found that parents in the audience react with surprised laughter: "I didn't realize they are listening." But as you will see, many are.

What is the worst thing about having a working father and mother?

In addition to asking older children about the best things about having a working father/a working mother, we asked them about the "worst thing." A considerable and impressive number of children said, "Nothing" (38 percent).

Other children, however, worry about their parents' stress level. "My father is stressed out by work," "My mother is stressed out by work," report 30 percent of the children. As parents, we might have guessed that our children would focus on not having enough time together. But time per se is not the major theme of children's concern. Almost twice as many children (30 percent) say that the worst thing about having a working mother/father is that their parent is stressed out by work as say, "I don't have enough time with my father/mother" (16 percent).

Children are sensitive to the stress and energy levels of their parents:

> *My mom's almost always tired. And my dad, if it's a hard client, then he'll be kind of grouchy because he had a hard time.*
>
> 9-YEAR-OLD GIRL

> *I wish that my parents wouldn't be so stressed out when they come home. 'Cause it usually bothers me to see them so stressed and tired. They can't concentrate. Just let them be like cool when they come home—not stressed out, but calmed down.*
>
> 12-YEAR-OLD GIRL

Obviously, parents at home can have bad days, just as parents at work can. The point here is that we probably are not considering how our bad days at work affect our children's picture of work. We are not using the bad days as an opportunity to tell children, "It's not your fault that I am upset." And we are not telling children the lessons we've learned about how to deal successfully with the frustrations and problems we encounter at work.

8.5

Children in the Seventh Through Twelfth Grades with Employed Parents: Worst Thing About Having a Working Father/Mother

What is the worst thing about having a working father/mother?	
My father/mother is stressed out by work?	30%
I do not have enough time with my father/mother?	16
I do not have my father/mother around when I need him/her?	8.5
My father/mother does not pay attention to me?	1
Other	6
Nothing	38

DO CHILDREN WORRY ABOUT THEIR PARENTS?

In our one-on-one interviews with children, we often heard them use the word *worry*. We expect parents to worry about their children—but children worrying about their parents?

Almost one third of the children (32 percent) 8 through 18 in our study say they worry about their parents "very often" or "often." That is an astounding number. When I add children's "sometimes" responses to this figure, the percentage goes up to almost two thirds (65 percent). Finding that two out of every three children worry about their parents on a fairly regular basis should be a wake-up call to us all. Because no one has ever "asked the children" about this before, we cannot tell whether this is an increase or a decrease in how much kids worry, but as a parent and professional, I find it troubling.

Who seems to be worrying? Our results indicate that girls are worrying more than boys. Other than that, there are no other differences in who worries.

What is the *main* reason they worry? Most (37 percent) say, "Because we are a family and families care about each other"—a heartwarming answer. Next, they say that that they worry because their parents are very stressed (25.5 percent). I've noted that many children wish that their parents would be less stressed by work, and that many also mention that the worst thing about having an employed parent is their parent's stress. As it turns out, that's why they worry about us, too. They also worry because their parents are very tired (11 percent).

These answers add yet another important piece to the puzzle I have been putting together throughout the book. Yes, there is a problem about our work, but it is not *that* we work. Once again, it is *how* we work. Work can be stressful. Work can be tiring. And stressed and tired parents cause children to worry. One 10-year-old girl we interviewed asked what used to be called the $64,000 question:

> *You know I'm proud of her, but I mean really, if she's so good, why do they make her work so hard?*

ARE OUR CHILDREN "PARENTING" US?

Worried children often say they "take care" of their parents in order to make them less stressed or tired. An 18-year-old girl tells us:

> *When I am home I help out with the house. Cleaning up and cooking dinner. I guess that I always try to help out as much as I can when she is tired. I know that she needs her rest. She is up all the time. She does not get much sleep 'cause she brings home her schedule and things like that she will stay up to get them done. We just let her catch up.*

A 12-year-old girl eases her mother's bad day through humor:

> *I try and make her feel better. My friend can make people laugh so easy. And so usually I'm like, "Chris, my mom feels kind of bad right now—you wanna come over and cheer her up?" and in just at least five minutes my mom is laughing so hard.*

Caring for parents in these ways is positive, but we also heard stories from children who felt that their parents had collapsed from the strain of work, who felt responsible for propping them up. They felt that their parents had become the children and that they were parenting them.

If you asked me, "When does parents' work harm children?" my answer would be, when children become their parents' parents—when they feel so responsible for their parents that they are weighed down by this responsibility.

So we asked the children, "When your father is in a bad mood or tired because of work, how often do you feel like you are taking care of him?" We also asked the same question about mothers.

Of course, a question like this can't really pinpoint the fine line between a child's normal feelings of being responsible and nurturing and a child's sense of being overburdened. It would take an observational study to assess this, and even then it could be a difficult call to make. But we could also ask children why they take care of their father or their mother. Although this question still can't differentiate between healthy and unhealthy care, it can provide a little more information about children's feelings.

How often do children feel that they are parenting their fathers?
Overall, 17 percent of children in the third through twelfth grades feel that they take care of their fathers often or very often. Another 26 percent feel that they do this sometimes; 56 percent say rarely or never.

Why do children take care of their fathers?
Children in the seventh through twelfth grades were asked to list the reasons why they sometimes take care of their fathers. Of the reasons given, I am really only concerned about the 12 percent who say that their fathers work too hard and are "too tired to take care of me" and the 3 percent who say that their fathers can't take of themselves:

8.6
Children in the Seventh Through Twelfth Grades with Employed Fathers: Parenting Their Fathers	
Why do you sometimes take care of your father?	
He can't take care of himself.	3%
He works too hard and is too tired to take care of me.	12
We are a family and we should help take care of each other.	50
It makes me feel important.	10
Some other reasons	13

How often do children feel that they are parenting their mothers?
More children report caring for their mothers than their fathers: Seventeen percent of children in the third through twelfth grades feel that they take care of their fathers often or very often compared with 29 percent who say that they care for their mothers this frequently. Another 24 percent feel that they do this sometimes, and 45.5 percent say rarely or never.

Why do children take care of their mothers?

It is striking that 20 percent of children in the seventh through twelfth grades explain that their mothers work too hard and are too tired to take care of their child. Another 5 percent say that their mothers can't take care of themselves, and almost half of the children endorse the notion of family responsibility as encompassing the care of one another.

8.7

Children in the Seventh Through Twelfth Grades with Employed Mothers: Parenting Their Mothers	
Why do you sometimes take care of your mother?	
She can't take care of herself.	5%
She works too hard and is too tired to take care of me.	20
We are a family and we should help take care of each other.	48.5
It makes me feel important.	12
Some other reasons	9

HOW OFTEN DO WE TALK ABOUT THE BAD THINGS AND THE GOOD THINGS ABOUT WORK?

Since children have such an obvious concern about how tired and stressed we are, I wondered how often children report hearing about the bad things versus the good things about work. Some children reported hearing good stories:

> Before she got her new job, when she worked on the floor as one of the nurses, I knew pretty much what she did. She would come home and tell us all the good stories.
>
> 18-YEAR-OLD GIRL

And some children talked about the bad things:

> She sometimes tells me like what this person did to her to make her mad. And how they all act like little kids.
>
> 16-YEAR-OLD BOY

When she comes home and she's had a bad day, I'll say "Did everything go well at work?" And she'll say "No." And she'll explain to me, "You know I have this somebody that . . . it's all [about] the bottom line. They don't care about the people anymore!" And you really get to understand, you know?

16-YEAR-OLD GIRL

Like sometimes she tells me that, you know the people are mean and stuff. And she say, sometimes she just go home and go to sleep, and it's all gone. And she tells me, sometimes she says she going to try and find her a different job.

11-YEAR-OLD BOY

Frank Newman, president of the Education Commission of the States, has a name for this negative communication: the skunk theory. He says that when you've had a bad day at work, you go home and "grump, grump, grump" about everything that's gone wrong. When you go back to work the next day, you find that the problem wasn't so awful, that the person you were upset with has a point, and you even resolve some of these problems. But then you don't go home to clear up the "stink" by sharing these resolutions. Without knowing "the rest of the story," your spouse and your kids "build up all of this bile," these negative feelings, which they don't have an opportunity to release.

We asked children in the third through twelfth grades how often they heard about the bad things about their parents' work and found that more than one out of every four children (27 percent) say that their mother/father talks with them about the *bad* things that happen at work often or very often. Another 27 percent say that this happens sometimes, and 46 percent say they rarely or never have conversations with their parents about the bad things. Children are more likely to hear about the bad things about work from their mothers than their fathers. Interestingly, younger and older children are equally likely to hear about the bad things about work.

Since just about half of the children hear about negative aspects of parents' work on a somewhat regular basis, is the glass then half full or half empty? Perhaps it is not *that* we talk about the bad things, but *how* we talk about them. Do we simply complain or are the problems described along with lessons learned? It also depends on whether parents talk about the good things, too.

When we compare the extent to which parents talk with children about good or bad things, good things have the edge: Thirty-nine percent of children hear about *good* things often or very often, compared with 27 percent who hear about bad things. The pattern of whom they hear from is also consistent: Children learn more about work (both good and bad) from their mothers than from their fathers. Just as mothers are the primary transmitters of information about the kinds of work they do, they are also the primary conduits of what happens at work.

HOW DO OUR COMMUNICATIONS ABOUT WORK AFFECT HOW CHILDREN SEE US AS PARENTS?

Thus far, I have been speculating about the future impact on children of our intentional or unintentional communications about work. But there is a definite "here and now" impact. I found that children assess their mothers' parenting competence more highly (that is, give their mothers higher grades) when:

▼ they know more about their mothers' work.
▼ they believe their mothers like their work more.
▼ they hear about the good things about work from their mothers more often.

Likewise, children assess their fathers' parenting competence more highly (that is, give their fathers higher grades) when:

▼ they know more about their fathers' work.
▼ they believe their fathers like their work more.
▼ they hear about the good things about work from their fathers more often.

It is interesting that the positive messages seem to carry the day, affecting how our children judge us more strongly than our complaints and negative feelings.

WHAT KIND OF WORK HAS THE MOST POSITIVE EFFECT ON HOW WE RAISE OUR CHILDREN?

There is also striking evidence that the nature of our jobs affects our child-rearing practices and our children's development far more than many other aspects of our lives.

In the 1970s and 1980s, researchers found that parents whose jobs entail working with ideas and symbols, completing complex tasks, and operating with greater autonomy and self-direction place more emphasis on self-direction and independence in their children than do parents whose jobs are rote, standardized, and closely supervised. Although more complex jobs tend to be white-collar jobs and more rote jobs tend to be blue-collar jobs, it was found that the specific characteristics of jobs, rather than the general type of occupation, are what matters most. In fact, they are quite powerful in their effects on children's socialization—more important than the parents' race, ethnicity, and religion.[10]

Several characteristics of jobs seem to make a difference. First, there is job complexity, which is repeatedly linked to the way that parents interact with their children. Parents whose jobs are very complex are more likely to value self-direction in their children, to encourage autonomy and intellectual flexibility, to provide intellectual stimulation and emotional warmth, to use child rearing practices that are firm but flexible, and to be less strict about discipline than parents with less complex jobs.[11]

A second job characteristic that is important is challenge. Parents—particularly fathers—who have more challenging jobs care for their children in firm but flexible ways and are less stringent disciplinarians than parents in less challenging jobs.[12]

A third important characteristic is the opportunity to make decisions. Mothers who have many opportunities to make decisions at work provide more emotional support and encouragement to their daughters and are more involved in their sons' schoolwork activities than mothers without such decision-making opportunities. Parents with self-directed jobs are also less authoritarian. Workers in settings that require teamwork and involvement in complex tasks engage in more problem solving with their families than workers who do not have these situations at work.[13]

Jobs not only affect parenting practice, they also affect children's development. Children of parents with more complex jobs exhibit fewer behavior problems. Children of mothers with complex jobs have been found to have better verbal facility. The more mothers use their skills at work, the higher their children's math achievement.[14]

All of these studies suggest that there are similarities between what is valued at parents' workplaces and the skills and values parents teach their children. Thus, the actual characteristics of our jobs have an impact on children's futures. Knowing this, we can be more deliberate about what we want to teach our children about work.

WHAT ARE CHILDREN LEARNING FROM US ABOUT HOW TO MANAGE WORK AND FAMILY RESPONSIBILITIES?

Ever the detectives, children are listening to us as we talk *with* them or *around* them about our work; they are also watching—looking at how we manage our work and family responsibilities. And they have opinions about what they see.

Do children think we work too much?

Just over two thirds of children 8 through 18 years old think that their parents work about the right amount. More than one fourth think their parents work too much, and very few (4 percent) think they work too little. It is fathers—more than mothers—whom children view as over-workers. As we saw in Chapter 4, fathers do in fact work longer hours than mothers, though mothers and fathers are equally likely to think they work too much.

Once again, children's perception of the family's economic health is a significant factor: Children who see their family in a more precarious position financially are much more likely to think their fathers work too much (43 percent) than children who see their families as having more than they need (27 percent). So yet another stereotype is challenged: It is not the overachieving father who sacrifices his family for his success, but the father who is struggling to make ends meet whom children are more likely to see as working too much.

Where there are differences—big differences—they are between parents' *assumptions* about what their children think and what kids actually think. We asked parents to guess, "Does your child think you work too much, too little, or about the right amount?" Almost twice as many mothers think that their child 8 through 18 years old believes they work too much (46 percent) as children that age who think their mother works too much (25 percent). Likewise, there is a large gap between what fathers assume their child thinks and what children think.

8.8

Comparison of Employed Parents and Children with Employed Parents: Work Too Much?

Does your child think you work too much, too little, or about the right amount?/Do you think your mother/father works too much, too little, or about the right amount?	Father about a child 8 through 18	Child 8 through 18 about father	Mother about a child 8 through 18	Child 8 through 19 about mother
Too much	49%	33%	46%	25%
About the right amount	49	64	53	70
Too little	2	3	1	5

Significance: *** = p <.0001.   *** = p <.0001.

Finding after finding in this study confirms the fact that nearly all children accept their parents' work as a given, as a fact of life, and that children are less judgmental than parents guess they are. Finding after finding also confirms that parents see the problem as time, whereas children are more attuned to the stress that their parents bring home from work than simply the amount of time they spend apart.

▼ | **How successful are parents in managing work and family life— according to children and parents?** Children in the third through twelfth grades see their parents in very positive terms when it comes to managing work and family life. Seventy-four percent see their mothers and 69 percent see their fathers as very successful. Parents are much less sanguine about their success. Only 34 percent of parents with a child from birth through 18 years old say that they are very successful at managing work and family life; 60 percent report being somewhat successful; and 6 percent say they are somewhat or very unsuccessful.

When we ran statistical comparisons of children 8 through 18 years old and parents with a child the same age, the gulf between the two generations becomes quite apparent: Children are more than twice as likely to say that their father is very successful (69 percent) as are fathers with a child of the same age (31 percent). The same pattern holds for children and mothers: 74 percent of children see their mothers as very successful compared with 34 percent of mothers who give themselves this high rating.

8.9

Comparison of Employed Parents and Children with Employed Parents: Parents' Success in Managing Work and Parenting Responsibilities

How successful are you in managing your work and parenting responsibilities?/How successful is your father/mother in managing his/her work and parenting responsibilities?	Father with a child 8 through 18	Child 8 through 18 about father	Mother with a child 8 through 18	Child 8 through 18 abuot mother
Very successful	31%	69%	34%	74%
Somewhat successful	65	26	60	21
Somewhat unsuccessful	3	3	6	3
Very successful	0	1.5	0	2

Significance: *** = p <.0001.   *** = p <.0001.

Whenever such large discontinuities exist, we have to ask ourselves why. Are children telling us what they think we want to hear? Or are parents being unrealistically tough on themselves, because of their ambivalence and guilt? Although only direct observation of families in action would enable us to answer this question, it seems evident that both interpretations have merit. Regardless, however, it is apparent that children are not questioning the success of parents' navigating work and family life to the extent parents are.

Do parents put their jobs before their family or their family before their jobs—according to children and parents?

How often do parents put their jobs before their family? This is the essential "value" question, and 80 percent of children 8 through 18 years old say rarely or never. Twelve percent say sometimes, and only 8 percent say very often or often.

Who are the parents whom kids see as putting their jobs first? There are only two demographic differences that matter. First, children are more likely to feel that their fathers rather than their mothers put their jobs first: 60 percent of children say their mothers never put their job before their family compared with 47.5 percent who say that their fathers never do. Second, the economic situation makes a difference in children's assessment of fathers. Children who feel their families are in poorer economic health are more likely to say their fathers put their job first—12.5 percent often or very often—compared with 7 percent of children in families with fewer financial constraints.

When we turn to parents, we find that almost one in four mothers and fathers with a child from birth through 18 years old says that he or she puts job before the family often or very often (24 percent), whereas 45 percent report that they rarely or ever do this.

In contrast to children, parents in families with higher annual incomes are more likely to say that they put their jobs before their families. This difference in perception is interesting—but could be related to the different family income measures used with children and parents. With parents, actual household incomes was used, whereas children estimated their families' economic health by assessing whether the family had less than enough or just enough to buy what they need versus more than enough. So it is not surprising that when children sense a financial pressure, they might see their parents struggling to redress it by putting their jobs first.

We also found that parents who work more hours are more likely to say that they put their jobs first than parents who work fewer hours. In addition, parents with an older child are more likely to say they put their job first. So parents' emphasis on work appears to increase as their children grow older and they themselves move forward in their prime working years.

When we compare children ages 8 though 18 and parents with a child of the same age, we find that children, once again, are much more positive about their parents than parents are. For example, children are more than three times as likely to say that their fathers never put their job before their family as fathers say they do (14 percent for fathers and 47.5 percent for children). For mothers, the discrepancy is even greater: Children are more than four times as likely to say that their mothers never put their job before their family as mothers say they do (60 percent of children compared with 13.5 percent of mothers).

8.10

Comparison of Employed Parents and Children with Employed Parents: Parents Put Job Before Family

How often do you put your job before your family?/How often do you feel that your father/mother puts his/her job before your family?	Father with a child 8 through 18	Child 8 through 18 about father	Mother with a child 8 through 18	Child 8 through 18 about mother
Very often	14%	4%	8%	4%
Often	19	5	13	3
Sometimes	32	16	39	9
Rarely	20.5	28	26	24
Never	14	47.5	13.5	60

Significance: *** = p <.0001.   *** = p <.0001.

We also asked the reverse question: How often do parents put their family before their job? As we have now come to expect, the large majority of children—three in four—see their parents as putting family before job often or very often. Children feel their mothers are more likely to put family first more often than their fathers.

Whereas children see a difference in the emphasis that mothers and fathers place on family versus work, parents' self-assessments do not conform. Mothers and fathers with a child from birth through 18 years old are *equally* likely to say that they put family first. This response indicates to me that the social climate around fathering has changed. Fathers seem to value parenting as much as mothers do, though according to children (who report differences between their fathers' and mothers' priorities), fathers' behavior may not yet have followed suit.

Parents with a younger child are more likely to say that they put their family before their job than those parents with an older child. And whereas children see a difference based on their perception of family economic health, parents' assessments reveal no differences. Rich and poor parents are equally likely to say that they put family first.

When we compare parents with a child 8 through 18 years old and children of this age, again it becomes clear that parents and children see the world through very different lenses. And the lenses that parents use are decidedly more self-critical.

8.11

Comparison of Employed Parents and Children with Employed Parents: Parents Put Family Before Job

How often do you put your *family* before your job?/How often do you feel that your father/mother puts his/her family before her/his *job*?	Father with a child 8 through 18	Child 8 through 18 about father	Mother with a child 8 through 18	Child 8 through 18 about mother
Very often	25%	47%	25%	60%
Often	28	26	26	18.5
Sometimes	31	17	34	13
Rarely	14	5	13.5	3
Never	2	4.5	2	4.5

Significance: *** = p <.0001.   *** = p <.0001.

Do our efforts in managing work and family life affect children's views of us?

Yes, they do. Children are more likely to grade their mothers more highly when they have mothers whom they see as:

▼ managing work and family more successfully.
▼ putting their jobs first less often.
▼ putting their families before their jobs more often.

Likewise, children are more likely to grade their fathers more highly on their parenting competence when they have fathers whom they see as:

▼ managing work and family more successfully.
▼ putting their jobs first less often.
▼ putting their families before their jobs more often.

LESSONS LEARNED

Taken together, the lessons learned from researching what we are teaching our children about our work and family life are clear:

▼ Let our children know about the kind of work we do.

▼ Share the good things about work in an intentional way.

▼ Take steps to relieve stress. "Even though work can be very stressful, don't take it out on your kids," says a boy, age 9. A girl of 12 puts it, "Please don't take the office home with you."

▼ Above all, put our family first. According to a girl, age 9: "Don't put your work before your kids, or they will think you don't love them."

What Does the Future Hold?

tudies show that we paint a very disparaging picture of kids today.[1] Although history indicates that "thus may be always so," the sentiment today seems especially pervasive. Where do we get such negative images? Clearly, one source of the pejorative imagery is the media. At a recent meeting that I attended at George Soros's Open Society Institute, the educator Herb Kohl held up one national newsmagazine cover after another portraying negative images of young people. Stories such as the school shootings absorb us because they become emblematic of a generation in trouble, emanating as they do not only from the inner cities, but also from rural areas of the country and from close-knit all-American towns.

Another source of negativity is our own experience. Seeing a pack of young people coming down the street or in the mall, many adults make a detour so as not to cross paths. And I find that there is no topic that generates more passion among business leaders than the assertion that the moral and intellectual glue is missing in our youth, that they won't have the wherewithal for thriving in the workplace of the twenty-first century.

Finally, there is what Douglas Copeland calls "clique maintenance": the desire of one generation to look good by putting down those who are younger.[2]

In our search for logical explanations for these views, we typically lay the problems of kids at the feet of their parents. Or we seek larger causes in society—divorce, working mothers, problem-ridden schools, lack of community support, and so forth.

The interesting aspect of this debate is that we often split ourselves off from the problem. For the most part, it is "those other parents," "those other children" who lack values—not us, not our children. It used to be "those other schools," but now we are increasingly seeing the problems in our own schools. By psychological distancing, we can maintain our own integrity as parents while also recognizing that problems do exist.[3]

There is no question that many young people feel maligned. At a recent town meeting held by the national nonprofit Do Something, the teenagers present said that they were sick of people's imputing negatives characteristics to their generation. But is there a split happening here as well? Is it "those other kids" who have problems, not me?

In this chapter, I try to separate fact from fiction. To do so, I turn to the study we conducted to see how children ages 8 through 18 feel about their futures and to gauge their attitudes about work and family issues. I also look at the attitudes and values of the generation just ahead of the children in the Ask the Children study to probe "the future that is now," using data from our National Study of the Changing Workforce. Finally, I examine the research of others who are studying work and family issues among young people both here and abroad.

WHAT IS THIS WORLD OUR CHILDREN WILL INHERIT?

Before we probe what children in our study think about what lies ahead of them, let's look at what we now know about the world our children inherit.

First, the world that our children will inherit will have a smaller proportion of young people, as the population ages. In the report *Children of 2010*, Harold Hodgkinson, director of the Center for Demographic Policy, notes that the number of children under 18 in the United States will increase by 2 percent between the years 2000 and 2010. At the same time, the number of young adults 18 through 44 years old will decrease by 1 percent. Those 45 through 64 years old will increase by 29 percent, adding 17 million more adults to this age range. Finally, the population 65 and older will increase by nearly 14 percent—adding 4 million more people in this age range. By mid 2000, there are expected to be 72,000 people 100 years and older.[4]

Second, the world that our children will inherit will be more diverse than in any other generation. Hodgkinson reports that the fastest growing ethnic group in the United States is Asian, with a 36 percent growth rate, followed by Hispanics or Latinos, with a 31 percent growth rate. African Americans have a 12 percent growth rate. In contrast, whites have only a 3 percent growth rate. Worldwide, 17 percent of the world's 5.7 billion people are now white; this number will drop to 9 percent by 2010. Put simply, in many parts of this country, minorities will become the majority as our children take their place in the world.

Third, this world will be more global. The experience of our children will not be limited by national boundaries. As *Workforce 2020*, a report on work and workers in the twenty-first century, notes, declining transportation and communication costs are leading to the "death of distance."[5]

Fourth, this world will be more economically bifurcated. In our children's world, there will be greater income disparity between the haves and the have nots.[6]

Fifth, this world will require our children to be continuous learners in order to prosper. We increasingly know that lifelong learning will make the critical difference between those who thrive and those who don't. In fact, successful companies are now referred to as "learning organizations."[7] A report prepared by NationsBanc Montgomery Securities asserts that knowledge will be "the ultimate source of competitive advantage whether for a nation, a company, or an individual."[8] The statistics cited are impressive:

▼ The salary gap between college and high school graduates has widened from 25 percent in 1980 to more than 100 percent in 1996.
▼ The Census Bureau estimates that by 2000, more than 85 percent of all jobs in the United States will require an education beyond high school, up from 65 percent in 1991.
▼ Lifelong learning will become the norm. As the chairman of the Federal Reserve Board, Alan Greenspan, has stated: "Human skills are subject to obsolescence at a rate perhaps unprecedented in American history."

Sixth, technology will shape how our children learn, live, and work. According to the Institute For The Future, a California-based global think tank, "The paramount human and organizational task for the next two decades will be cultivating knowledge in the garden of information chaos." Because of technology and the Internet, they expect the routes to knowledge to be increasingly varied and global, and its forms increasingly multimedia. We will be able to access knowledge on demand.[9]

Technology is also changing the way we work. In an article for *Harvard Business Review*, Thomas Malone and Robert Laubacher of MIT refer to the "e-lance economy." Speculating that this new economy will be based on the individual rather than the organization, individuals (I would add, in some types of jobs) will join in temporarily connected electronic networks to do a job, then disband and form new networks for the next job. They assert that the e-lance economy is already upon us, as evidenced by the increase in temporary workers, outsourcing, telecommuting, and creation of "virtual companies."[10]

Seventh, our children will combine work and family life. Our generation has lived through what *Workforce 2020* calls "the most significant change in the history of the American workplace": the increase in women in the work force. Although women now account for about 46 percent of the work force—up from 29 percent in 1950—it is expected that there will be equal numbers of men and women in the work force in the years to come. So our children can expect to deal with issues of navigating work and family life in the future, just as we do today.[11]

Finally, work as we know it is changing. Ending is the idea of a job for life, replaced by shifting jobs and careers throughout the life cycle, into the so-called retirement years. Ending is the career ladder with each rung leading to a higher position, replaced by a career lattice with lateral spirals as well as upward moves. Ending is the chain of command and control and patriarchal management, replaced by the notion of leadership within us all and the assumption of personal responsibility for the path our work lives take. Ending is the individual worker, a cog in the workplace structure, replaced by teams that form, break up, and re-form. And ending is the one central workplace, replaced by people working off site and at home as well as at the workplace.[12]

This workplace of the future will clearly call for different skills. In addition to basic skills, when they join the work force our children will need to know how to take personal responsibility for their work lives, remain ongoing learners, analyze and synthesize information, communicate, work well with people, work in diverse teams, think outside the box, take risks, and solve problems. Yet, few schools are teaching these skills, so necessary for succeeding in life beyond graduation. If children are truly to succeed in this new workplace, schools and parents must teach them, by explanation and example.

DO CHILDREN WANT TO EMULATE THE WORK AND FAMILY LIVES OF THEIR PARENTS?

Now, we turn to children's views. Where, in their opinion, are they headed, and how well prepared do they feel?

Do children want to work as much as their parents?

Very few children 8 through 18 years old with an employed father want to work more than their fathers: [13] 8 percent, to be exact. Almost a third (32 percent) want to work less, and 56 percent say that they want to work the same amount.

Are children turning their backs on the escalating cycle of work and more work? It certainly seems that way, but to understand what is going on fully, it's important to look beneath these averages to understand which children take which positions.

Girls feel more strongly than boys that they want to work less than their fathers (39 percent of girls compared with 27 percent of boys). But the most striking finding is that children whose fathers work the longest and hardest are the most likely to want to work less time. This includes the following children:

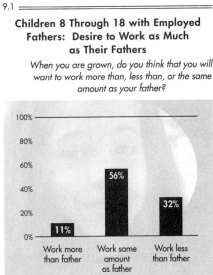

9.1

Children 8 Through 18 with Employed Fathers: Desire to Work as Much as Their Fathers

When you are grown, do you think that you will want to work more than, less than, or the same amount as your father?

Work more than father — 11%
Work same amount as father — 56%
Work less than father — 32%

▼ children with fathers who work full-time.
▼ children with fathers who work 6 to 7 days a week.
▼ children whose fathers work nondaytime shifts.

Perceptions also matter. Sixty-one percent of children who feel that their fathers work too much say that they want to work less than their fathers do. Finally, children who feel that their fathers find it difficult to focus on them when they are together don't want to work as much as their fathers do.

This is an important finding: The children of seemingly "overworked"

9.2

Children 8 Through 18 with Employed Mothers: Desire to Work as Much as Their Mothers

When you are grown, do you think that you will want to work more than, less than, or the same amount as your mother?

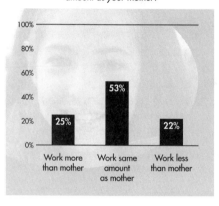

fathers do not want to follow in their footsteps. But does it hold for children's feelings about their mothers as well? Considering the fact that mothers work fewer hours on average than fathers, it is not surprising to find that one in four children with an employed mother (25 percent) wants to work more than his or her mother; 53 percent want to work about the same amount; and 22 percent want to work less.

Though children's age and gender don't make a difference, other aspects of their lives do. Children are more likely to want to work less than their mothers who have mothers who:

▼ work full time.
▼ work 6 to 7 days a week.
▼ work nondaytime shifts.
▼ work multiple jobs.
▼ don't like their jobs.
▼ work too much.
▼ put their jobs before their family more frequently.

So the pattern holds in terms of mothers too. Does this mean that the surging wave of work-and-more-work will lose its swell? Of course, it is hard to tell. We can feel one way as a young person and act a different way as an adult. We can also feel and do different things. But the fact that only 21 percent of children overall want to work more than their mothers and fathers could—underscore could—mean that the next generation of workers will put the brakes on over-work.

We are beginning to see the tip of this trend now with Generation Xers. Although these young workers log in long hours and work as hard as baby boomers, they appear less willing to do so on other people's terms. They are more entrepreneurial, quicker to leave the establishment and step out on their own. They seek ways of getting more control over all of the aspects of their lives.[13] I suspect that our children may follow the trail blazed by Generation Xers: When work and more work is thrown at them, especially under difficult work conditions, they may not catch the pass, but instead create their own game.

Do children want to manage work and family life as their parents do?

We asked the children, "If you have a family of your own someday, how much like your father/mother do you want to manage your work and family?"

Although there has been speculation that today's kids might not want to have their own kids someday, only 4 percent said that they did not plan to have a family. Boys and girls, older and younger children, are equally likely to want to have children. Though it appears that some children are turning away from the rising tide of work, they do not seem to be turning their backs on having families.

Among those who plan to have children, more than one third of the children 8 through 18 years old (36 percent) say that they want to manage work and family life very similarly to their fathers, 37 percent say somewhat similarly, 16 percent say somewhat differently, and 11 percent say very differently.

9.3

Children 8 Through 18 with Employed Fathers: Manage Work and Family Life Like Father	
If you have a family someday, how much like your father do you want to manage your work and family?	
Very similar to my father	36%
Somewhat similar to my father	37
Somewhat different from my father	16
Very different from my father	11

The children who want to model themselves after their fathers are more likely to:

▼ live in families that they see as having what they need economically.

▼ have fathers who work daytime hours.

▼ know more about the kind of work their fathers do.

▼ hear about the good things at work from their fathers more frequently.

▼ have fathers who like their work more.

▼ feel that their fathers put their job before their family infrequently.

▼ feel that their fathers put their family before their job more frequently.

▼ have fathers who find it easy really to focus on them when they are together.

Similar proportions of children want to manage work and family as their mothers do, but here there are age differences. Younger children are more likely to want to emulate their mothers than older children are.

9.4

Children 8 Through 18 with Employed Mothers: Manage Work and Family Life Like Mother			
If you have a family someday, how much like your mother do you want to manage your work and family?	8- through 12-year-olds	13- through 18-year-olds	Total
Very similar to my mother	51.5%	32.5%	41%
Somewhat similar to my mother	26	39.5	33.5
Somewhat different from my mother	12	17	15
Very different from my mother	10	11	11

Significance: ** = p <.001.

It is interesting that boys and girls do not differ in the desire to be like their fathers, but they do differ in wanting to model their work and family responsibilities after their mothers. As psychoanalytic theory would predict, girls are more likely to identify with their mothers than boys are.

In addition, the children who want to manage work and family as their mothers do are more likely to:

▼ live in families whom they see as having what they need economically.

▼ live in two-parent families (as opposed to single-parent families headed by mothers).

▼ hear about the good things at work from their mothers more frequently.

▼ have mothers who like their work more.

▼ feel that their mothers put their job before their family infrequently.

▼ feel that their mothers do put their family before their job more frequently.

▼ have mothers who find it easy really to focus on them when they are together.

It is very important to note that children are influenced by the work side of parents' lives as well as the family side. As I noted in the previous chapter, we don't pay very much attention to the way we communicate about work to our children, but these results indicate that we should. I hope we use them as a call to action—to communicate about our jobs and the frictions between our jobs and family life in ways that help children begin to fashion healthy work and family lives in the future.

WHAT ARE CHILDREN'S ATTITUDES ABOUT MEN'S AND WOMEN'S ROLES AND ABOUT WORK AND FAMILY?

In Chapter 1, we looked at how employed parents feel about the hot issues of our times. Now we turn to children, including those with employed and nonemployed parents, to see where they stand.

Should men earn the money and women care for the children?

Children in the third through twelfth grades were asked how strongly they agree or disagree with the statement "It is much better for everyone involved if the man earns the money and the woman takes care of the home and the children."

Interestingly, more than two in five children (43 percent) strongly or somewhat agree that the traditional gender division of labor is better for "everyone involved." But there are big differences between older and younger children: More than twice as many 8- through 12-year-olds strongly agree with this statement (22 percent) as older children 13 through 18 years old (10 percent).

Equally striking are the gender differences between boys and girls in their feelings about traditional gender roles: Almost twice as many boys strongly agree (19 percent) as girls (11 percent). The omnipresent polling in this country has made us aware that there is a gender gap in politics. But here we find a gender gap in children's views of the proper roles of men and women! And it occurs early.

This led to two logical follow-up questions. Since older children have less traditional views than younger children, I wondered whether the overall differences between boys and girls diminish as both get older. I also wondered whether boys' opinions change as they get older. The answers to both of my queries is no. Older boys and older girls continue to differ in the way they see gender roles. And although the raw numbers show that a slightly smaller proportion of boys 13 through 18 years of age feel that it is better if men earn the money and women care for the family than of boys 8 through 12 years old, these differences do not reach the level of statistical significance.

Not surprisingly, children's home life affects their opinions. Children with a mother at home are almost twice as likely to agree strongly that it is better for the man to earn the money and the woman to care for the family (24 percent) than those with an employed mother (14 percent). It stands to reason that children would support the life-style choices they see their parents making.

That 43 percent of children endorse traditional gender roles in this era when having a working mother is the norm is fascinating. Are chil-

9.5

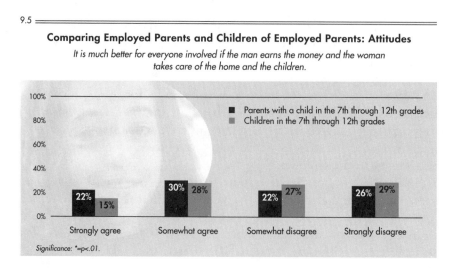

Comparing Employed Parents and Children of Employed Parents: Attitudes

It is much better for everyone involved if the man earns the money and the woman takes care of the home and the children.

■ Parents with a child in the 7th through 12th grades
■ Children in the 7th through 12th grades

	Strongly agree	Somewhat agree	Somewhat disagree	Strongly disagree
Parents	22%	30%	22%	26%
Children	15%	28%	27%	29%

Significance: *=p<.01.

dren turning their backs on societal change? Do they feel that the path that many of their parents have followed is wrong?

To put children's views in perspective, we compared the views of older children with employed parents with those of employed parents who have a child the same age. The result: Children's views are less traditional than parents'. For example, 22 percent of employed parents strongly agree with the statement "It is much better for everyone involved if the man earns the money and the woman takes care of the home and the children," and only 15 percent of children with employed parents do.

The tentative conclusion to be drawn is that attitudes don't change as quickly as behavior, but they are changing. Although mothers have been entering the work force in record numbers, just more than half of employed parents and just under half of the children of employed parents continue to support traditional role ideology.

Can mothers who work have a relationship with their children just as good as can mothers who don't work?

Children in the seventh through the twelfth grades were asked how strongly they agree or disagree with the following statement: "A mother who works outside the home can have just as good a relationship with her children as can a mother who does not work."

The large majority of older children agree with this statement either strongly (48 percent) or somewhat (33 percent). In contrast, 13 percent somewhat disagree and 6 percent strongly disagree.

As before, however, there are gender differences. Girls are more likely than boys to feel that mothers can have equally good relationships with their children regardless of whether they work. Whereas one fourth of the boys disagree strongly or somewhat with this statement (25 percent), only 12 percent of girls do. It is interesting that boys and girls of the gender revolution have such strongly contrasting views of men's and women's roles.

Experience also plays a part in children's attitudes. The more time the mother works, the more likely her kids are to feel that mothers who work can have as good a relationship with their children as mothers who are at home. In addition, children are more likely to feel that employed mothers can have just as good a relationship with their children as mothers who don't work when they have mothers who:

▼ talk about the good things about work more frequently.
▼ like their jobs more.

▼ put their family before their job more often.
▼ put their job before their family less often.
▼ find it easy to focus on them (their children) when they are together.

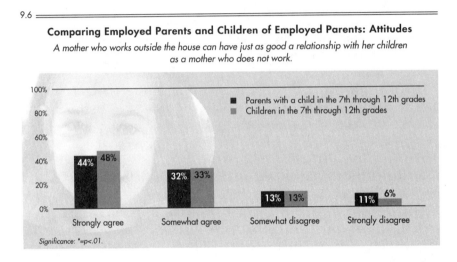

9.6

Comparing Employed Parents and Children of Employed Parents: Attitudes

A mother who works outside the house can have just as good a relationship with her children as a mother who does not work.

■ Parents with a child in the 7th through 12th grades
■ Children in the 7th through 12th grades

Strongly agree: 44% / 48%
Somewhat agree: 32% / 33%
Somewhat disagree: 13% / 13%
Strongly disagree: 11% / 6%

*Significance: *=p<.01.*

When comparing responses of children in seventh through twelfth grades who have employed parents with those of employed parents who have a child in the same grades, we again see that children are somewhat more likely than parents to feel that a working mother can have just as good a relationship with her children as a mother who does not work. Once again, it appears that the ideology around employed mothers is slowly changing.

Do children do as well if mothers are the breadwinners and fathers the nurturers?

Children in the seventh through twelfth grades were asked how strongly they agree or disagree with the statement "Children do just as well if the mother has primary responsibility for earning the money and the father has primary responsibility for caring for the children."

One third of these older children (33 percent) strongly agree with this statement, and another 37 percent somewhat agree. Thus although seven in ten children agree, 22 percent somewhat disagree and 8 percent strongly disagree.

Again, there are gender differences: 42 percent of girls strongly agree that it is okay if men and women don't follow traditional gender roles compared with 25 percent of boys.

Children are more likely to endorse this idea when, in children's view, their mothers:

▼ talk about the good things about work more frequently.
▼ like their jobs more.
▼ put their family before their job more often.
▼ find it easy to focus on them when they are together.

Whereas there have been generational differences in the previous attitudinal issues we have examined, employed parents and children with employed parents don't differ as to whether "children do just as well if the mother has primary responsibility for earning the money and the father has primary responsibility for caring for the children."

When attitudes are in transition, people can hold seemingly contradictory truths to be self-evident at the same time. When we compare older children on the last three issues, we see this pattern: Although 43 percent strongly or somewhat agree that traditional gender roles are best, 82 percent also support the idea that employed mothers can have just as good relationships with their children as mothers at home, and 70 percent feel that fathers can be competent primary care givers.

Is it okay for mothers to work if they really need money?

Three quarters of children 8 through 18 years of age strongly agree, "It is okay for mothers to work if they really do need money." Another 17 percent somewhat agree and only 8 percent disagree, somewhat or strongly. The notion that mothers should work when they need the money has become commonly accepted, so the gender differences we found in children's answers to the other questions do not emerge here. Neither are there differences between employed parents and children 8 through 18 years old with employed parents.

Should mothers work if they don't need the money?

Our findings reveal a greater ambivalence among children 8 through 18 about whether mothers should work when they can afford to stay at home. When we asked children how strongly they agree or disagree with the statement "Mothers who don't really need to earn money shouldn't work," almost one third of the children 8 through 18 years old

(33 percent) either somewhat or strongly agree with this position; comparable proportions disagree somewhat (34 percent) or disagree strongly (33 percent).

Boys are far more likely than girls to think that mothers who do not really need the money should not work. In fact, there is a 20-percentage-point difference between girls (78 percent) and boys (58 percent) who strongly or somewhat disagree with the statement!

The children more likely to disagree with the statement that mothers who really don't need the money should not work have:

▼ fathers who like their work more.
▼ mothers who are employed.
▼ mothers who work more time.

So when it comes to the question of whether or not mothers who don't need the money should work, children tend to "vote" their experience. The finding about fathers' liking their work is puzzling. Do children with fathers who like their work see that work can be fulfilling and feel that their mothers should have access to a similar experience?

The generational difference we have found continues here. Children with employed parents are far more likely (67 percent) than employed parents (53 percent) to disagree with the notion that mothers who don't really need to earn money shouldn't work.

9.7

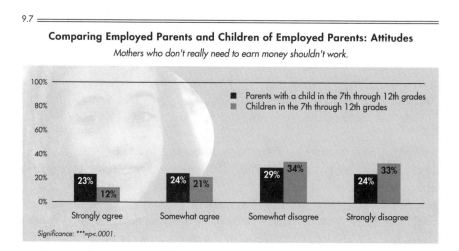

Comparing Employed Parents and Children of Employed Parents: Attitudes

Mothers who don't really need to earn money shouldn't work.

■ Parents with a child in the 7th through 12th grades
■ Children in the 7th through 12th grades

	Strongly agree	Somewhat agree	Somewhat disagree	Strongly disagree
Parents	23%	24%	29%	24%
Children	12%	21%	34%	33%

*Significance: ***=p<.0001.*

Do mothers care more about being successful at work than meeting the needs of their children?

When the debate about working parents becomes fervent, the fire is fueled by contentions that parents are selfish, materialistic, driven by their own desires for success and money, neglectful of their children. So it is with great interest that I look at how children feel about these claims. Do children feel that "many working mothers seem to care more about being successful at work than meeting the needs of their children?"

More than one in five children 8 through 18 (22.5 percent) agree with this statement, although only 9 percent do so strongly and 13.5 percent do so somewhat. While these percentages aren't huge, it is troubling that one in five children sees employed mothers as selfish. On the other hand, 50 percent strongly disagree and 27 percent somewhat disagree. Younger children are more likely to disagree. So are girls.

In addition, children who disagree that working mothers put their success above the needs of their children are more likely to have:

▼ fathers who work daytime schedules.
▼ fathers who like their work more.
▼ fathers who put their family before their job more often.
▼ fathers who find it easy to focus on them when they are with their fathers.
▼ mothers who are employed.
▼ mothers who work more time.
▼ mothers who put their family before their job more often.
▼ mothers who put their job before their family less often.
▼ mothers who find it easy to focus on them when they are together.

Compared to the other attitudinal issues we've investigated, children's assessments of mothers' altruism or selfishness seem to be more sensitive to the conditions of *both* mothers' and fathers' jobs and parenting. Why are fathers important here? The only explanation I can see relates to the literature on what is called *social support*. These studies find that when employed mothers receive little support or help from their husbands, they are more likely to be stressed.[14] So perhaps fathers who like their jobs provide more support to their wives, who in turn are better able to nurture their children. Children who experience

7.8

Comparing Employed Parents and Children of Employed Parents: Attitudes

*Many working **mothers** seem to care more about being successful than meeting the needs of their children.*

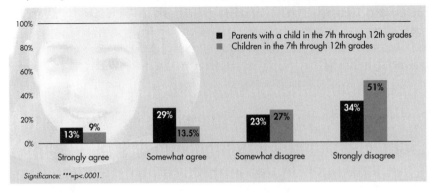

Significance: ***=p<.0001.

these circumstances may in turn see mothers as less selfish and more nurturing.

When comparing children in grades seven through twelve who have employed parents with employed parents who have a child in the same grades, we find that children are more likely than parents to disagree with the statement that mothers care more about being successful at work than meeting the needs of their children. Perhaps children are less cynical than parents about the ways of the adult world, or perhaps they are less absorbed in the societal pattern of blaming parents, but they obviously see mothers in a more favorable light than employed parents do.

Do fathers care more about being successful at work than meeting the needs of their children?

Children 8 though 18 years old were asked the same question about their fathers. Recall that more than one in five agree that mothers put their needs for success ahead of their children. With fathers, it is an even higher proportion—almost one in three (32 percent). These are alarming numbers. Although only 10 percent strongly agree with this statement, 22 percent somewhat agree. On the other hand, 23 percent somewhat disagree and 45 percent strongly disagree.

As we continue to discover, there is a difference between older and younger children: Younger children are less likely to see fathers as placing their desire for success ahead of meeting the needs of their children.

Boys and girls do not disagree on their views of fathers. This is very interesting because as we've seen, boys and girls certainly disagree on many of the opinions they hold about employed mothers, with the exception of whether mothers should work when they really need the money—an idea that has general support.

As occurred with children's assessments of mothers' altruism, when we look at children's views of fathers' altruism or selfishness, aspects of *both* parents' lives matter. Children who disagree that employed fathers put their success above the needs of their children are more likely to have:

▼ fathers who like their work.
▼ two-parent families.
▼ fathers who work daytime schedules.
▼ fathers who put their family before their jobs more often.
▼ fathers who find it easy to focus on them when they are with them.
▼ mothers who do not have multiple jobs.
▼ mothers who like their jobs.
▼ mothers who put their family before their jobs more often.
▼ mothers who put their job before their family less often.
▼ mothers who find it easy to focus on them when they're together.

These findings support the pattern we have been seeing throughout. When we ask the children, we see that the intense public focus on employed mothers misses the mark. For one thing, children are more critical of their employed fathers than of their mothers—they give them lower grades as parents and see them as more selfish. For another, they yearn for more time with them. And—as the preceding analyses reveal—those fathers who do put their children first, who do pay attention to their children, are seen quite positively.

It is telling that employed parents are even harder on fathers than the children of employed parents are. Whereas close to one third of the children see fathers as putting their success at work ahead of meeting the needs of their children, 62 percent of employed parents endorse this point of view either somewhat or strongly. Fathering tends to be overlooked in the work-family debate, but it is very clear that we must pay more attention to this issue.

9.9

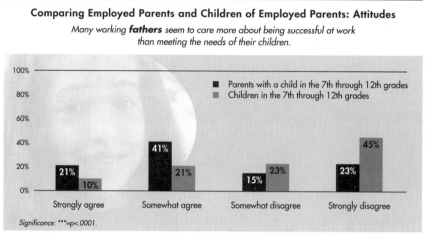

Comparing Employed Parents and Children of Employed Parents: Attitudes

*Many working **fathers** seem to care more about being successful at work than meeting the needs of their children.*

■ Parents with a child in the 7th through 12th grades
■ Children in the 7th through 12th grades

	Strongly agree	Somewhat agree	Somewhat disagree	Strongly disagree
Parents	21%	41%	15%	23%
Children	10%	21%	23%	45%

*Significance: ***=p<.0001.*

Do children have to grow up too fast because of their parents' work and family lives?

Our images of childhood are of dusty lots and baseball games, of lemonade stands and paper dolls, of exploring an attic and trying on old clothes, of fishing in a pond with a pole, or of putting on a play for the relatives. In other words, childhood should be a time of freedom and fun, of play and of leisurely pastimes, of antics and closeness. In contrast is the popular view that the cycle of earn and spend has become a monster, needing constant feeding, pushing parents to run faster and faster on the treadmill of work, and thus depriving the parents and children of these idyllic experiences.

To what extent do children ages 13 through 18 agree that children have to grow up too fast because of the pressures of their parents' work and family life? Almost half, 48 percent, agree: 18 percent strongly and 29 percent somewhat. No wonder so few of them want to work more than their mothers and their fathers! Is this yet another indication that the tide could turn on the escalating cycle of work and more work?

The age and gender of the child don't make a difference here, but work and parenting style do. Children who disagree that children have to grow up too fast are, from their perspective, more likely to have:

▼ fathers who like their work.
▼ fathers who work part-time.
▼ fathers who put their family before their jobs more often.
▼ fathers who find it easy to focus on them when they are with them.

▼ mothers who put their jobs before their family less often.

▼ mothers who find it easy to focus on them when they're together.

Although children are less likely than parents to think that children have to grow up too fast because of the pressures of their parents' work and family lives, sizable and alarming proportions of both groups feel that this is a problem: 48 percent of the children and 70.5 percent of the parents.

9.10

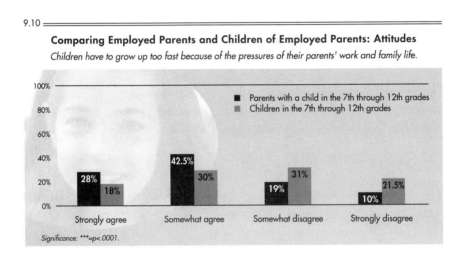

Comparing Employed Parents and Children of Employed Parents: Attitudes

Children have to grow up too fast because of the pressures of their parents' work and family life.

■ Parents with a child in the 7th through 12th grades
■ Children in the 7th through 12th grades

Significance: ***=p<.0001.

WHAT INFLUENCES CHILDREN'S ATTITUDES ABOUT WORK AND FAMILY LIFE?

All in all, we find that children hold more positive views of work and family life and somewhat less traditional views of gender roles than parents do. This finding indicates that the twenty-first century might see slow but incremental change in work and family roles and responsibilities. Are there other patterns in the findings that can provide guidance to us today as parents? I think that there are.

The age of the child

Younger children are more likely to think it would be better for all concerned if men earn the money and women take care of the children and family—that is, follow traditional gender roles. This is not surprising.

The research on gender roles shows that younger children tend to adopt more "black-and-white" views, but as they age, they begin to pay attention to the subtleties and nuances of what is expected of men and women.[15] Conversely, older children are more likely than younger children to feel that mothers and fathers care more about success than about meeting the needs of their children. Again, this perspective is not unexpected, though it is unsettling.

We have found—and parents know from firsthand experience—that teenagers are more critical of parents than are elementary school–age children. In the process of becoming adults, they need to separate themselves from us before they can reconnect as young adults. When my own children were teenagers—and were sometimes in "deep freeze" or hypercritical mode—I found it comforting to know that if I could handle the impenetrable silences or the flare-ups well, if I could try to keep the lines of communication open whether they appeared to want me to or not, and if I could listen to their criticism nondefensively, attending to the complaints that were well founded and changing what wasn't working, that "this too shall pass." And it did!

The gender of the child

There is a substantial gap between what girls and boys think about a number of issues. Girls are more likely than boys to *disagree* with the notion of traditional gender roles and the idea that mothers put their own success before their children. They are also more likely to *agree* that it is okay for mothers to work even if they don't need the money, that working mothers can have as good relationships with their children as at-home mothers, and that fathers can be nurturers and mothers breadwinners. In other words, girls have less conventional ideas about gender roles than boys. Furthermore, our analyses indicate that boys' attitudes do not change as they grow older.

Differences between males' and females' views obviously begin early in childhood. Is it that males pass on one ideology to their sons and females pass on another to their daughters? Or do the experiences of the sons and daughters of employed mothers differ, as some studies suggest?[16] Recall that we found some gender differences in this study, including the fact that girls gave their employed mothers higher ratings than boys for several parenting skills (see Chapter 2).

The fact that girls and boys have different views of gender roles and responsibilities could have serious implications for the adult relationships they will form in the future. Are gender roles being discussed in most families? My guess is, not very often. As one parent I interviewed said, "I can't remember *ever* having a conversation with my children about what they think about the roles of men and women in terms of work and family life." Is this issue being discussed among young people? Probably not often, either. Are there other forums for these discussions? Not many. As one mother said, "If young men and women don't see eye to eye on their expectations, they will simply replay some of the conflict-ridden scripts our generation has been playing." I would certainly hope that parents will use the findings from this study to have open discussions with their children about their expectations of the roles of men and women at work and at home.

Family structure
There are several instances in which having an at-home mother makes a difference. Children whose mothers are not employed are more likely to think that it is better if women assume the care-giving role and men earn the money, that women shouldn't work if they don't need to, and that mothers are putting their own success ahead of their children's well-being. On the other hand, they are no more likely than the children of employed mothers to think that it is all right for fathers to care for children and for mothers to be the economic providers, and that mothers who are employed can have equally good relationships with their children as mothers who are not employed. Thus, their views seem to reflect an ideological perspective about working mothers that also acknowledges that having an employed mother can be okay, too.

Children in single-parent homes are also more likely to feel that fathers care more about being successful than meeting the needs of their children. Recall that when we looked at how children grade their parents, children with nonresident fathers give their fathers much lower grades than the children in families in which the fathers are present. It is my strong hope that this study can amplify the voices of children in a way that nonresident fathers can hear. Although divorce and separation present some obstacles to good relationships with children, these problems aren't inevitable. It is really up to us.

The structure of parents' jobs
How much time the parent works is also linked to children's beliefs about work and family life. On one hand, children whose mothers work full-time are more likely to feel that having a working mother does not harm the child's relationship with her and that working is all right even if the money isn't essential to family survival than children whose

mothers work less than full-time. On the other hand, children whose mothers work less than full-time are more likely to see mothers as sacrificing their children on the altar of their own success than those who work full-time.

The fathers' work schedule also comes into play. Children whose fathers work part-time are more likely to feel that children today are growing up too fast—perhaps because those families are under more economic pressure. Children also have more positive views about parents' meeting children's needs and not just being preoccupied with their own success when their fathers work daytime schedules.

Children's views of their parents' feelings

It is very clear that children's convictions about work and family life are shaped by how they see their mothers' and fathers' working. On many fronts, children have more positive views about working parents when their mothers and/or fathers are seen as liking their jobs and when they bring home stories about the good things that are going on at work. Although many of us do not think of our day-in and day-out conversations about work as "teaching" our children about the world of work, as we saw in Chapter 8, these conversations not only affect how children assess our parenting competence, but also color children's views about their future. The obvious implication is that we should be more thoughtful about how we talk about work with our children.

Children's views of their parents' parenting skill and setting of priorities

Children's attitudes about work and family are heavily influenced by whether or not they see their parents putting family first. Children who feel that they are primary in their parents' lives are more positive about mothers' and fathers' working.

And repeatedly, the importance of focus comes to the fore. When children feel that their parents really focus on them when they are together, they are more open to the variety of choices that parents make with regard to work and family life. If there is one key lesson of these findings, it is that we need to "be there" for our children.

What's missing?

Four factors that were *not* significant were surprises:

    ▼ *The child's assessment of the family's economic health*: It appears that attitudes about work and family are formed independently of the family's perceived economic need, though, as you will recall, children's grades of their parents are strongly linked to family economics.

▼ *The child's knowledge of the kind of work their mothers and fathers do*: Rather, it is children's views of parents' *feelings* about their work that matter.

▼ *Whether the parent talks about the bad things that happened at work*: Talking about the good things is what counts.

▼ *The child's view of whether the mother/father works too much*: Although parents' actual part-time/full-time status does make a difference in some instances, children's perceptions of how hard their parents work is not significant.

As I review these findings, I am reminded of an interview I conducted with an employed mother of three young children. She said that she used to think that the best times she spent with her children were simply a matter of what they did together, the one-on-one moments they had with each other: It was as if she were in a cocoon with her children. But lately she had come to realize that the walls of the cocoon are quite porous. Things that are going on in her life at work and with her spouse seep into that cocoon and affect her time with her children:

> It is the environment I am creating, my sense of well-being, how my husband and I are interacting and what else is going on [at work]. To me, that affects quality time. Period.
>
> If there is stress in this house you can't have quality time. The [children] can't have it by themselves and they can't have it with us.

I suspect that our findings are saying the same thing: If mothers *and* fathers have jobs that they don't like, if they have difficult working conditions, they are less able to meet the needs of their children. It goes back to my conclusion in Chapter 4: It's not *that* we work that matters most; it's *how* we work.

▼ WHAT ABOUT THE FUTURE THAT IS NOW?

We may be able to get a glimpse of what the future holds in store for the children we interviewed by looking at young people in their late teens, twenties, and early thirties. Much of how this generation is depicted has been written by market researchers who examine the views of people born between 1965 and 1982—commonly referred to as Generation X, Gen Xers, Xers, or twenty-somethings.

These young people grew up with divorce and latchkey kids in their families; pictures of missing children on their milk cartons; deteriorating and unsafe schools, racial strife, gangs, homelessness, and AIDS in their communities; junk food, the depleted ozone layer and global warming in their environment; downsizing, job loss, and escalating executive salaries in the job market; the threat and reality of war in the Middle East; fear of the collapse of social security for their old age; and mainstream media that have become like the tabloids featuring entertainment like *Beavis and Butthead* and *The Simpsons* and real-life serials like Joey Buttafuoco, Clarence Thomas, the Menendez brothers, O. J. Simpson, the Starr Report, and the impeachment of the president.

What Are Gen Xers Supposedly Like?

Generation watchers describe Gen Xers as follows:

▼ *Cynical:* "Everything from the presidency to our parents' own marriage was exposed to us long ago. It turned more than a few of us into philosophical nomads, believing very little of what we hear."[17]

▼ *Independent:* Seeing the world full of uncertainties and trade-offs, they resist rigid solutions. "Xers are determined to be involved, to be responsible, to be in control—and to stop being victimized by life's uncertainties." Because they spent a lot of time alone as children, "they learned that they could fend for themselves." And because they came of age in the aftermath of downsizing and reengineering, their loyalty is to themselves and their work rather than to institutions.[18]

▼ *Open to information:* They want hard facts, delivered by experts; are comfortable with technology and multifocus; and are less concerned with introspection.[19]

▼ *Focused on the present:* "Ask an Xer about the future and what you'll hear about is the here and now," according to a book on this subject, *Rocking the Ages*. This is a way to manage a world full of insecurity. It also makes this generation more open to taking risks.[20]

▼ *Aware of career possibilities:* Interested in jobs that provide "just-in-time leadership" (feedback that is frequent, accurate, specific, and timely); that will help them develop marketable skills, relationships with decision makers, creative challenges, increasing responsibilities, and control over their schedules, according to Bruce Tulgan, who has written extensively on managing Xers.[21]

To what extent are these proposed characteristics accurate? If they are accurate, then to what extent do they reflect changes in all of us, not just in the younger generation? In other words, to what extent do they represent youthful bravado that will mellow with age? The most careful researchers compare the past with the present, looking at an age group such as 18- to 32-year-olds then and now. They also look at how attitudes have changed over time within the total population. One such analysis found that the sense of being disaffected—that is, feeling bleak, cynical, and sad—has influenced all age groups, not just the youngest adult generation.[22]

How do Gen Xers feel about work and family issues?

Several qualitative studies both in the United States and abroad have explored how younger people view work and family. Kathleen Gerson at New York University is in the process of interviewing late adolescents and young adults between the ages of 18 and 30 years old randomly selected from a range of urban and suburban neighborhoods in the New York metropolitan area. She finds that most of these young people are "coping with a world in which high hopes and aspirations collide with subtle fears and constricted realities."[23] There is no going back to an era in which marriages are forever, women stay at home and raise children, and men are the ultimate authorities. And the era ahead of them will be extremely challenging. Across all the income and ethnic groups she interviewed, Gerson finds that young people feel that good jobs may be difficult to find, good marriages elusive, and the combining of work and family life fraught with challenges and hampered by a lack of institutional support. So they support diversity in how they want to live, seeking not the one ideal, but the best tradeoffs for each individual:

▽ *Work*: Although young women and men alike have high aspirations, those who are less advantaged are less optimistic. They want satisfying and secure jobs but aren't sure that they can find either. Men don't believe that they can support a family alone, and women don't feel secure in counting on men to support them, so each attempts to be economically independent. At the same time, both long for a respite from the demands of work.

▼ *Marriage*: Both men and women expect to be in dual-earner marriages. They think that it will be easier to find a good job than a good marriage and would prefer to be alone than to be trapped in a bad relationship. Women are attuned to the need to remain financially self-sufficient.

▼ *Parenthood*: Women and men believe that children thrive when there is a happy marriage, but that a child is better off with one parent who is happy than with two parents who are at war with each other. They both think that men and women should share parenting, but women doubt that men will do so and men doubt that their employers will give them the flexibility to do so.

▼ *Children*: Young people worry about the worsening situation of children. They don't blame the problems of children on working mothers or on changing families, but on community decline.

Suzan Lewis and Janet Smithson at Manchester Metropolitan University in the United Kingdom have worked with an international team to explore the orientations of young people, ages 18 through 30, by conducting focus groups in five European countries: Great Britain, Ireland, Portugal, Norway, and Sweden. Overall, they find that because of an elongated period spent in education and training and because of the growing insecurities of work, young people seem to live "in an extended present." "Settling down" is what will happen in the future, but not before they "live" their lives and find a secure job.[24]

▼ *Work*: Although young people do not expect to find a job that they will stay in for the rest of their lives, they are finding it difficult to find secure jobs, leading to doubts of financial independence and stability.

▼ *Marriage*: Young people recognize that families have become more diverse, but when they think of settling down, they think in the traditional sense of having a partner and having children. Yet many do not expect lifelong partners.

▼ *Parenthood*: Just as in the United States, the young people interviewed in Europe "hope to be able to work and to have a life outside work." Many see parenthood as a "joint effort" of women and men; however, their views of the roles of men and women vary across the five countries. Expectations for having employers support work-life issues are fairly low in all of the countries.

Gen Xers: A Reality Check

Our 1997 National Study of the Changing Workforce (NSCW) provides an opportunity to do a reality check on some of the issues that have emerged in these studies. Because many of same questions were asked both in 1997 and in the Department of Labor's 1997 Quality of Employment Survey, we can compare the views of nationally representative samples of 18- through 32-year-olds in the United States then and now. We can also assess how the views of the baby boomers (who were twenty-somethings themselves two decades ago) have changed over the past 20 years.[25]

Is family life more diverse?

According to the 1997 NSCW, the answer is overwhelmingly yes:

- ▼ Young workers today are less likely (40 percent) to be legally married than employees of comparable ages in 1977 were (52 percent). However, the same proportion live in marriagelike relationships then and now: 52 percent.
- ▼ Young workers today are much more likely to live in dual-earner households. In 1997, 82 percent of married young workers lived in dual-earner households compared with 69 percent of married workers in 1977.
- ▼ Despite the fact that fewer young workers today are married, they are just as likely to have children as their age peers 20 years ago: 41 percent have children under 18.

Thus, it appears that in the United States, at least, young people who are working are no more likely than those two decades ago to "live in an extended present" by putting off work and family challenges.

Do young people have more egalitarian views about parenthood?

Again according to the 1997 NSCW, the answer is yes.

- ▼ Whereas 36 percent of today's young workers feel that it is "better for everyone involved if the man earns the money and the woman takes care of the home and children," fully 56 percent of young workers felt that way 20 years ago.

▼ Today's baby boomers, who were the young workers 20 years ago, have also become more accepting of working mothers. Now 41 percent of baby boomers agree that it is better when women stay at home. But this figure is still somewhat higher than that of young workers today, 36 percent of whom support a more traditional division of labor.

Our research also shows that fathers are expected to be more involved in family life today than they were 20 years ago. For example, 46 percent of mothers 18 through 32 years old in 1977 thought that fathers should spend more time with their children compared with 63 percent of mothers of this age range in 1997.

Is work less secure?
Our findings from the 1997 NSCW agree with those of Kathleen Gerson, Suzan Lewis, and others that young people see jobs as a lot less secure:

▼ More than one quarter of young workers (27 percent) in 1997 felt that it was very or somewhat likely that they would lose their jobs within the next couple of years, compared with 15 percent 20 years earlier.

When the Quality of Employment Survey was conducted, the notion of a job for life was pretty much taken for granted, so questions about this issue were not included. However, in 1997, we did ask employees of all ages whether they imagined that they would remain with the same employer for most of their work lives when they first began working. So we are able to compare the views of the Xers with those of baby boomers.

▼ Gen Xers are less likely (41 percent) than baby boomers (54 percent) to report that when they first began working they imagined they would spend their working lives mainly with one company or organization.

▼ About half (51 percent) of both groups now believe that they shouldn't expect any company to provide lifelong employment. As an indication of the conflict-ridden nature of this issue, comparable proportions of both groups think that employers *should* provide job security.

Xers, however, are no more likely than their counterparts 20 years ago to job-hop. Only 22 percent of young workers then and now said that they would make a genuine effort to find a new job with a new employer in the coming year.

Do young people long for a respite from work?

Young workers today work longer total hours (both paid and unpaid) than their counterparts did 20 years ago (47 hours at all jobs for 18-through 32-year-olds now, compared with 43 hours for 18- through 32-year-olds then). Young workers today also see themselves working harder, working faster, and having too little time to get everything done.

Since our Ask the Children study found that only 21 percent of children want to work more than their parents, I wanted to know whether resistance to overwork is also manifested in the twenty-something generation. I certainly hear it from the young people I know and from their parents:

> *I am in a job where I am expected to stay to the middle of the night if we are finishing a project. Nobody says you have to but when one of the men here left at 8 o'clock, the boss made jokes that this man really didn't care about the project. And he does care. And he's good, too. So night after night I was working away, when I realized that I was turning into my mother. I didn't come this far in life to become just like my mother!*
>
> DESIGNER, 26 YEARS OLD

> *My daughter tells me that the feminists got it all wrong. She says, "Whose idea was it to invent the superwomen?" Why would anyone want to "do it all to have it all?" She thinks the way we live (working hard) is a joke.*
>
> MOTHER OF A COLLEGE STUDENT

If we simply compare Gen Xers with baby boomers using our 1997 NSCW data, we find that boomers (68 percent) are more likely than Xers (59 percent) to prefer to work fewer hours than they actually do each week. Why? Perhaps because the boomers work longer hours to begin with. And perhaps because more baby boomers are married, and married people want to work fewer hours. Interestingly enough, when we look at employees with children in both generational groups, there is no difference: 65 percent want to work fewer hours! That's a very large number.

What about trading a day's pay for an occasional day off? There we find that Gen Xers (63 percent) are more willing to make this tradeoff than boomers (55 percent). Here the difference seems to be due to unmarried Xers, who are more willing to trade money for time off than unmarried boomers. There is no difference between boomers and Xers with children in their willingness to make this tradeoff: 57 percent say they would trade a day's pay for an occasional day off.

Are Gen Xers more likely to put family first?

When we compare Gen Xer parents with those who are baby boomers using Ask the Children data, we find that Xers put a much higher priority on family than baby boomers do. However, since our earlier analyses showed that parents with younger children are more likely to put family first than parents with older children, we wondered whether Xers prioritize their family life more highly because they have younger children than boomers. The answer to that question is yes. When we use statistical controls for the age of the youngest child, we find no differences between Gen Xers and baby boomers: Regardless of their generation, parents with young children stress the importance of family life equally. Moreover, whereas one might expect fathers to put work above family and mothers to put family above work, this doesn't happen. Both fathers and mothers seem to see their roles as nurturing their families and providing for them economically.

The majority of parents (54 percent) put a higher priority on family than on work; a small minority (16 percent) put a higher priority on work; and 30.5 percent give equal priority to work and family.

9.11

Employed Boomer and Gen Xer Parents with a Child Birth Through 18: Priorities				
Much higher priority on family	Higher priority on family	Equal priority on family and work	Higher priority on work	Much higher priority on work
32%	22%	30.5%	12%	4%

Data from public opinion polls suggest that the country as a whole has become more family-oriented over the years. For example, according to the Yankelovich MONITOR, 56 percent of boomers when they were in their twenties and thirties in 1978 espoused a return to traditional standards in family life; in 1998 both 80 percent of boomers and 76 percent of Xers called for this. In addition, people in both groups are more likely to say that their satisfaction comes from home and family than they were 10 years ago.

In sum, many children, Gen Xers, and baby boomers alike appear to want to reduce the mounting pressures of work. Will they do so? I suspect they will.

How Do We Navigate Work and Family, and How Do We Ask the Children?

rom a living room in Albuquerque to a backyard in Portland, from a conference room in Bethesda to a newsroom in Denver, from a café in Boston to a beachfront restaurant in Miami's South Beach, we heard from parents about what works and what doesn't work in navigating the responsibilities of work and parenting. Using the conceptual framework, with the able assistance of Judy David, we have developed for this book and the results of our research, we share parents' and my own advice in this chapter.

HOW TO NAVIGATE WORK

As I've noted, it is not *that* we work, but *how* we work that makes the difference. But what does this mean in everyday life? Our research indicates it means keeping *job demands* at a level that feels reasonable; organizing our work so that we can *focus* on what's important without too many tasks to do at the same time or too many interruptions; improving the *quality of our job* so that our work feels meaningful, provides an opportunity to learn, and gives us some autonomy; and enlisting the *support at work* of coworkers and supervisors.

Job demands

I say keep job demands at a "reasonable" level because what's reasonable for one person may not be so for another. Each of us has a different threshold for pressure—a boundary between what feels exciting and challenging and what feels overwhelming. More specifically, our analyses reveal that when we work longer hours and more days per week, when we take work home, and when we feel that we don't have enough time to get everything done, we are more likely to be stressed. Likewise, when we feel that we don't have enough time to get everything done, we are less likely to feel successful at work.

▼ **Seek the flexibility you need to manage your work and family responsibilities.**

▼ Determine your needs for flexibility. Do you want what is called *traditional flextime*, in which you select arrival and departure times and stick with them? Do you want *daily flextime*, varying your arrival and departure times daily? Do you want to work at home occasionally or on a more regular basis? Or do you want to reduce your hours?

▼ Find out about your employer's policies and practices on flexibility. Talk to other employees who have used these policies to learn what's worked, what hasn't, and what they would do differently if they had it all to do again.

▼ **If you would like to have greater flexibility in your work schedule and it's not immediately available, make a "business case" for having this flexibility.**

In order to make a business case, you need to assume a dual perspective—yours and your employer's. You need to show how it is in your employer's self-interest to provide greater flexibility. Here are the steps you can take:

▼ Find a champion or champions within your organization to work with you. These champions need to be well enough respected by your employer to carry credibility in espousing this issue. Depending on the circumstances, these champions may advise you behind the scenes or take a more public role. Also depending on the circumstances, you may want to suggest the creation of a new policy or simply advocate a change in your own schedule.

▽ Develop several options to ensure that your work will get done on time and at least as productively as before. This can include doing your work but at different times or in different places such as at home or coming in an hour earlier and then leaving an hour earlier. Or it may mean that others take over some of your responsibilities.

▽ Before you present your business case, think about your supervisor's decision-making style. Does your boss make better decisions if he or she sees things in writing first? Does your boss like to be handed a written memo when you meet? Or does your boss prefer a discussion, perhaps followed by a written memo? Use the approach that best suits your supervisor.

▽ If you develop a written memo, it should include your "business case" and the options you suggest.

▽ Suggest a trial period so that you and your employer can work the kinks out of the systems and make changes where necessary.

▽ Where there are problems, try to work them out collaboratively.

▽ Stick to the trial period and come back to your employer at the end of this time with "It's working" or "Here's what I would do to improve this plan."

Employers are much more enthusiastic about flexibility if they feel you are not assuming that it is an entitlement, owed to you—leaving coworkers and your boss to pick up the pieces—but rather that you are working as partners to ensure that the work gets done while you get more flexibility.

Whether or not you decide to advocate and then take advantage of greater flexibility, here are some other suggestions for managing work demands:

▼ **Prioritize what's most important for you to accomplish at work.**

An illness or a dramatic event in our lives should not be necessary to make us sift through all of the demands on us and decide what's most important. It's much better to live our lives this way on an everyday basis.

▼ **Set realistic expectations of what you can accomplish.**

A parent describes how she has learned to set doable expectations:

> *I used to have these endless to-do lists and of course there was no way that I could ever get everything on my list done, so I would always feel bad about myself. Now I go to work every day with no more than three top priorities. If I do more than that—and I almost always do—I feel really great.*

▼ Say no when you need to.

Another parent says:

> *I've learned only this past month to say to people, "I can't do that on that day. I'm not available." And when they say, "Oh, well, what are you doing? Maybe you can switch your plans," I just say, "No, I wish I could help, but I really can't." I used to say, "Maybe I can," and I used to tell them what I was doing, as if it was their responsibility to determine what I should do.*

When you say no, it is important to do so with respect. Or you can say, "I can't do this today. Would next Tuesday be okay?" Sometimes people who have always tried to please go to the opposite extreme and turn into vehement naysayers, offending everyone in sight, when that kind of adamancy is really not necessary and is often counterproductive.

▼ Use problem-solving techniques.

I am amazed again and again at how useful problem-solving techniques are for reducing job demands and at how few people use them:

▼ Identify the problem.
▼ Generate multiple ways to solve the problem. At this stage, there is no one right answer—the more solutions you have, the better.
▼ Evaluate what would work and what wouldn't for each of your possible solutions. Look at the impact of each solution on you, on the other people involved, and on the results you hope to achieve.
▼ Select one solution to try out on the basis of your evaluation. Remember there is no one right answer—think of this solution

as an idea you are testing, rather than as the answer to all of your prayers.

▼ After a trial period, review your solution. If it is working, keep at it. If not, try another solution. Or if necessary, redefine your definition of the problem and begin the process again.

The following is a real life example of how this technique works. An employed parent of twins served as an office manager of a small company. On her commute to work every morning, she composed her must-do list. Soon into her day, she confronted the day's emergencies: The copier needed new toner but no one had ordered it; the phone company was doing repairs on the phone lines outside the building so the phone system would be down for a hour or so; the receptionist was out of work with a stomach virus and it was necessary to find a replacement; a vendor needed more detailed information on the specifications of an order before he could provide a bid; several employers needed help understanding their new software; and someone was reporting a new virulent computer virus. Her must-do list curled up in smoke!

Using this problem-solving technique, the office manager identified her major problem: She was bombarded by daily emergencies—all urgent to the employees in question. This identification process was useful because she further realized that this situation wasn't going to go away. It was her "real" job to respond to employee problems. Thus, the problem wasn't really the external situation; it was her attitude about it. When she saw employees' requests as interfering with her must-do list, she resisted and resented people who went to her for help. When she redefined her job as providing service to employees, she approached their problems from a different and more constructive vantage point: She wanted to meet their needs in the best possible way. In fact, she made a sign that she tacked above her desk: "Customer service."

Her change of attitude notwithstanding, she was still faced with too much to do each day. Thus, she brainstormed possible solutions:

▼ She could tell employees all the things that stood in the way of meeting their requests.
▼ She could prioritize employees' requests.
▼ She could work with employees to evaluate the "real" urgency of their requests.

When she looked at the pros and cons of each solution, she concluded that telling employees about other people's problems wasn't going to win friends and influence people. Likewise, it would be hard for her to prioritize employee requests without more information from them. Therefore, she selected the third option for her trial. She could work with employees to evaluate the urgency of their request. And if she couldn't fulfill it as needed, she would work with them to provide stopgap measures until she could resolve their problem.

When the office manager tested this solution, things changed—employees became less demanding. She realized that when she approached employees with more empathy and respect, they treated her likewise. And though she had more than enough to accomplish each day, she felt that she was swimming with the tide rather than against it.

▼ Use technology.

A parent who has a high-powered job finds that technology has helped her manage its demands. She can sort out what she needs to do at work and what she can do at home either early in the morning or after her children have gone to sleep—such as responding to email. Now, she can linger with her child in the morning because she has already dealt with the pressing work-related issues at home via computer.

▼ Get help when you need it.

Saying that you need help in managing your workload is not an admission of failure. In fact, it is an admission of strength. I have known people who would get overburdened (the everyday tasks were piling up) but who couldn't accept help even when it was freely offered. In a sense, we are setting ourselves up for more failure this way rather than concentrating on the goal—the work tasks we want to accomplish.

▼ Take stock regularly.

It is like a New Year's resolution. We can start out determined not to let work overwhelm us, but slowly, surely, the stress starts to escalate. Pick a time, such as the first day of the month, to check in with yourself to see how things are going and to make changes.

Focus at work

Our open-ended interviews with employed parents uncovered the issue of maintaining "focus at work" as an essential component of feeling productive. These interviews helped us define "focus" as being able to pay attention to your work without feeling pulled away or distracted by constant interruptions or by the demands of other tasks. We then used our survey of a nationally representative sample of employed parents to determine how often employed parents feel that they can really focus on their work. We found that:

▼ 19 percent find it very difficult to focus on the work that they have to do often or very often.
▼ 55.5 percent say that they work on too many tasks at the same time often or very often.
▼ 41 percent report that they are interrupted during the workday often or very often, making it difficult for them to get their work done.

Our analyses revealed that parents who find it easier to focus on the work they have to do, who don't work on too many tasks at the same time, and who aren't interrupted too frequently feel less stressed. They also feel more successful at work. Here are some strategies for assessing and improving your focus at work.

▼ Uncover the assumptions that guide when and how work gets done.

Expectations underlie the way we behave at work. They govern when and how we work as well as how we react to problems and their solutions. In the study at Xerox discussed in Chapter 4, researchers unearthed the following assumptions about that particular worksite:

▼ We should operate as if we are in perpetual crisis mode.
▼ If there is a problem, we throw more time at it.
▼ Time—at least at work—is an infinite resource.
▼ The hero at work is the individual who slaves long hours and solves the crisis at the very last minute.

Obviously, it is very hard to maintain focus when one remains in a perpetual crisis mode. So step back for a minute and try to observe yourself at work as if you were an anthropologist in a foreign land. Why do you behave as you do? What are the assumptions you are making about how work should be done, about who gets rewarded, and about what it takes to get ahead? Ask yourself whether you think these assumptions are realistic and/or effective for you at work and at home. If not, try to change these assumptions to others that make you feel more fulfilled and successful.

To try to make changes, seek the help of a supervisor or colleagues in determining what to do about the assumptions that you think are undermining your own (and perhaps others') effectiveness at work. For example, one new employee in a company thought it was expected that everyone take piles of work home over the weekend. He sought the advice of a veteran employee, who told him that the results of his accomplishments were what mattered most, not the bulging briefcase he carried out of the office on Friday evenings.

▼ **Restructure your time or working space so that you have fewer interruptions.**

At many worksites I have studied, employees feel that they can't get their "real" work done during the workday—there are too many interruptions. So "real" work is consigned to "the edges," at the beginning or end of the day. Problem solving together or alone, employees can come up with many solutions, including the following:

▼ Post a sign (it can be humorous) near your workspace saying "No interruptions."
▼ Arrange to arrive at work later and get the essentials done at home before you go to work.
▼ Find a quiet place to work.
▼ Set up your workspace so that it minimizes distractions.
▼ Wear a Walkman and play soothing music to screen out noise.

Each of us has a different tolerance for interruptions. Be aware of when you are most productive and find ways to make that happen more frequently. By making others aware of what you are doing and by seeking help when necessary, you can improve your capacity to focus and you can enlist the support of others to help you do so. Sometimes all you need is half an hour of uninterrupted time to finish a task that has been hanging over your head—and when it's completed, you'll feel a deep sense of accomplishment and relief.

▼ **Help others around you maintain focus.**

A working mother with a young child makes an interesting point about how she applies her parenting techniques to the workplace:

> *Sticking to the facts is hard for kids and adults. When a child wants to get out of a jam, he'll try to cloud the issue with other stuff; your employees do the same thing. You have to listen to them, remaining very patient and calm, and help them focus on the issue.*

▼ Find a satisfactory level of multitasking.

Just as each of us has a different tolerance for interruptions, we also respond differently to doing many things at the same time. Some of us (me included) are more productive if we have a number of balls in the air at the same time, and others like to do one thing at a time.

If you fall into that majority (55 percent) who feel you have too many balls in the air, you can try to structure your time so that your work tasks are more sequential. This may mean talking with your boss and your coworkers about how you work best and seeing whether they can support your working style.

One way to remove some of the "clutter" in our work lives is to focus on what's most important. As one parent explains:

> *A rule I have for myself is trying not to do work that's not truly valuable, trying to eliminate it, trying to focus on what's most important.*

Job quality

We looked at four aspects of a good-quality job—job autonomy, learning opportunities, job challenge, and meaningful work. We found that:

- ▼ almost three quarters of parents with children 18 and younger feel that they have freedom to decide what to do on their jobs (74 percent) and a lot of say about what happens on their jobs (73 percent).
- ▼ about four in five employed parents agree "somewhat" or "strongly" that they are satisfied with the opportunities they have at work to learn new skills (79 percent), that their jobs require that they keep learning new things (85 percent), and that their jobs require that they be creative (79 percent).
- ▼ likewise, the vast majority of employed parents agree either

somewhat or strongly that the work they do is meaningful to them (89 percent).

Parents who have better-quality jobs are less stressed at work and feel more satisfied. A parent says:

> Being able to use the skills that I have that I've acquired over the years makes me feel fulfilled. I'm very proud of what I've accomplished, of what I'm doing. Even though at any moment I may feel guilty about the 42 things I haven't done yet, overall I'm pretty pleased with what's happening. I feel that you can find a job where there are new challenges all the time.

▼ Look for opportunities to have a say in how to do your work.

Some workplaces solicit and use the feedback of employees, and others are based on the "command and control" notion of management. Whatever your situation, look for the moments to offer your ideas.

It is important that your suggestions be offered in a way that can be heard. It is much easier for a boss to avoid the whiners, the complainers, the glass-half-empty types, and the gossipers than to listen to them and to heed their advice. Here are some suggestions for how to present your ideas constructively:

▼ Start by saying what you appreciate about the situation.
▼ Identify the problems you want to address without blaming or criticizing.
▼ Take both employees' and employers' views into account.
▼ Make a business case for addressing the problem, showing that the benefits for taking action outweigh the cost of the situation's remaining the same.
▼ Suggest several ways of solving the problem.
▼ Make suggestions for how the proposed solution could be evaluated.

I have noticed that the moments when I feel I have no control are the moments when I can become most rattled: I have plans to do something I feel I must do, and all of a sudden those plans are swept away by a momentary squall. I have had to learn to distinguish between when it is viable to regain control and when it isn't. When reestablishing control is not within the realm of possibility, I find it's better to go with the flow than either to try to turn things around or to feel upset that my well-laid plans have crashed. It is the same skill we use in parenting and it serves us well at work, too.

▼ **Create a learning environment for yourself at work.**

Although our analyses showed that parents with more education and with higher incomes are more likely to feel that their jobs offer opportunities to learn, my guess from working with both low- and high-wage workers is that attitudes have something to do with these judgments as well. Two people can be in the same job, one of them always seeking ways to learn more and the other absorbing only what is necessary and then becoming static. One manager says that she tells prospective assistants:

> *You can make this job as boring or as interesting as you want. There will always be scut work to do. It's up to you whether you want to open the mail and hand it to me, or open the mail, read it, and hand it to me. Same thing with a copying job. It is up to you to decide to learn.*

It comes down to curiosity and a verve for learning. In this era of "employability" in which workers are expected to take personal responsibility for their careers (as opposed to getting on a path and then being pulled forward along a set course like a carnival car on a track), the people who value and enjoy learning will fare better.

▼ Identify what interests and intrigues you about your job.
▼ Find ways to learn more about this by talking with people, reading, attending classes or conferences.
▼ Become the resident expert on this subject for your work group.
▼ Follow this pursuit on to the next set of questions, the next frontier of your learning.

By intensifying your opportunities to learn, you may feel as if you are only adding to an already crammed schedule, but in fact, if you are learning on the job, you will probably enjoy your job more and the work will seem less arduous.

If you have been given a task at work that seems beyond your grasp, reach out to others to learn from them. These helpers don't have to be within your workplace. For example, my daughter was asked to organize a town hall–style meeting in which well-known figures in the media and politics would listen to the concerns of middle school and high school students. What topics should she include? How should she organize the day? Where should she find the students? Where should she hold the event? What would be the incentive for young people to attend? There were an overwhelming number of considerations, and she had never done anything like this before. But she turned to her coworkers, to a network of community leaders she had established across the country in the course of her regular job, and to other young people. With advice and help, she was able to develop an outstanding plan.

▼ **Look for meaning in your work.**

In our efforts not to see our work as competing with our children, many of us have probably overemphasized the money we earn and underemphasized the meaning of our work. Yet as I noted in Chapter 8, it is important for our children to know that work can be meaningful because they are more likely to judge us as more competent and to want to emulate us if we like our jobs. Moreover, our study reveals that parents who feel their work is meaningful experience less stress.

The other night I was talking with a young person I know. She works at a law firm in a secretarial pool. Work exhausts her. She goes home at the end of the day too tired to do anything but get ready for the next day. But it's not simply the hours she works that drain her—it's the complete lack of meaning in this work. She feels like "chattel," with no real connection to the lawyers. A lawyer whom she has assisted several times will say, "Nice to meet you," not remembering her. She sees only slices of the tasks she does—the beginning or the middle or the end. She never has a sense of what the full task is or why it is being done. In sum, she faces an "off the scale" lack of meaning in her work. In extreme cases like this, it might be better to look for another job. But if there are possibilities in your work, mine them:

▼ Take a moment to reflect on the importance of what you do: How does your work contribute to a larger good?
▼ Find meaning in the relationships you have at work. If you have been curt and rushed with clients, customers, students, or patients—whoever is the recipient of your efforts—try to build relationships that are more worthwhile to them and to you.

Support at work

We have defined support at work as three-pronged: feeling supported by your supervisor, by your coworkers, and by the company culture. We found the following:

▼ 85 percent of employed parents somewhat or strongly agree that their supervisors are understanding when they talk about the personal or family issues that affect their work; 69 percent feel comfortable bringing up personal or family issues; and 74.5 percent feel that their supervisors really care about the effect that work demands have on their personal and family life.

▼ 88 percent somewhat or strongly agree that they feel a part of the group of people they work with, and 89 percent look forward to being with their coworkers each day.

▼ 30 percent of employed fathers and mothers somewhat or strongly agree that it is not acceptable at their organization to take care of family needs on company time. Another 41.5 percent agree that employees who put their family or personal needs ahead of their jobs are not looked upon favorably.

A working parent describes the difference a supportive administrator can make:

> *He knows I do my job. He's not looking at his watch wondering where I am. I don't have to ask to leave or that I need time off. I just inform him and I leave.*

We found that employed parents in more supportive work environments experience less stress and feel more successful. A parent we interviewed described how a bad relationship at work can eat at you:

> *You can feel good about the work you do, the tasks you do. But if someone treats you badly, then all of that goes away real fast. It's so aggravating at a very personal, visceral level.*

Even some children recognize that an unfair boss contributes to their parents' work-related stress. A 10-year-old boy observes:

> *[My mother's boss] is not that nice or polite to her; he screams at her over deadlines.*

He wishes she would change jobs and bosses.

▼ **Try to bring out the best in your boss.**

▽ Appreciate your boss when he or she is supportive and remember to say thank you.

▽ If you have to miss work because of your children, explain this to your boss and have a plan prepared for how your work will get done.

▽ Figure out a way to tell your boss when she or he treats you in a way that is counterproductive.

To discuss problems with your boss, it is best to know his or her style. For example, a boss who dishes it out might hear you best if you dish it right back. Being apologetic or subservient would only encourage more bullying. In a case like this, an employee said to her supervisor, "If someone else acted the way you just did, you would have a fit. Come on; don't treat me that way." And it worked.

This tactic could backfire with a different personality. When her boss got wound up and agitated, another employee was able to say to him: "I really hate seeing you so upset. Let's talk in a few minutes." And that worked.

Another person could be made aware of his or her actions with humor. Sometimes a constructive voice mail or email message can be effective, especially for someone who needs time to think. Waiting for the right moment always helps: "I know budgets are due this week and your days are pretty hectic. Let's talk next week."

When my daughter graduated from college, one of the commencement speakers advised her graduating class that the world is populated with people "you went to junior high school with" (i.e., jerks), but "you should be nice to them because one of them may be your boss someday." It was good advice.

▼ **See whether "people skills" can become a part of your organization's performance appraisals.**

In the Families and Work Institute's 1998 Business Work-Life Study, a representative study of employers with 100 or more employees, we asked whether companies "consider how well supervisors manage the work-family issues of employees in making job performance appraisals." We were pleasantly surprised to find that 44 percent say that they do.

If your organization doesn't do this, see whether "people skills," including managing work-family issues, can be considered part of job performance appraisals and can be tied to pay increases. This is perhaps one of the most effective ways to improve management's responsiveness to work-family problems.

▼ Find support for dealing with your boss.

It is a good idea to have someone who can help you when problems arise with your boss. This person can help you figure out what's really going on, talk through how to approach your boss, and give you feedback on how your actions might be contributing to the problem. Pick your support person or persons carefully. You need someone who appreciates you, who will be honest, and who will not break your confidence. It's also important that your boss not see your relationship with this person as a betrayal.

▼ Build positive relationship with coworkers.

So many people think of their coworker relationships as a given without realizing how they can shape these relationships to be more supportive. The process starts with the following steps:

- ▼ acknowledging the positive work your coworkers do.
- ▼ being thoughtful—giving your coworker Post-it notes with a funny message or a new kind of pencil.
- ▼ pitching in for your coworkers when they need help or when they have a work-family problem.
- ▼ refraining from spreading information that coworkers told you in confidence and refraining from backbiting.

An employed mother adds:

> I avoid situations and people at work who drain me. If I have to work with them, I try to be humble and figure out what it will take to make the situation work.

▼ Contribute to a supportive culture.

At my organization, we begin each year by talking about what we want our organizational culture to be like. We post these "resolutions" for all to see. We also build cultural expectations into performance appraisals. We describe the culture we want and then each of us is assessed on his or her efforts to contribute to realizing this culture (recognizing that the development of an organizational culture is always a work in progress).

▼ **Keep your perspective when all else fails.**

Putting matters into perspective when you're under high pressure helps. An educator in a high-stress inner-city school shares his technique:

> *My theme song is "Row, row, row your boat, gently down the stream." We've got to live with some joy and gentleness. It's a mental conversation I have with myself: "Have you done your best? Okay. Then let it go. Don't keep holding on, trying to control." We just have to do our best and bring good energy.*

HOW TO NAVIGATE THE TRANSITION FROM HOME TO WORK AND FROM WORK TO HOME

Successfully navigating the transition from home to work and back again can help minimize negative spillover while maximizing the chances of positive spillover that will help you and your children thrive when you are apart and when you are together.

From home to work
▼ **Get as organized as you can the night before.**

Getting clothes set out, lunches made, and homework or work ready to go the night before can prevent the very familiar last-minute crises:

> *Where is my blue shirt? I need to wear it today.*
> *I can't find the permission slip I'm supposed to bring to school.*
> *Why do we only have peanut butter for lunch? I'm sick of peanut butter.*
> *Where did I put those papers that I need to bring to work?*

▼ **Get up in time so that you aren't rushed.**

A mother of two school-age children advises:

> *This may not work for nonmorning people, but I always feel so much better if I can have some time to myself before everyone else in the household gets up.*

Another says:

> *I trained myself in 15-minute increments to get up one hour earlier. Now I have time for a leisurely shower, coffee, and time with a good book before the morning madness begins. I firmly resist the temptation to do work or chores during this time. My rule is "What can I do that is fun?"*

▼ **Set up rituals for saying good-bye.**

A father who drops off his children at child care before he heads for work says:

> *We would have terrible struggles in the morning until I set up a game we do every morning. We play Simon Says: Simon Says get your coat. Simon Says get your lunch. Go out the door. Whoops—I caught you because I didn't say Simon Says so you can't go out the door until I say Simon Says.*

▼ **Change your perspective on good-bye.**

My perspective on good-bye is that we are teaching our children how to venture out. So rather than seeing good-bye as a loss, a rupture, something we are inflicting on our kids, I saw it as an opportunity to teach my children how to approach the world with enthusiasm and anticipation of what the new day can bring!

▼ **Leave your child with care givers or teachers you trust.**

All the parents we interviewed felt so much better about leaving their children if they were leaving them with people who enriched and enlarged their children's lives, who were like extended family:

I don't carry the guilt of leaving my children unless their health is questionable. I leave my parent self as soon as I hug my last child good-bye in the morning. I can do that because my child care is phenomenal.

▼ **Have a backup plan for emergencies.**

Don't wait until your child is slightly sick, it's a snow day, or your child care falls apart to make a backup plan. Find people or a place in your community for backup care.

▼ **Create a going-to-work transition for yourself.**

When a parent with older children was going through a tough divorce, she found the drive to work helped her relax, let go of her home problems, and focus on the workday ahead:

Driving in the car is wonderful therapy because I can turn on Christian music. I can put in a classical tape if I want. Or I can just have quiet. There is a point on the interstate and when I drive over it in the morning, I realize this issue [of the divorce] is gone, because I can't fix it right now. That part of my day I'll take care of when I get back home. There's a line— I don't know where it is, but I can feel it. When I drive to work in that car and I'm by myself, I can feel the tension leave and I'm okay.

From work to home
▼ **Phase out work at the end of the workday.**

Some parents use their last moments at work to "switch out of the work mode":

I meditate at my desk for a few minutes before I leave.

Another describes the technique that a friend uses:

I have a friend who freshens her makeup and spritzes on perfume as a closure to her day before she leaves the office. It's a way for her to affirm herself as a person and a woman, not just a worker or a parent.

Another parent says:

It takes about twenty minutes to come home from work. When I'm closer to work, I think about the things that have happened through the day. As I get closer to home, I start thinking more about things at home, or what needs to happen when I get home. And what I need to be doing when I get home. It's the drive that makes the transition for me.

▼ **Develop rituals to help you make the transition.**

It is fascinating how many parents change their clothes as a symbolic act of shifting from their work selves to their parent selves. A father takes off his uniform before he leaves work:

Maybe it's the act of changing in the locker room [that helps me], putting my street clothes back on, my Levi's and T-shirt.

A mother of two preschoolers changes her clothes as soon as she gets home:

When I pick [my children] up at child care, I'm in my work clothes. As soon as we got in the door, they used to say, "I need the snack, the juice," all this. So now I ask them in the car, on the ride home, "What would you like for a snack or a drink when we get home?" Then I know what they want—they can express their needs and I say, "Okay, I'll do that. Before I give it to you, though, what does Mommy need to do?" And they both yell out, "Change her clothes."

It just takes a few minutes for me to change, but they know they've got my undivided attention afterward. But before I did that, I was so frustrated with them for placing all these demands on me when I couldn't even change my clothes. I do realize they're young children; it's not fair. It's not their fault that I'm wearing work clothes.

Another mother describes this process as transforming her sense of self:

> *As soon as I get home, I take those work clothes off, the panty-hose come off and the sweat pants go on. There definitely is a transition in the person you become because at work you're a professional and you're all dressed up. As soon as I take those work clothes off, I feel like I can relax and the environment is much more homey. It's two different people, two different types of individuals, and sometimes it's hard to shut one off.*

I have always thought of changing clothes as the Mister Rogers technique. Remember how Fred Rogers always takes off his jacket and puts on his sweater and sneakers at the beginning of his television show, *Mister Rogers' Neighborhood?*

For one mother, it goes beyond changing clothes. The transition into her "home" versus her "work" sense involves changing her tone of voice, her demeanor, everything:

> *Sometimes when I answer the phone at home I answer it "May I help you?" because I just can't get out of the work mode. I definitely try to transition into a different person because my son knows. He'll ask me why [I answer the phone the way I do]? Funny, but until he says something like that, you don't even know you're doing it.*

It's her son's reactions, more than her own needs, that have triggered this mother to shed her work demeanor. Her son has made it clear that he wants a "mother, not an employee" to be at home.

▼ **Make sure your children's needs are met when you see them.**

If the children are tired or hungry, there is a greater chance that "arsenic hour" (my term, because when things get crazy you want to give it to them or take it yourself) will erupt in full force. I always had a snack with me when I picked up my children or tried to have a healthy snack already prepared in the refrigerator. Rather than seeing this snack as spoiling dinner, I treated cut-up vegetables or fruit, for example, as one of the courses of dinner.

▼ **Develop "hello" rituals for your children.**

Hello rituals make it easier to reconnect with your children. In our family, I always sang a song to them: "What did you do in school today, what did you do in school today, what did you do in school today, dear little boy—or girl—of mine?" Although they wouldn't always answer a straight question about what happened in school, this song was so embedded as a family tradition that they would usually sing their response back to me.

▼ **Expect your children to save their troubles for you.**

Children typically save their pent-up feelings from the day for the people they feel most comfortable with—their parents. Although it doesn't seem fair that they are on their best behavior with others and not us, the fact that they can share their feelings is an indication that they feel safer and more supported by us than by others.

Rather than resist "arsenic hour," it is better to accept it and plan for it, as this mother does:

> When I pick [my children] up from their after school program, they're pretty exhausted and grumpy and tired of negotiating with people. So the car ride home is often sort of a blowing off steam time.

Another parent checks in with her children before the end of the day to assess their level of tension:

> I call home in the afternoon, after school, and I can get a sense of how things have gone, what the noise level is, and whether they're fighting.

Her response depends on how her own day has gone:

> When I have the energy, I can engage and set up something. When I don't have the energy, when I'm physically exhausted, it's harder. Sometimes I can think of something for them to do that I don't have to be involved in.

Knowing what to expect helps her prepare.

▼ **If you have had "one of those days," take care of yourself if you can and be straight with your children about it.**

On tough days, some mothers and fathers often say they walk in the door and head for a quiet room, where they rest or compose themselves.

Even 5 minutes alone can help. When children are very young, you obviously need someone to supervise them while you take some time for yourself. Perhaps your child care provider or spouse can take care of the children for a few extra minutes while you shower and change, have a snack, open up the mail, or otherwise decompress behind closed doors.

It is important to be honest with your children, saying that you are tired, you need some time to recover, and when you're in a better mood you can have a better time together. If children have waited for you for a long time, they may find this additional wait difficult so provide a realistic answer to how long you need "time out." If it's hard for them to gauge time, set a kitchen timer so they can watch the numbers. Some children think it is their fault that you're upset or that you're rejecting them, so it is important to dispel these feelings: "You didn't do anything to upset me. I just had a tough day at work."

HOW TO SET UP REASONABLE BOUNDARIES

As I listened to parents talk about the transitions between work and home, I heard what I came to think of as "rules." Parents didn't describe them as rules, but each of us has certain standards that we feel we *must* maintain to preserve and protect the boundaries between work and family—particularly as the boundaries between these domains of life have become more blurred and permeable. For one father, it is leaving on time:

> Five o'clock, I'm out of there. Quality time is important, but a half hour of quality time before they go to bed as opposed to being home to help make dinner, eat with them, give them baths, help them do their homework isn't the same. All time has to be quality, but there's a quantitative aspect of it too, which just has to be there, because the kids will notice that.

For another parent, it is pickup time at child care. If she's later than 5:45 P.M., she feels that she's a bad parent; if she's earlier, she is a good parent.

Some parents hold dinner hour as sacrosanct. One family used to watch television during dinner, but now they don't:

> I make it a point for all of us to sit down and just say, "No, I'm sorry we're not watching that TV show; we're going to take these

> *30 minutes." Once you put your foot down and say this sharing*
> *time is important, then it's okay.*

Minimizing work at home is another "rule" that a number of parents follow. This may mean not taking phone calls (including work phone calls) during family time:

> *If my husband is reading to one child and I'm reading to the other and the phone rings, the answering machine picks up. I don't let the interruptions happen.*
>
> *I used to have clients calling me at all hours and I felt as though I needed to respond to them—they're paying the bills. I didn't have clear end times for my frequent phone calls and the kids would be needing something. It just felt really unprofessional and I was pulled in two different directions. Now I have stopped the phone calls after a certain hour at night.*

A father tries to avoid taking work home "like the plague," but if he must do it, he has a strategy:

> *I'll bring home light stuff, like I'll write a short memo or outline a presentation. Or I'll read some because I like to keep up on the technical aspects of my job.*

Another parent always takes off time when the children are sick—no matter what.

> *The major conflict that's always been there was working when the kids were sick. We just did the best we could. Now I'm finally able to say I need this job, I like this job, but my kids come first. I'm finally able to shove the guilt of needing to be at work. And it's just too bad that it took me 12 years to do it. I wish I had been able to learn this a lot sooner, when the girls were younger.*

Another parent notes that staying at home with a sick child involves more than changing your attitude—it can involve taking on a work culture that frowns on absence:

> *Please learn early not to let your employer make you feel guilty for wanting to be with your children when they're sick. Your kids aren't going to be there forever.*

Not missing a special event in their child's life is a rule for some. Because he was clear in his own mind and communicated his priorities to his superiors, "everything just fell in line" for this father:

> *If the kids were involved in something that was important, don't count on me being [at work].*

A single parent who is a nurse with adolescent children describes her rule as being on call for her kids:

> *Nursing is very much a part of me and my children know that. But they also know, all they have to do is pick up that phone and I'm out of here. If they need me to come home, if they need me to do something, I'll do it.*

There is no one rule that is important to everyone. We need to set our own rules. These rules become very important to us. In the pioneering world we are all in, these rules serve as our litmus test that we are living up to our expectations, that we are being the kind of parent we want to be. But sometimes our expectations turn out to be unreasonable. For example:

> *Dinner on the table by 6:30 was the rule in my house growing up. So I tried to do that. It was a hopeless guilt trip in my life today. So I ditched it!*

This woman was wise to revise her expectation, to resolve the dissonance between her expectation and reality. So ask yourself what is the basis of your expectation: Does it come from your parents? Your friends? Does it really embody your values and priorities? If not, update your rules so they work for you and for your family.

HOW TO NAVIGATE WHEN WORK RESPONSIBILITIES CONFLICT WITH FAMILY RESPONSIBILITIES

There are many times when regardless of the boundaries we have created, there is spillover. Rather than resist or blame yourself, find ways to cope:

▼ Provide explanations when work must interfere with family life. When you need to change the routine and leave for work earlier or come home later, let your children know why. If there are phone calls that you need to take at home also explain why.
▼ Tell children about deadlines. A university professor explains:

As my kids have gotten older, I just say I have this deadline. If I get totally crazy, I will apologize when I'm done. I say to them, "Let me know if I'm too impossible but expect me to be a little cuckoo for a while."

▼ Set up a system so children know when they can interrupt you when you are working and when they can't. If they call you at work, how can they get through? When can they have you paged? When should they wait? And if you are taking calls at home, when is it an emergency and when is it routine? A mother who is a physician signals the urgency of a phone call with colored cards. When a phone call is truly an emergency she holds up a green card to indicate "absolutely no interruptions." When a phone call is important, but she can be interrupted if necessary, she holds up a blue card.
▼ Work to resolve problems that emerge when work and family conflict with each other. If you always promise that you will be off the phone in "a minute" but the minutes tick away into hours and your children get more and more distraught, problem-solve with your kids. You might decide that you will try to be more accurate about the amount of time you are going to be on the phone. You might place a timer by the phone to help you keep track. And you might pack a bag of special "phone toys" that your kids can play with when you must talk on the telephone.

HOW TO NAVIGATE FAMILY LIFE

I found in this study that the same aspects of life that are important at work are important at home as well: demands, focus, autonomy, and support. In other words, the demands of your life as a parent, your capacity to focus on your child, the autonomy you have in raising your child the way you want to, and the support you have from family and friends are linked to how successful you feel at home.

Family demands and focus

When I was initially developing this conceptual model for how work and family fit together, I cast the notion of family demands in negative shades (just as work demands can feel negative). But in fact, we found that the *more time* that parents spend with their child, the *more activities* they are engaged in together, the *less rushed* they feel their time with their child is, and the easier they find it to *focus* on their child, the better they feel about their parental competence and success. I call this *intentional parenting*. Parents who put more into being a parent—by spending more time with their child and doing more together—feel better about the job they do.

The findings for children are exactly the same. The more time they spend with their parents, the more activities they do together, the less their time is rushed, the more they feel it is easy for their parents to focus on them when they are together, the more positive children feel about their parents' competence and the way their parents manage work and family life.

▼ Reframe the way you think about time with your children.

When we ask the children, we see that there is a need to change how we think about time with children. Recently, I was interviewed by the *New York Times* on the question of whether parents should get off the fast track and devote more time to their children and by *Time* magazine on mothers who have cut back their work hours to spend more time with their children. To both of these reporters, *simply* spending more time was *the* answer to all of our problems. The amount of time parents and children spend together is certainly important, but we continue to separate—almost surgically—the amount of time parents and children spend together from *what they do in that time*. Therein is the crux of the quantity time versus quality time debate. As I have argued throughout, this is an outmoded concept because it is based on an either/or notion. It is not an either/or proposition. *Both* the amount of time *and* what happens in that time matter. These aspects of time with our children cannot be separated.

Another reason that the quality time versus quantity time debate is outmoded is that the word *quality* has come to have a meaning that is virtually unattainable on an everyday basis. Nothing ever goes wrong in quality time. No children throw food at each other across the dining room table. No children are ever surly with us. No children are ever too busy to be with us. There are no disagreements, no arguments, no fights, no icy silences. But that's not reality in my house, or probably, in yours.

We need a new language for talking about time with children. When we asked children and parents about "what works," the words they chose described focused time and hang-around time.

▼ So spend time with your children.

Spending time with your children counts. As I have noted in previous chapters, children whose parents spend more time with them view their parents' competence more positively and are more likely to see them as role models. Is there a magic amount of time? No, but it should feel like enough time to both you and your children.

▼ Spend hang-around time with your children.

Hang-around time is time when you don't feel rushed and frantic. Two in five children somewhat or strongly agree that their time with their mothers and fathers is rushed. When children have less rushed time with their parents, they tend to see them more positively. There are, of course, moments when we do have to rush, but it is important that children also experience some moments with us that are calm.

Hang-around time is time when you are not necessarily interacting, but are nearby. You are doing something and so are they. Several parents we talked with set aside special time to just hang out. They stay in their pajamas on Saturday morning. They putter around the house while the kids are doing their things. They play with the dog. Now that my children are older, I often find that the best conversations start when we are hanging out. It is almost as if we need this warm-up period before we can really talk.

▼ Spend focused time with your children.

Most of the children in our study say that it is easy for their parents to focus on them when they are together. When children feel that their mothers and fathers can focus on them, they are much more likely to feel that their parents manage their work and family responsibilities more successfully and put their families before their work, and they give their parents much higher marks for their parenting skills.

Focus means being attuned to the child's cues and clues. It means paying attention. It means being responsive. As I've noted before, responsiveness is a useful concept because it encompasses emotional as well as intellectual attention. It includes listening to a child when the child wants to talk. It includes comforting a child who is unhappy, whether that child is a preschooler or a teenager. It also includes caring about the child's learning and extending it, whether this is a young child who is excited about the world around him or her or an older child studying about science or math. Here are the words of parents.

Focused time is:

> *reading to my children . . . doing splish, splash in the pool with them together.*

> *finding some little thing I can do with each of [my children] separately . . . whether it is just going to the drugstore and getting to where we're going in the car for 10, 15 minutes.*

> *planning with my 13-year-old son how he can earn the money to purchase the pair of Michael Jordan tennis shoes he wants.*

> *making sure the channels of communication are open.*

> *being good listeners if there are problems.*

Focused time is building trust in children:

> *that you are there for them.*

And sometimes, it is shutting out the rest of the world so they can put on a play for you:

> *They put on the show—the phone was ringing off the hook like crazy, and I said, "Don't answer it. Just let the phone ring." I [didn't] want to hear from anybody, I [didn't] want to talk to anyone else. I was totally focused on them and that worked.*

It is not always easy to do this. A single mother with an 8-year-old says:

> *He needs me to spend more time focused on him mentally. You can be there for a child and not [be really] there. I'm with him, but sometimes my mind is not there. I guess when he was smaller, he didn't notice, but now that he's getting older, he sees it.*

She notes that the less she pays attention to him, the more demanding and clingy he becomes. So she has learned how to be with him in such a way that she is deeply connected to the way he feels:

> *I start going into his business, besides what he is trying to tell me. When he's done, I ask him questions. That seems to make him happy when I ask and I want more details. Then he'll come closer and we just sit and talk.*
>
> *He starts to smile and he wants to talk more. So that works, but sometimes it takes my conditioning myself, telling myself, "If I don't do this, my son is going to grow away from me."*

Focusing can be difficult if you have a child who has trouble paying attention. One father with a son likes to play chess with him because the game can provide a structure for them to be together.

And it can be hard because of the timing. One mother talks about being out of sync with her child. If she were there when he came home from school, he would want to talk. But by the time she gets home at 6:00 P.M., she has lost her moment. He has drifted away. As she says, "It is her time, not his time then." So she has her son pick up the phone and call her as soon as he walks into the house. That way she doesn't miss his moment of wanting some focused time with her.

Does not having a parent focus on them harm children? We found that although relatively few children—10 to 15 percent—believe that their parents have trouble paying attention to them, those who do clearly see their mothers and their fathers quite negatively.

The importance of focused time has to be considered in context with other factors. Witness the story of a colleague of mine. She told of going to visit her daughter in her junior year abroad program and meeting her daughter's new international friends. They asked her in front of her mother what it was like to grow up with her parents. "They are great," she said. "I know they really care about me. The only hard thing was that my mother was usually operating on two channels at once. A lot of the time she was there, but she wasn't really there." Importantly, she noted, others did focus on her.

Having a mother who was typically on two tracks was difficult, but this young woman grew up to be caring and competent. It was a loss, but it was not devastating.

Or listen to the eulogy that Jennifer Helbraun, the adult daughter of a friend of mine, gave when her mother, Phyllis Helbraun, died of brain cancer in the summer of 1998. Phyllis didn't have paid work when her children were young, but she was an outstanding volunteer and community activist.

> *I learned social activism in the most personal way, at Phyllis's knee. Literally. When I was knee-high, I'd come running in to her with my latest upset, and I know I'd find her on the phone while she worked in the kitchen, involved with whatever campaign she was running at the time. She'd be distracted, and between her activism and three other children, sometimes she wouldn't be able to help me with what was upsetting me. Or she'd come home from one of many meetings, and my brother David would run for her "stay-at-home" shoes. Those were the comfortable ones that she'd never leave the house in, so he called them stay-at-home shoes in hopes she'd stay at home longer.*
>
> *As soon as Mom got sick, I realized that if I had to choose, I would rather have had the mother I had than the kind of attention I wished she could have lavished on me as a child. Because I grew up with a model that women can be hugely and concretely powerful. That we can lead lives of enormous integrity. From my child's eye view, Mom started the Fresh Air Fund in Rockland [New York] so that a Puerto Rican girl, Lizette, could come and live with us over the summers, and so I could fall in love with things Latin American. She ran campaigns to build the finest school district possible, so that I could have teachers that I loved and who inspired me.*
>
> *Last year at her 75th birthday, my husband, Dave, asked her what was her secret, what advice would she give for raising such wonderful children. "Always let them know that the rest of the world is important, too," she said. "Show them that there is a bigger world to be involved in, and that they're needed."*

Our study has shown we have a hard time focusing on our children when work is consuming us. But there is also a personal style element in play here. Jennifer Helbraun says that her mother "hated surface niceties. She didn't think she was good at it, and she was supremely impatient with it."

My colleague with the daughter in the junior year abroad program says that even if she hadn't been so busy creating a business, she is the kind of person who operates on two tracks. And lest we think that this is a woman's issue, it's not. Recall that children see their fathers as having a harder time focusing on them than their mothers.

Although having trouble focusing may result in part from the lives we lead and in part from our personal style, we can learn to change. In fact, Jennifer says that her mother worked at changing herself:

> *Phyllis's greatest strength as a mother was her capacity to learn and to grow. Whatever her own childhood issues which she brought to mothering, over time she learned to be more self-reflective as a mother, and increasingly she set aside those issues in favor of nurturing each child's ability to be their own very individual person.*

Whereas as a parent of young children, Phyllis had trouble focusing and listening, she learned to do so when her children were grown.

> *Once the brain cancer started moving so fast, Phyllis never again had the wherewithal to settle affairs or clean up relationships—if she needed to. But we all talked about it and realized we had nothing to clean up with her. Nothing needed to be said. All my adult life, before any visit ended, she'd say, "Is there anything we need to talk about?" And as the years went on, more and more often there was nothing that needed to be said.*

Learning about the importance of focus from the interviews and from this study has changed the way I parent. Both of my children are grown, but there are times when they become what I think of as "hover-crafts." Because I have been on such a pressured deadline to finish this book, I used to feel I needed to keep working, no matter what. But as the findings of the study emerged, I began responding differently. I now try to put my work aside to listen, to talk, and to focus. It is a gift we can give our children.

It's important to bear in mind that focused time is not always conflict-free. Dealing with an irate child is just as important as reading peacefully to him or her. And we are not always perfect in our responses. But think of what Jennifer Helbraun learned from her mother's attempts to change. In fact, Jennifer says that "Phyllis's greatest strength as a mother was her capacity to learn and to grow." I am reminded of the 13-year-old boy quoted in Chapter 7 who noted that if parents try, and if they lead by example, "kids will turn out pretty good."

▼ Get involved in activities with them.

We found that children who are engaged in activities with their parents see their parents more positively. What activities? Something that you like and they like: playing Scrabble, having a jigsaw puzzle in progress, doing art projects at the kitchen table, coaching their soccer or T-ball team.

But aren't children's lives today too structured? Aren't we pushing them too hard? This continues to be a subject of debate. A University of Michigan study compared the experiences of a representative sample of children 3 through 11 years old in 1997 with those of children in 1981. According to the principal investigator, Sandra Hofferth, "Today's children spend about 30 minutes less a day, on average, in unstructured play and outdoor activities."[1] In fact, free time has decreased from 40 percent of a child's day to 25 percent. Among the other findings:

▼ Participation in sports by boys and girls rose more than 50 percent.

▼ Time spent eating meals decreased by nearly 20 percent.

▼ Daily television viewing declined from 2 hours in 1981 to 1.5 hours in 1997.

▼ In the 17 hours that children under 13 spend directly with parents per week, they shop, clean the house, prepare food, read books, do homework, talk about the family, and participate in sports or outdoor activities.

So children's time has become more structured. Is that bad? Katie Couric asked me this question when I appeared on the *Today* show to discuss this trend. My answer probably won't surprise you. We have an idyllic vision of free time, so our knee-jerk reaction is that these changes are bad. We see children spending less time running out of their yards with the white picket fences and congregating in the neighborhood with their friends—riding bikes, playing jump rope, or joining in back lot games of baseball. We don't think of free time as being idle with nothing to do, bored and lonely. Naturally, the impact depends on what the free time and the activities entail.

Like our study, the University of Michigan study found that parent-child activities can be constructive. Their study concludes that "parents with high expectations [for their children], who report a warm relationship, and who do more activities with their children have children who have less aggressive behavior problems, have many good qualities, are less withdrawn, and seem happier." As always, the relationship between the parent and the child is what makes the critical difference in how children fare.[2]

Here's my advice on activities:

▼ Do things that you like to do and that your children like to do.
▼ If it is a new activity and they profess not to like it, have them give it a good chance. If you feel it is something that's important for your child to learn (such as music lessons) explain why and try to ensure that it is fun as well as work.
▼ Be mindful whether you are pushing your children to please you or to further their own interests. If it is just for you, ease up.
▼ Be mindful of whether your children are on a treadmill and need some downtime. They will tell you if you are open to listening. And if they do need downtime, ensure that they get it.
▼ Do activities *with* them, not just *for* them.

One mother of school-age children found herself very involved in her children's lives, but doing things for them rather than with them.

> *One of the ways that I try to be more involved in my children's lives is to participate in PTA and Class Mom and soccer coach and all of that stuff. However, it is very time consuming. I'm in meetings . . . and the details and the DJ [for a class party] and the decorations. I mean it was a HUGE amount of work.*

She realized that her time would be better spent if she became involved in activities for the school in which her children could participate, such as making decorations for the school fair.

▼ **Promote their "lemonade stands."**

Years ago, I conducted a seminar at Exxon for employed parents. Parents had selected the topic of the seminar—"communicating with their children." Many of them, particularly the dads, had older children who would be leaving home in a few years. Their question was how to communicate with their teenagers.

To answer the question, I brought in a panel of teenagers. I began the seminar by asking the kids on the panel to tell about a time when their mother or father wanted to tell them something, it was a disaster, and why they thought it was. We then talked about times when the communication was effective and why. Pretty soon the employed men and women in the audience were asking these teenagers questions. In a sense, the seminar was a model of what they could do at home with their own children.

The main question the parents asked was "What gets kids into trouble?" They wondered why some kids fall by the wayside and others don't. They wondered whether the kids on the panel had seen any patterns in how these two groups of kids were raised.

The teenagers' answer has always stayed with me. They said that the kids who got into trouble had no real interests. They had nothing outside themselves that they cared about. They had no larger reason for living.

Perhaps because my own children at the time were at the stage of having lemonade stands, I have always thought of this advice as encouraging children to have lemonade stands. The teenagers told the parents in the audience not to get uptight if they didn't like their kid's interests. Let it be rock music or skateboarding. It doesn't matter. What matters is that your child cares about and pursues something beyond himself or herself that is constructive. Remember that teenage fads come and go.

Parenting autonomy and support

Our study also revealed that being able to raise your child the way you want to and having the support of family and friends—particularly if you experience difficulties with your child—contribute to better parenting.

▼ **Think about how you want to raise your children and try to live up to these expectations.**

In my book *The Six Stages of Parenthood*, I found that our expectations are critical in our views of ourselves as parents. When we are upset, angry, or depressed, typically at the core of our distress is an expectation that we haven't lived up to. I also found that growth in parenthood results from bridging the gap between what we expect and what has occurred—in reconciling our expectations with reality. We can do this in two ways: either by changing our expectation to be more realistic (my child is not going to be a sports star, but she or he is very good at art) or by changing ourselves to live up to our expectations (I am not happy with myself when I lose my temper, so I am going to work on that).

We do have expectations about how we want to raise our children, though these expectations may lie beneath the surface of our thoughts. Autonomy entails bringing your expectations to the surface and evaluating them.

▼ Ask yourself how you really want to raise your child. Another way of getting at this is to ask yourself whether you will feel good about the decision you are making in a year, in 5 years, in 10 years.

▼ If there is a disparity between your expectations and reality, try to reconcile it by changing your expectation to be more realistic or by changing yourself to live up to your expectation.

▼ Find people who support you.

As I have said earlier, I never feel comfortable as a parent unless I know that there is someone around to whom I could turn "at 3 o'clock in the morning." I have never had to call anyone in the middle of the night, but knowing that there are people who wouldn't ask questions if I did call has been a source of comfort.

As a parent, I also found that there are some parents who always see what you do or say as moves in a competition—a game that they need to win. If you say your child did something wonderful, their child did something better. If you say your child has a problem, their child would never have such a problem. My advice: Stay away from such parents at all costs—even if they are your relatives.

Instead, surround yourself with people who make you feel good as a parent. If you turn to them with a problem, they help you feel you can solve it. If you turn to them because you are upset with your child, they can help you laugh at yourself and your child. If you turn to them because you feel like throwing your child out of the house, they help you calm down and find a more effective strategy. They are honest with you, yet supportive. And after you are with them, you feel, "I can be a good parent." I call it "finding a Jeannie" or "finding a Nancy" because these are two of the people who have provided this kind of support to me throughout my years of parenthood.

Support can come in many forms. Obviously, the support of a partner is important. A mother praises her husband:

I'm very lucky to have a partner who has a big hand in raising our daughter. It's not all on me. He has a pretty high-powered job with a lot of stress, and yet, he takes time out to be with the family, to be with his daughter.

She describes how they share care for their daughter:

From day one when our daughter was born, and I went back to work, we shared the responsibility of getting her up and taking her to school or day care for the whole day. I have Monday, Wednesday, and Friday. He has Tuesday, Thursday, and basically does a lot on the weekend. He gets her up, gets her lunch, takes her to school, picks her up, [gives her] dinner, [puts her to] bed—the whole day. So that gives me a break.

In some families, older children help out at home, thereby easing the stress on working parents. Some children have regular chores, such as getting dinner ready or helping the younger ones bathe. Coworkers, friends, and neighbors can also help one another. Whomever you turn to for support, try to ensure that it is real support that builds—not diminishes—your strength as a parent.

▼ **Take care of yourself.**

Stewart Friedman, coauthor of *Allies or Enemies? How Choices About Work and Family Affect the Quality of Men's and Women's Lives*, has found—as have we—that when parents take care of themselves, they are better parents. But because we tend to think of work and family life as a zero-sum balancing act (if you give to yourself, you take away from your children), we often skimp on taking care of ourselves.[3] Our 1997 National Study of the Changing Workforce found that in the past 20 years, both mothers and fathers have cut back on the time they spend on personal activities. One parent describes her realization that time for herself doesn't detract from her parenting; it adds to it:

I used to feel guilty thinking every minute I exercise is a minute away from my kids. But now I realize that's not true. One day I absolutely had to get a workout in because of the stress in my office. I went to pick up my children, probably at six o'clock, which is fifteen minutes later than my cutoff. We had a delightful time and I thought, "It's not my children, because they're the same they always have been. They're always delightful." I just didn't see it as much before because I was stressed.

HOW TO COMMUNICATE WITH CHILDREN ABOUT WORK AND FAMILY ISSUES

Two thirds of children 8 through 18 years old know "a lot" about the kind of work their mothers do, and 54 percent know "a lot" about the kind of work their fathers do. Yet, our research also indicates that we don't necessarily make *intentional* efforts to explain, discuss, or show our children what we do. What children are learning about work is often learned indirectly—from overheard conversations, from passing comments, from their observations of us. Kids are piecing together shreds of evidence as they try to make sense of what's going on in their parents' work world. Why is their dad upset? Is he about to be fired? Or is it just a conflict with a coworker? Why is their mom so tired? Is she sick? Is something happening at work? Or is something happening at home?

Parents' work is an integral part of children's daily experience—it's what triggers separation from their parents at the beginning of the day; it's what draws their parents' attention after dinner and on weekends; it's what provides the family with necessities and "special things"; it's what contributes to parents' stress and satisfaction. Whether we tell them or not, children are learning about our world of work. In fact, it's in their own self-interest to know about this aspect of our lives, as they *must* know about the world of work in order to become the workers of the future.

When we don't intentionally tell children about our work lives, we run several risks. We risk that our children come away with misinformation and misunderstanding about what we do and thus we have lost the opportunity to introduce them to the world of work. We also risk that they will think of work in more negative terms than we do. Our research indicates that children underestimate by a large margin the extent to which parents like their work.

Thus, I think that working parents need to make deliberate efforts to tell their children about their work. We need to decide what information we want to share and not just leave it to chance eavesdropping. In this way, we provide an accurate window onto the world of work to help prepare children for the future. We need to emphasize the pluses and pleasures of our jobs as well as the problems. And when we mention the problems, we ought to include how we are tackling them so that they can learn how to address challenges and problem-solve.

Many of the families we interviewed have found successful strategies for managing work and family. It is my hope that as a result of this book, parents will share their work lives with their children in a more intentional fashion. Our children are waiting and ready to listen and learn.

▼ Find the right time and the right place for talking.

The setting and timing have to be right for good communication to occur. Some parents note that you can't absolutely prescript the right time. You can't necessarily say:

> *"Well, we're going to have four hours on Thursday evening at 6."*
> *I think I would screw that up royally. I think that would be just*
> *a disaster.*

For a number of parents, the best times for connecting are in bits and spurts:

> *Sometimes it's when I sit down to look at the newspaper, and my*
> *son decides he wants to sit down beside me and talk. And some-*
> *times he'll follow me into the bedroom and I'll say, "Well, I'm*
> *going to get dressed." And he'll say, "I want to talk to you, Mom."*
> *I'll say, "Well, okay, you sit right there and talk."*

For many parents, it is the *time in-between* that provides fertile ground for conversation. It happens:

> *on the way to the grocery store, on the way to soccer practice, or*
> *on the way home from soccer practice.*

> *[during] car time—you're just stuck in the car and if there's*
> *something on your mind you can talk about it.*

Other families do prescript times when conversation will occur, such as dinnertime:

> *For us, the most important time is dinnertime. It establishes a*
> *pattern where we talk to our kids about what's going on every*
> *day in a fairly in-depth manner. Certainly the level of discussion*
> *has changed dramatically since they were much younger, but this*
> *process of going through the day was something we started when*
> *they were very little.*

Regular family meetings in which family members get together to talk and to solve problems also offer an ideal opportunity for talking together. For other families, it is time after dinner, as a father says:

> *Instead of turning on the TV, we do have a rule. During school nights, there is no television from the time we get home to the time our daughter is in bed. So all of our attention is focused on her, her school work, and whatever else comes up.*

For still other families, special outings provide time for talking:

> *Monday nights we have a routine that we both now love. I take her to the music class after school, we have dinner, then we go to the library and read together. And there're no dishes. Monday nights are always special and they sort of fortify us both for the whole week.*

Bedtime rituals also offer an opportunity for talking. And having a bedtime ritual doesn't just apply to little children. A number of parents spend time talking to older children when they "tuck them in."

In our family, we continued reading stories aloud at bedtime until the children were fairly old. I found that reading stories about "other people" often offered the best opportunity for in-depth discussions with my children. We could talk about a "hot topic"—fears and challenges—in the context of the characters in the story and each express our real feelings and points of view in a noncharged atmosphere. Talking about movies and television shows offers a similar safe haven for intimate conversation.

In fact, with older children, some of the best opportunities to talk occur when you don't have to make eye contact such as in the car or at bedtime when the lights are dimmed. One mother of teenagers would ask her children to go on night walks with her.

> *I would take them, one by one, for walks in the dark, because they'll tell you anything in the dark, because they have that cover. They're safe. I wouldn't say, "We need to talk because something's bothering you," I'd say, "I really need you to go walk with me tonight." "Sure, Mom." He's helping me. So he would go with me and we'd walk around the block. We might walk for an hour and I'd hear everything that's going on. I'd hear everything in his mind and heart. That's how I knew my kids. Because we walked in the dark.*

Get them in the car, turn the music on low, and talk. They'll talk to you there, because they're safe. You're driving. You're not gonna hit them and you're not gonna yell. In the house if they say something to you and you don't like it, they risk being yelled at. Walking in the dark, driving in the car, you're not going to yell at them, and they know that.

▼ Find out what has gone on in your child's day.

A father who now has a daily conversation about his day with his daughter began this process a long time ago, when he asked her about her day. After feeling that she has been listened to, she now listens to her father talk about his day.

▼ Listen well.

Communication involves both talking and listening, but it is listening that leads to more talking and sharing. Think about the people you avoid talking to. They probably are the people who haven't heard what you are trying to say. They probably are the people who butt in, interrupt, give unwanted advice, change the subject, don't pay attention. So:

▼ Ask your children specific rather than general questions. "What did you do at school today?" will not yield as much as asking about a specific project your child is working on, a specific book your child is reading, a specific activity your child was looking forward to. Ask about the out-of-school times, too. For children, these are important parts of their day: the school bus ride, lunch, recess, after-school activities, time spent with friends.

▼ Ask leading questions: "What do you think will happen tomorrow?"

▼ Ask how-did-you-feel questions: "How did you feel when the teacher gave that pop quiz?" "How did you feel when you got to go on a field trip?"

▼ Repeat what your child has said as a way of moving the conversation forward: "You had a sandwich for lunch."

▼ Withhold immediate judgment if it will cut off conversation right away. "I want some time to think about this."

▼ Say how you feel by using "I" messages, not "you" messages: "It upsets me when I hear that you took something from your friend" rather than "You are a bad person."

▼ State your values and use empathy to convey how you feel. "Taking something from a friend is wrong. Remember how you felt when your friend took something from you."

▼ Ask your children how they feel about the way you are navigating work and family life.

Because we have been afraid of the answer, we haven't asked this question. But as the results of our study indicate, children aren't necessarily going to say what we fear most—stay home. When parents open up this topic of conversation, they find it a relief:

> *I don't know why it took me so long but a few years ago, I talked to my children about my work and how it affected them. They had things they wanted to say—some things that I had never thought about. Like one of my children was upset when I seem preoccupied. When I knew what was going on, I could address it.*

▼ Be open to listening to what's really on your children's minds.

This advice came from children, and I think it is very wise advice. When I consider what was one of my mother's greatest gifts to me, it was permission to talk about what was or wasn't working in our family life. So rather than complain or rebel (of course I did that, too), I could tell her how I felt about her parenting and she listened with true respect. This child makes the same observation about her parents.

> *I think the most important thing about being a good parent is making sure everything's okay with your child. Every day when I come home, my parents ask me, "How was school?" and "Is there something we need to talk about?"*
>
> *They ask me if they're messing up anywhere and if they can make any improvements. And I think if everybody's parents did that, there would be a lot more happy children.*

Although this approach may feel as if we are abdicating our authority as parents, it doesn't have to be. We can ask the children within the context of our being in charge, yet gather their input. I found that when my children had some say about family decisions as appropriate, they were more likely to go along with the decisions we made.

A child sums up the importance of keeping the lines of communication open:

What makes for a good relationship? It's talking, communication. [You tell] your parents about your day and they tell you about theirs. That's what we do. I'm at that preteen age where I thought I knew everything, but I'm trying to get out of that now, because I don't know everything.

HOW TO HELP CHILDREN LEARN ABOUT THE WORLD OF WORK

Many parents take deliberate steps to teach their children about the kind of work they do, about why they work, and about the world of work. Here are some ways to do it:

▼ Arrange for your children to visit you at work, if possible. When this is planned, children have a chance to meet coworkers and even help out. A 10-year-old boy remarks with pride, "I like to help with the time sheets in my mother's office." How many preschoolers have been thrilled to make a photocopy of their stuffed animal on an office machine?

▼ If you can't take your kids to work, take pictures of your workplace so they have a visual image of where you spend your time.

▼ Share information about your job. Talk about your day; share what is most interesting about your work now; talk about the lessons you've learned from working.

▼ Encourage children to ask questions. A 7-year-old child asks her parents, "Is it fun to work?" "Did you have a rough day at work?" Instead of treating her questions as a nuisance at the end of a long workday, they answer directly and honestly. These parents are glad their daughter shows interest, concern, and curiosity about their work.

▼ Encourage young children to play out "work scenarios." Young children learn through play; they deepen their understanding by trying our different roles and by using realistic materials. An airplane pilot helps his children build planes out of large cardboard boxes and arrange kitchen chairs for passenger seats. They're well supplied with old headsets and maps. A secretary helps her preschoolers set up an office, complete with phones, intercom, and an old computer. She also finds some "dress-up clothes" and used train tickets they can play with.

▼ When you have guests in your home, ask them about their work so children can learn about different occupations.

▼ Relate to children the interesting experiences you have as part of your work. Whether you work as a doctor, a designer, a secretary, a computer specialist, or a salesperson, your work is related to experiences you and your children have together. For example, my research on the changing work force has taken me into factories where candy is made, pills are produced, and crayons are manufactured. As the opportunities arose, I was able to share what I had learned from those visits with my children.

▼ Know when to stop talking about work. A single parent, a lawyer, says her 9-year-old is interested in what she does. "But there are times when I start telling her things and she'll say, 'I have no idea what you're talking about.' It's pretty clear she's also saying I really don't care. So I try to stop telling things at that point."

▼ Tell your children the many reasons why you work.

We work for money but we also work for a lot of other reasons. I think that it is very important for children to understand the full spectrum of reasons we work—we are shortchanging them if we just say we are working for money, we are just working to buy them special things, or we are just working because we have to.

A mother of preschool-age children recently found that her kids didn't think that she liked work because she, like so many parents, had said, "I *have* to go to work. I wish I could stay with you." She now says, "Mommy likes her work and she likes to be with you. Just like you like school and you like to be with me." Another parent says:

> *Over and over, I've told them about the importance of what I do, so they don't think I'm just running off. I know they don't want me to be away from home. So I feel like I need to let them know that what I do is important, that it means a lot to me, that I feel good about what I do.*

Another mother who had stayed home until her daughter was 4 years old initially had a tough time explaining her return to work:

> *I tried to be as reassuring as I could, but I told her that I needed to go to work. I told her I needed to do it so that we can have money for some of the things we wanted to do. I always tried to emphasize that I needed to do it for myself too, for my own growth and to keep me feeling like I have enough to do, that I was an important person and a grown-up and not just a mom. She didn't understand at first, but I think she has come to some understanding of that. Now she's proud of me and she brags about me. It's nice. I like it.*

If you don't like your work, share the reasons why as well. A mother who works two jobs in order to support her three children says:

> *I'm in a situation I don't want them to be in. I try to educate them more than I got educated by letting them know there are a lot more things for them to do than working at [a fast-food chain]. You have to also put your best foot forward to get ahead. And I tell them they can be anything they want to be, as long as they keep focused on it.*

▼ Be thoughtful about what you want to teach your children about work.

Most children learn lessons about work indirectly, by watching and overhearing their parents. But some parents do think about the lessons they want their children to learn about work. One parent wants her children to know "you reap what you sow." Her daughter summarizes this lesson:

> *A job will be whatever you make it out to be. If you think it's a terrible job, or if you're not doing your best, it is going to be a terrible job.*

Parents also mentioned other lessons:

▼ You need to learn to get along with all kinds of people.
▼ Don't just complain about what's wrong; try to fix it.

▼ You can manage difficult situations.
▼ It is important to do what you say you are going to do.

▼ Share your feelings about work.

Children are particularly attuned to our feelings about work. So whether we intend it or not, they are learning about work by picking up on our moods. If you are feeling burned out by work, how much should you share with your children? That of course depends on the children's age. If your mood is going to affect them, it is important to let them know so that they don't think it is their fault. One parent who used to mask her feelings found that this approach backfired:

Because when they see me in a bad mood, they don't know if it's because of them, or it's because of something else.

Before this realization, this parent found that her kids would act up, fight, or worry that they had done something wrong.

It is also important to tell children when you need some time to recover. One parent says:

Boy, this was a pretty hard day. Mommy's tired. Mommy's gonna lie down. Give me 30 or 15 minutes when I get home. Go ahead and look over your homework and give Mommy some time.

A parent of two school-aged children explains why she must tell her children when she's burned out by work:

If I don't take the time to sit and tell them that something's going on with me, then they'll just escalate . . . their whining and begging and wanting me to do something now. So we have to stop and sit down as a family and talk about what's going on and so forth. We try to prevent as much as we can by talking.

A teenager urges parents to talk about what's happening at work. When parents are stressed by work and the children don't know why, they sometimes feel neglected:

Make sure that your kids know what you do. I think that's always important just because they'll understand more about your behavior and why you come home tired or exhausted if they know what kind of day you had and what you had to do. Especially if you have a very strenuous job or something that puts a lot of stress on you, your kids are going to think, "Ahh, look at this, she's not taking care of me, she's not giving the time I need."

She adds that parents should be honest and not try to protect their children from the tough realities of the workplace. She believes that even young children can be told the truth at a level they can understand. And in the end, the children will have learned an important lesson—that their parents work hard—and they will come to appreciate what their parents do for them.

If you have a job where it's sharks and cutthroats—corporate America can be that way—you need to tell them enough that their age group would understand. They'll appreciate what they have more if they know how hard their parents work.

Don't just share your negative feelings; share your good feelings too. Our research shows that talking about the good things about work affects children in many positive ways. A parent says:

The main thing is that I want [my children] to know you can have a job you're excited about and that's what work should be. Work shouldn't just be about making money and dragging through the day.

This mother's view is seconded by an adolescent, who passes on this advice to working parents:

It's amazing how many kids don't know what their own parents do for a living. I think parents should be telling their kids what they do. All of us need to share in what we succeed in and love to do.

"KIDS HAVE GREAT IDEAS"

What children have to say is less scary than we might think. Most children seem to be proud and impressed with their parents' ability to be both good parents and good workers. A 9-year-old says:

I want to be just like my parents because I think they both work hard and they both get things done. And I want to be like that. I don't want to put stress on myself like they do sometimes because of work. But other than that, ever since I was . . . well, as long as I can remember, I've always wanted to be exactly like my parents.

A child of 12 sums up what we have found:

Listen. Listen to what your kids say, because you know, sometimes it's very important. And sometimes a kid can have a great idea and it could even affect you. Because, you know, kids are people. Kids have great ideas, as great as you, as great as ideas that adults have.

What Children Want to Tell the Working Parents of America

n the one-on-one interviews we conducted with children across the country, we asked, "What would you like to tell the working parents of America?" That question was often particularly revealing, opening up children to talk about their own families in the guise of talking about other working families. I therefore included this question on the survey we conducted with more than 1,000 children—children from all different kinds of backgrounds, including dual-earner families, traditional families, and single-parent-employed families. Their answers tell a compelling story. Here are ten messages from children to the working parents of America:

MESSAGE 1: WORK IF YOU WANT TO WORK!

Because so many of us—mothers and fathers alike—believe that children secretly (or not so secretly) wish we would be at home full-time, we have never asked them how they feel about our work.

Altogether, 5 percent of children[1] wrote about the issues of working mothers. Of those, most children support the idea of mothers—or both parents—working and/or of fathers being at home:

> *The father is not the only one who has to work. The mother can work if she wants. She has a right to be independent.*
>
> GIRL, AGE 13, divorced parents:
> father works full-time, mother works about half-time

> *Mothers should work and make more money to provide things.*
>
> BOY, AGE 14, married parents: both work full-time

> *I think that it doesn't matter who works as long as you get the money you need and take care of your family.*
>
> BOY, AGE 9, married parents: both work full-time

One child echoes the research finding on the impact of maternal employment on children:

> *It's okay to work. The kid is going to turn out the same way if you work, or if you don't work.*
>
> GIRL, AGE 15, married parents: both work full-time

Another reassures parents that their children will accept their working, if not now, then later:

> *Your children may not like you working now, but it will pay off later on.*
>
> GIRL, AGE 15, married parents:
> father works full-time, mother does not work

And in the tradition of "You go, girl," one child says:

> *Work if you want to work!*
>
> GIRL, AGE 11, divorced parents: both work full-time

One child, however, comments on the "second shift" that some employed mothers have:

> *I feel that mothers have a much bigger responsibility if they work because when they get home they have to do everything that a nonworking mother has to do, plus their own job. But I do believe that both parents should work and make a decent living to raise their children the best way they know how.*
>
> GIRL, AGE 14, married parents: both work full-time

Another child advocates more egalitarian roles:

> *If parents wish to provide some of the better things in life, both parents need to work and share the home and children responsibilities.*
>
> BOY, AGE 12, married parents: both work full-time

Of 265 written responses, only 5 children (2 percent) say, "Stay home":

> *Stay home, talk with, and care for your children.*
>
> BOY, AGE 14, married parents: father works about half-time, mother works full-time

> *Fathers, get a good job that provides a stable home environment for your family. Mothers, stay home with your kids if you can and teach them good moral values and give them love.*
>
> GIRL, AGE 15, married parents: father works full-time, mother does not work

MESSAGE 2: WE ARE PROUD OF YOU

In addition to worrying that children would say "stay home," parents were concerned that their children would be very critical of them. In fact, whenever I have mentioned that I am working on a book about how children see their working parents, high intensity and self-conscious joking often ensues: "My kids might say that I was nice—maybe a couple of times a year!" Parents are often surprised to learn that many children notice that their parents are working hard and respect the time and effort they are putting in. Ten percent of the children spontaneously wrote of their pride in their parents:

> *Thank you for making America great!*
>
> BOY, AGE 11, married parents: father works about half-time, mother works about half-time

> *I would tell the working parents of America to keep up the good work, because it's paying off.*
>
> GIRL, AGE 17, married parents: both work full-time

People that work are very strong people.

> BOY, AGE 14, married parents: both work full-time

I am proud that my parents work.

> GIRL, AGE 11, married parents: both work full-time

Some children note how hard parents work:

As hard as it may be, you're doing a good job, and keep up the good work.

> BOY, AGE 14, married parents: both work full-time

Some children prefer work to welfare:

I'm very proud that they're doing it instead of being on welfare! There's no reason why people can't work!

> GIRL, AGE 14, divorced parents: both work full-time

If you are a single parent with children—WORK!

> GIRL, AGE 10, divorced parents:
> father works full-time, mother works about half-time

Another feels that parents should work, even when they don't need the money:

It is very important to work. Just because you may be very wealthy and probably don't need the money from work, you should still do it. It is healthy and should be a goal in everyone's life.

> GIRL, AGE 16, married parents: both work full-time

It is interesting that children see working as meeting adult needs:

I commend them for their effort! I think that parents' working is necessary to provide, to keep them busy, and for them to maintain a normal adult life.

> GIRL, AGE 13, married parents:
> father works full-time, mother works about half-time

And they feel that parents can both work and take care of their children.

Keep on working—just because you work does not mean you don't care for your children.

BOY, AGE 14, married parents: both work full-time

You are doing great keeping your children happy and well brought up.

GIRL, AGE 12, married parents: both work full-time

An appreciable number of children remark on the stress of today's parents and—sometimes in a way that makes them sound adult beyond their years—say they understand:

We appreciate you. We love you. We understand when you're stressed, tired, and upset about work.

GIRL, AGE 12, divorced parents:
father works full-time, mother works about half-time

You deserve a vacation.

BOY, AGE 8, divorced parents: both work full-time

I would like to thank the working parents of America for working so hard to earn money. I feel they do this out of love so they will be able to support us. I know that a working parent goes through so much for their children, and I am appreciative [of] that.

GIRL, AGE 15, married parents:
father does not work, mother works full-time

MESSAGE 3: LOVE US; RAISE US WELL

In academic circles, there are debates about how much effect parents have on the way their children turn out. Is it nature (our genetic endowment) or nurture (our environment) that matters? How is nurture defined? Does nurture include our parents and/or our peers?

It is unclear why this debate continues to resurface. A careful reading of the research supports the idea that the expression of our genetic endowment is sculpted by experience—and this experience includes family first and foremost but also all the other people who are important in the child's life. Urie Bronfenbrenner, a very wise developmental psychologist at Cornell University, laid out a model to explain development more than two decades ago. It is an ecological model of concentric circles whereby the child, an active player in his or her own development, is influenced by family, by neighborhood, by community, and by his or her ever-widening world. Development continues throughout the life cycle. Once again, the issue is not either/or. It is both/and.[2]

One has only to ask the children to obtain their views on the difference that parents make in their lives. And 11 percent have plenty of advice for us.

First and foremost, they say, "Love us":

> *Make sure that your child knows that you love him/her, and show them whenever you get the chance.*
>
> GIRL, AGE 17, divorced parents:
> no father figure, mother works full-time

Interestingly, they also tell children to love their parents:

> *Love your kids for who they are, and kids, love your parents for who they are!*
>
> GIRL, AGE 12, married parents: both work full-time

Love us, they say, even when we are difficult and life is difficult:

> *No matter how bad or irresponsible your son/daughter is, let them know that you still love them.*
>
> GIRL, AGE 16, married parents: both work full-time

> *It's hard enough on kids growing up in the environment that we live in; try to make this long and hard road called life not so hard and long.*
>
> BOY, AGE 15, married parents:
> father works full-time, mother works about half-time

Want us:

> *If you want children, treat them like you want them.*
>
> BOY, AGE 10, married parents:
> father works full-time, mother does not work

Keep your kids happy and make them feel needed.
> BOY, AGE 11, parents never married: mother works full-time

Listen to us, respect us, appreciate us, encourage us:

Listen to your kids and believe [in] them. But don't make them uncomfortable, and encourage them as much as possible.
> BOY, AGE 12, married parents:
> father works full-time, mother works about half-time

Encourage your children in whatever they do, and be there for your children when they need you most. Family values should be your #1 priority.
> GIRL, AGE 17, married parents: both work full-time

Help your children if they are in trouble, try to make as much money as possible, and try to appreciate your children for what they are.
> BOY, AGE 12, married parents:
> father works full-time, mother works about half-time

Discipline us without being harsh or judgmental, and don't tell us we are "going through a phase":

Take care of your kids and watch what they do, please.
> GIRL, AGE 11, married parents: both work full-time

Keep kids well disciplined, spend time with them, and be present at their activities.
> BOY, AGE 15, married parents:
> father works full-time, mother does not work

Think about what you say to your children, even if it's a joke. Care about what they do; don't just think everything is a phase that they're going through. Talk to them without yelling a lot.
> GIRL, AGE 12, divorced parents:
> no father figure, mother works full-time

Be involved in our lives—and keep your promises:

> *Just remember that you should always stay active and involved in your child's life. Every child needs a full-time mother and father—not just a mother and not just a father.*
>
> GIRL, AGE 15, divorced parents: both work full-time

> *When your child is asking for attention, give it to them. Don't keep working and not talk to your child. Go to games when they are in sports. Don't promise them something you can't keep. It will hurt them.*
>
> GIRL, AGE 14, married parents:
> father works full-time, mother does not work

Have fun with us—in everyday activities:

> *Have fun with your kids, like take them to the beach, ice cream, the parks, or watch a movie.*
>
> GIRL, AGE 12, married parents:
> father works full-time, mother does not work

Don't let the rest of the world—work or personal problems—intrude on your relationship with us:

> *Children need to feel loved and cared about. If you spend all your time at work and dedicate your life to work, then you are not doing your job as a parent.*
>
> GIRL, AGE 13, divorced parents: both work full-time

> *Take care of your kids no matter what kinds of problems you are having.*
>
> GIRL, AGE 12, parents never married:
> father works full-time, stepmother works full-time

> *Don't get too caught up in life and forget about the best thing you have: a family.*
>
> BOY, AGE 14, married parents: both work full-time

Understand us:

> *If you have kids, try and understand them even if you are tired. Spend time with them and make them feel loved.*
>
> GIRL, AGE 12, married parents: both work full-time

Importantly, be there for us:

Be there for your children—there is nothing like not having a mother and father.

GIRL, AGE 11, married parents: both work full-time

I would like to tell them to keep up the good work, but if a child is sick or needs help, help them.

GIRL, AGE 12, married parents:
father works full-time, mother works about half-time

But also, in that wonderfully contradictory way, revealing the push and pull of the parent/child relationship, children say "give us space":

You should spend just enough time with your children to make us feel loved and be excited to see you, but don't spend SO much time with us. We want to get away from you.

GIRL, AGE 11, married parents:
father works about half-time, mother works about half-time

Children's words parallel many of the research findings about the important parenting skills we identified: making children feel important and loved, being someone children can go to when upset, spending time talking with children, knowing what is really going on in children's lives, encouraging children to want to learn and to enjoy learning, appreciating children for who they are, raising children with good values, controlling one's temper when children make parents angry, providing rituals and traditions, being involved with what is happening to children at school, being there for children when they are sick, and attending the important events in children's lives.

MESSAGE 4: KEEP ON WORKING AND SUPPORTING YOUR CHILDREN

When we asked the children to make a wish that would change the way that their parents' work affects their lives, the most frequently mentioned wish was that their parents make more money. On hearing this finding, some people have said to me that the children of today are just too materialistic. They want their parents to work hard so that they can have the right pair of sneakers, the right clothes, the right CDs, the right stereos. Given our data, I can't fully know what children mean by that response. But given how often children mention their parents' fatigue and stress level, I suspect that children see money not only as a means of providing food and shelter (as well as buying special things) but also as a means of reducing the pressure that parents feel.

When asked what they want to tell the working parents of America, many children (9 percent) talk about money. A number say they appreciate the financial support their parents' jobs bring:

> *I appreciate you for trying to support your family.*
> BOY, AGE 8, married parents:
> father works about half-time, mother works about half-time

> *Keep on working and supporting your children.*
> BOY, AGE 13, married parents: both work full-time

> *They are wonderful, caring people for supporting their families.*
> GIRL, AGE 12, married parents: both work full-time

> *Thanks for working and giving your kids the things they need.*
> BOY, AGE 13, married parents: both work full-time

A few children speak enthusiastically about money and what it can buy:

> *Work hard and earn that money!*
> BOY, AGE 12, divorced parents:
> father works full-time, mother does not work

> *Working is good because everyone needs money in today's world in order to live a wealthy long life.*
> BOY, AGE 15, married parents:
> father works full-time, mother works about half-time

> *Keep earning those big bucks.*
> GIRL, AGE 17, divorced parents:
> father works full-time, mother works about half-time

One child even has advice for parents about how to spend their money:

It's good to be a working parent because even if you don't need the money, you could save it for a special occasion: a wedding, college, a birthday party, or yourself.

GIRL, AGE 15, married parents: both work full-time

Numerous children, however, advise parents not to be too materialistic:

I know making money is important because it pays the bills, but sometimes you must sacrifice work for love.

GIRL, AGE 17, married parents:
father does not work, mother works full-time

I know you may feel you're doing good by trying to earn all the money you can, so you can buy stuff for your child. Sure, we sometimes need new stuff, but still . . . What a child really needs is someone there.

GIRL, AGE 12, divorced parents:
stepfather recently fired, mother handicapped and does not work

It's okay to work to provide for your family, but make sure you pay attention to your kids.

GIRL, AGE 15, divorced parents: both work full-time

I know work is hard for you, and about 50% of the reason you work is to support your children, but money won't buy them love and good guidance throughout their lives.

GIRL, AGE 14, divorced parents:
father works full-time, mother works about half-time

Some children appear to be (or are) speaking from difficult family situations:

The primary reasons parents work [are] to live and to put food on the table. They have to work to give their children the necessities of life. The only thing I hope I do when I am a parent is to get a career I love so everything would be easier.

GIRL, AGE 18, parents never married:
no father figure, mother works about half-time

They need to get a job with more money.

BOY, AGE 12, no father, mother works full-time

From my experiences, it's great to have parents who have good jobs and can buy you nice things and extra stuff, but sometimes I would rather give up my luxuries and have my parents around to support me, love me, and share in my life. It makes me very upset sometimes when all my other friends do stuff with their parents and I'm stuck at home with my brothers because my parents are working. I basically had to grow up at the age of ten and start doing laundry and things around the house. [When I was] ten, my mom was working from 8 A.M. to 11 P.M. I had become the mother-figure to my brothers. At dinner-time and around the house, it was like our mother didn't exist. It was just me, my dad, and my two brothers. If it wasn't for my dad, I would be completely alone. I will be 17 in a month and my mom has already missed my childhood and teen years. I wish to God that she would at least become involved in my brothers' lives before they grow up. They don't really know what it's like to have a mom and I think it's really sad.

GIRL, AGE 16, married parents: both work full-time

The message from one child is

Enjoy your kids, because material things don't last.

GIRL, AGE 16, divorced parents: both work full-time

Or put another way:

Make money and spend time with your family.

BOY, AGE 11, married parents: both work full-time

MESSAGE 5: SPEND FOCUSED AND HANG-AROUND TIME WITH YOUR CHILDREN

Our analyses have shown that the amount of time children say they spend with their parents affects how they feel about their parents. So, not unexpectedly, many of the comments—12 percent—concern time. (If we include the fact that children mention time as a part of other messages, it brings the figure to 27.5 percent of the messages in which time is mentioned.)

Children speak in a very authoritative voice on this subject, admonishing their parents to increase the amount of time they spend with them:

> *Because you are working, you really have to take time out in order to be involved with your kids, especially when they're very young.*
>
> BOY, AGE 17, married parents: both work full-time

> *Spend more time with [your] children. Really make an effort in establishing values, morals, and self-esteem. Most importantly, just pay attention.*
>
> GIRL, AGE 16, divorced parents: both work full-time

> *I would like to tell [parents] that they need not to work so hard and [they need to] spend more time with their children and know what is going on in their lives. Take some quality time off for your family and friends.*
>
> GIRL, AGE 16, divorced parents:
> father works about half-time, mother works about half-time

> *The more time you spend with your kids, the stronger the bond between you. If you can't find time, make time.*
>
> BOY, AGE 12, divorced parents: both work full-time

For some children, work (including the boss) is seen as the culprit:

> *I wish you would stop working so much and spend more time with us.*
>
> BOY, AGE 12, married parents:
> father works full-time, mother works about half-time

> *You don't always have to work so hard (especially dads).*
>
> BOY, AGE 11, married parents: both work full-time

> *You people should have more time off. I think you should tell your boss just to leave you alone.*
>
> BOY, AGE 13, married parents: both work full-time

> *The worst thing you can ever do is to neglect your children for your job. Always make time for your family. You don't know how much it hurts when you think your parents love their job more than you.*
>
> GIRL, AGE 11, married parents: both work full-time

For other children, it is other adults who draw their parents away:

> *I would like my mother and father to spend more time with us, and not just themselves—they just spend too much time together.*
> GIRL, AGE 13, married parents: both work full-time

> *If they have extra time, they should spend it with their children instead of with their friends because their children are more important than spending time with their friends.*
> GIRL, AGE 16, divorced parents: both work full-time

As we found in our analyses, the quantity of time parents spend with their children is always colored by what happens during that time. Some children argue for more relaxed, less rushed time:

> *You need to relax more and take some time OFF!*
> GIRL, AGE 10, divorced parents: both work full-time

> *Slow down and spend time with your family. People are more important than things!*
> GIRL, AGE 18, married parents: both work full-time

> *Go home and spend more time with families and get more sleep.*
> BOY, AGE 14, divorced parents: both work full-time

Finally, some children warn parents of the repercussions of not spending time with their children:

> *Spend a lot of time with your children, because when you're gone, there is a big hole in our hearts that makes some or most of us want to cry.*
> GIRL, AGE 12, married parents: both work full-time

> *Spend time with your children, no matter what the circumstance is. They grow up too fast and are grown before you know it.*
> GIRL, AGE 18, married parents:
> father works full-time, mother does not work

MESSAGE 6: PUT YOUR FAMILY FIRST

One of the most frequent messages to the working parents of America is to prioritize, to put their family first. Nineteen percent of the children write this to parents—and if one includes how often this message is embedded in other messages, it brings the figure to 22 percent. This response—and the intensity of children's words about this issue—are interesting in light of the fact that more than three in four children feel that their fathers and their mothers rarely or never put their job before their family (75.5 percent for fathers and 84 percent for mothers). Studies on a number of issues show that the public is likely to feel their own situation is all right, but everyone else's is not.[3] Perhaps this is the case here or perhaps writing about "other people" gives children a safe way to talk about their own families.

> *Unless you are dying of starvation or are strongly in need of money, PUT YOUR FAMILY BEFORE THE WORK.*
>
> BOY, AGE 11, married parents:
> father works full-time, mother works about half-time

> *Your children are the most important part of your life—love them more than work.*
>
> GIRL, AGE 10, divorced parents:
> father works full-time, mother works about half-time

> *It is okay to have a career as long as the parent is active in their child's life—not only in school situations, but other obstacles in life as well.*
>
> GIRL, AGE 17, married parents:
> father works full-time, mother works about half-time

Children point out that parents may not be aware of how their children feel:

> *You should always put your kids first. They need your help more than you think they do.*
>
> GIRL, AGE 11, divorced parents:
> no father figure, mother works full-time

Parents should never put work before kids. It makes kids feel like they're not wanted. Parents should spend time [with] and love children. If you don't, then ask yourself: "Why do I put this before them? Do I really love my children?"

GIRL, AGE 11, married parents:
father works full-time, mother works about half-time

Some children are very critical of parents for putting their work first:

You are pathetic. You put work before anyone else, and you don't ever care about anyone.

BOY, AGE 12, married parents: both work full-time

However, children don't want parents to neglect their work:

Pay attention to your kids, but don't lose interest in your job.

GIRL, AGE 12, married parents:
father works full-time, mother does not work

Parents should try very hard to equally balance the time that they work and the time that they spend with their children.

GIRL, AGE 13, married parents:
father works full-time, mother works about half-time

As long as children come first and remain the top priority in [your] life, then go ahead and make the most out of yourself.

BOY, AGE 16, married parents: both work full-time

Children warn of the consequences of not putting children first:

Never put your job before your children because they will think that you don't love them and that would cause them to run away. Always put your children first no matter what because your job won't always be there. Your children are your life.

GIRL, AGE 14, divorced parents:
father works full-time, stepmother works full-time

I was struck by the fact that some children use the phrase "Don't forget" in urging parents to put their children and families first:

[Try] to do [your] best at what you do, and don't forget about the other people in your life.

GIRL, AGE 12, divorced parents: both work full-time

The parents of America should keep on working strong, but not forget about us children. Sometimes we feel left out.

GIRL, AGE 15, divorced parents:
father works full-time, mother does not work

One child writes adamantly, then plaintively:

"I'd like to tell working parents of America to ALWAYS put your kids before your work. Your kids are more important . . . I hope.

GIRL, AGE 12, married parents: both work full-time

MESSAGE 7: BE THERE FOR YOUR CHILDREN—OR ELSE

As you can see, many children include positive or negative consequences in their statements to the working parents of America. Overall, 15 percent of the children mention consequences in their statements.

If you raise us well, there will be positive consequences for us—the children:

Spend time with your children because it will help them be successful during life.

GIRL, AGE 11, parents never married: both work full-time

I think that if the parents spend more time with their children, they will become better people in life.

BOY, AGE 12, married parents:
father works about half-time, mother does not work

If you want us to be good people with good morals, it's up to you.

BOY, AGE 15, married parents:
father works full-time, mother works about half-time

There will be positive consequences for you—the parents:

Keep on working and taking care of your children so they can be like you when they grow up.

GIRL, AGE 12, parents never married:
no father figure, mother works full-time

Remember that your children are more important than your work. Make sure that they realize this while they're young so they can have a better relationship with you and with their future children.

BOY, AGE 16, married parents: both work full-time

Take care of your children to secure your future.

BOY, AGE 15, married parents: both work full-time

Parents, take care of your children. You're going to need them someday.

BOY, AGE 11, parents never married: both work full-time

There also will be positive consequences for this country. A number of children pointed out what child advocacy slogans have said for years: "Children are our future":

Take time to show love for your children, because we are the future of America.

GIRL, AGE 18, divorced parents:
adopted by grandparents, who do not work

In addition to positive consequences, many children predict negative consequences for parents who are not there for their children. Among the consequences are children's feeling bereft *now*:

If you work a lot, you need to spend a lot of time with your kids so they can feel important and not feel lonely. They need you.

GIRL, AGE 14, divorced parents: both work full-time

I would like to tell them that it's all right to work, but don't work too much or you will make your kids feel unwanted.

BOY, AGE 15, raised by grandmother and uncle:
grandmother doesn't work, uncle works full-time

From a child, words that sound as if they come from an adult:

Please take care of your children because they can only be a child once.

GIRL, AGE 12, divorced parents: both work full-time

Two other consequences are mentioned—children grow up too fast and have problems later on:

Don't make your children grow up too fast.

BOY, AGE 14, married parents:
father works about half-time, mother works about half-time

Pay attention to your children, because if you ignore them they're going to grow up and not have good friends.

GIRL, AGE 14, married parents:
father works about half-time, mother does not work

I would tell them that they should spend a lot of time with their children. If not, they might grow up and be a bad person.

GIRL, AGE 12, divorced parents:
father does not work, mother works full-time

Don't forget you have children at home. Don't put your work before family, because you never know it might come and slap you on the face one of these days. Don't be surprised if a daughter becomes pregnant.

GIRL, AGE 15, married parents: both work full-time

Still another consequence—the children won't be there for parents when the parents need them:

Don't leave your kids in the dark—you'll always have your job, but you may not always have them. Make time!

GIRL, AGE 16, married parents: both work full-time

Always put your children first before any job because if you don't they will grow up to always put you to the side when you need them.

GIRL, AGE 14, married parents: both work full-time

Spend more time with your kids and focus on being a good parent, or your children will grow up hating you.

> BOY, AGE 15, no father figure, mother works full-time

Finally, children warn parents that neglected children could become an actual menace to society now or in the future:

It is good to work, and it definitely makes finances better for a family with two sources of income. Just don't alienate your children or let them do whatever they want whenever they want because that could get them in trouble.

> GIRL, AGE 16, married parents:
> father works full-time, mother does not wor

If you don't spend enough time with your children, they grow farther and farther away towards drugs and violence. So stay close to your children and learn what's going on in their lives.

> GIRL, AGE 12, divorced parents:
> father works full-time, mother does not work

Take care of your kids, or else they'll go nuts and kill people.

> BOY, AGE 15, divorced parents:
> father works about half-time, mother works full-time

Some children remind us that the time when children are at home passes quickly:

I would like to tell the working parents of America to try more to put their families first and then your job, to take more time to think, talk with, and love your children as much as they love you. Because one day, they are not going to be there anymore.

> GIRL AGE 12, married parents: both work full-time

Always be there for your kids because if you mess up, you probably will never get another chance.

> BOY, AGE 10, parents never married:
> father does not work, mother works full-time

MESSAGE 8: DON'T BRING THE STRESS FROM WORK INTO THE HOME

Children's messages to parents about stress amplify the findings in our study about spillover. Parents' work spills over into family life, affecting their mood and energy. That's why so many children wish that their parents would be less stressed out, less tired from work. And that's why numerous children (10 percent) tell their parents to leave their work stress at work.

Leave your work at work, and put on your parenting suit at home.
GIRL, AGE 18, parents never married: both work full-time

Some children talk about their parents' anger:

Not to be angry and so grumpy when you get home from work, and don't be so stressful so much at work.
GIRL, AGE 10, divorced parents:
father works full-time, mother does not work

Others talk about how tired their parents are:

I would tell them that my mother works hard, and she comes home every day tired.
GIRL, AGE 13, parents never married:
father does not work, mother works about half-time

Although only one child wrote here that he is worried about his parents, more than one third of the children in the survey say that they worry about their parents very often or often. Thus, I think that it is a point worth making:

Children are worried about their parents.
BOY, AGE 12, married parents:
father works full-time, mother works about half-time

Among those who wrote about their parents' stress and exhaustion, most have suggestions for how to manage better:

Don't work too hard. Know when to quit, because if you don't, you'll get all stressed out and take it out on us.

> GIRL, AGE 15, married parents: both work full-time

Try to get less stressful jobs.

> BOY, AGE 14, married parents: both work full-time

[Parents] need to calm down and work fewer hours. In Spain, they take a 2- to 3-hour nap in the middle of the day. We need that here. Parents need to be able to sit down, relax, and enjoy what they're doing.

> BOY, AGE 16, married parents:
> father works full-time, mother works about half-time

I know all of you are trying to help your children, but if you have to, take a rest.

> BOY, AGE 11, married parents:
> father does not work, mother works full-time

If your work is too stressful, take a vacation and don't take it out on your family. Also, [parents should not] yell at their children as much [because] that kills their confidence. Applaud them, encourage them, and love them.

> BOY, AGE 11, married parents:
> father works full-time, mother works about half-time

Work when you need to work, but put your family first. Work to live, don't live to work.

> BOY, AGE 11, divorced parents:
> father works full-time, mother works about half-time

I am sure that the astute reader has noticed that not all of these children have parents working full-time schedules. Work demands—the stress that comes home from work, the exhaustion that work can engender—are not the sole province of dual-earner families.

Children say that if parents can't get less stressful jobs, "don't take it out on your children":

If you are going to have a job that stresses you out, don't take it out on your children.

> GIRL, AGE 15, divorced parents:
> father works about half-time, mother works full-time

Think about children, not about work, when you are with them:

> *Go to work, but when it is time to go home—STOP THINK-ING about work.*
>
> GIRL, AGE 18, divorced parents: both work full-time

Don't tell children about the bad stuff about work all the time:

> *If you have a bad day at work, don't tell your kids so much, because it puts them down and makes them feel that the parent isn't happy with their lives, and that makes them feel bad.*
>
> BOY, AGE 13, married parents:
> father works about half-time, mother works full-time

Finally, understand that children have stressful lives, too:

> *I'd just like to say that I know you're tired and stressed when coming home from work, but you have to understand we go to school and that's work for us, too. We do need attention, affection, and love. Work is important, but your family should come first.*
>
> GIRL, AGE 15, father has died: mother works full-time

MESSAGE 9: FIND OUT WHAT IS GOING ON IN YOUR CHILDREN'S LIVES AND TELL THEM ABOUT YOURS

Seven percent of the children write about the importance of improved communication between parents and their children. This starts with knowing what is really going on in the child's life:

> *If a child has something to say, listen to them. They might teach you something.*
>
> GIRL, AGE 14, divorced parents: both work full-time

> *I think parents should try to open up to their children and see what is going on in their children's lives.*
>
> GIRL, AGE 17, divorced parents: both work full-time

Try to communicate with their children more, because in today's society, a lot of parents don't even know what's going on with their children.

GIRL, AGE 16, married parents: both work full-time

Be a resource to children in helping them solve their problems:

Have or build a good enough relationship with them so they can talk to you easily when they need a person to talk to them.

GIRL, AGE 15, married parents:
father works full-time, mother does not work

To try to ask your kids questions—especially personal ones. Solve them. Please plan one to two nights for only family. Play games, solve problems, etc.

GIRL, AGE 11, married parents: both work full-time

Treat your children special—we need adults to talk to.

GIRL, AGE 12, married parents: both work full-time

Take the time to sit down and ask your kids how their day was, or if you can help them with their homework.

BOY, AGE 13, divorced parents: both work full-time

For those parents who feel they try to communicate, only to be rebuffed, children advise parents to hang in there. Don't be put off when they push us away, because they do want to talk with us. Good communication, they say, requires that parents try to understand children's viewpoints and problems (which are just as important as parents' problems).

Furthermore, children advise us not to lecture:

Don't be afraid to talk to your kids. They may act like they don't want you talking to them, but actually it's very important you do. Talking to your kids is great and they want you to whether you think they do or not.

BOY, AGE 14, divorced parents:
no father figure, mother works full-time

Give your child their space. Let them have their own opinion, way of life, beliefs, and ways of living. Let them express themselves in their own way.

GIRL, AGE 15, married parents: both work full-time

You are not your children—respect and understand our viewpoints and needs. We need your love and support unconditionally. Many of the things we struggle with in life are just as hard for us as they are for you. We don't do these to make you angry. In fact our own frustration is hard enough to handle. We need your love rather than your lectures.

GIRL, AGE 16, married parents: both work full-time

Children need to be talked to and listened to. Our problems are just as big as yours.

GIRL, AGE 14, married parents: both work full-time

Finally, although only one child wrote about this in the questionnaires, we heard a great deal about this subject from our one-on-one interviews. We parents need to talk with children about our work:

Try to find time to sit and talk to your children. Ask them how they feel about your work hours.

BOY, AGE 13, married parents:
father works full-time, mother does not work

MESSAGE 10: TEACH YOUR CHILDREN HOW TO WORK

Although only two children wrote about parents' role in teaching children about the world of work, I think that by doing so, we are helping prepare them with information and insight that will help them when they move into the work force. Parents not only affect their children's psychological development, they also introduce them to the world of work:

You have to work and teach your children how to work. Also, let them know how to do something they'll enjoy. You have to work to have to get what you want in life.

BOY, AGE 15, divorced parents: both work full-time

What do I hope will happen as a result of the publication of this book? I hope that the conversations around work and family will change. I hope that we will move from seeing the issues that surround working and parenting as either/or issues to seeing them as both/and issues. But most of all, I hope that we will ask the children.

I know all too well what happens when there are no conversations. Time and time again, I heard misunderstanding and misinformation from children when there was no talking. I heard about fears and grievances. I heard "secrets."

One child thought that her mother had stopped working at home because she was too noisy, when in fact her mother's plan to move from her home office had been in the works for a long time and had nothing to do with the child's making noise. Several children hated their child care providers (and for very good reason) but had never said so.

When parents and children talk together about these issues, reasonable changes can be made. One teenager had wished for years that her parents had gone on school field trips when she was young. As a result of a conversation, this family is now planning a field trip. It's a lark, but it's not a lark either. It was unfinished business that was eating away at the child. Also as a result of a conversation, a mother whose business calls had interrupted her time with her child will no longer put her child off with "just a minute" but will be realistic about the time the calls will take and will try not to schedule calls that interrupt family time.

Why does the bank in my neighborhood have the slogan "It's the right relationship"? Because even with the bank, it is all about relationships. We are the parents—we set the rules and the traditions, and we navigate the course that our work and family lives take. Within that context, however, it is important to create a climate in which we can listen to and talk to our children about whatever is important in their lives.

Children will tell us that it isn't *that* we work, but *how* we work, that matters. They will probably tell us how some things could be better, if we are willing to listen. Yes, they will still try to push our guilt buttons. Yes, they will still try to read our moods and wait for the right moments to plead their case for whatever they want—because kids will be kids. But we are the adults, and we create the tone for our relationship with our child.

I repeat the wisdom of a 12-year-old child:

> *Listen. Listen to what your kids say, because you know, sometimes it's very important. And sometimes a kid can have a great idea and it could even affect you. Because, you know, kids are people. Kids have great ideas, as great as you, as great as ideas that adults have.*

So let's ask the children.

Research Notes
and References

Introduction

1. E. Galinsky, D. Hughes, M. Love, & P. Braggioner, *Family Study* (New York: Bank Street College, 1985).

2. E. Greenberger, R. O'Neil, & S. K. Nagel, "Linking Workplace and Home-place: Relations Between the Nature of Adults' Work and Their Parenting Behaviors," *Developmental Psychology* 30 (1994): 990–1002; R. Repetti & J. Wood, "The Effects of Daily Stress at Work on Mother-Child Interactions," Poster presented at the Biennial Meetings of the Society for Research on Child Development, Indianapolis, 1995; R. O'Neil, "Maternal Work Experiences, Psychological Well-being and Achievement-Fostering Parenting," unpublished manuscript (Los Angeles: University of California, Los Angeles, 1992); C. Howes, L. M. Sakai, M. Shinn, D. Phillips, E. Galinsky, & Mr. Whitebook, "Race, Social Class, and Maternal Working Conditions as Influences on Children's Behavior in Child Care," *Journal of Applied Developmental Psychology* 16 (1995): 107.

3. The cooperation rate for the randomly selected parents sample was 62 percent (total contacts/[total contacts + refusals]). The maximum sample error for parents is ± 4 percent at a 95 percent confidence interval.

Harris takes several steps at different stages of the survey process to ensure the representativeness of the sample of children. The first stage involves the selection of the sample. This is a two-stage, stratified, and clustered sampling process. Stratification variables include school type (public, private, and parochial), grade coverage, urbanicity, and region.

Within the basic strata, defined by these dimensions, stratification is carried out by state, grade enrollment, and zip code. The second stage involves maintaining a representative sample. If a particular school cannot participate, it is replaced by a school with similar demographic characteristics so as to preserve the integrity of the primary selection. The cooperation rate for randomly selected schools was 31 percent (total contacts/[total contacts + refusals]). Virtually all students in cooperating classrooms completed the questionnaires that were distributed by their teachers.

The third stage is weighting the data to correct any biases. A two-stage weighting process, based on data from the U.S. National Center of Education Statistics was used. These control the distribution of students by grade, region, size of place, gender, and race/ethnicity. The maximum sample error for children is ± 3 percent.

Chapter 1: Reframing the Debate About Working and Children
1. J. Bowlby, *Attachment and Loss*, Vol. 1, *Attachment* (New York: Basic Books, 1969).
2. U. Bronfenbrenner & A. C. Crouter, "Work and Family Through Time and Space," in S. B. Kamerman & C. D. Hayes (eds.), *Families That Work: Children in a Changing World* (Washington, DC: National Academy Press, 1982), 39–83; T. J. Gamble & E. Zigler, "Effects of Infant Day Care: Another Look at the Evidence," *Journal of Orthopsychiatry* 56, 1 (1986): 26–41; L. W. Hoffman, "Effects of Maternal Employment in the Two-Parent Family," *American Psychologist* 44 (1989): 283–292; C. Hayes, J. Palmer, & M. Zaslow, *Who Cares for America's Children? Child Care Policy for the 1990's* (Washington, DC: National Academy Press, 1990); J. Belsky, "The Effects of Infant Day Care Reconsidered," *Early Childhood Research Quarterly* 3 (1988), 235–272.
3. In this and subsequent analyses of attitudinal questions, we asked the following questions in our data analyses:
   ▼ Is there a difference between mothers and fathers on their views?
   ▼ Is there a difference among parents who are white (non-Hispanic), African American, and Hispanic?
   ▼ Is there a difference between mothers in dual-earner couples (mothers who are married or living in a committed relationship and have an employed spouse) and fathers in dual-earner couples (fathers who are married or living in a committed relationship and have an employed spouse)?
   ▼ Is there a difference between fathers in dual-earner families and in traditional families (employed father and mother who is nonemployed or at home)?
   ▼ Is there a difference among parents who are living as a couple, single mothers, and single fathers?
   ▼ Is there a difference among parents whose total household income

in 1997 was $25,000 or less, more than $25,000 to $50,000, more than $50,000 to $75,000, and more than $75,000?

▼ Is there a difference among parents who work less than 35 hours per week and those who work 35 hours or more per week?

▼ Is there a difference among parents who have a high school diploma or less, those who have completed some secondary education, and those who have completed a 4-year degree or more?

We set the threshold for statistical significance at p < .01 level. For the sake of brevity, we occasionally report some of the significant findings in the research notes rather than in the text.

4. J. T. Bond, E. Galinsky, & J. Swanberg, *The 1997 National Study of the Changing Workforce* (New York: Families and Work Institute, 1998); R. P. Quinn & G. L. Staines, *The 1977 Quality of Employment Survey* (Ann Arbor, MI: Institute for Social Research, University of Michigan, 1979).

5. NICHD Early Child Care Research Network, "The Effects of Child Care on Infant-Mother Attachment Security: Results of the NICHD Study of Early Child Care," *Child Development* 68 Number 5 (1997): 860–879.

6. Bond, Galinsky, & Swanberg, *The 1997 National Study*, 1998.

7. A. Skolnick, *Embattled Paradise: The American Family in an Age of Uncertainty* (New York: Basic Books, 1991).

8. In addition, employed mothers and fathers who are in the lowest quartile in terms of household income (their annual household income in 1997 was $25,000 a year or less) agree with the statement "It is OK for mothers to work if they really do need the money" more fervently than their higher-income counterparts. And an overwhelming 93 percent of African-American parents "strongly agree" with this statement compared with 70 percent of white parents.

9. G. J. Duncan & J. Brooks-Gunn (eds.), *Consequences of Growing Up Poor* (New York: Russell Sage Foundation, 1997); J. Brooks-Gunn, G. Guo, & F. F. Furstenberg, "Who Drops Out of and Who Continues Beyond High School? A 20-Year Follow-up of Black Urban Youth," *Journal of Research on Adolescence* 37 (1993): 271–294; K. A. Moore, D. R. Morrison, M. Zaslow, & D. A. Glei, "Ebbing and Flowing, Learning and Growing: Family Economic Resources and Children's Development," paper presented at research briefing, Board on Children and Families (Washington, DC: Child Trends, Inc., December 5–6, 1994); Carnegie Corporation of New York, *Starting Points: Meeting the Needs of Our Youngest Children* (New York: Author, 1994); E. F. Dubow & M. F. Ippolito, "Effects of Poverty and Home Environment on Changes in the Academic and Behavioral Adjustment of Elementary School-Age Children," *Journal of Clinical Child Psychology* 23 (1994): 401–412; G. Duncan, J. Brooks-Gunn, & P. Klebanov, "Economic Deprivation and Early Childhood Development," *Child Development* 65 (1994): 296–318.

10. A. R. Hochschild, *The Time Bind* (New York: Henry Holt & Company, 1997).

11. C. Goldberg, "A Murder Trial about More than a Nanny," *New York Times*, 24 October 1997, A18.

12. M. Jackson, "On the Job, Goodbye Superwoman," Associated Press, 8 October 1997.

13. In addition, there are differences among parents in different racial and ethnic groups. African-American parents are more likely than white parents and Hispanic parents to disagree with the statement "Mothers who really don't need the money shouldn't work."

14. L. Harvey, "Short-Term and Long-Term Effects of Early Parental Employment on Children of the National Longitudinal Survey of Youth," *Developmental Psychology* 35 (1999): 445.

15. A. S. Fuligni, E. Galinsky, & M. Poris, *The Impact of Parental Employment on Children* (New York: Families and Work Institute, 1995).

16. In addition, there are two other significant findings. First, 60 percent of parents who work less than 35 hours a week agree that "many working mothers seem to care more about being successful at work than meeting the needs of their children" compared with 40 percent of those who work more than 35 hours a week. Second, white non-Hispanic parents are more likely to agree with this statement than are Hispanic parents.

17. Parents with fewer years of education are less likely than parents with more years of education to feel that fathers put their career success ahead of their concern for meeting the needs of their children; for example, 53 percent of parents with a high school degree or less agree compared with 75 percent of those with a 4-year degree or more. White parents are also more likely than Hispanic parents to support this statement.

18. Bond, Galinsky, & Swanberg, *The 1997 National Study*, 1998; B. Holcomb, *Not Guilty: The Good News About Working Mothers* (New York: Scribner, 1998).

19. Ibid. *The 1997 National Study*, 1988.

20. Ibid.

21. Child Care Law Center, *Child Care Not a Proper Basis for Custody Change*, media advisory, 9 November 1995.

22. Unpublished data from *The 1997 National Study*.

23. M. Petersen, "The Short End of Long Hours: A Female Lawyer's Job Puts Child Custody at Risk," *New York Times*, 18 July 1998, D1.

24. J. A. Levine & T. L. Pittinsky, *Working Fathers: New Strategies for Balancing Work and Family* (New York: Harcourt Brace & Co., 1997), 35.

25. F. A. Pedersen, N. Zaslow, J. Suwalsky, & R. Caine, "Parent-Infant and Husband-Wife Interactions Observed at Five Months," in F. Pederson (ed.), *The Father-Infant Relationship* (New York: Praeger, 1980), 82–92.

26. R. D. Parke, *Fathers* (Cambridge, MA: Harvard University Press, 1996).

27. N. Radin, "The Role of the Father in Cognitive, Academic, and Intellectual Development," in M. E. Lamb (ed.), *The Role of the Father in Child Development* (New York: John Wiley & Sons, 1981).

28. Harris, Furstenburg, & Marmer, 1996, cited in Levine & Pittinsky, *Working Fathers*, 26.
29. Lamb, 1986, cited in Levine & Pittinsky, *Working Fathers*, 41.
30. K. Pruett, *The Nurturing Father* (New York: Warner Books, 1987).
31. M. Whitebook, C. Howes, & D. A. Phillips, *Who Cares? Child Care Teachers and the Quality of Care in America*, Final Report of the National Child Care Staffing Study (Oakland, CA: Child Care Employee Project, 1990); E. Galinsky, C. Howes, S. Kontos, & M. Shinn, *The Study of Children in Family Child Care and Relative Care: Highlights and Findings* (New York: Families and Work Institute, 1994); Cost, Quality & Child Outcomes Study Team, *Cost, Quality, and Child Outcomes in Child Care Centers* (Denver: Economics Department, University of Colorado, 1995).
32. NICHD Early Child Care Research Network, "The Effects of Child Care," 860–879; Fuligni, Galinsky, & Poris, *Impact of Parental Employment*.
33. R. M. Kanter, *Work and Family Life in the United States: A Critical Review and Agenda for Research and Policy* (New York: Russell Sage Foundation, 1977).
34. R. Barnett, presentation at Working Mother Congress, September, 1997.
35. B. Thorne, *Selected Bibliography on the Sociology of Children* (Berkeley: University of California, Berkeley, 1998).

Chapter 2: How Children See Their Parents' Parenting Skills

1. L. A. Sroufe, "Infant-Caregiver Attachment and Patterns of Adaptation in Preschool: The Roots of Maladaptation and Competence," in M. Perlmutter (ed.), *Minnesota Symposium in Child Psychology: Development and Policy Concerning Children with Special Needs* 16 (Hillsdale, NJ: Lawrence Erlbaum Associates, 1983) 41–83; L. A. Sroufe & B. Egeland, "Illustrations of Person-Environment Interaction from a Longitudinal Study," in T. Wachs and R. Plomin (eds.), *Conceptualization and Measurement of Organism-Environment Interaction* (Washington, DC: American Psychological Association, 1991); M. F. Erickson, J. Korfmacher, & B. Egeland, "Attachments Past and Present: Implications for Therapeutic Intervention with Mother-Infant Dyads," *Development and Psychopathology* (Cambridge: Cambridge University Press, 1992).
2. M. A. Hofer, "Hidden Regulators: Implications for a New Understanding of Attachment, Separation, and Loss," in S. Goldberg, R. Muir, & J. Kerr (eds.), *Attachment Theory: Social, Developmental, and Clinical Perspectives* (Hillsdale, NJ: The Analytic Press, 1995); R. Shore, *Rethinking the Brain: New Insights into Early Development* (New York: Families and Work Institute, 1997).
3. D. J. Siegel, *The Developing Mind: Toward a Neurobiology of Interpersonal Experience* (New York: Guilford Press, 1999).

4. M. R. Gunnar, "Quality of Care and the Buffering of Stress Physiology: Its Potential in Protecting the Developing Human Brain," University of Minnesota Institute of Child Development, 1996.

5. D. R. Powell, "Strengthening Parental Contributions to School Readiness and Early School Learning," prepared for the U.S. Department of Education, Office of Educational Research and Improvement, 1991, ii.

6. S. Scarr & K. McCartney, "Far from Home: An Experimental Evaluation of the Mother-Child Home Program in Bermuda," *Child Development* 59 (1988): 531–543.

7. I. E. Sigel, "The Relationship Between Parents' Distancing Strategies and the Child's Cognitive Behavior," in L. M. Laosa & I. E. Sigel (eds.), *Families as Learning Environments for Children* (New York: Plenum, 1982), 47–86.

8. Powell, "Strengthening Parental Contributions," ii.

9. U.S. Department of Education, *What Works: Research About Teaching and Learning* (Washington, DC: Author, 1987).

10. Powell, "Strengthening Parental Contributions," 5.

11. J. Kagan, *The Nature of the Child* (New York: Basic Books, 1984).

12. P. Leach, personal communication, August 1996.

13. OERI Goal 1 Work Group, "Review of Research on Achieving the Nation's Readiness Goal," Technical Report (Office of Research, U.S. Department of Education, Office of Educational Research and Improvement, 1993); Powell, "Strengthening Parental Contributions."

14. J. M. Hunt & J. Parashevopoulos, "Children's Psychological Development as a Function of the Inaccuracy of Their Mothers' Knowledge of Their Abilities," *The Journal of Genetic Psychology* 136 (1980):285–298.

15. R. D. Hess & S. D. Holloway, "Family and School as Educational Institutions," in R. Parke (ed.), *Review of Child Development Research*, Vol. 7, *The Family* (Chicago: University of Chicago Press, 1984): 179–222; J. S. Eccles, *School and Family Effects on the Ontogeny of Children's Interests, Self-Perceptions, and Activity Choice*, Nebraska Symposium on Motivation, 1992.

16. R. Seginer, "Parents' Educational Expectations and Children's Academic Achievements: A Literature Review," *Merrill-Palmer Quarterly* 29 (1) (1983): 1–23.

17. S. Farkas & J. Johnson, *Kids These Days: What Americans Really Think About the Next Generation* (New York: Public Agenda, 1997).

18. S. L. Hanson & A. Ginsberg, "Gaining Ground: Values and High School Success," prepared for the U.S. Department of Education, 1985.

19. OERI Goal 1 Work Group, "Review of Research," 1993; L. Steinberg, S. M. Dornbusch, & B. B. Brown, "Ethnic Differences in Adolescent Achievement: An Ecological Perspective," *American Psychologist* 47 (1992): 723–729.

20. D. Baumrind, "Current Patterns of Parental Authority," *Developmental Psychology Monographs* 4, Number 1, Part 2 (1971): 1–103; H. Lytton & W.

Zwirner, "Compliance and Its Controlling Stimuli Observed in a Natural Setting," *Developmental Psychology* 11 (1975): 769–779; S. M. Dornbush, P. L. Ritter, P. H. Leiderman, D. F. Roberts, & M. J. Fraleigh, "The Relation of Parenting Style to Adolescent School Performance," *Child Development* 58 (1987): 1244–1257; NICHD Early Child Care Research Network, "Early Child Care and Self-Control, Compliance, and Problem Behavior at 24 and 36 Months," *Child Development* 69 (1988a): 1145–1170.

21. H. R. Schaffer & C. K. Crook, "Child Compliance and Maternal Control Techniques," *Developmental Psychology* 16, Number 1 (1980): 54–61.

22. H. Lytton, "Three Approaches to the Study of Parent-Child Interaction: Ethological, Interview and Experimental," *Journal of Child Psychology and Psychiatry* 14 (1973): 1–17.

23. M. L. Hoffman, "Parent Discipline and the Child's Consideration for Others," *Child Development* 34 (1963): 573–588.

24. M. B. Shure & G. Spivak, "The Problem-Solving Approach to Adjustment: A Competency-Building Model of Primary Prevention," *Prevention in Human Services* 1.5 Fall/Winter (1981): 87–103; M. B. Shure & G. Spivak, "Interpersonal Problem-Solving in Young Children: A Cognitive Approach to Prevention," *American Journal of Community Psychology* 10, Number 3, (1982): 341–356.

25. G. R. Patterson, *A Social Learning Approach to Family Intervention*, Vol. 3, *Coercive Family Process* (Eugene, OR: Castalia, 1982); G. R. Patterson, J. C. Reid, & T. J. Dishion, *Antisocial Boys* (Eugene, OR: Castalia, 1992).

26. Powell, "Strengthening Parental Contributions."

27. W. J. Doherty, *The Intentional Family* (New York: Addison Wesley Longman, Inc., 1997).

28. Siegel," *The Developing Mind*, 1999.

29. T. Z. Keith & T. M. Reimers, P. G. Fehrmann, S. M. Pottebaum, & L. W. Aubrey, "Parental Involvement, Homework, and TV Time: Direct and Indirect Effects on High School Achievement," *Journal of Educational Psychology* 78 (1986): 373–380.

30. S. L. Dauber & J. L. Epstein, "Parents' Attitudes and Practices of Involvement in Inner-City Elementary and Middle Schools," in N. F. Chavkin (ed.), *Families and Schools in a Pluralistic Society* (Albany: SUNY Press, 1993).

31. The differences we investigated are as follows:

▼ Are there differences between the grades given by boys compared to girls?

▼ Are there differences among children in different racial or ethnic groups—white (non-Hispanic), African-American, and Hispanic?

▼ Are there differences between younger children (third through sixth grades) and older children (seventh though twelfth grades)?

▼ Are there differences between children in two-parent families and those in single-parent families headed by a mother?

▼ Are there differences between children in two-parent families and those in single-parent families headed by a father?

▼ Are there differences between children who perceive the economic health of their families as marginal (the child reports that the family has "a hard time buying the things we need" or "My family has just enough money for the things we need") and children who see their families as economically healthy (the child reports, "My family has no problem buying the things we need and we can also buy special things")?

▼ Are there differences between children whose mothers are employed and whose mothers are not employed or are at home?

▼ Are there differences between children whose fathers are employed and whose fathers are not employed or are at home?

▼ Are there differences between children whose mothers work full-time and those whose mothers work part-time?

▼ Are there differences between children whose fathers work full-time and those whose fathers work part-time?

▼ Are there differences between children in dual-earner families and those in traditional families (employed father and nonemployed mother)?

▼ Are there differences between children whose father lives with them (resident fathers) and those whose father does not live with them (nonresident fathers)?

32. We set the threshold for statistical significance at $p < .01$. This means that differences would only occur 1 time in 100 by chance. In other words, 99 times out of 100, such a finding reflects a real difference among or between the groups. However, many of the differences we discuss are far less likely to have occurred by chance than 1 time in 100; they occur 1 time in 1,000 by chance ($p < .001$), 1 time in 10,000 by chance ($p < .0001$), or even less often.

33. M. Pipher, *Reviving Ophelia* (New York: Putnam Publishing Group, 1994); W. Pollack, *Real Boys: Rescuing Our Sons from the Myths of Boyhood* (New York: Random House, 1998).

34. Farkas & Johnson, *Kids These Days,* 13.

35. Ibid., 21.

36. NICHD Early Child Care Research Network, "The Effects of Infant Child Care on Infant-Mother Attachment Security: Results of the NICHD Study of Early Child Care," *Child Development* 68 (1997): 860–879; V. C. McLoyd, "The Impact of Economic Hardship on Black Families and Children: Psychological Distress, Parenting and Socioemotional Development," *Child Development* 61 (1990): 311–346.

37. B. Egeland, E. Carlson, & L. A. Sroufe, "Resilience as Process," in *Development and Psychopathology* (Cambridge: Cambridge University Press, 1993), 250.
38. R. Parke, personal communication, 1998.
39. G. H. Elder & A. Caspi, "Economic Stress in Lives: Developmental Perspectives," *Journal of Social Issues* 44 (1988): 22–45.
40. U. Bronfenbrenner & A. C. Crouter, "Work and Family Through Time and Space," in S. B. Kamerman & C. D. Hayes (eds.), *Families That Work: Children in a Changing World* (Washington, DC: National Academy Press, 1982), 39–83.
41. M. Siegal, "Economic Deprivation and the Quality of Parent-Child Relations: A Trickle-Down Framework," *Journal of Applied Developmental Psychology* 5 (1984): 127–144.
42. M.D.S. Ainsworth & B. Wittig, "Attachment and Exploratory Behavior of One-Year-Olds in a Strange Situation," in B. Foss (ed.), *Determinants of Infant Behavior* 4: (London: Methuen, 1969) 111–136; J. Belsky, L. D. Steinberg, & A. Walker, "The Ecology of Day Care," in M. E. Lamb (ed.), *Non-Traditional Families: Parenting and Child Development* (Hillsdale, NJ: Lawrence Erlbaum Associates, 1982), 71–116; T. J. Gamble & E. Zigler, "Effects of Infant Day Care: Another Look at the Evidence," *Journal of Orthopsychiatry* 56 (1986): 26–42; B. E. Vaughn, F. L. Gove, & B. Egeland, "The Relationship Between Out-of-Home Care and the Quality of Infant-Mother Attachment in an Economically Disadvantaged Population," *Child Development* 51 (1980): 1203–1214.
43. R. A. Arend, L. Gove, & L. A. Sroufe, "Continuity of Individual Adaptation from Infancy to Kindergarten: A Predictive Study of Ego-Resiliency and Curiosity in Preschoolers," *Child Development* 50 (1979): 950–959; E.A. Farber & B. Egeland, "Developmental Consequences of Out-of-Home Care for Infants in a Low-Income Population," in E. F. Zigler & E.W. Gordon (eds.), *Day Care: Scientific and Social Policy Issues* (Boston: Auburn House, 1982); S. Londerville & M. Main, "Security of Attachment, Compliance, and Maternal Training Methods in the Second Year of Life," *Developmental Psychology* 17 (1981): 289–299; Sroufe & Egeland, "Illustrations," 1991.
44. L. A. Sroufe, "Infant-Caregiver Attachment." 1983.
45. J. Belsky & M. Rovine, "Temperament and Attachment Security in the Strange Situation: An Empirical Rapprochement," *Child Development* 58 (1987): 787–795.
46. K. A. Clarke-Stewart, "Infant Day-Care: Maligned or Malignant?" *American Psychologist* 44(1989): 266–273; M. Lamb & K. Sternberg, "Do We Really Know How Day-Care Affects Children?" *Journal of Applied Developmental Psychology* 11 (1990): 351–379. L. Roggman, J. Langois, L. Hubbs-Tait, & L. Reiser-Danner, "Infant Day-Care, Attachment, and the 'File-Drawer problem,' " *Child Development* 65 (1994): 1429–1443.

47. NICHD Early Child Care Research Network, "Effects of Infant Child Care," 875.

48. Ibid., 876.

49. NICHD Early Child Care Research Network, "Relations Between Family Predictors and Child Outcomes: Are They Weaker for Children in Child Care?" *Developmental Psychology* 34 (1998): 1119–1128.

50. Ibid.

51. This discussion is drawn from the literature review conducted at the Families and Work Institute: A. S. Fuligni, E. Galinsky, & M. Poris, *The Impact of Parental Employment on Children* (New York: Families and Work Institute, 1995).

52. L.W. Hoffman, "Effects of Maternal Employment in the Two-Parent Family," *American Psychologist* 44 (1989): 283–292.

53. S. M. Alessandri, "Effects of Maternal Work Status in Single-Parent Families on Children's Perception of Self and Family and School Achievement," *Journal of Experimental Psychology* 54 (1992): 417–433.

54. N. Colangelo, D. M. Rosenthal, & D. F. Dettman, "Maternal Employment and Job Satisfaction and Their Relationship to Children's Perceptions and Behaviors," *Sex Roles* 10 (1984): 693–702.

55. L.W. Hoffman, "The Effects on Children of Maternal and Paternal Employment," in N. Gerstel & H. E. Gross (eds.), *Families and Work* (Philadelphia: Temple University Press, 1987); F. J. Crosby, *Juggling: The Unexpected Advantages of Balancing Career and Home for Women and Their Families* (New York: Free Press, 1991).

56. F. F. Schachter, "Toddlers with Employed Mothers," *Child Development* 52 (1981): 958–964.

57. Alessandri, "Effects of Maternal Work," 417–433.

58. Schachter, "Toddlers," 958–964.

59. L. Armistead, M. Wierson, & R. Forehand, "Adolescents and Maternal Employment: Is It Harmful for a Young Adolescent to Have an Employed Mother?" *Journal of Early Adolescence* 10 (1990): 260–278.

60. S. Crockenberg & C. Litman, "Effects of Maternal Employment on Maternal and Two-Year-Old Child Behavior," *Child Development* 62 (1991): 930–953; Armistead et al. "Adolescents and Maternal Employment," 260–278.

61. D. Gold & D. Andres, "Developmental Comparisons Between 10-Year-Old Children with Employed and Nonemployed Mothers," *Child Development* 49 (1978): 75–84.

62. N. W. Finkelstein, "Aggression: Is It Stimulated by Day Care?" *Young Children* 37 (1982): 3–9; J. Rubenstein & C. Howes, "Adaptation to Infant Day Care," in Sally Kilmer (ed.), *Advances in Early Education and Day Care* (Greenwich, CT: JAI Press, 1983); J. Belsky, "The 'Effects' of Infant Day Care Reconsidered," *Early Childhood Research Quarterly* 3 (1988), 235-272.

63. A E. Gottfried, A.W. Gottfried, & K. Bathurst, "Maternal Employment, Family Environment, and Children's Development: Infancy Through the School Years," in A. E. Gottfried & A.W. Gottfried (eds.), *Maternal Employment and Children's Development: Longitudinal Research* (New York: Plenum Press, 1988), 11–58.

64. E. Hock, "Working and Nonworking Mothers and Their Infants: A Comparative Study of Maternal Caregiving Characteristics and Infant Social Behavior," *Merrill-Palmer Quarterly* 26 (1980): 79–101; M. Weintraub, E. Jaeger, & L. Hoffman, "Predicting Infant Outcomes in Families of Employed and Nonemployed Mothers," *Early Childhood Research Quarterly* 3 (1988): 361–378.

65. N. Baydar & J. Brooks-Gunn, "Effects of Maternal Employment and Child-Care Arrangements on Preschoolers' Cognitive and Behavioral Outcomes: Evidence from the Children of the National Longitudinal Survey of Youth," *Developmental Psychology* 27 (1991): 932–945.

66. F. F. Cherry & E. L. Eaton, "Physical and Cognitive Development in Children of Low-Income Mothers Working in the Child's Early Years," *Child Development* 48 (1977): 158–166; D. L. Vandell & J. Ramanan, "Effects of Early and Recent Maternal Employment on Children from Low-Income Families," *Child Development* 63 (1992): 938–949; A. S. Fuligni, "Effects of Parental Involvement and Family Context on the Academic Achievement of Third- and Fourth-Grade Children," unpublished doctoral dissertation, University of Michigan, 1995.

67. Armistead et al., "Adolescents and Maternal Employment," 260–278; Gold & Andres, "Developmental Comparisons," 75–84.

68. C. B. Asha, "Creativity of Children of Working Mothers," *Psychological Studies* 28 (1983): 104–106.

69. Gottfried et al., "Maternal Employment," 11–58.

70. J. Barling, C. Fullager, & J. Marchl-Dingle, "Employment Commitment as a Moderator of the Maternal Employment Status/Child Behavior Relationship," *Journal of Organizational Behavior* 9 (1988): 113–122; A. M. Farel, "Effects of Preferred Maternal Roles, Maternal Employment, and Sociodemographic Status on School Adjustment and Competence," *Child Development* 51 (1980): 1179–1186.

71. J. G. Webster, J. C. Pearson, & D. B. Webster, "Children's Television Viewing as Affected by Contextual Variables in the Home," *Communication Research Reports* 3 (1986): 1–8.

72. NICHD Early Child Care Research Network, "Effects of Infant Child Care," 860–879; V. C. McLoyd, "Employment Among African American Mothers in Dual-Earner Families: Antecedents and Consequences for Family Life and Child Development," in J. Frankel (ed.), *The Employed Mother and the Family Context* (New York: Springer, 1993).

73. Baydar & Brooks-Gunn, "Effects of Maternal Employments," 932–945; B. Heyns & S. Catsambis, "Mother's Employment and Children's Achievement: A Critique," *Sociology of Education* 59 (1986): 140–151.

Chapter 3: Is It Quality Time or Quantity Time?

1. J. T. Bond, E. Galinsky, & J. Swanberg, *The 1997 National Study of the Changing Workforce* (New York: Families and Work Institute, 1998). R. P. Quinn & G. L. Staines, *The 1977 Quality of Employment Survey* (Ann Arbor, MI: Institute for Social Research, University of Michigan, 1979).
2. The sample size for single parents in the 1977 Quality of Employment Survey is too small to make comparisons with the 1997 National Study of the Changing Workforce. Therefore, we focus on parents in dual-earner couples when making 20-year comparisons.
3. C. Rubinstein, "Superdad Needs a Reality Check," *New York Times*, 17 April 1998, A23.
4. E. Galinsky & J. Swanberg, "Employed Mothers and Fathers in the United States: Understanding How Work and Family Life Fit Together," in L. L. Haas, P. Hwang, & G. Russell (eds.), *Organizational Change and Gender Equity: International Perspectives on Fathers and Mothers at the Workplace* (Thousand Oaks, CA: Sage Publications, Inc., in press).
5. Galinsky & Swanberg, in press.
6. Bond, Galinsky, & Swanberg, *The 1997 National Study*, 1998.
7. There are two differences in the way we asked about time in this study and the 1997 National Study of the Changing Workforce (NSCW). First, the study for *Ask the Children* asks employed parents about just *one* of their children, who was 18 years or younger and living with them at least half-time. In order to make this selection random, parents were asked to report on the child "who most recently had a birthday"; researchers term this the *target child* or *focal child*. In order not to use research language, I simply refer here to the child, but it is important to keep in mind that parents are reporting on just *one—not all—*of their children. The second difference is that the Ask the Children study includes children *18 years old and under* (because I assessed children in the third through the twelfth grades), whereas 1997 NSCW asks employed parents about their children *under 18*. Employed mothers and employed fathers were asked how much time they spend taking care of and doing things with their child on days when they are working and on days when they aren't working.
8. Because we found that time spent with one child in the Ask the Children study is higher in absolute terms than time spent with all children in the 1997 National Study of the Changing Workforce, we conducted a series of analyses to determine whether these represented statistically significant differences for comparable groups of parents. Only one comparison—that of mothers on a typical workday—reaches significance at the $p < .01$ level.
9. The reader may notice that the differences between mothers and fathers with a child 8 through 12 years old are significant for a typical workday but not significant for a typical nonworkday, whereas the absolute differences between mothers and fathers are very similar for the two ratings. There is more variability in parents' ratings for non-

workdays than for workdays, making it less likely that the findings for nonworkdays will be significant.

10. Children in the third through the sixth grades were asked to check categories: 30 minutes or less, less than an hour but more than 30 minutes, 1–2 hours, 2–4 hours, 5–6 hours, and more than 6 hours. Children in the seventh through twelfth grades were asked for actual time estimates. The questions asked of parents and children are therefore not strictly the same, so I do not make comparisons between what children say and what parents say. Finally, because this book primarily concerns parents who are employed, children were only asked these questions about their employed mother and/or employed father. In order to make the information from children as close as possible to that from parents, we only include information about parents who reside in the same household most of the time.

11. Since children were only asked about engaging in activities with at least one of their parents, we cannot know whether the parent the child is referring to is employed or not employed. So for this set of analyses, we enlarge the lens to include *all* children who live with their parents most of the time, whether or not their parents are employed. However, when we make direct comparisons between children and parents, we restrict the analyses to focus on families with dual-earner parents and single-parent-employed families to ensure that the parent referred to is employed.

12. S. Hofferth, "Children's Time: Child Development Supplement of the Panel Study of Income Dynamics" (Ann Arbor: Institute for Social Research, University of Michigan, 1998).

13. There is a fundamental difference in how children in our study were asked about activities and about their parents' effectiveness (or what researchers call *outcomes*). In terms of activities, they were asked about how often they engaged in activities with at least *one* of their parents, whereas in terms of outcomes, they were asked to judge *each parent separately*. By design, then, we can't link a child's involvement in an activity with a mother or a father to the child's judgments about both parents' effectiveness. Thus, these analyses should be considered exploratory.

14. S. Shellenbarger, "Teens Are Inheriting Parents' Tendencies Toward Work Overload," *Wall Street Journal*, 3 June 1998, B1.

15. D. Siegel, personal communication, September 23, 1998.

16. J. Schor, "Time and Money: Households Under Pressure" (New York: Radcliffe Public Policy Institute Forum, 1999).

Chapter 4: There Is Something About Work

1. K. Gerson, "Children's Experiences of Work, Family, and Community Change," presentation at Radcliffe Public Policy Institute, November 1997, 3.

2. Ibid.; Ad Council, cited in A. L. Dombro, N. Sazer O'Donnell, E. Galin-
sky, S. G. Melcher, & A. Farber, *Community Mobilization: Strategies to
Support Young Children and Their Families* (New York: Families and
Work Institute, 1996).

3. E. Galinsky, *The Six Stages of Parenthood* (Reading, MA: Addison-
Wesley, 1987), 75.

4. R. C. Barnett & G. K. Baruch, "Women's Involvement in Multiple Roles
and Psychological Distress," *Journal of Personality and Social Psychology*
49 (1985): 135–145; F. J. Crosby, *Juggling: The Unexpected Advantages of
Balancing Career and Home for Women and Their Families* (New York:
Free Press, 1991); P. R. Pietromonaco, J. Manis, & K. Frohardt-Lane,
"Psychological Consequences of Multiple Social Roles," *Psychology of
Women Quarterly* 10 (1986): 373–381; S. Lewis & C. L. Cooper,
"The Stress of Combining Occupational and Parental Roles: A Review
of the Literature," *Bulletin of the British Psychological Society* 36 (1983):
341–345.

5. C. Madole, Presentation at the Association for Work/Life Professionals
conference, February 1997.

6. When we examine each component of the model, we assess how parents in this study are doing, looking at the differences among various
groups of parents—for example, differences between fathers and mothers, differences among parents with different family incomes and levels
of educational attainment—reporting only the findings that are statistically significant.

7. As a backdrop to the model, we looked at the different industries and
occupations in which mothers and fathers work. Not surprisingly, there
are large differences between fathers and mothers. For example, about
one in two mothers (51 percent) works in the professional service
industry compared with one in five fathers (18 percent). More than
twice as many fathers (20 percent) as mothers (9 percent) work in
manufacturing. Although there are also differences in occupation, these
are slighter. For example, comparable numbers of fathers and mothers
are managers, executives, or proprietors (of small business). Likewise,
comparable numbers are professionals. Other research, however, indicates that within these occupations, fathers are at a higher level than
mothers.

8. P. M. Keith & R. B. Schafer, "Role Strain and Depression in Two-Job
Families," *Family Relations* 29 (1980): 483-488; M. H. Katz & C. S.
Piotrkowski, "Correlates of Family Role Strain Among Employed Black
Women," *Family Relations* 32 (1983): 331–339; G. L. Staines & J. H.
Pleck, *The Impact of Work Schedules in the Family* (Ann Arbor, MI: Insti-
tute for Social Research, University of Michigan, 1983); P. Moen &
D. I. Dempster-McClain, "Employed Parents, Role Strain, Work Time,
and Preferences for Working Less," *Journal of Marriage and the Family*
49 (1987): 579–590; P. Voydanoff, "Work-Family Life Cycles," paper

presented at the Workshop on Theory Construction and Research Methodology, National Council of Family Relations, 1980; P. Voydanoff, "Work Role Characteristics, Family Structure Demands, and Work/Family Conflict," *Journal of Marriage and the Family* 50 (1980): 749–761; P. Voydanoff & R. F. Kelly, "Determinants of Work-Related Family Problems Among Employed Parents," *Journal of Marriage and the Family* 46 (1984): 881–892.

9. E. Galinsky & J. Swanberg, "Employed Mothers and Fathers in the United States: Understanding How Work and Family Life Fit Together," in L. L. Haas, P. Hwang, & G. Russell (eds.), *Organizational Change and Gender Equity: International Perspectives on Fathers and Mothers at the Workplace* (Thousand Oaks, CA: Sage Publications, Inc., in press).

10. In addition, we found that employed mothers and fathers in families with higher total household income (calculated in 1997 dollars) work longer hours. More than twice as many parents in households with annual incomes of more than $75,000 work more than 50 hours per week compared with those with annual household income of $25,000 or less, 27 percent versus 12 percent, respectively.

11. R. A. Karasek, D. Baker, F. Marxer, A. Ahlbom, & T. T. Theorell, "Job Decision Latitude, Job Demands and Cardiovascular Disease: A Prospective Study of Swedish Men," *American Journal of Public Health* 71 (1981): 694–705.

12. L. Alfredsson, R. A. Karasek, & T. T. Theorell, "Myocardial Infarction Risk and Psychosocial Environment: An Analysis of the Male Swedish Working Force," *Social Science Medicine* 3 (1982): 463–467; P. A. Landsbergis, "Occupational Stress Among Health Care Workers: A Test of the Job Demands-Control Model," *Journal of Organ Behavior* 9 (1988): 217–239; A. Falk, B. S. Hanson, S. Isaccson, & P. Ostergren, "Job Strain and Mortality in Elderly Men: Social Network, Support, and Influence as Buffers," *American Journal of Public Health* 82 (1992): 1136–1139.

13. D. Lerner, S. Levine, S. Malspeis, & R.B. D'Agostino, "Job Strain and Health Related Quality of Life in a National Sample," *American Journal of Public Health* 84 No. 10 (1994): 1580–1585.

14. Parents with higher levels of education and with higher household income clearly feel a time crunch. For example, more than twice as many parents with a 4-year degree or more (47 percent) than those with high school or less (21 percent) strongly agree that they never have enough time to get everything done.

15. Galinsky & Swanberg, "Employed Mothers," in press.

16. J. T. Bond, E. Galinsky, & J. Swanberg, *The 1997 National Study of the Changing Workforce* (New York: Families and Work Institute, 1998).

17. R. Rapoport & L. Bailyn, *Relinking Life and Work: Toward a Better Future* (New York: Ford Foundation, 1996).

18. In addition, employed parents with higher levels of education and with higher household income are more likely to report that they work on

too many tasks at the same time. For example, 46 percent of employed parents in families with annual household income above $75,000 report that they work on too many tasks at the same time very often, compared with 31 percent of those in households with incomes at or below $25,000.

19. Additionally, parents with higher levels of education and with higher household income report more interruptions than their counterparts with less education and with lower household income.
20. Galinsky & Swanberg, "Employed Mothers," in press.
21. Parents with higher household income are more likely to report that they have autonomy in their job, as are employed parents in professional and managerial occupations.
22. Galinsky & Swanberg, "Employed Mothers," in press.
23. Ibid.
24. E. Galinsky, R. R. Ruopp, K. Blum, *The Work and Family Life Studies* (New York: Bank Street College of Education, 1983).
25. Families and Work Institute, *An Evaluation of Johnson & Johnson's Work-Family Initiative* (New York: Author, 1993).
26. E. Galinsky, J. T. Bond, & D. Friedman, *National Study of the Changing Workforce* (New York: Families and Work Institute, 1993).
27. Families and Work Institute, *Evaluation*, 1993.
28. Galinsky, Bond, & Friedman, 1993.
29. Bond, Galinsky & Swanberg, *The 1997 National*, 1998.
30. Galinsky & Swanberg, "Employed Mothers."
31. Galinsky, Bond, & Friedman, 1993.
32. Families and Work Institute, *Evaluation*, 1993.
33. Galinsky & Swanberg, "Employed Mothers."

Chapter 5: There's Something About Family Life, Too

1. S. Farkas & J. Johnson, *Kids These Days: What Americans Really Think About the Next Generation* (New York: Public Agenda, 1997), 8, 11.
2. To make these comparisons, the letter grades were transformed into numerical scores and averaged.
3. These grades were also reduced to numerical scores to provide a more stringent test of the findings.
4. One explanation for the difference in findings between children and mothers may relate to the way the questions were asked. Mothers were asked to report the actual number of hours they work, whereas children reported their mothers' work hours in categories: full-time, about half-time, or less than half-time.
5. K. J. Daly, "Deconstructing Family Time," paper presented at conference on Work and Family sponsored by the Alfred P. Sloan Foundation, the Business and Professional Women's Foundation, and the Wellesley College Center for Research on Women, November 1998.

6. E. Galinsky, *The Six Stages of Parenthood* (Reading, MA: Addison-Wesley, 1987).

7. E. Galinsky & J. T. Bond, "Work and Family: The Experiences of Mothers and Fathers in the U.S. Labor Force," in C. Costello & B. Kivimaekrimgold (eds.), *The American Woman 1996–97: Where We Stand, Women and Work* (Washington, DC: Women's Research Education Institute, 1996), 79–103; E. Galinsky, J. T. Bond, & D. Friedman, *National Study of the Changing Workforce* (New York: Families and Work Institute, 1993); T. Bond, E. Galinsky, & J. Swanberg, *The 1997 National Study of the Changing Workforce* (New York: Families and Work Institute, 1998).

8. R. C. Barnett, N. L. Marshall, S. W. Raudenbush, & R. T. Brennan, "Gender and the Relationship Between Job Experiences and Psychological Distress: A Study of Dual-Earner Couples," *Journal of Personality and Social Psychology* 64 no. 5 (1993): 794–806.

9. L. Pearlin & C. Schooler, "The Structure of Coping," *Journal of Health and Social Behavior* 19 (1978): 2–21; D. Unger & D. Powell, "Supporting Families Under Stress: The Role of Social Networks," *Family Relations* 29 (1980): 566–574; R. L. Repetti & J. Wood, "Families Accommodating to Chronic Stress: Unintended and Unnoticed Processes," in B. H. Gottlieb (ed.), *Coping with Chronic Stress* (New York: Plenum Publishing, 1997), 191–220.

10. J. S. House, *Work Stress and Social Support* (Reading, MA: Addison-Wesley, 1981); Pearlin & Schooler, "Structure of Coping," 2–21.

11. D. Belle, *Social Support, Lives in Stress: Women in Depression* (Thousand Oaks, CA: Sage Publications, Inc., 1982).

12. D. Entwistle & S. Doeinger, *The First Birth: A Family Turning Point* (Baltimore, MD: Johns Hopkins University Press, 1981); R. S. Weiss, *Staying the Course: The Emotional and Social Lives of Men Who Do Well at Work* (New York: Free Press, 1990); Galinsky, Bond, & Friedman, *National Study*.

13. Bond, Galinsky, & Swanberg, *The 1997 National Study*, 1998.

14. S. Yogev & S. Brett, *Patterns of Work and Family Involvement Among Single and Dual-Earner Couples: Two Competing Analytical Approaches* (Washington, DC: Office of Naval Research, 1983); L. Pearlin, "Role Strains and Personal Stress," in H. B. Kaplan (ed.), *Psychological Stress: Trends in Theory and Research* (New York: Academic Press, 1983); J. Glass & T. Fujimoto, "Housework, Paid Work, and Depression Among Husbands and Wives," *Journal of Health and Social Behavior* 35 (1994): 179–91; C. E. Bird, M. L. Rogers, & P. S. Webster, "Gender, Paid Work, and Housework: The Division of Labor Within Couples, Perceived Role Quality, and Depression," PSTC Working Paper #97–15, Brown University Population Studies and Training Center, 1997; S. L. Coltrane & M. A. Adams, "Experiencing Gendered Divisions of Labor in American

Households: Resources, Entitlement, and Perceptions of Fairness," paper presented at conference on Work and Family sponsored by the Alfred P. Sloan Foundation, the Business and Professional Women's Foundation, and the Wellesley College Center for Research on Women, November 1998.

15. C. E. Bird & M. L. Rogers, "Parenting and Depression: The Impact of the Division of Labor Within Couples and Perceptions of Equity," PSTC Working Paper #98–09, Brown University Population Studies and Training Center, 1998; Barnett & Shen, "Gender."

16. E. Galinsky & W. H. Hooks, *The New Extended Family: Day Care That Works* (Boston: Houghton Mifflin, 1977); E. Galinsky, C. Howes, S. Kontos, & M. Shinn, *The Study of Children in Family Child Care and Relative Care: Highlights and Findings* (New York: Families and Work Institute, 1994).

17. M. Whitebook, C. Howes, & D. A. Phillips, *Who Cares? Child Care Teachers and the Quality of Care in America*, Final Report of the National Child Care Staffing Study (Oakland, CA: Child Care Employee Project, 1990); E. Galinsky, C. Howes, S. Kontos, & M. Shinn, *The Study of Children*, 1994; Cost, Quality & Child Outcomes Study Team, *Cost, Quality, and Child Outcomes in Child Care Centers* (Denver, CO: Economics Department, University of Colorado, 1995).

18. Galinsky, Howes, Kontos, & Shinn, *The Study of Children*, 1994.

19. A. R. Hochschild, *The Time Bind* (New York: Henry Holt & Company, 1997).

20. Ibid.

21. R.W. Larson, M. H. Richards, & M. Perry-Jenkins, "Divergent Worlds: The Daily Emotional Experience of Mothers and Fathers in the Domestic and Public Spheres," *Journal of Personality and Social Psychology* 67, No. 6, (1994): 1034–1046.

22. N. Zill, Behavior Problem Index based on Parent Report, Washington, DC Child Trends (1990).

23. NICHD Early Child Care Research Network, "The Effects of Child Care on Infant-Mother Attachment Security: Results of the NICHD Study of Early Child Care," *Child Development* 68 (1997): 860–879.

Chapter 6: Spillover

1. C. S. Piotrkowski, *Work and the Family System* (New York: Macmillan, 1979); D. Hughes, "Relationships Between Characteristics of the Job, Work/Family Interference, and Marital Outcomes," doctoral dissertation (Ann Arbor: University of Michigan), 1985.

2. R.W. Larson, M. H. Richards, & M. Perry-Jenkins, "Divergent Worlds: The Daily Emotional Experience of Mothers and Fathers in the Domestic and Public Spheres," *Journal of Personality and Social Psychology* 67, Number 6 (1994): 1034–1046.

3. J. P. Robinson & G. Godbey, *Time for Life: The Surprising Ways Americans Use Their Time* (University Park, PA: Pennsylvania State University, 1997); Larson, Richards, & Perry-Jenkins, "Divergent Worlds," 1042.

4. D. M. Almeida & R. C. Kessler, "Everyday Stressors and Gender Differences in Daily Distress," *Journal of Personality and Social Psychology* 75 (1998): 678.

5. K. J. Williams & G. Alliger, "Role Stressors, Mood Spillover, and Perceptions of Work-Family Conflict in Employed Parents," *Academy of Management Journal* 37, Number 4 (1994): 837–888.

6. They also assessed household chores, personal or leisure activities, and transportation, but these are not included in the present analyses.

7. Williams & Alliger, "Role Stressors."

8. E. Galinsky, J. T. Bond, & D. Friedman, *National Study of the Changing Workforce* (New York: Families and Work Institute, 1993); T. Bond, E. Galinsky, & J. Swanberg, *The 1997 National Study of the Changing Workforce* (New York: Families and Work Institute, 1998).

9. L.W. Hoffman, "Work, Family, and the Child," in M. S. Pallak and R. O. Perloff (eds.), *Psychology and Work: Productivity, Change, and Employment: The Master Lectures* 5 (Washington, DC: American Psychological Association, 1986); E. Greenberger, R. O'Neil, & S. K. Nagel, "Linking Workplace and Homeplace: Relations Between the Nature of Adults' Work and Their Parenting Behaviors," *Developmental Psychology* 30, Number 6 (1994): 990–1002.

10. R. L. Repetti, "Short-Term and Long-Term Processes Linking Job Stressors to Father-Child Interaction," *Social Development* 3 (1994): 1–15.

11. R. L. Repetti, "Effects of Daily Workload on Subsequent Behavior During Marital Interaction: The Roles of Social Withdrawal and Spouse Support," *Journal of Personality and Social Psychology* 57 (1989): 651–659; R. L. Repetti, "Social Withdrawal as a Short-term Coping Response to Daily Stressor," in H. S. Friedman (ed.), *Hostility, Coping, and Health* (Washington, DC: American Psychological Association, 1992), 151–165; R. L. Repetti & J. Wood, "Families Accommodating to Chronic Stress: Unintended and Unnoticed Processes," in B. H. Gottlieb (ed.), *Coping with Chronic Stress* (New York: Plenum Publishing, 1997), 191–220.

12. Repetti, "Short-Term and Long-Term."

13. Repetti & Wood, "Families Accommodating"; R. L. Repetti & J. Wood, "The Effects of Daily Stress at Work on Mothers' Interactions with Preschoolers," *Journal of Family Psychology* 11 (1997): 90–108.

14. R. L. Repetti, "The Effects of Daily Job Stress on Parent Behavior with Preadolescents," paper presented at the biennial meeting of the Society for Research in Child Development, Washington DC, April 1997.

15. The relationships between predictor variables and the work-family interference index were evaluated using Spearman nonparametric correlation.

16. E. Galinsky & J. Swanberg, "Employed Mothers and Fathers in the United States: Understanding How Work and Family Life Fit Together," in L. L.

Haas, P. Hwang, & G. Russell (eds.), *Organizational Change and Gender Equity: International Perspectives on Fathers and Mothers at the Workplace* (Thousand Oaks, CA: Sage Publications, Inc., in press).

17. Galinsky & Swanberg, "Employed Mothers"; A. C. Crouter, "Spillover from Family to Work: The Neglected Side of the Work-Family Interface," *Human Relations* 37 (1984): 425–442.

18. Repetti, "The Effects of Daily Job Stress," 1–2.

19. S. D. Friedman & J. H. Greenhaus, *Allies or Enemies? How Choices About Work and Family Affect the Quality of Men's and Women's Lives* (New York: Oxford University Press, in press).

20. E. Galinsky & A. Johnson, *Reframing the Business Case for Work-Life Initiatives* (New York: Families and Work Institute, 1998); J. G. Grzywacz & N. F. Marks, *Reconceptualizing the Work-Family Interface: An Ecological Perspective on the Correlates of Positive and Negative Spillover Between Work and Family* (Irvine: University of California, School of Social Ecology, Psychology and Social Behavior, 1999).

21. Williams & Alliger, "Role Stressors," 1994, 837–888.

22. S. Friedman, personal communication, 1999.

23. Note that when we examined work's spilling over into parenting, we asked parents about just one of their children (the child we focus on for the purpose of this study), whereas when we looked at how family life spills over into work, we asked parents about all of their children. For looking at spillover in this direction, it didn't make any sense to limit the discussion to just one child.

24. E. Galinsky & S. S. Kim, *A Work-Life Scan of Endeavors to Improve Work-Life Connections Around the Globe* (New York: Families and Work Institute & The Center for Work & Family, Boston College, 1999).

25. Bond, Galinsky, & Swanberg, *The 1997 National Study.*

Chapter 7: How Do Work and Family Life Affect Us as Parents?

1. J. Levine, "The Other Working Parent," *New York Times*, 4 March 1999, A25.

2. A. K. Harris, "Linking Family Work and Wage Work: An Historical View," paper presented at conference, Time of Transition: Work, Family, and Community After 2001, Families and Work Institute, Tarrytown, New York, February 25, 1999.

3. The discussion in this chapter is guided by multiple regression analyses that include a large number of variables (previously examined pair by pair) within the same analytic framework. Regression analyses provide the basis for reaching the more general conclusions presented here.

4. "New Longitudinal Study Finds That Having a Working Mother Does No Significant Harm to Children," APA news release, February 18, 1999; "UMass Researcher Finds No Developmental Differences in Children with Working Moms Versus Non-Working Moms," University of Massachusetts Amherst press release, March 1, 1999.

5. P. Fonagy, M. Steele, H. Steele, G. S. Moran & A. C. Higgitt, "The Capability for Understanding Mental States: The Reflective Self in Parent and Child and Its Significance for Security of Attachment," *Infant Mental Health Journal* 12 (1991): 201–218; A. N. Schore, *Affect Regulation and the Origin of the Self: The Neurobiology of Emotional Development* (Hillsdale, NJ: Lawrence Erlbaum Associates, 1994); D. J. Siegel, *The Developing Mind: Toward a Neurobiology of Interpersonal Experience* (New York: Guilford Press, 1999).

6. B. Romer, personal communication, 1997.

7. First and last names of all family members have been changed.

8. S. D. Friedman, P. Christensen, & J. DeGroot, "Work and Life: The End of the Zero-Sum Game," *Harvard Business Review*, Reprint 98605, November–December 1998, 119–129.

9. P. Moen & Y. Yu, "The Changing Work/Family Interface," prepared for presentation at the annual meetings of the American Association for the Advancement of Science, Anaheim, CA, January 1999.

10. S. Mitchell. *Tao Te Ching* (New York: HarperPerennial, 1988), 8.

Chapter 8: What Are We Teaching Children About Work and Family Life?

1. F. Rogers, personal communication, December 11, 1998.

2. E. R. Shell, "Mommy, Why Do You Work?" *Parents* magazine, April 1999, 106–112.

3. A. R. Hochschild, "Childhood and Cultures of Care," presentation at Work and Family: Today's Realities, Tomorrow's Vision, presented by the Alfred P. Sloan Foundation, the Business and Professional Women's Foundation, and the Wellesley College Center for Research on Women, Boston, November 6, 1998.

4. C. S. Piotrkowski & E. Stark, "Children and Adolescents Look at Their Parents' Jobs," in J. H. Lewko (ed.), *How Children and Adolescents View the World of Work, New Directions for Child Development* 35 (San Francisco: Jossey-Bass, 1987).

5. J. T. Bond, E. Galinsky, & J. S. Swanberg, *The 1997 National Study of the Changing Workforce* (New York: Families and Work Institute, 1998).

6. Piotrkowski & Stark, "Children and Adolescents," 4.

7. A. Skolnick, *Rethinking Childhood: Perspectives on Development and Society* (Boston: Little, Brown and Company, 1976), 59–60.

8. V. A. Zelizer, *Pricing the Priceless Child: The Changing Social Value of Children* (Princeton, NJ: Princeton University Press, 1994), 6.

9. D. Ehrensaft, "The Kinderdult: The New Child Born to Work-Family Conflict," presentation at Work and Family: Today's Realities, Tomorrow's Vision, presented by the Alfred P. Sloan Foundation, the Business and Professional Women's Foundation, and the Wellesley College Center for Research on Women, Boston, November 6, 1998.

10. M. L. Kohn, *Class and Conformity: A Study in Values*, 2nd ed. (Chicago: University of Chicago Press, 1977); M. L. Kohn & C. Schooler, "Job Conditions and Personality: A Longitudinal Assessment of Their Reciprocal Effects," *American Journal of Sociology* 87 (1982): 1257–1286); M. L. Kohn & C. Schooler, *Work and Personality: An Inquiry into the Impact of Social Stratification* (Norwood, NJ: Ablex, 1983).

11. A. E. Gottfried & A. W. Gottfried, "Maternal Employment and Children's Development: An Integration of Longitudinal Findings with Implications for Social Policy," in A. E. Gottfried & A. W. Gottfried (eds.), *Maternal Employment and Children's Development: Longitudinal Research* (New York: Plenum, 1988) 269–278; C. Schooler, "Psychological Effects of Complex Environments During the Life Span: A Review and Theory," in C. Schooler & K.W. Schaie, *Cognitive Functioning and Social Structure over the Life Course* (Norwood, NJ: Ablex, 1987), 24–49; T. L. Parcel & E. G. Menaghan, "Maternal Working Conditions and Children's Verbal Facility: Studying the Intergenerational Transmission of Inequality from Mothers to Young Children," *Social Psychology Quarterly* 53 (1990): 132–147; T. Luster, K. Rhoades, & B. Haas, "The Relation Between Parental Values and Parenting Behavior: A Test of the Kohn Hypothesis," *Journal of Marriage and the Family* 51 (1989): 139–147; S. Bloom-Feshbach, J. Bloom-Feshbach, & K. A. Heller, "Work, Family, and Children's Perceptions of the World" in S. B. Kamerman & C. D. Hayes (eds.), *Families That Work: Children in a Changing World* (Washington, DC: National Academy Press, 1992); E. Greenberger, R. O'Neil, & S. K. Nagel, "Linking Workplace and Homeplace: Relations Between the Nature of Adults' Work and Their Parenting Behaviors," *Developmental Psychology* 30, Number 6 (1994): 990–1002.

12. Greenberger, O'Neil, & Nagel, "Linking Workplace and Homeplace," 990–1002.

13. R. O'Neil, "Maternal Occupational Experiences and Psychological Well-Being: Influences on Parental Achievement and Children's Academic Achievement," unpublished doctoral dissertation (Irvine, CA: University of California at Irvine, 1991); Bloom-Feshbach & Heller, "Work, Family," 1992; A. C. Crouter, "Spillover from Family to Work: The Neglected Side of the Work-Family Interface," *Human Relations* 37 (1984): 425–441.

14. T. L. Parcel & E. G. Menaghan, "Early Parental Work, Family Social Capital, and Early Childhood Outcomes," *American Journal of Sociology* 99, Number 4 (1994): 972–1009; Parcel & Menaghan, "Maternal Working Conditions," 132–147; C. S. Piotrkowski & M. H. Katz, "Indirect Socialization of Children: The Effect of Mother's Job on Academic Behavior," *Child Development* 53 (1982): 409–415.

Chapter 9: What Does the Future Hold?

1. S. Farkas & J. Johnson, *Kids These Days: What Americans Really Think About the Next Generation* (New York: Public Agenda, 1997).
2. D. Copeland, *Generation X: Tales for an Accelerated Culture* (New York: St. Martin's Press, 1991); J. W. Smith & A. Clurman, *Rocking the Ages: The Yankelovich Report on Generational Marketing* (New York: Harper Business, 1997).
3. D. Wadsworth, presentation at The Open Society Institute, 1998.
4. V. Washington & J. D. Andrews (eds.), *Children of 2010* (Washington, DC: National Association for the Education of Young Children, 1998); U.S. Bureau of the Census, "Resident Population of the United States: Middle Series Projections, 1996–2000, by Age and Sex," (Washington, DC, U.S. Bureau of the Census, March 1996).
5. R.W. Judy & C. D'Amico, *Workforce 2020: Work and Workers in the 21st Century* (Indianapolis: Hudson Institute, 1997).
6. Washington & Andrews, *Children of 2010*, 1998.
7. P. M. Senge, *The Fifth Discipline: The Art and Practice of the Learning Organization* (New York: Doubleday Currency, 1990).
8. NationsBanc Montgomery Securities, *The Age of Knowledge* (San Francisco: NationsBanc Montgomery Securities LLC, 1998), 2.
9. Institute For The Future, *Emerging Technologies: A Map of the Horizon* (Menlo Park, CA: Institute For The Future, 1997), 5.
10. T. W. Malone & R. J. Laubacher, "The Dawn of the E-Lance Economy," *Harvard Business Review*, Reprint 98605 (1998): 145–152.
11. Judy & D'Amico, *Workforce 2020*, 52.
12. Institute For The Future, *Ten-Year Forecast* (Menlo Park, CA: Institute For The Future, 1998).
13. J. T. Bond, E. Galinsky, & J. S. Swanberg, *The 1997 National Study of the Changing Workforce* (New York: Families and Work Institute, 1998); data from The Yankelowich MONITOR, Yankelowich Partners, Inc., 1998.
14. S. Scarr, D. Phillips, & K. McCartney, "Working Mothers and Their Families," *American Psychologist* 44 (1989): 1402–1409.
15. E. Galinsky and J. David, *The Preschool Years* (New York: Ballantine Books, 1991).
16. D. Gold & D. Andres, "Developmental Comparisons Between 10-Year-Old Children with Employed and Nonemployed Mothers," *Child Development* 49 (1978): 75–84; F. F. Cherry & E. L. Eaton, "Physical and Cognitive Development in Children of Low-Income Mothers Working in the Child's Early Years," *Child Development* 48 (1977): 158–166.
17. Williams, 1994 in D. B. Grusky & E. Rice, *Is There a Generation X?* (Stanford, CA: Stanford University, 1998).
18. Smith & Clurman, *Rocking the Ages*, 84; B. Tulgan, *The Manager's Pocket Guide to Generation X* (Amherst, MA: HRD Press, 1997).

19. N. D. Murrray, "Welcome to the Future: The Millennial Generation," *Journal of Career Planning & Employment*, 1997, 36–42.
20. Smith & Clurman, *Rocking the Ages*, 86.
21. Tulgan, *Manager's Pocket Guide*.
22. Grusky & Rice, "Is There a Generation X?"
23. K. Gerson, "Children of the Gender Revolution: Some Theoretical Questions and Preliminary Notes from the Field," in V.W. Marshall, W. R. Heinz, H. Krueger, & A. Verma, *Restructuring Work and the Life Course* (Toronto: University of Toronto Press, in press).
24. S. Lewis, J. Smithson, J. Brannen, M. Das Dores Guerreiro, C. Kugelberg, A. Nilsen, & P. O'Connor, *Futures on Hold: Young Europeans Talk About Combining Work and Family* (London: Work-Life Research Centre, 1998).
25. Bond, Galinsky, & Swanberg, *The 1997 National Study*.

Chapter 10: How Do We Navigate Work and Family, and How Do We Ask the Children?

1. D. Elkind, *The Hurried Child: Growing Up Too Fast Too Soon* (Reading, MA: Addison-Wesley, 1989); S. Hofferth, *Children's Time: Child Development Supplement of the Panel Study of Income Dynamics* (Ann Arbor: Institute for Social Research, University of Michigan, 1998); press release, University of Michigan, November 9, 1998, 2.
2. Hofferth, *Children's Time*, 16.
3. S. Friedman, personal communication, February 4, 1999; S. D. Friedman & J. H. Greenhaus, *Allies or Enemies? How Choices About Work and Family Affect the Quality of Men's and Women's Lives* (New York: Oxford University Press, in press).

Chapter 11: What Children Want to Tell the Working Parents of America

1. Although we reference the percentage of children whose responses can be categorized in each of the ten messages, children often mention more than one topic in their statements. Thus, there is a great deal of overlap in these groupings.
2. D. J. Siegel, *The Developing Mind: Toward a Neurobiology of Interpersonal Experience* (New York: Guilford Press, 1999); U. Bronfenbrenner, *The Ecology of Human Development: Experiments by Nature and Design* (Cambridge, MA: Harvard University Press, 1979).
3. D. Wadsworth, presentation at the Open Society Institute, 1998.

A Word About the Photographs

In keeping with the spirit of the Ask the Children study, I wanted to see how children would demonstrate their views of their parents' work. I asked children to "do something" that reminded them of their parents' work. My photographs of their responses—an informal mini-study of sorts—appear throughout this book. The parents' occupations are listed below:

Title Page—(*top*) guardian is a private duty certified nursing assistant, (*center*) father is a taxi driver, (*bottom*) mother is a food service worker

Overview: Why Ask the Children, and Why Now?—mother is a marketing consultant

Introduction: Why and How This Study Was Conducted—father is a banker

Chapter 1: Reframing the Debate About Working and Children— mother is a policy and media consultant

Chapter 2: How Children See Their Parents' Parenting Skills— father is an underwriter, insurance risk management

Chapter 3: Is It Quality Time or Quantity Time?—father is a health care management executive

Chapter 4: There Is Something About Work—mother is a marketing consultant

Chapter 5: There's Something About Family Life, Too—mother is a pediatrician

Chapter 6: Spillover—mother is a program associate in a nonprofit

Chapter 7: How Do Work and Family Life Affect Us as Parents?—father owns a dry cleaning business

Chapter 8: What Are We Teaching Children About Work and Family Life?—father is a banker

Chapter 9: What Does the Future Hold?—mother is a freelance television producer

Chapter 10: How Do We Navigate Work and Family, and How Do We Ask the Children?—mother and father are partners in a graphic design firm

Chapter 11: What Children Want to Tell the Working Parents of America—mother is an administrative assistant

Afterword—mother is a program associate in a nonprofit

Research Notes and References—mother and father own a water bottling and distributing company

A Word About the Photographs—mother is a jewelry designer

INDEX

Page numbers in *italics* refer to charts.